D0031827

ENGLISH AND ITS HISTORY

The Evolution Of A Language

ROBERT D. STEVICK

University of Washington

ALLYN AND BACON, INC.
BOSTON

Library of Congress Catalog Card Number:
68-18990

PRINTED IN THE UNITED STATES OF AMERICA.

Second printing . . . September, 1970

PREFACE

If I have accomplished my intent fully and correctly, this book will do much more than store information on paper to be read and stored in turn by students. My purpose is to induce the kinds of academic thinking and disciplines that go under the names of science and history. To record data or formulations of facts about English one writes dictionaries, grammars, scholarly articles, monographs. To establish certain accurate attitudes towards the English language one writes histories or handbooks showing that English is not One English and English teachers its chief priests. To show that the evolution of the language may be a subject of inexhaustible and fascinating study, one undertakes to write a textbook dealing with this evolution.

Regarded in the ways indicated, the subject of English and its history belongs to university-level study and in advanced courses, for which this book is designed. A specific feature of the book is that the materials included fall clearly within the topic named in the title; hence it omits a capsule history of England and other English-speaking nations; it begins with English rather than with Indo-European; it does not tell the story of the alphabet or recount the development of lexicography and linguistics or comment on the literary style of famous authors or assess impressionistically the character or the virtues of the language. Another feature is a dominant approach—not to be construed as adherence to a "brand" or "school" of language study; that is, the essentially systemic nature of a language is emphasized in both the descriptive and historical accounts. The linguistic items at any given stage in the development of English are presented in terms of the systems of which they are components, and change in the language is presented as a modification of existing systems and patterns. In several places the systemic approach produces analysis or integration of materials never before presented in comparable textbooks.

A technical feature is that the book has been written without footnotes. At no place did relegation of information, acknowledgements, or references to a remote place seem to offer anything but inconvenience to a reader, especially a student reader. Subsidiary information has been subordinated within the text; acknowledgements have also been made within the text without inconvenience and where their prominence is more commensurate with the scholarly debts they record; references are kept to a minimum, not to obscure the abundant resources upon which the author has drawn and to which a reader should turn, but to sustain the continuity of the exposition in substance and in a reader's attention.

All publications to which specific acknowledgement or reference was due have been listed in the bibliography. This list also includes a number of additional publications selected specifically for students using this book; the selection is slanted to direct sources of knowledge of early English rather than to scholarly commentary on the language. To these publications acknowledgement is due and is made here with the observation that many of them—especially dictionaries, grammars, and manuals—have served as constant and invaluable resources in the writing of this book. Other diverse acknowledgements can only be generally expressed here; these are to the countless writings, conversations, and students' questions that have helped create and sustain my own continuing interest in English and its history, from which this book derives.

R.D.S.

CONTENTS

Introduction

THE STUDY OF ENGLISH

FACT, STORY, OR SYSTEM OF KNOWLEDGE

0.1 If every fact about English, present and past, were recorded on cards—one fact to a card—and all the cards collected into one enormous basket, the collection would be useless to anyone interested in English or its history. If the cards were sorted into smaller baskets—one for words and their meanings, another for speech sounds and spellings, another for words with various grammatical inflections, and so on—still the baskets and their contents would be of doubtful value. Reading one card after another as they were drawn from any one set, we should have neither narrative nor description that we could comprehend, let alone use. The collection would be only a monstrosity, unless the facts had been sorted into much smaller sets, the sets had been labeled, grouped and cross-referenced, and the grouping and identification had been carried out according to some plan we understood. Even the orderly collection would have value only as a source of information about discrete facts. It would resemble somewhat a combination of large dictionaries, traditional grammars and histories, and dialect atlases of the language. The collection would serve our interests once we began connecting facts together, especially if we had them arranged in patterns serving as a model of English at specified times or as patterns which together made clear the development of the language.

If, instead of a file of facts, a book-length series of statements about English were compiled so as to tell the story of the language, the collection of statements would be worth the attention of those concerned with the language and its history. However, any story or history has an end and our interest in a history cannot legitimately go beyond the narration itself, for once the story is completed, we can do nothing more with it except go over it again. (It may, of course, arouse our interest in its subject, thereby taking us into additional study.) A continuing interest in the historical study of English requires us to avoid the dead end of merely learning a history and to get beyond the static collection of facts on file. It is necessary for us to deal with the English language as a system of knowledge that is open rather than finished, in formulations that are analytic as well as narrative or descriptive. This point can be restated briefly. English will be continually interesting if studied in the manner of history, or scientific description, or both.

LEARNING VS. STUDYING A LANGUAGE

0.2 The study of English that has given each of us a user's knowledge of the language was neither descriptive nor historical. The normal process of learning one's native language—effective and remarkable as that process is—can hardly be characterized as study: the learning is nearly complete, except for vocabulary, before a person reaches the first grade in school. A person who learns English as a second language may well study the language, but that study is characteristically a practice for establishing another set of language habits, that is, learning another language. The study of English (language, not literature) in primary and secondary schools is rarely scientific or historical, since that study usually is concerned with such paralinguistic matters as writing and reading, the organization of paragraphs and essays, some aspects of rhetoric, and the "correct" use of the language—the last of these perhaps better described as the etiquette of English. In none of these is the language, present or past, the specific object of systematic study. In all of them the goal is to gain practical skills involving the use of the language.

Neither descriptive nor historical studies are inherently practical, but the knowledge they produce is often used to solve practical problems; and the solutions based on sound knowledge have a better chance of succeeding than solutions not based on extensive and disinterested study. The prevention of disease or the acceleration of language learning was not managed very well until medicine or linguistics, as sciences, provided the basic and reliable knowledge. Hence, practical ends are served by the historical and descriptive study of English as an object in itself.

THREE LAYERS OF STUDY

0.3 Both historical study and scientific description have more than one layer; one involves the accumulation and general sorting of data, on the order of the card-and-basket illustration above. Suppose we had sorted the facts about English into groups according to the century from which the data were recorded. Then, if we drew cards from the tenth and the thirteenth centuries and compared them where the data were comparable, we would note many differences: earlier *hlaford* corresponds to later *laverd, lord* 'lord'; earlier *word* (plural) matches later *wordes* 'words'; negation of a verb would be marked by *ne* preceding the verb in both centuries but *noght* or *not* following the verb would appear as well only in the later examples; some words, like *prouesse* 'prowess' would appear only in collections from the later century; and so on. Another layer of study involves analysis of these data, eventuating in statements about elements of the language, their relationships, and the relation of language-facts to relevant non-language facts (such as geographical distribution, social classes of speakers, or historical period of occurrence). From this type of study come many of the historical accounts of the language. Some accounts concern changes in pronunciation, others concern changes in grammatical inflections, or word meanings, or sentence structures. Here is one generalized account of the development of English in the centuries associated with Norman Conquest:

> **The Norman Conquest.** This great event, while it undoubtedly marks a new departure in many ways in our social and political history, is by no means such a revolutionary factor in the history of our language as some writers lead one to believe. Its main effects are seen in our vocabulary. . . . In fact, there is no ground for assuming that the history of English sounds would have been other than we know it, had the Norman Conquest never taken place. . . . We are to consider the changes in sounds and inflexions which we associate with the [Middle English] period, not as due in any way to the great historical cataclysm which befell in 1066, but as the natural outcome of forces that were at work long before Duke William was born. (Henry Cecil Wyld, *A Short History of English,* 3rd ed., pp. 81–82; quoted with permission of John Murray (Publishers) Ltd.).

Another statement concerning the Conquest-facts and English language-facts gives the opposite impression of their relationship:

> **The Norman Conquest.** Towards the close of the Old English period an event occurred which had a greater effect on the English language than any other in the course of its history. This event was the Norman Conquest in 1066. . . . The Norman Conquest changed the whole course of the English Language. (Albert C. Baugh, *A History of the English Language,* 2nd edition, p. 127. Copyright ©1957 by Appleton-Century-Crofts, Inc. Reprinted by permission).

In the matter of history we resist contradictory statements, assuming that "the way things were," no matter how complex that way may have been, was *one* way and was not two or more ways that could admit contrary states of affairs.

In the face of ostensibly contradictory historical accounts, we must make a choice or make a distinction. Random choice marks us as mere gamblers in the pursuit of knowledge. Accepting the more recent statement is an act of faith in not only the advance of knowledge, but the reliability of the more recent author as well. Better than asking, "Which shall I believe?" is to ask directly, "What is the case?" For the statements about the effect of the Norman Conquest on the development of English we should ask specifically, "Which description squares best with the facts?" Also, if we are alert, we must ask, "Does the term *language* refer to the same things in both statements?" Problems of the kind illustrated here will often lead to a third level of study—explicating and testing assumptions about the language or about its history.

Taking English and its history as a body of knowledge, the first level of study involves apprehending the data of that body, the second consists of constructing that body—putting the data into their systematic relations—and the third is the analysis of the body of knowledge itself.

TINKERING VS. ANALYSIS

0.4 To learn parts of speech and rules of grammar is simple enough; memory is sufficient to the task. For the conservation of knowledge or for the attainment of certain modest social standing or vocational status, this seems to be enough. If we learn to distinguish nouns from adjectives, and then learn that an adjective may be "used as" a noun and a noun in possessive case may work like an adjective in a sentence, we are liable to frustration if we then begin to reflect on the definitions and rules we have learned. If *good* is an adjective, how can it be a sentence subject in *The good go to Glory?* (It doesn't help to say that the subject is understood though not expressed.) If *men* is a noun, how can it "modify" *quarrel* in *The men's quarrel was over a trivial matter?*

Fitting rules and definitions together by merely tinkering with one and then another is seldom successful. Two hundred years of this tinkering produced nothing better than the noun and adjective paradoxes just mentioned. Obviously, what was needed was analysis of English at another level at the same time. When this analysis was done, the consistency among the definitions and rules was increased many fold: one way was to introduce a simple distinction between the classes of words (nouns, verbs, etc.) based on their sets of inflections and the classes based on sentence position. In *The* —— *go to Glory* the position marked can be filled only by something nounlike, and if it is not a noun (in having an *-s* plural or *men*-type plural, or the like), it can be called a nominal; while in *The —— grain was left in the fields to rot* the position can be filled only by something adjectivelike. *Good* can be used in both; hence we shall have to distinguish between *good* (noun) and *good* (adjective).

Making these distinctions and describing their historical background involves the three-layer study inherent in both history and science. This book is an introduction to the history and (scientific) analysis of English. Without the facts about English, the analysis of data and explication of assumptions cannot be carried out. Hence the presentation of facts about the language must dominate the book as a whole. However, problems in methodology and structure and in the continual correction and extension of a body of knowledge are essential materials of mature college-level study. In addition, presentation of linguistic techniques and their complexity is basic to any study which is to be more than dilettantism.

History, as well as science, needs no apology. When history and science combine, as they may in the study of English, each discipline complements the other, and together they can lead to fuller knowledge of a subject than either can provide by itself.

Chapter 1

SCIENCE AND HISTORY OF ENGLISH

DEFINITIONS FOR A SYSTEMATIC STUDY

1.1 Little is gained in attempting a comprehensive, abstract definition for certain kinds of concepts, for example those designated by the terms "life," "society," "goodness," and "the British Commonwealth" or those like "language" and "history." To serve a solid, practical purpose, definition of terms such as these must be made narrow and specific: for precisely identifying that to which a term refers, for supplying the clear basis for an argument of exposition, or for establishing the postulates of a systematic body of knowledge such as that of a science or a history. Only definitions constructed to provide working ideas in systematic study of English and its history fall within our concern here.

PROBLEMS OF DEFINITION

1.2 Definition of the English language may be introduced as a problem rather than a statement. English, we say, is a language, and we can designate abundant instances of speech that are properly called "English." Can we, however, describe as "English" a wide range of samples of speech of North America, New Zealand, Scotland, and Jamaica, as well as of England? Can we include the earliest speech of children whose parents speak English? Or the speech of students in a Japanese, Lebanese, or Peruvian classroom who are making first attempts to use English? Or the special auxiliary speech of native peddlars, policemen, and prostitutes associating with English speakers in a foreign-speaking area? Is it possible to include utterances as diverse as the following (all three are translations of a passage of Boethius' *Consolation of Philosophy*)?

> (a) If anyone wants nothing more than unbridled will and unlimited fame (thinking that these are the greatest goods), let him look into the vast areas of the heavens and the small space of the earth. . . . [20th century]
>
> (b) Whoso that with overthrowynge thought oonly seketh

glorie of fame, and weneth that it be sovereyn good, lat him looke upon the brode schewynge contrees of the hevene, and upon the streyte sete of this erthe. . . . [14th century (Chaucer)]

(c) Swa hwa swa wilnige to habbene þone idelan hlisan and þone unnytan gilp, behealde he on feower healfe his hu widgille þæs heofones hwealfa bið, and hu neara þære eorðan stede is. . . . [10th century (King Alfred)]

These questions indicate the nature of the problem of defining a language, in this instance, English.

The English language, let us say, is the characteristic speech of peoples inhabiting certain geographical areas, when they speak to each other with mutual intelligibility in a natural or habitual manner in a wide variety of circumstances. It is true that English is the language most frequently spoken and understood by most people in Great Britain. The statement implies a limitation in time to contemporaneous speakers; a broad measure of contemporaneity in this sense is the normal life-span. Yet, life-spans of speakers overlap and a person's language system (under normal circumstances) never seems to suffer disruptions in form and efficacy within his own community; we may then have to allow for English a time-span reaching into the past and future to an indefinite extent.

What happens to our trial definition when we allow indefinite extension into the past of what we have called the English language? As the parallel translations of Boethius cited above show, Chaucer's speech was different from our own, and the writings of King Alfred indicate that a thousand years ago the inhabitants of the geographical area now called Great Britain spoke in such a way as not to be intelligible to modern inhabitants of England or America. Although intervening generations have been continuous and their speech systems presumably have had continuous existence and efficacy, the older and the newer inhabitants obviously could not speak to one another in a wide variety of circumstances in a natural manner, with mutual intelligibility. Thus, in accommodating one aspect of our provisional definition of English (its time-span) we have rejected, because we have contradicted, another aspect—mutual intelligibility in normal speech under widely varied circumstances.

Defining a language may be analyzed as a problem in classification. From one point of view a language is collective, manifest in all the utterances, actual and potential, of a group of speakers. If we are to deal scientifically or historically with a language, it is necessary to classify all utterances, and to formulate these classes to a purpose. We can define a language, for instance, as the habitual closely similar speech systems used by a relatively homogenous speech group—a speech community—within a stipulated narrow span of time. Or we can define a language as the broad system of speech elements exhibiting continuous modification while in shared use by a continuous cultural succession of human generations. In the first instance the definition serves the purpose of description based on contrastive analysis, and belongs to what is called synchronic study of a language. In the second instance the definition serves comparative and historical analysis, falling under what is called diachronic study of a language. That each of these definitions may lead to difficulties or contradictions when inappropriately applied is the result of differences in the interests and disciplines they serve.

The science of biology provides a parallel. For a taxonomist a species is defined by the thoroughgoing structural resemblance of individual organisms, their inhabitance of a continuous geographical area, and their ability to interbreed freely in the wild; this last criterion implies that they exist within a single geological period. Organisms are classed in one species if they conform to all these criteria; they are classed in *separate* species if they do not conform to all these criteria. The paleontologist also classifies organisms; and because it is convenient, he uses a classification system based on that of the taxonomist: at the latter end of the time-scale their classifications must be congruent. Since the paleontologist classifies organisms that lived in different geological periods, he cannot use the full set of criteria adopted by a taxonomist. Instead, he classes organisms in separate species when the degree of difference between past organisms corresponds to the degree of difference between species of living organisms. Taxonomy and paleontology are separate disciplines and make separate classifications of the variations among organisms: they define "species" differently. Each science proceeds without difficulty from its own postulates, including its definition of species. If contradictions were to arise, as they might in an attempt to describe the history of two species that have developed from a single earlier species from which in turn both later species are held to be distinct, then the definitions from the two disciplines would not have been kept distinct.

In dealing with both the description and the history of the English language, we must have two types of definition. We must deal with English as both taxonomists and paleontologists. On the one hand, we can make models based upon synchronic analysis of observed relatively uniform speech (or its records), and, on the other, we can make models based on diachronic analysis of observed speech elements (or their records). Descriptive and historical linguistics are related in a way like taxonomy and paleontology. To the extent that they are related, it is convenient when dealing with the history of English to base many categories, concepts, and designations on the working ideas and terminology of descriptive analysis. The two disciplines are separate, though, and their statements—like those expressed in their definitions of "English"—must be kept distinct.

VARIATION IN SPEECH SOUNDS

1.3 Dual interest in the structure of the English language and in relations between its various stages requires two different procedures operating with two different definitions of English. Nevertheless, a close, complementary relationship exists between the procedures and definitions; this relationship may be suggested first by saying that description and history deal with English as it is used in normal, habitual ways within communities of native speakers of the language.

It is a commonplace of both theory and precise observation that no two utterances are exactly alike. To take the simplest example, a one-syllable word spoken by different persons may differ in pitch, speed, or loudness. One person cannot easily repeat a word without differences noticeable even to an average listener. The more refined the techniques of measurement, the more unlikely that two utterances cannot be distinguished. Ultimately we know them to be not identical because they are at least numerically different—they originate from different sources, they occur at different times, or both. As language is actually used in speech communities, however, many of the differences noticeable even to average hearers are ignored, and within a large, random collection of utterances the differences that are regularly observed are relatively few. To look at this circumstance from the opposite point of view, a great many utterances are considered by users of a language to be alike; the likeness may be in patterns of sounds that have meaning (such as individual words), sounds that in themselves do not have meaning (*k*-sounds, for example), or in sequences of meaningful sounds (phrases and sentences). We have, then, on the one hand, the fact of constant variation in speech utterances. On the other, we have the fact that a great many variations, though continually apparent as an aspect of actual speech, are not recognized as a significant part of the language of the speakers.

"SAMES" AND "DIFFERENTS" IN LANGUAGE DESIGN

1.4 The characteristic of language reflected in the recognition of "sames" and "differents" in utterances has been termed "telegraphic" as opposed to "telephonic" by Martin Joos, in "Description of Language Design." The characteristic is one of language *design.* In so far as language is something that can be analyzed and described systematically and completely, a description can deal with its design. When analyzed for their design, languages are always found to have "sames" and "differents" but not to have continuous gradations. A speech sound such as a vowel in any given utterance is distinguished in one language in either one way or another; it is never ambiguous or ambivalent. When *pen* is pronounced with a quick and less open vowel than usual it may be understood as *pin* but it is never understood as both *pin* and *pen* at the same time, or as referring to a cross between a pin and a pen; if social or physical contexts suggest to the hearer that *pin* is inappropriate he may ask which was meant—*pen* or *pin.* At all events he will decide. Even though utterances may have various durations for the sequence of the sounds represented by *p–e–n,* these variations are not used continuously in English to signify, say, variations in length or brand or color of a pen. From this point of view of "telegraphic" design, descriptions of a language are concerned with discrete units. The terms "phoneme" and "morpheme" designate two such types of language elements. Phonemes are discrete, contrastive units of speech sounds like those represented by *e* and *i* in *pen* and *pin* or by *p* and *d* in *pin* and *din;* morphemes are discrete, contrastive meaningful forms, such as *pen* and *pencil.* They will be defined in some detail in Chapters 3 and 11, respectively.

Differences and identities among utterances are referable to the two kinds of material that constitute language: the symbolic material, consisting of speech sounds, their combinations, and the relations among their combinations, and the referent material, consisting of the experience complex associated with the symbolic material. The latter has been described by H. A. Gleason, Jr., as the "ideas, social situations, meanings— . . . the facts or fantasies about man's existence, the things man reacts to and tries to convey to his fellows" (*An Introduction to Descriptive Linguistics,* revised edition, p. 2) . The two kinds of material are commonly called "expression" and "content."

Some identical features of expression and some identical features of content occur, for example, in the following utterances:

(a) Pitch the ball!
(b) He pitched the ball.
(c) It was a wild pitch.
(d) Pitch the ball?
(e) He's a second-rate pitcher.
(f) A bucket of pitch.

(g) They refined radium from pitchblende.
(h) That water pitcher.
(i) A pitchier appearance.
(j) Musical pitch.

All ten contain the expression *pitch.* Three of them *(a, b, d)* contain the expression *ball;* three *(c, h, i)* contain *er;* three *(e, f, j)* contain a *k*-sound; the intonation of *c* and *e* (and some others) is the same, and *a* and *d* differ only in intonation. Identical content features occur in *a* and *d* (and some others) ; the *–ed* in two instances *(b* and *g)* are the same in content but not in expression; the *er* (in *e, h, i*) is the same but differs by indicating agentive function in *e,* comparative degree in *i,* and nothing at all by itself in *h (water).* Other examples are the two meanings 'permit' and 'hinder' for *let,* the two meanings for identical matter serving to distinguish two distinct forms. In *to ring a bell* and in *the ring of a bell* differences in the forms spelled *ring* are inherent in the differences in contexts—in syntactic frames —so that one is a verb form and the other a noun form.

"SAMES" AND "DIFFERENTS" IN LANGUAGE HISTORY

1.5 Historical analysis of a language, based on the discrete characteristics of language design, must account for differences of design structure that may occur in continuing use of a language by a continuing speech community. The problem is one of connecting systems in which patterns of "sames" and "differents" of utterances do not exactly correspond. At an early stage of English "*f*-sounds" and "*v*-sounds" were the "same" (in respect to distinguishing one word from another), and at a later stage they were different; the past tense verb corresponding to present tense *go* was *yode* until replaced by *went;* at one time negation was expressed by *ne* before the finite verb of a clause, but at a later time it came to be expressed by *not* following the verb. In one aspect, historical analysis differs from structural or descriptive analysis only in having simultaneous interest in two or more structures (or designs) of language considered to have a relation of continuous development. That is, historical analysis involves descriptions of two or more developmentally related language systems. However, to describe the changes in language design that connect two successive systems the analysis must include something about the nature or processes of persistence with modification of a language system. It is the range and variety of ever-present variations that enables historical study to make plausible analyses. Thus the treatment of change and variations in utterances differs in synchronic and diachronic studies of a language: in the first they are classed by an either-or procedure within a fixed system, while in the second they are charted in a process of change. To put it informally, the first kind of analysis makes "cuts," while the second traces "drifts."

Let us describe this discourse through another analogy from biology. The evolution of organic forms does not occur within individual organisms themselves; the genetic systems of individual organisms are not in continuous transition. (Even the incidence of mutation—a sudden change—within an organic system is extremely infrequent.) Furthermore, the variations that occur within a biological group (such as a species) are not infinite, but represent a continuous gradation in which differences are very small indeed. Evolutionary change in biology, then, arises from differential reproduction of discrete biological systems (individual organisms), and is described as the drifts of averages or centers of genetic variations. In short, it is not organisms that evolve, it is species, or populations.

The analogy is closely apposite to language history. A language system, as already mentioned, does not contain variations of the kind we can call transitions. From the point of view of description and design, an utterance is not transitional; it can be that only from an historical point of view. As evidence of past language systems shows, however, the average of variations within closely similar speech systems (a language) does change in the course of time. The change we analyze in historical study of a language is therefore a feature of shift in ranges and averages of variations among language structures. Finally, the variations among speech systems are not infinite, though they too represent continuous gradation in which differences are small enough seldom to be noticed within a speech community. Thus, the study of change in a language concerns the historical succession of speech systems; it deals with drifts in the makeup of the system of utterances within continuing language communities.

DIFFERENCES OF ANALYSIS FOR DESIGN AND CHANGE

1.6 Analysis of English for purposes of description and historical study must be twofold. In so far as we deal with the language as a speech system in normal use by a group of speakers, we will analyze systems of discrete elements with absolute distinctions of the "sames" and "differents" among utterances whose sounds, forms, constructions, and meanings exhibit continual variation. The analysis is atomistic, based on contrastive principles yielding classes of facts and rules of their relations. In dealing with change of the language we will analyze not a language as it functions at a given time for a speech community, but the shifts and differences that can be observed between successive language systems and their materials. The analysis is ultimately statistical, based on extrapolation of norms, gradations, and trends in successive language systems. Science and history are different, and they are complementary.

Chapter 2

SOME BACKGROUND INFORMATION

SOCIAL HISTORY VS. LANGUAGE HISTORY

2.1 The relation of speakers and their language with respect to mutual influence is understood differently now than it was a few decades ago. National, tribal, or racial traits are no longer credited directly with shaping language, environment does not automatically account for the characteristics of a community's speech, and it is linguistic systems that mold thought and not the other way around. Although culture and language are believed to have had close formal as well as lexical correlations in the remote past, "the [grammatical] forms of language will in course of time cease to symbolize those of culture," as Edward Sapir observed more than half a century ago ("Language and Environment," in *The American Anthropologist,* Vol. 14, for 1912, p. 241, used with permission); while linguistic structure and culture apparently never lose all relation to one another, "the relative rates of change of the two differ so materially as to make it practically impossible to detect the relationship" (Ibid.). The vocabulary of a language, however, always reflects the culture and environment of its speakers.

The history of English, therefore, may be expected to differ markedly from the history of its speakers. The first is often distinguished as the "internal" history of English and the second as the "external" or "social" history of English. The internal history of the language appears as a much slower, steadier, more self-determining process of change than does the external history of English-speaking peoples. The course of change of the language shows nothing comparable to the revolutions, conquests, changes in manners, and migrations in the social history of its speakers. For all the variety and rapidity of changes in social, political, economic, scientific, and other cultural characteristics of the peoples, the course of events nonetheless exhibits at all points a coherence and continuity enabling a history to show causes of change except where evidence is insufficient. Language history, too, operates from assumptions shared with history and science, particularly the assumptions of cause and coherence. The assumption of coherence in language history may be formulated thus: The behavior of past language elements in chronological succession does not differ in any of its principles from the behavior of presently observable language elements in chronological succession. This assumption is supported in two reciprocal ways. First, having observed no interruption or sudden, large change in continuing use of various aspects of a current language, we postulate that no interruptions or gross changes occurred in any successive past stages of linguistic change. The coherence and continuity within any observed span of a language permit the assumption of coherence and continuity in all similar spans of language in the past. It is also found that in every instance yet encountered, the more dense the chronological set of factual data, the smaller the differences within the set. Second, the assumption is consistent with the knowledge we have of human affairs generally and of linguistic facts in particular; and its converse is not. If we fail to recognize the continuity embodied in the history of English, we shall miss full appreciation of the fact that the language has an identity in its developmental as well as in its contemporary aspects.

THE HISTORICAL PERIODS OF ENGLISH

2.2 It is practical, nonetheless, to divide any lengthy history into parts or periods and to set the point of its beginning. For English the conventional major divisions are three: Old English, for the period from beginnings to about 1100; Middle English, for about 1100 to 1450/1500; Modern English, for the language from the sixteenth century to the present. The principal basis for these divisions lies in changes in the systems of grammatical inflections: the times of most rapid change in the inflectional system are represented by approximate dates. The inherent practicality of using changes in the inflectional system as the criterion for dividing the history of English into periods will become increasingly apparent in the chapters that follow. Suffice it to say here that the sounds of English speech constitute a system whose evolution is in many ways independent of other aspects of the language; the vocabulary has a flexibility and independence that does not identify the basic, structural features of the language; the grammatical inflections, however, have been related to the syntax in such ways as to function as an index of extensive structural characteristics of the language. To recall the analogy in 1.2, inflections provide an index by which, as linguistic paleontologists, we can distinguish differences among successive stages of English comparable to taxonomic differences between developmentally related languages. The beginning of English cannot be set quite so specifically, partly because records of the language and of the languages from which it became differentiated do not exist. Even if records did exist the stipulation of even a half-century date would be difficult because of the gradualness of language change and differentiation. As practical as any criterion, perhaps, is the period of major settlement in England by speakers whose language came to be known as English: the beginnings of English may be put in the sixth century. The written records of Old English nevertheless come mostly from the ninth, tenth, and eleventh centuries.

Prior to its differentiation as a separate, "English" language, the language systems in use by fifth and sixth century conquerors of England constituted closely related dialects within a variety of dialects labeled collectively in language history as West Germanic. The larger set of dialects in turn were developmentally related to other large sets of dialects—North Germanic and East Germanic. The names imply a still larger grouping—Germanic—that constitutes one of the major divisions of the group of Indo-European languages. As a Germanic language English began with some of the characteristics that distinguish Germanic from other, related language groups. It had two major patterns of verb inflection, as will be described in Chapter 16; it had a twofold declension of adjectives, as will appear in Chapter 14; it also had a stock of words in common with other Germanic languages; it had as well a fixed stress accent, a feature that will be illustrated in several contexts in subsequent chapters; and it shared a difference from non-Germanic major language groups in certain consonants resulting from the "First Germanic Consonant Shift," commonly referred to as an effect of "Grimm's Law," the heading under which it is defined and illustrated usually in collegiate dictionaries.

Because it lies outside the scope of our topic, the prehistory of English is only mentioned here. We shall have enough to do in working through the recorded history of the language without working through linguistic reconstruction back to the antecedents of English.

DIALECT AREAS OF EARLY ENGLISH

2.3 Throughout its recorded history English has been a collection of dialects. The differences among dialects, the influence of one dialect on another, and the rise of dialects to the status of "standard" will be recurrent themes in many of the chapters following. At the outset it will be useful to name the major dialect areas for the periods of Old English and Middle English in order to have a terminology for regional differences that must be mentioned frequently in describing the language and the changes it has undergone. Figure 2A shows the dialect divisions of Old English in block letters and those of Middle English in italic. No boundary lines have been drawn in the figure because their presence would even further oversimplify the gradations and overlaps

Figure 2A. Major dialect areas of England for Old English (block letters) and Middle English (italic).

and shifts among variations in the language as they were distributed geographically. It may be noted that the shape of the land mass in the map roughly approximates that in "The Gough Map," a mid-fourteenth century map showing the principal population centers and roads, as well as rivers and a few other topographical data. Reproduction of that early map here would be impractical; the map is available in facsimile, however, and is well worth examining for its picture of population distribution and routes of travel in early England. The map can provide valuable aid to understanding dialect distribution and change for much of the early history of English.

THE VOCAL TRACT

2.4 With one additional kind of background information we shall be ready to begin direct description of English in its various stages and trace some of the main lines of its historical development. The diagram of the "vocal tract" in Figure 2B labels the principal positions of artic-

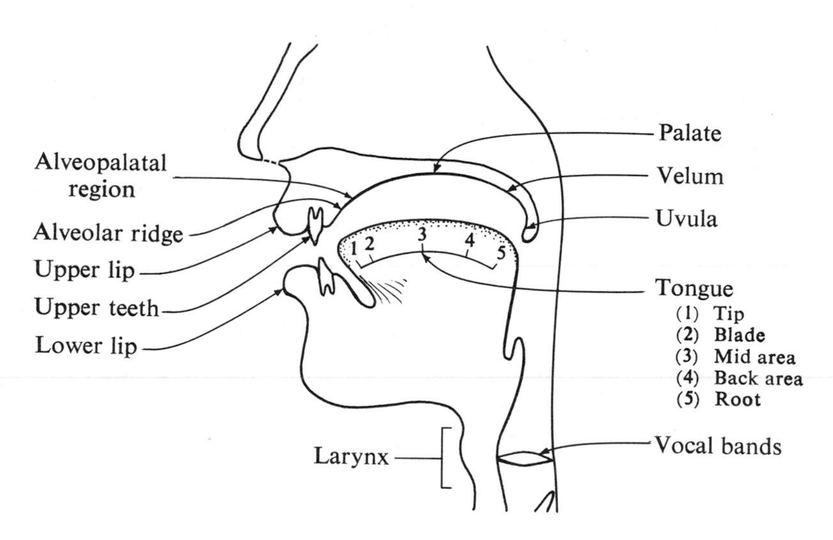

Figure 2B. The "vocal tract," with labels for principal areas of articulation of speech.

ulation of vowels and consonants. Figure 2C diagrams the positioning of the principal articulators for two representative consonant sounds, *n* (as in *no*) and *g* (as in *go*). Speech also requires a breath stream, supplied from the lungs. The muscles controlling the flow of air need not be included in the diagram, since their function provides no differentiation of English vowels and consonants. Their operation is significant, however, in differentiating some other speech signals of a kind to be described in Chapter 24. Finally, it may be noted that there is no reason to doubt that the vocal tract has been essentially the same for all speakers of English, whatever their racial characteristics, through all the history of the language.

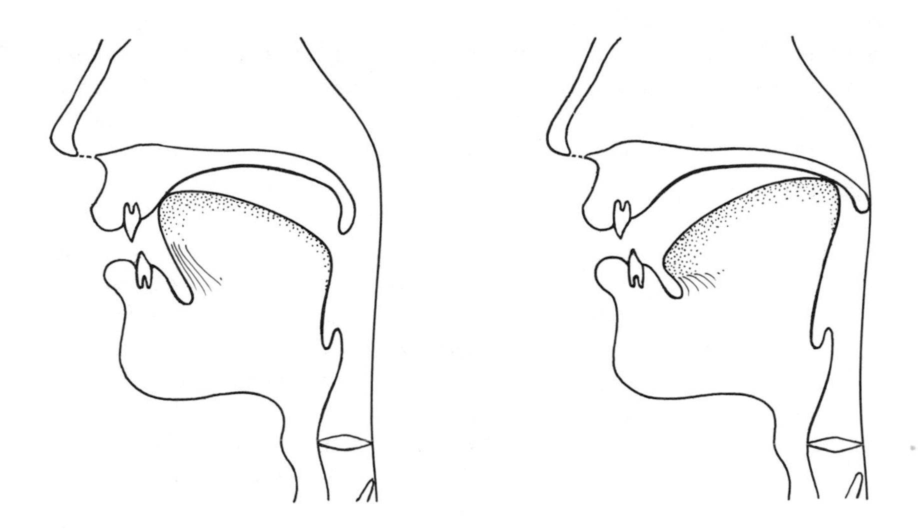

Figure 2C. Positions of principal articulators for [n], left, and [g], right.

Chapter 3

INDIVIDUAL CONSONANTS

SPEECH SOUNDS AND PHONOLOGICAL UNITS

3.1 Normal speech is in sentences. The sentences are made up of units that we can delete, add, or rearrange in order to say one thing rather than another. In this respect the general small units we tend to think of are "words." Within words are other obvious units, as in the instance of *book* vs. *books, sing* vs. *sang, you* vs. *your.* Then there are smaller units by which we differentiate *mouse* from *house, pan* from *pun, at* from *mat,* and so on. It must be assumed that throughout the history of English speakers normally spoke in sentences. Changes occurred in the ways sentences were put together from words, but sentence patterns did not change as a result of substituting *uncle* for *em, despair* for *wanhope, names* for *namen.* Nor was there significant change in sentence construction when case inflection of adjectives (similar to *they–their–them*) was no longer used, or when a past-tense verb no longer had different shapes for singular and plural—*hē drāf, wē drifon* 'he drove,' 'we drove,' for example. The same action was symbolized when *sneeze* began with *fn–* rather than *sn–*. Some changes in one aspect of the language, however, did occasion, or accompany, changes in other aspects: for example, when a whole set of forms—*se, ðæs, ðǣm, ðā, ðone, ðāra, ðæt*—was replaced by *ðe* = *the,* relative pronouns (pronominals) and the clauses they introduced were extensively modified. The history of English concerns changes in all these aspects of the language; in so far as it is history and all the elements of sounds, forms, constructions, and meanings were present in all utterances in English at all times, the history concerns all these at once. To *deal* with the history, however, we must start with one part of it, proceed to another and then another, and concern ourselves with the relations—one at a time—of its various aspects. We shall begin with the speech sounds, first in present-day English.

This study must deal with the sounds, considered for themselves, and the way in which speakers of English use and react to those sounds. The study concerns the empirical data of the sounds and the pragmatic treatment of them by people speaking and hearing English. As speakers of English we may talk about the "*y*-sounds" and there is no question about what the term means when we further specify "*y*-sounds at the beginning of words." We mean, for example, the sounds that distinguish *yet* from *wet, yawl* from *ball* or *all.* In fact we tend to prefer "the sound 'y' " to "the sounds 'y.' " It is "the sounds," though, as may be readily discovered by greatly slowing down the articulation of what we represent in writing by the letter *y*. In the word *yawl* the "sound" begins similar to the vowel in *fit* or perhaps in *feet;* it ends as a glide into the vowel spelled here *aw,* rhyming with *ball,* and in between has passed through a range of sounds some of which resemble the vowel of *numb*. The initial "y" of *yummy* is much like that of *yawl* except that the glide is shorter. In *yes* it is also shorter but not quite the same as in the other two words. The sounds making up the glide are different in other ways for *you* and different again for *yeast.* For *yeast,* the glide ends in the vowel like that of *feet,* that is, in the sound with which it may begin in *yawl*; it begins with a sound made with greater tenseness of muscles in the throat and mouth than the sound of the vowel in *feet*; and the glide is extremely short. The differences in these "y-sounds" beginning *yeast, yes, you, yummy, yawl* are indeed great when we listen to them simply as sounds. It will be obvious, too, that not only do they differ among themselves, but that any articulation of "y" beginning a word is a continuous sequence—a slur—of distinguishable sounds; the slur continues right into a following vowel.

Nevertheless we do speak of "the *y*-sound" in English. It is this "sound" that distinguished *yet* from *met, bet, wet,* etc. and *yawl* from *maul, ball, wall, all,* etc. As good pragmatists we say that there is no difference unless it makes a difference. Since the length of the "*y*–glides" or the particular sequence of sounds we can hear in them makes no difference to us by itself in distinguishing words, we say that there is no difference, at least in our language: whatever their differences, they are "the same." The differences in sounds that we can detect, by carefully observing and comparing, are designated as phonetic differences. The differences that are singled out—segmented—as only pertinent to the language we speak, the ones we recognize pragmatically in using the language, are designated as phonemic differences. Sounds that are phonetically different but regarded for all practical purposes as being the same (such as the different "y's") are designated as allophones of a phoneme.

It would be both out of place and out of proportion here to derive the phonemes of English step-by-step. The phonemes will merely be listed and certain of their attributes will be described directly. Because English contains more distinctive speech sounds (phonemes) than can be symbolized by the conventional alphabet—and because English spelling does not spell most phonemes in a single and consistent way, a single symbol is used for each phoneme. Phonemic notation is enclosed in slants (virgules) to distinguish it from spelling notation which is given in italic; thus /y/ is read "the phoneme 'y' " and it is spelled variously, as in *you, onion, use.*

FACTORS OF ARTICULATION: STOPS AND NASALS

3.2 The words *lamb, lab, lap* are distinguished in speech solely by means of the terminal sounds; that is, speakers of English use one segment in each series of sounds making up the words to differentiate between an utterance referring to a certain kind of animal, to a place where experiments are conducted, and to the front part of a person from waist to knees when he is sitting. The segments are respectively the phonemes /m b p/. The sounds that manifest these different phonemes are obviously different and can be described in various ways. To isolate the sounds—to utter "–m–," "–b–," "–p–"—is one way to begin. Even if each can be recognized easily, to state how they sound different is difficult. How the sounds differ *as sounds* can be shown when the phonemic segments are analyzed by special equipment that represents graphically the acoustic (or the physical) features of the disturbances of air we call sound. Our present concern will be simply to deal with the differences in phonemes in terms of readily accessible correlations, the concomitants of the production of the distinctive sounds: our description of differences will be based on the factors of their articulation.

The articulation of /m b p/ involves closure of both lips; /m/ consists of a continuing voice sound, while /p/ and /b/ do not, and /p/ and /b/ cannot be continuant sounds, as anyone may discover by trying to sustain them. For /m/ the breath is allowed to escape through the nose (by lowering the velum), while for /b/ and /p/ sounds the breath is stopped from escaping through either the nose or the mouth —so long as the characteristic articulation of these particular sounds is taking place. In uttering *lamb, sum, rim,* the final distinctive sound of /m/ is articulated, then, by closing the lips, opening the passage from throat to nose, and continuing the voice; the /m/ ceases when the voice stops, and nothing more is utilized as a speech sound (the rest is mere breathing). In uttering *man, mill, mumps,* the initial /m/ involves onset of voice, closed lips, and open passage to the nasal area. Initial and final /m/'s are clearly different in their beginnings. Put into larger utterances, though, these differences diminish: *The lamb is hungry* has /m/ following a vowel and, as in *mill,* the same /m/

precedes a vowel. Finally, the distinctiveness of the articulating factors of /m/ may be reduced to bilabial (that is, two-lip) closure, velar lowering (for nasal breath stream), and voice.

The thoroughness of articulatory description for the sounds manifesting /m/ will permit description of the distinguishing phonetic features of the other two phonemes to proceed more rapidly. It was shown that /p/ and /b/ are bilabial and nonnasal. In final positions, as in *lab, sub, rib* and *lap, sup, rip,* the closure of the lips may or may not be followed by an opening of the lips after voice has stopped. In initial position—before a vowel—the closure is of course followed by an opening of the lips to provide for articulation of the subsequent sound. Closure, thus, is the only constant factor in this aspect of articulation of the /p/ and /b/ sounds. The raised velum, blocking the breath from the nasal area, has already been mentioned—hence the articulation is oral (taking place in the mouth only). Now to consider how the sounds for /b/ and /p/ differ. At the beginning of an utterance, both involve stoppage then release of breath; at the end of an utterance they need only involve stoppage of breath. Voice will cease when the air flow is fully stopped; or it will diminish rapidly between the time it is blocked and the time the build-up of air pressure in the mouth brings the flow toward a stop; or in the reverse process it will change rapidly as the air flow increases to full speech force. The onset or cessation of voice for /p/ is more rapid than it is for /b/. The difference in rate is great enough to be distinctive—to distinguish *lab–lap, rib–rip, bill–pill, bumps–pumps.* The customary terminology designates /b/ as a voiced consonant, /p/ as an unvoiced consonant. With economy of linguistic terminology they may be labeled voiced bilabial stop /b/ and unvoiced (or voiceless) bilabial stop /p/.

In exactly parallel procedure /n d t/ are distinguished; *rain, raid, rate* and *near, deer, tear* will provide illustration. Instead of bilabial closure, the stoppage of the breath stream in the mouth (for most English speakers) involves the forward part of the tongue in contact with the alveolar ridge—the gum-ridge behind the upper front teeth. To /n/ is assigned the descriptive formula of (voiced) alveolar nasal; /d/ and /t/ are respectively voiced and unvoiced alveolar stop consonants.

Three more consonants, /ŋ g k/, fit into the same scheme of distinctions. They are illustrated in *ring, rig, rick,* or in *slang, slag, slack;* initially *goal* and *coal* are contrastive, but /ŋ/ does not occur at the beginning of English words. Again we have a nasal and two stops, articulated in one area of the mouth. In English the area is relatively extensive, allowing variations in /k/ articulations, for example, that are easily distinguishable phonetically. By isolating the "*k*–sounds" in *keel* and *call* or in *leak* and *lock* the differences can easily be heard. Where the surface of the tongue closes against the top of the mouth is the palatal area for *keel* and *leak;* it is the velar area for *call* and *lock.* An area intermediate between these provides the point of breath stoppage for *lake* and *came.* Because of the variation of position in articulation, English /ŋ g k/ are given the joint label of palatal-velar consonants—/ŋ/ a (voiced) nasal, /g/ and /k/ voiced and unvoiced stops, respectively.

Two more phonemes /č ǰ/, contrasting in *char* and *jar,* will be listed among the stop consonants. Description of them may be postponed, however, until the next series has been sketched in.

FACTORS OF ARTICULATION: SPIRANTS

3.3 The phonemes /s z/ are manifest as continuant sounds utilizing the oral rather than the nasal breath passages. The distinction between them stems from the absence or presence of voice tone, as in *sink, zinc* and *rise, rice.* Otherwise they share distinctive features of continuant manner of articulation having characteristic noise produced by a grooved configuration of the surface of the tongue placed so that the breath stream, in passing over it, is squeezed then released in a turbulence of "hiss" or "buzz." The position is to the front of the (hard) palate; the noisy constriction of breath, contrasting with stoppage of breath for /p b t d k g/, is a distinctive characteristic for which the label "spirant" is assigned: /s/ and /z/ are described as unvoiced (or voiceless) and voiced prepalatal (grooved) spirants.

Parallel description for /f/ and /v/ requires only the stipulation of the position at which the spirant "noise" is produced; the voice feature is illustrated as absent in *fail, fat, few* and present in *vale, vat, view.* The squeeze of the breath stream is made by lower lip and upper teeth—a labiodental position. Two additional spirants /θ/ and /ð/ are also distinguished from each other by voiced and unvoiced production, and from other spirants by their place of articulation: the blade of the tongue constricts the air passage in the region of the upper teeth and gums: the consonant /θ/ in *thigh, wreath* and /ð/ in *thy, wreathe* are thus called dental spirants. Two others are similarly distinguished: /š/ is an unvoiced spirant, with a grooved passage made by the tongue farther back than for /s/, in a palatal position, as in *shoe, crush.* /ž/ is the voiced member of this pair occurring between vowels as in *treasure;* initially and finally it occurs only in nonnative words when the foreign pronunciation is imitated, as in French-derived *gendarme, mirage.*

THREE PHONEMES OF EARLY ENGLISH

3.4 Three additional consonants will be described here, phonemes in early English which appear no longer in most dialects of Modern English. Two of them are spirants differing from each other as unvoiced vs. voiced, like /f/ and /v/, /θ/ and /ð/. They are articulated in the same positions as /k/ and /g/, with corresponding range from palatal to velar areas. The unvoiced palatal-velar spirant is /x/; the voiced palatal-velar spirant is /ǥ/.

The other consonant, symbolized as /ġ/, is of less certain phonetic reconstruction. That it was voiced is clear enough, and that its articulation was generally palatal is hardly to be questioned. It presumably had a spirant quality and may be inferred to have had glide articulation as well: it was apparently in the nature of "*y*-sounds" with spirant "noise." The uncertainty concerns the priority of glide or spirant character as the distinguishing feature. The consonant will be designated provisionally as a spirant with nondistinctive glide in Old English, with the observation that the phoneme continues in English and is analyzed as a glide /y/ by the beginning of Middle English and perhaps earlier.

ASSIBILATED STOPS

3.5 Let us now return to the consonants /č ǰ/, illustrated in *char* and *jar, larch* and *large*. Each of these can be analyzed phonetically into two elements, /č/ being a sequence of [t] and [š], and /ǰ/ a parallel sequence of [d] and [ž]. (The square brackets indicate phonetic as opposed to phonemic notation; the alphabetic symbols in this illustration are identical for both standard systems of notation) . As phonemes, their articulation can be described as follows. Both begin with a stop-articulation followed by a noisy release of air like that for /š/ and /ž/. The forward position of the stop-articulation is the alveolar ridge, like that of /t/ and /d/; besides the tip of the tongue, however, the area behind the tip is also used so that the release of the stop has the noise of [š] or [ž] to which the term "sibilance" is assigned. The articulation, then, of /č/ and /ǰ/ is conveyed in the formula "assibilated stop," voiceless or voiced. Because of the position of air stoppage and that involved in producing sibilance, the palatal position (that is, front of the palate) is designated for these consonant articulations.

LINGUALS

3.6 The consonants /l/ and /r/ do not differ from each other by means of any of the distinguishing features so far described. They are both voiced, and their positions of articulation are not distinctive. The variety of labels that have been applied to them—laterals, liquids, linguals—suggests something of the difficulty in isolating and describing their most usable distinguishing characteristics within the system of English consonants. Acoustically, both have resonance like that of vowels. Essentially, /l/ is produced as a voiced sound during which normally the tip of the tongue is in contact with the upper gums, with space left by the tongue for the breath stream to pass laterally along its sides. A number of variations occur, especially as a result of the back of the tongue being raised or lowered; these variations are nondistinctive. A great variety of "*r*-sounds" are automatically assigned to /r/ by speakers of English. Some include "retroflex" articulation, the tip of the tongue turned upward and backward toward the top of the mouth; some include the tip of the tongue touching the upper gum ridge during the articulation, while for others the tip of the tongue is only put near the gum ridge. The essential characteristic of articulation may be suggested to consist of modifying the voice tone by "cupping" the back of the tongue and allowing the breath stream to escape over and around the more front part of the tongue, the tip of which is raised to some extent. To distinguish it from a vowel, /r/ has glide articulation that /l/ does not have. Though the varieties and characteristics of /l/ and /r/ cannot be described so simply as those of other consonants, the place of these phonemes in the system of English consonants is clear enough. The term "linguals" will be applied to both.

GLIDES

3.7 Two consonants articulated as glides are /y/ and /w/. The illustration of phonetic and phonemic distinctions above (3.1) has characterized /y/ in part. If either of these glides were cut into sections and any section were prolonged to vowel duration, the lengthened section would in effect be one of the vowels: it was pointed out that /y/ may begin with articulation like that of the vowel in *feet*. The beginning of /w/ is a sound typified by the vowel in *blew, to,* or *through*. Glides may be short or long depending on the distance of tongue or lip and jaw movement from their onset to their termination in a following vowel. The exact positions for the onset of their articulations varies, as we saw for /y/ in the examples of *yawl, yes, yeast,* etc.; the variations for /w/ may be illustrated in *want, west, woo.*

In all the examples thus far, glides have preceded vowels in the same syllable: the articulation involves "gliding onto" a vowel. In phonetic terms English also has glides away from a vowel to a following consonant still in the same syllable or to silence. The former are called "on-glides," the latter are called "off-glides." Phonetically, the two "*y*-glides" and the two "*w*-glides" are simply reversals of each other, each pair beginning or ending with approximately the same sound. Some illustration may be helpful. After the /m/ in *my* follows a vowel sound similar to the vowel in *rob, nod* in many American dialects; a glide in the direction of the vowel in *rib* follows from that vowel sound; there is only one syllable. Sounds in *I, tie, lie, fly,* and others are similar. The glide in *cow, now, bough* may be distinguished in the same way. A few pairs of words in English are especially useful in illustrating these glides both preceding and following a vowel—the pairs use the same sounds in exactly opposite orders: *yes* is the reverse of *say, wan* is the reverse of *now.* Both on-glide and off-glide of a single type occur in a single syllable in the exclamation *wow* and the common noun *woe.*

The symbol /y/ will be assigned to the consonantal on-glide in which the tongue begins in a tense configuration close to the palatal area of the mouth; /w/ will be assigned to the on-glide which begins with lips narrowly rounded and the back of the tongue raised (producing an "*oo*-sound") . Both glides are voiced. As on-glides, /y/ and /w/ appear in English words only at the beginning of a syllable, hence only initially (alone or after another consonant) or medially in a word: *yes, music, few, west, quest, fewer,* and the like.

THE GLOTTAL SPIRANT

3.8 English /h/ is a spirant produced with the vocal bands ("vocal cords") partially open so that the breath stream passes noisily over them. It is classed as a voiceless phoneme. Unlike the other consonants, which are articulated in the mouth region, /h/ is a laryngeal or glottal consonant. Because its articulation is independent of the disposition of tongue and lip positionings, to produce any "*h*-sound" also involves producing one or another of the vowel or glide sounds.

SHARED ARTICULATORY CHARACTERISTICS

3.9 Sorting consonants according to certain shared articulatory characteristics will put them into groups more convenient for further study of English phonemes and their history. They may be grouped first on the basis of contrasts in voicing.

Unvoiced: /p t k č f θ s š h/ (earlier, /x /)
Voiced: /b d g ǰ v ð z ž m n ŋ y w / (earlier, /ɡ ġ/)

The manner in which they are articulated provides another basis for grouping.

Stop: /p b t d k g č ǰ/
Spirant: /f v θ ð s z š ž h/ (earlier, /x ɡ ġ/)
Lingual: /l r/
Nasal: /m n ŋ/
Glide: /y w/

The point at which the positioning of speech organs is determinative provides another basis for grouping consonants. Combining this classification with a listing of descriptive labels for all the consonants is convenient.

Bilabial (two lips):
- /p/ unvoiced bilabial stop
- /b/ voiced bilabial stop
- /m/ (voiced) bilabial nasal
- /w/ (voiced) bilabial glide (and see below under *Velar*)

Labiodental (lip-teeth):
- /f/ unvoiced labiodental spirant
- /v/ voiced labiodental spirant

(Inter-) Dental ([tongue with] teeth):
- /θ/ unvoiced dental spirant
- /ð/ voiced dental spirant

Alveolar (gum ridge behind upper front teeth):
- /t/ unvoiced alveolar stop
- /d/ voiced alveolar stop
- /n/ (voiced) alveolar nasal
- /l/ (voiced) alveolar "lateral" (lingual)
- /r/ (voiced) alveolar "cupped" (lingual)

Prepalatal (front of the palate):
- /s/ unvoiced prepalatal (grooved) spirant
- /z/ voiced prepalatal (grooved) spirant

Palatal:
- /č/ unvoiced (assibilated) palatal stop
- /ǰ/ voiced (assibilated) palatal stop
- /š/ unvoiced (alveo-) palatal (grooved) spirant
- /ž/ voiced (alveo-) palatal (grooved) spirant
- /y/ (voiced) palatal glide
- (/ġ/) (voiced) palatal spirant, with glide (> /y/)

Velar ("soft" palate):
/k/ unvoiced palatal-velar stop
/g/ voiced palatal-velar stop
/ŋ/ (voiced) palatal-velar nasal
/w/ (voiced) labiovelar glide (but see 4.3)
(/x/) unvoiced palatal-velar spirant
(/ɡ̶/) voiced palatal-velar spirant
Glottal (larynx):
/h/ voiceless glottal (or laryngeal) spirant

Further sorting of the consonants, involving more complex relationships, will appear in subsequent chapters.

Chapter 4

CONSONANT SYSTEMS

PROBLEMS OF RECONSTRUCTING PAST SPEECH

4.1 Materials from our own speech were used in Chapter 3 in listing the consonant phonemes of Modern English and in describing and sorting them according to the phonetic features of their allophones. Divergences between phonology and spelling will have been fully apparent. To deal with the phonology of earlier stages of English, however, we must depend primarily on written records. Some consideration of the problems of reconstructing past speech is therefore in order.

Interpretation of written records of past speech is in some respects a difficult operation, requiring the skills of cryptography, the ingenuity of riddle solving, and linguistic training of great thoroughness. These qualifications are important in dealing with any language, though they are seldom tasked so heavily as they are with a thousand years of written records of English. The continuity of records of English (the longest among modern Germanic languages), the fact that the records terminate at one end of the scale in the living speech of our own time, and their relationships with other extensive records of related languages eliminate a great many "unknowns"; these circumstances make possible the extensive reconstruction of past phonology, morphology, and semantic data. English writing, furthermore, has been essentially alphabetic from the beginning, and except for a few early instances of runic writing, has been based on the roman alphabet; it has never been logographic or syllabic—that is, having a full set of separate symbols to represent words or syllables. In the course of its history, English has also retained one writing system.

The relation between spelling and speech, however, has been anything but constant. If eighteenth and twentieth century printed texts look very much alike, while sixteenth and eighteenth century texts look somewhat less alike, we cannot automatically conclude that English changed more rapidly in the time of Shakespeare and Milton than it did in the time of Wordsworth and Hardy. From comparing a group of fourteenth century literary texts and a group of nineteenth century literary texts we cannot conclude that diversity of dialects had all but disappeared during the intervening five hundred years. Differences in pronunciation of English—both among contemporaneous dialects and successive periods—are increasingly obscured especially during the last three hundred years in most printed materials and other writing by educated persons: the reason is simply that spelling has been progressively standardized and fixed within that period while the language has continued to change. (The spelling of English is taken up as a separate topic in Chapter 23.) Until dialect surveys were undertaken only in the last hundred years, the written sources of evidence for language variation during the period of Modern English lie generally in the occasional aberrant spellings of practiced writers and in the writings of persons less practiced or less schooled. Evidence of change and variation is more direct and transparent in spelling of fifteenth, sixteenth, and early seventeenth century documents; during that period the number of persons who wrote rapidly increased, together with a decrease in the proportion of professional scribes and printers whose records have survived. Working back from the fifteenth century to the twelfth century, we can observe a decrease and disappearance of a dominating, standard dialect for writing; the evidence from this period reflects much of the diversity and change in English speech. It is only in the earliest documents, however, that English spelling seems to record vowels and consonants with close, though never perfect, consistency.

Besides the evidence of spelling, at any period rhyme, alliteration, and puns are of great value for reconstructing past speech. Further evidence is given by orthoepists and others who, since the sixteenth century, have attempted to describe the pronunciation of English; some of them, it is true, are either unreliable or obscure. Still further evidence can be discovered by the method of internal reconstruction. This method proceeds from data within a synchronic description of a language, and attempts to infer historical development of those data. The only data for which the method is specifically designed are those of morphophonemic variation—the alternation of [f] and [v] in *life – lives,* for example. In most instances in Modern English the alternation of [f] and [v] makes a difference in meaning: *fat – vat, safe – save,* etc., which is to say that Modern English includes the two phonemes /f/ and /v/. Because sound changes are known to occur regularly in given phonetic situations regardless of whether in word-roots, suffixes, or prefixes, an inference can be made about the development of the alternation of [f] and [v] in *life – lives, knife – knives, wife–wives,* etc.: at one time alternation of [f] and [v] made no difference in meaning. That is, Modern English has two phonemes /f/ and /v/, but an earlier stage of English had only one phoneme corresponding to them, with allophones [f] and [v]. Similar reconstructions within the inflectional variations of Modern English can be made from alternations typified by *house–houses* and *bath–baths* to the effect that /s/ and /z/ correspond to one phoneme in earlier English, as /θ/ and /ð/ correspond to another single earlier phoneme.

Reconstruction of phonological, morphological, and semantic factors of earlier stages of English has been carried out in the past hundred years with great thoroughness, and the results are presented in orderly form notably in the historical grammars and in the *Oxford English Dictionary*. Most of this work was done prior to the development of the concepts of modern structural linguistics, and many details of structural formulation of the data are still to be worked out; however, enough has been established to enable us to undertake historical study of most periods of English on the basis of material now available with assurance of the general accuracy of the data and the procedures.

CONSONANT SYSTEMS OF EARLIER ENGLISH

4.2 Consonant systems of earlier stages of English correspond in several ways to the system of Modern English. It will be practical therefore to introduce consonants of the principal earlier periods first by way of parallel lists, remarking only on those particular consonants that differ significantly from our own.

MnE /p b t d k g č ǰ f v θ ð s z š ž m n l r w y h/
ME /p b t d k g č ǰ f v θ ð s z š x m n l r w y h/
OE /p b t d k g k̭ ĝ f þ s x ǥ m n l r w ġ h/

In both Middle English and Old English /r/ was probably manifest as a trilled consonant, and /t/, /d/, /n/ were probably dental rather than alveolar in point of articulation. It will be recalled that /ǥ/ was a voiced palatal-velar spirant and /ġ/, whose Middle English reflex is symbolized as /y/, probably had spirant articulation. /x/ was a patatal-velar spirant having unvoiced [x] and voiced [γ] allophones. /k̭/ was an unvoiced stop, in a more fronted position than /k/ and to some extent assibilated; its reflex in Middle and Modern English has been given the notation /č/. /ĝ/ was a voiced assibilated stop pairing with /k̭/ in position of articulation and in assibilation; its reflex in later stages of English has been given the notation /ǰ/. (The different symbols for the Old English stops with assibilation are useful in implying the origin of the stops, as we shall see later, and in suggesting the historical transition from stops with nondistinctive assibilation to later assibilated stops; the Old English /k̭/ and /ĝ/ nevertheless do closely correspond phonetically and systemically to later /č/ and /ǰ/.) Until late Middle English /n/ had two allophones, dental [n] and velar [ŋ]. In Old English /f/, /þ/, and /s/ had unvoiced and voiced allophones [f, v], [θ, ð], and [s, z], respectively; Old English /þ/ is the only readily adaptable symbol for distinguishing the spirants of Old English from those of Middle English.

The consonants of Old English are illustrated in the following list:

/p/ pæð *path,* grāp *(he) seized,* uppan *on*
/b/ bæð *bath,* lamb *lamb,* hæbbe *(I) have*
/t/ tūn *enclosure, town,* sealt *salt,* winter *winter*
/d/ dūn *hill, down,* tīd *time, while,* wurdon *(they) became*
/k/ cēne *bold,* dranc *(he) drank,* drincan *(to) drink*
/g/ gār *spear,* sprang *(he) sprang,* springan *(to) spring*
/k̲/ ċēn *torch,* iċ *I,* miċel *much*
/ĝ/ secg (/seĝ/) *man, warrior,* sengan *(to) singe*
/f/ [f] for *for,* wulf *(he-) wolf,* drifst *drivest*
[v] wulfas *wolves,* hæfde *(he) had*
/þ/ [θ] þorn *thorn,* āð *oath,* seofoða *seventh*
[ð] āþas *oaths,* eorðe *earth, land*
/s/ [s] stān *stone,* ċēas *(he) chose,* mǣst *most*
[z] ċēosan *(to) choose,* rǣsde *(he) rushed,* bosm *bosom*
/x/ [x] rūh *rough,* uht *dusk*
[γ] beorgan *(to) protect*
/ǥ/ dragan *(to) draw*
/m/ mā *more,* eom *(I) am,* lamb *lamb*
/n/ [n] nā *not, no,* ān *one,* ond *and*
[ŋ] dranc *(he) drank,* springan *(to) spring*
/l/ lār *learning, lore,* hāl *whole, sound,* willan *(to) wish*
/r/ rād *(he) rode,* lār *lore,* word *word*
/w/ wē *we,* hrēaw *raw,* sāwol *soul*
/ġ/ ġēar *year,* weġ *way,* þeġn *thane*
/h/ horn *horn*

The consonants of later Middle English are illustrated in the following list:

/p/ path *path,* grop, grap *(he) seized,* upper *more upward*
/b/ bath *bath,* lamb *lamb,* labbe *blab, tell-tale*
/t/ toun *town,* salt *salt,* wynter *winter*
/d/ doun, dun *a hill, down,* tyde *time, while,* briddes *birds*
/k/ kene *keen, sharp,* drank *drank,* drynke *(to) drink*
/g/ gere *gear, equipment,* sprang *sprang,* sprynge *(to) spring*
/č/ chekes *cheeks,* ich *I,* muchel *much*
/ǰ/ wegge *wedge,* senge *(to) singe*
/f/ fyn (e) *fine,* wolf *wolf*
/v/ vyne *vine,* wolves *wolves*
/θ/ thorn *thorn,* oth *oath,* erthe *earth*
/ð/ scathe *harm, misfortune,* rathe *quickly*

/s/ ston, stoon *stone,* ches *(he) chose,* moost *most*
/z/ chese *(to) choose*
/š/ shal *shall,* dissh *dish,* wasshe *(to) wash*
/x/ rough *rough,* thoghte *(he) thought*
/m/ mo, more *more,* am *am,* doumb *dumb*
/n/ [n] no *no,* oon *one,* and *and*
[ŋ] drank, *drank,* synge *(to) sing*
/l/ loore, lore *teaching, lore,* hool *whole, sound,* wylle *(to) will*
/r/ rood, rod *(he) rode,* soore, *sore (-ly),* word *word*
/w/ we *we,* fewe *few,* drawe *(to) draw*
/h/ he *he,* hond *hand*

SYSTEMIC RELATIONS OF CONSONANTS

4.3 In the remaining sections of this chapter we shall be connecting consonant phonemes in various ways so as to understand the patterns which they form. To some extent the arranging of consonants, for each of the three principal periods of English, resembles a game with the object of finding patternings that may be represented in diagrams. The serious object of the "game" will become apparent in Chapter 6.

To extend our description of English consonants beyond sorting the phonemes according to shared distinctive features of the allophones of each of them, let us consider more complex systematic relations of the consonants to each other. The relations among phonemes are a specially important part of their descriptions in that a phoneme is defined in part by its differences from other phonemes of the same language. We shall continue to use phonetic features. Certain systems of arrangement appear among these features. For instance, the first sixteen consonants in the above list for Modern English can be arranged in sets of eight, one unvoiced set, one voiced set. Consonants can also be arranged in sets of stops and spirants by using additional classification of shared phonetic features (Figure 4A). The diagram-

		Bilabial	Labio-dental	Dental	Alveolar	Prepalatal	Velar
Stops	unvoiced	p			t		k
	voiced	b			d		g
Assibilated stops	unvoiced					č	
	voiced					ǰ	
Spirants	unvoiced		f	θ	s	š	
	voiced		v	ð	z	ž	

Figure 4A. Stop and spirant consonants of Modern English arranged according to articulatory features.

matic representation in the figure also shows the phonemes in a sequence from left to right corresponding to that of the points of articulation from the front to the back of the mouth. That is, the relation of /p/ is "more front" than all other consonants except its voiced counterpart /b/; or the relation of /s/ to /f/, /b/, etc. is "more back," but with respect to /č/, /g/, etc. it is "more front."

This set of consonants can be given further desrcription: the eight spirants are related by two patterns—voiced vs. unvoiced, and by position of articulation along the scale front-to-back. Using the symbol ">" to mean "more front than," the spirants can be described in two sets /f/>/θ/>/s/>/š/ and /v/>/ð/>/z/>/ž/. To unite these two sets of relations, the diagram in Figure 4B is the simplest form of

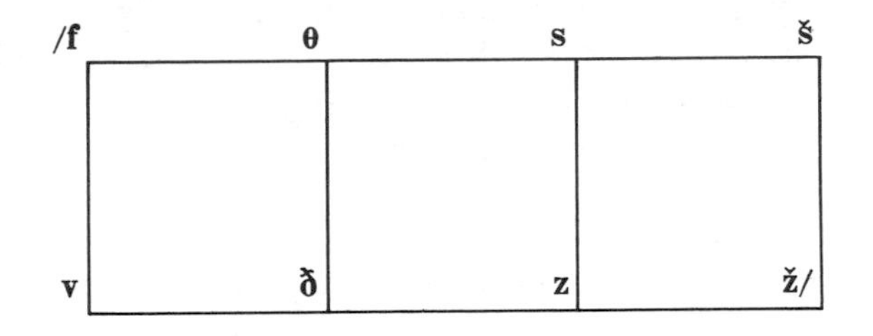

Figure 4B. Spirant consonants of Modern English arranged to show symmetrical contrastive relations of phonetic features.

statement. The vertical lines represent the unvoiced-voiced distinction, the horizontal lines represent distinctions in point of articulation. We have also graphically expressed the fact that each phoneme of the set is differentiated from the others by at least one distinctive phonetic feature.

By themselves the stops /p t k b d g/, apart from the assibilated stops (or "affricates") /č/ and /ǰ/, present a six-member pattern of relations much like the pattern for spirants. The assibilated stops appear then as an isolated pair. From a structural point of view of Modern English alone, the evidence for regarding assibilated stops as a separate set or as members of the set of other stops is not conclusive. Choice between the alternatives of classification, for synchronic analysis of Modern English, depends on such factors as the degree to which symmetry of language subsystems is believed to be real or important. Let us choose for the moment to assign /č ǰ/ to the set of stops, allowing the justification to appear in the next two chapters. We can express the relations among the other consonants paired by voice distinctions as /p/>/t/>/č/>/k/ and /b/>/d/>/ǰ/>/g/ or, diagrammatically, as they appear in Figure 4C. The two diagrams representing the rela-

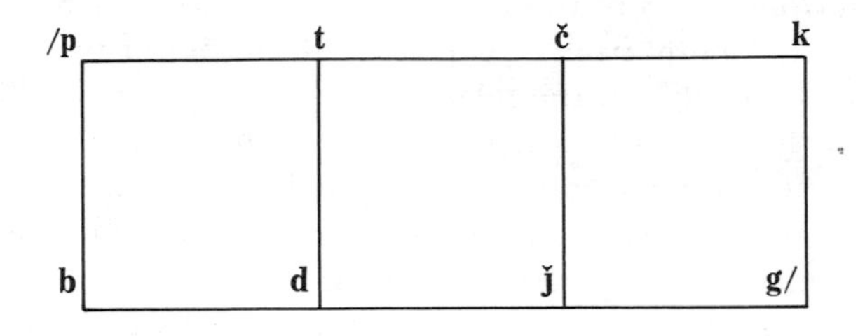

Figure 4C. Stop consonants of Modern English arranged to show symmetrical contrastive relations of phonetic features.

tions of spirant and stop consonants, respectively (Figures 4B and 4C), are congruent, suggesting that Modern English spirants and stops are structured symmetrically. Phonetically they are not congruent, as the first representation (Figure 4A) shows. In so far as their relations to each other are concerned, both spirants and stops do, however, form similar structural sets. Phonemically, though not phonetically, they are congruent. We can extend our description of these sixteen phonemes, again using a diagram; Figure 4D shows stops and spirants

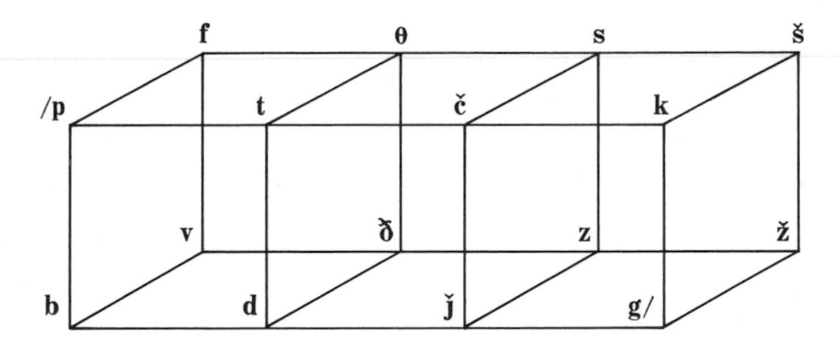

Figure 4D. The obstruent system—stops and spirants—of Modern English arranged to show symmetry of contrastive relations among phonetic features.

united in a single system; together they constitute the obstruent system of Modern English. The lines in the diagram connecting the two earlier sets represent a distinctive contrast in manner of articulation—stop vs. spirant.

The other consonants occur in less extensive structural patterns. Modern English /m n ŋ/ are characterized by nasality; they are voiced only and are distinguished from each other only in position of articulation; they are represented in Figure 4E, left to right, on a scale

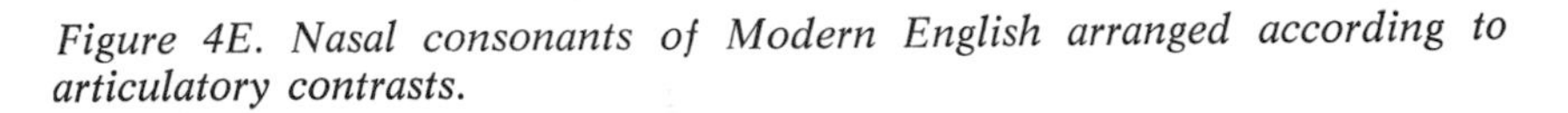

Figure 4E. Nasal consonants of Modern English arranged according to articulatory contrasts.

front-to-back of position of articulation. The glides (or semivowels) /w y/ are characterized by nonfixed position, already illustrated in their glide articulation. Length of the glides was shown to be noncontrastive. Their contrasts with each other are sometimes described in terms of the location of the resonance area at the beginning of articulation of the allophones: /y/ is classified as the more front, /w/ as the more back; this scheme takes its departure from the technique of classifying vowels. It seems better to arrange the glides according to the position of the articulating speech organs, so that /w/, articulated with the lips, is classified as more front. The latter way of describing structural relations of these consonants produces the pattern in Figure 4F. The linguals /l r/ are distinguished only as lateral vs. nonlateral,

/w ———————————————— **y/**

Figure 4F. Glide consonants of Modern English arranged according to articulatory contrasts.

giving the pattern represented in Figure 4G. Spirant /h/, the only

/l
———
r/

Figure 4G. Lingual consonants of Modern English arranged according to articulatory contrasts.

common English consonant with glottal articulation, forms a set of one member only.

To emphasize the fact that the preceding section, including its diagrams, is only descriptive, two alternate diagrammatic representations may be given. The first, in Figure 4H, is based on one by Wallace L. Chafe, "Phonetics, Semantics, and Language," (*Language*, 38 [1962], 338; used with permission). Points along horizontal lines represent mutually exclusive phonetic features based on differences in point of articulation. Voiced and unvoiced features stand in a second type of mutually exclusive set. Recurrence of features is indicated by

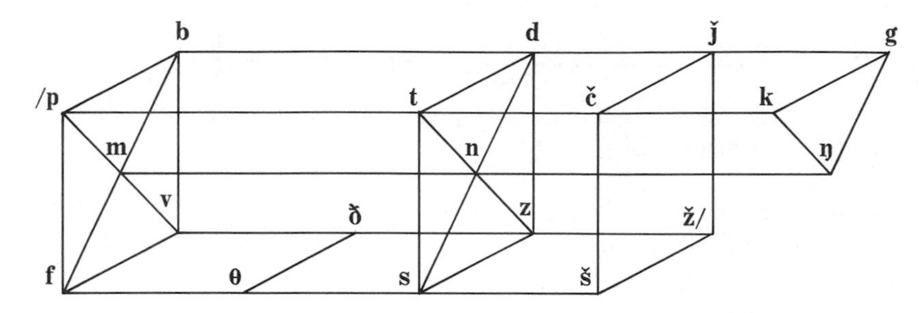

Figure 4H. Alternate representation of consonants, uniting stop, spirant, and nasal consonants of Modern English.

lines of equal length when they are either parallel or when they converge. This strategy unites stops, spirants, and nasals. The other, in Figure 4I, is based on one by Robert A. Hall, Jr., *Introductory Linguistics,* p. 96; used with permission. It combines all spirants, including /h/, stops, nasals, and linguals.

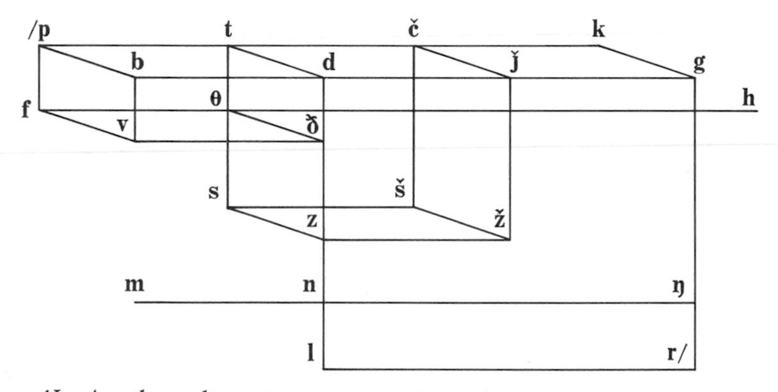

Figure 4I. Another alternate representation of consonants, uniting stop, spirant, nasal, and lingual consonants of Modern English.

No way has yet been found to arrange all English consonants in a single relational pattern (except as they all contrast with all the vowels). Unless such a way is found, we can add what seems to be another accurate descriptive statement about English consonants: they are constituted of patterned sets of distinctive features, but the sets of features are constructed according to three or more patterns. The history of consonants in English also implies multiple patterns or subsystems of the consonants.

Chapter 5

CONSONANT CLUSTERS

INITIAL THREE-MEMBER CLUSTERS

5.1 English consonants have still another set of patterning characteristics besides those based on distinctive articulatory features. This other patterning—"clustering"—is also significant for the formulation of history of the language. By "consonant clusters" is meant a sequence of phonemes consisting only of consonants, such as /skw–/ in square, /st–/ in *stop,* /šr–/ in *shrink,* /by–/ in *beautiful,* /–rst/ in *worst,* /–mp/ in *hump,* /–rm/ in *warm.* To describe patterns of successive consonants is simply to describe further the phonemes of English, characterizing them on the basis of a facet of their distribution. The relations of consonant clustering patterns at various stages in the development of English reflect the gradualness as well as the selectiveness of the evolution of the language. To some extent this chapter continues the "game" of working out patterns, still regarding the consonants somewhat abstractly. By working out the patterns formed by these clusters, we shall be able to see the historical changes in English as something more ordered and comprehensible than mere lists of corresponding elements from the different periods can ever show.

In Modern English the maximum number of consonants in sequence at the beginning of a word or syllable (and before a vowel) is three. These initial clusters can be arranged conveniently in this way:

/spl–		skl–
spr–	str–	skr–
spyu–	styu–	skyu–
		skw–/

This first description provides only enumeration and simple arrangement. Further description of these clusters includes the following. (1) The pattern of sequence is *spirant, unvoiced stop, lingual* or *glide.* (2) The sequence is invariable. (3) The members of each position in the sequence are limited to consonants articulated in the same manner—spirant or stop articulation—or with the shared feature of no voicing distinction—lingual or glide:

1	2	3
sibilant	unvoiced stop	lingual or glide
/s/	/p t k/	/l r y w/

(4) Frequency of clusters: /spr– str– skr–/ occur in a good many words, and /spl– skw–/ are fairly common—*spring, spread, string, straw, screen, scratch, spleen, splendid, square, squib;* /styu–/ occurs commonly but (in American speech, at least) as an alternate to /stu–/, as in *student;* /skyu–/ occurs in only a small number of words such as *skew, skewer;* /spyu–/ in still fewer, e.g., *spew,* and /skl–/ only rarely, e.g., *sclerosis.*

INITIAL TWO-MEMBER CLUSTERS

5.2 Two-member clusters of consonants in the same position also conform to fixed patterns. They are listed schematically for economy of exposition. While frequency of occurrence of these clusters varies greatly, both in terms of the number of syllables in which they occur and in frequency of occurrence of any given syllable, all are common except those marked by an asterisk. These rare clusters may not occur in the speech of many English speakers since they are limited to variants *(suitor* as /syu–/ or /su–/, *duty* as /dyu–/ or /du–/, etc.), to proper names (šm–/ *Schmidt,* /šw–/ *Schweppes,* /vl–/ *Vladimir,* etc.), to words borrowed with foreign pronunciation (*bwana, pueblo, noire,* etc.) and some anomalies such as /zw–/ *zwieback.*

/sp	st–	sk–				syu–*	sm–	sn–
šp–*	št–*	šk–*	šr–	šl–*	šw–*		šm–*	šn–*
					zw–*			
			fr–	fl–		fyu–		
			vr–*	vl–*		vyu–		
			θr–		θw–	θyu–		
			pr–	pl–	pw–*	pyu–		
			by–	bl–	bw–*	byu		
			tr–		tw–	tyu–*		
			dr–		dw–	dyu–*		

	kr–	kl–	kw–	kyu–		
	gr–	gl–	gw–	gyu–		
			hw–	hyu–		
sf–*						
sv–*						
					mw–*	myu–
					nw–*	nyu–*/

The following are but a few of the observations that can be made about these clusters. The position classes already assigned for three–member clusters were (1) spirant /s/ (sibilant), (2) voiceless stop /p t k/, and (3) linguals and glides /l r y w/, and the sequence was found to be invariable. In two-member clusters the sequence is spirant followed by lingual, glide, or nasal; spirant followed by stop; stop followed by lingual or glide; and a few others mostly of rare occurrence. In other words, nearly all two-member clusters well established in English, excepting /myu–/ and perhaps /nyu–/, fit a pattern similar to that of the three-member clusters. Expanding the earlier pattern we have then the following:

1			2			3	
spirant			stop			lingual, glide, nasal	
/s	š					l	r
f	θ	h	p	t	k	y	w
v*		z*	b	d	g	m	n/

The patterns by which these are combined are 1–2, 1–3, 2–3; /sf– sv–/ are rare, as noted, consisting within this analysis of 1–1 combinations; /mw– nw–/, are also rare and essentially foreign, appearing as 3–3 combinations. The patterns are sufficiently regular for the established, common clusters to warrant the broad statement that the sequence by position class for two member clusters is also invariable. Certainly we have no instances of 3–1, 3–2, or 2–1.

Additional reason for employing position-class analysis lies in the dominant symmetry of clusters in which the first members are pairs distinguished by voice—particularly the 2–3 clusters. The pairs beginning with stops are symmetrical, including the rare /pw– bw–/. Except for the deliberate retention of foreign or spelling pronunciation of words containing /zw– vr– vl–/, the 1–3 clusters contain only one cluster /vyu–/ with a voiced member in the Position 1 consonants.

The initial clusters do not include sequences of stops and spirants in which members of each class differ in voice distinctions; for example, */zt–/ and */sg–/ do not occur. Stops and spirants are paired by voice features. Nasals, linguals, and glides do not have voiced vs. unvoiced distinctions, and 1–3 and 2–3 clusters are not restricted by the rule about voice distinctions. The pattern of clusters is without the dental consonant followed by /l/ or /m n/—*/dl– θl– tl– dn– tn–/ etc. do not occur; nor in Modern English do labiodentals cluster with nasals —there is no */fn– fm–/ and the like.

ALTERNATIVE FORMULATION FOR INITIAL CLUSTERS

5.3 The preceding pattern for the ordering of consonants in initial clusters is conventional, based on the characteristics of three-member clusters. To consider an alternative way of formulating the sequence characteristics of all initial clusters in English is important for two reasons. First, a simpler formulation will probably be more usable and exact. Secondly, an alternative formulation may clarify processes of change in the history of English. There are no reverse-order clusters, as we have seen; but the 1–1 and 3–3 combinations do not conform to a specifiable progressive sequence as the other combinations do. For the 1–1 clusters, it is easy enough to split Position 1 into 1 (a) for /s/ and 1 (b) for the other spirants: thus /sf– sv–/ become 1 (a)–1 (b) combinations. The *a* and *b* designations are more apposite than expanding the set with additional numerals, since no more than three consonants ever occur in these initial clusters. As defined by the earlier pattern, the 3–3 combinations should not simply be split as, for example, nasals separate from linguals and glides. For these, as in /myu– nyu–/ *music, news,* it will be better to place the nasals in Position 2 as a second group: 2 (a) stops /p t k b d g/ and 2 (b) nasals /m n/. Thus, 2 (a)–2 (b) combinations do not occur, but /myu– nyu–/ are distinguished as 2 (b)–3 combinations. Still further reason for this reformulation will appear subsequently in the patterns for earlier English consonant clusters and in the historical relations of the successive consonant systems of English. We now have an alternative pattern for initial clusters, as follows.

	1		2	3
	spirant		stop; nasal	lingual; glide
(a)	/s	(a)	/p t k	/l r
(b)	/f θ š h		b d g/	y w/
	v* z*/	(b)	m n/	

CLUSTER DIFFERENCES AMONG DIALECTS

5.4 Speech systems within English are not entirely coextensive in the number and particular inventories of consonant clusters they utilize in initial position in words or syllables, but their congruence is evident. Any dialect in which the less common clusters marked (*) do not occur manifests the same general structural patterns as a dialect containing all the clusters listed. None has more than three consonants together in this position. No reverse-order clusters will occur, no matter how diverse the dialects, so long as the words considered can on other grounds be classified as English. Even in terms of frequency of occurrence, minimum-inventory and maximum-inventory dialects are much the same at least in general proportions of the occurrences taken up by the various clusters. In short, an important set of rules or descriptions can be drawn up for initial clusters of consonants in English, and these rules are equally applicable at the language and dialect levels.

FINAL CONSONANT CLUSTERS

5.5 Final consonant clusters are more conveniently presented by beginning with those having two members. Illustrative words are supplied in the listings, for some final clusters are less easy to recognize than are most initial ones.

/–ps/ lapse	/–ts/ mats		/–ks/ backs
/–pt/ lapped		/–čt/ latched	/–kt/ backed
/–pθ/ depth			

	/–bd/ robed	/–bz/ robes		
		/–dz/ roads		/–dθ/width
	/–ǰd/ judged			
	/–gd/ fogged	/–gz/ dogs		
/–ft/ left		/–fs/ laughs		/–fθ/ fifth
	/–vd/ waved	/–vz/ waves		
	/–θt/ frothed	/–θs/ myths		
	/–ðd/ seethed	/–ðz/ lathes		
/–sp/ lisp	/–st/ list		/–sk/ risk	
	/–zd/ raised			
	/–št/ rushed			
	/–žd/ rouged			
/–mp/ lump				
	/–md/ numbed			
	/–mf/ lymph	/–mz/ rooms		
	/–nt/ want	/–nč/ lunch		
	/–nd/ bound	/–nǰ/ lunge		
			/–ns/ rinse	/–nθ/ month
			/–nz/ buns	
	/–ŋd/ ringed		/–ŋk/ rink	
			/–ŋz/ rings	/–ŋθ/length
/–lp/ help	/–lt/ welt	/–lč/ gulch	/–lk/ silk	
/–lb/ bulb	/–ld/ weld	/–lǰ/ bulge		
/–lf/ self	/–lθ/ wealth	/–ls/ false		/–lš/ welsh
/–lv/ valve		/–lz/ falls		

/–lm/ film /–ln/ kiln

/–rp/ harp /–rt/ heart /–rč/ larch /–rk/ ark

/–rb/ barb /–rd/ lard /–rǰ/ large /–rg/ berg

/–rf/ scarf /–rθ/ hearth /–rs/ farce /–rš/ marsh

/–rv/ carve /–rz/ mars

/–rm/ warm /–rn/ warn

/–rl/ whirl

Three-member clusters in final position consist almost entirely of two-member clusters with one following consonant from the set /s z t d θ/; the one exception in the list given is /–dst/ *midst.*

/–pst/ lapsed /–tst/ blitzed /–kst/ fixed

/–ksθ/ sixth

/–pts/ scripts /–kts/ facts

/–pθs/ depths

/–dθs/ widths

/–fts/ lifts /–fθs/ fifths

/–sps/ lisps /–sts/ lists /–sks/ risks

/–spt/ lisped /–skt/ risked

/–mps/ ramps

/–mpt/ tempt

/–mfs/ nymphs

/–nts/ wants /–nčt/ lunched

/–nds/ bounds /–nǰd/ lunged

/–nθs/ months /–nst/ rinsed

/–nzd/ bronzed

/–dst/ midst /–ŋks/ rinks

/–ŋkt/ linked

/–ŋkθ/ strength

/–ŋθs/ lengths

/–lps/ helps /–lts/ welts /–lks/ silks

/–lpt/ helped /–lkt/ milked

/–lbz/ bulbs /–ldz/ welds

/–lbd/ bulbed /–lčt/ mulched

/–lǰd/ bulged

/–lfs/ shelf's /–lθs/ healths

/–lft/ shelfed

/–lfθ/ twelfth

/–lvz/ shelves

/–lvd/ shelved

/–lšt/ welshed

/–lmz/ films /–lnz/ kilns

/–lmd/ filmed /–lnd/ kilned

/–rps/ harps /–rts/ hearts /–rks/ marks

/–rpt/ harped /–rčt/ lurched /–rkt/ marked

/–rbz/ barbs /–rdz/ bards /–rgz/ bergs

/–rbd/ barbed /–rǰd/ barged

/–rfs/ scarf's /–rθs/ berths /–rst/ burst

/–rft/ scarfed /–rθt/ berthed

/–rvz/ carves

/–rvd/ carved

/–rmz/ warms /–rnz/ warns

/–rmd/ warmed /–rnd/ warned

/–rnt/ aren't

/–rmθ/ warmth

/–rlz/ whirls

/–rld/ whirled

There are also a few four-member consonant clusters in final position.

/–ksts/ texts

/–ksθs/ sixths

/–mpts/ tempts

/–mpst/ glimpsed

/–ŋkθs/ strengths

/–ŋkst/ jinxed

/–lpts/ sculpts /–ltst/ waltzed

/–lfθs/ twelfths

/–rsts/ bursts

/–rmθs/ warmths /–rnst/ Ernst

With the one exception noted, /–dst/ *midst,* all three-member clusters are extensions of two-member clusters. With the one exception of /–rnst/ *Ernst,* all four-member clusters are extensions of three-member clusters with the final consonant being limited to /s/ or /t/. The regularities are more important, though. In all final clusters, whether with two, three, or four members, the last consonant is unvoiced or voiced according to whether the preceding consonant is unvoiced or voiced if the next-to-last consonant is voice-distinguished: /–st –zd –ft –vd/ etc. occur, but */–zt –sd –vt –fd/ and the like do not. This characteristic exactly parallels the rules of sequence for initial stops and spirants. (/–dθ *width* is an exception, involving two consonants articulated with one tongue position.) Consonants with greater loudness come nearest the vowel—just preceding the vowel in initial clusters, just following it in final clusters. When two consonants come together in a final cluster, both without voice distinction, the nasal is the latter of the two—*warn, helm,* etc.

THREE-MEMBER CLUSTERS OF EARLY ENGLISH

5.6 Consonants in Old English, as in Modern English, cluster in initial position in groups of no more than three:

/spl–*

spr– str– skr–/

The pattern of sequence is sibilant, voiceless stop, lingual—congruent with that of Modern English and lacking only glides in Position 3. It is difficult to determine just when /skr–/ was replaced by /šr–/ as a result of /sk/ being replaced by the new phoneme /š/. (The problem is taken up in 6.5.) The sequence was invariable, and the position groups were (1) /s/, (2) /p t k/, and (3) /l r/. The three clusters that include /r/ were common, but the /spl–/ cluster was rare, being a pattern limited to a few words borrowed from Latin. In what follows, Old English examples of /spl–/ will not be included because they apparently occurred only when a deliberate borrowing from Latin was used in the speech (or writing) of the learned few.

Juxtaposing pattern descriptions of three-member initial consonant clusters of English speech from periods separated by about one thousand years would show sufficient congruence and coextensiveness to suggest historical identity of the language systems to which the patterns belong. But if we introduce descriptions of two intervening stages of English, the patterns of progression and the identity become more apparent. The vocabulary of the *Ormulum* (c. 1200) and of Chaucer's writings (c. 1400) have been used as a basis for the descriptions; if the descriptions of these samples of early and late Middle English do not contain all clusters to be found in the dialects they represent, they nevertheless are based on large enough samples to include all but the very infrequent clusters.

Old English (c. 900)	Middle English (c. 1200)	Middle English (c. 1400)	Modern English (c. 1950)
		skl–	/spl–

/spr– str– skr–/	/spr– str– skr–/	/spr– str– skr–	spr– str– skr–
			spyu– styu– skyu–
		skw–/	skw–/

In the Chaucerian sample (c. 1400) /skl–/ is of low frequency.

Three observations can be made on the basis of data thus far presented. First, if the list of clusters were revised for each of the periods of English represented above by eliminating those clusters of rare occurrence, the coextensiveness of the patterns would be greatly increased. In Modern English, for example, a sample comparable to those used for early and late Middle English might not include /skl–/ and might even fail to exhibit /spyu– styu– skyu–/. Second, the interval between the Middle English and Modern English materials is two or three times longer than between the earlier stages, perhaps accounting for the greater difference between the latest two patterns listed. Third, while the sample from c. 1400 contains no instances of /spl–/, this cluster appears in a number of words that have continued from the same period to the present to form part of the normal vocabulary of English. Significantly, a great many of these /spl–/ words came into English through translations from Latin, well-illustrated in the texts translated by Trevisa.

TWO-MEMBER CLUSTERS OF EARLY ENGLISH

5.7 Two-member clusters in the initial position are more numerous than three-member clusters, and generally of higher frequency. These clusters are given in full in tabular form but without detailed commentary.

OE (c. 900)			EME (c. 1200)			LME (c. 1400)			MnE (c. 1950)		
/sp–	st–	sk–	/sp–	st–	sk–	/sp–	st–	sk–	/sp–	st–	sk–
pr–	tr–	kr–	pr–	tr–	kr–	pr–	tr–	kr–	pr–	tr–	kr–
pl–		kl–	pl–		kl–	pl–		kl–	pl–		kl–
									pyu–		kyu–
		kw–			kw–			kw–			kw–
		sl–			sl–			sl–			sl–

		sw–			sw–			sw–			sw–
											pw–
		tw–			tw–			tw–			tw–
bl–		gl–	bl–		gl–	bl–		gl–	bl–		gl–
br–	dr–	gr–	br–	dr–	gr–	br–	dr–	gr–	br–	dr–	gr–
									byu–	dyu–	gyu–
	dw–			dw–			dw–	gw–	bw–	dw–	gw–
		gn–						gn–			
fl–			fl–			fl–			fl–		
fr–	θr–		fr–	θr–	šr–	fr–	θr–	šr–	fr–	θr–	šr–
									fyu–	θyu–	
	θw–			θw–			θw–			θw–	šw–
fn–						fn–					
		hl–			hl–						
		hr–			hr–			hr–			
		hw–			hw–			hw–			hw–
		hn–									
					hy–						
											hyu–
		kn–			kn–			kn–			
		sn–			sn–			sn–			sn–
		sm–			sm–			sm–			sm–
										nyu–	myu–
										nw–	mw–
		wl–			wl–			wl–			

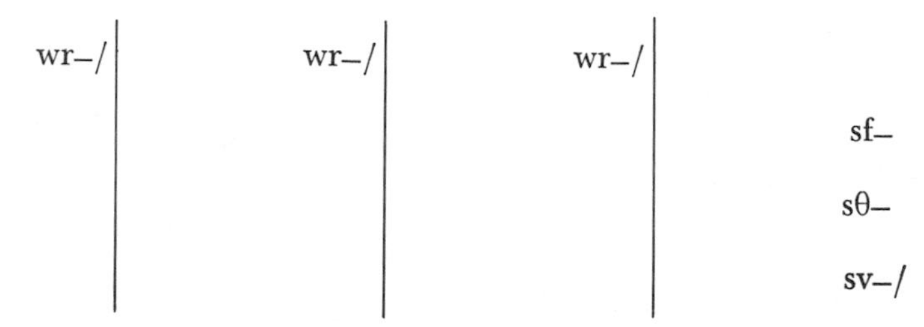

wr–/	wr–/	wr–/	
			sf–
			sθ–
			sv–/

Again, if Modern English rare clusters were eliminated as the rare clusters probably are in the other lists, the similarity among the cluster patterns would be increased. For instance, /pw–/ occurs in some pronunciations of *pueblo* and a few other words, but is rare; /bw–/ occurs in *bwana* but seldom elsewhere; /nyu–/ is uncommon except as a dialectal alternate to /nu–/ as in *news;* /šl– šw– šm– θyu– θw–/ as in *Schlitz, Schweppes, schmalz, thewes, thwack* are rare and chiefly in recently borrowed words and in proper names; /hyu–/ is not common; /sv–/ occurs only in careful pronunciation of *svelte* and the like, /sθ/ is unique in *sthenia, sthenic,* and /sf–/ is infrequent in a few borrowings such as *sphere;* /nw–/ occurs when French pronunciation is imitated for *noire,* etc. Inclusion of /hyu–/ in the early Middle English list is conjectural, based on little more than occurrence of *ȝho* in the *Ormulum.* On the other hand, /fn–/ as in *fnæst,* 'puff, blast, breath' was rare in both Old English and Middle English.

POSITION CLASSES OF CLUSTERS

5.8 The data on initial consonant clusters can be subjected to a number of analyses, of which the following is only one. Position classes can be set up as in 5.3, using three-member clusters as a model since that group is the largest. Listing all consonants in the various combinations of both two- and three-member clusters under these position headings produces the tabulation that follows. (Whether /y/ should be included in early Middle English Position 3 is not certain; see 5.7.)

	Position 1	Position 2	Position 3
	(a) /s/	(a) /p t k	/r l
OE (c. 900)	(b) /f þ h/	b d g/	w /
		(b) /m n/	
EME (c. 1200)	(a) /s/	(a) /p t k	/r l

	(b) /f θ š h/	b d g/	w /
		(b) /m n/	
	(a) /s/	(a) /p t k	/r l
ME (c. 1400)	(b) /f θ š h/	b d g/	w /
		(b) /m n/	
	(a) /s/	(a) /p t k	/r l
MnE (c. 1950)	(b) /f θ š h	b d g/	w y/
	v* z*/	(b) /m n/	

The following tabulation shows some of the clustering patterns in initial clusters, arranged by position-class combinations.

	1 (a)–2 (a)	1 (a)–2 (b)	1 (a)–3
OE	/s p– t– k–/	/s m– n–/	/s l– w– /
EME	/s p– t– k–/	/s m– n–/	/s l– w– /
ME	/s p– t– k–/	/s m– n–/	/s l– w– /
MnE	/s p– t– k–/	/s m– n–/	/s l– w– y–/

	1 (b)–2 (b)	1 (b)–3
OE	/f n– /	/f r– l– /
EME	/f (n–)/	/f r– l– /
ME	/f n– /	/f r– l– /
MnE	——	/f r– l– y– /
OE	——	/þ r– w– /
EME	——	/θ r– w– /
ME	——	/θ r– w– /
MnE	——	/θ r– w– y–/
OE	——	——————

EME ——	/š r– /
ME ——	/š r– /
MnE /š m– n–/	/š r– l– w– /
OE /h n–/	/h r– l– w– /
EME ——	/h r– l– w– /
ME ——	/h r– w– /
MnE ——	/h w– y–/

1 (a)–1 (b)	2 (b)–3
OE ————	————
EME ————	————
ME ————	————
MnE /s f– θ v–/	/m w– y–/ /n w–y–/

2 (a)–3

OE	/p r– l– /	/t r– w– /	/k r– l– w– /
	/b r– l– /	/d r– w– /	/g r– l– /
EME	/p r– l– /	/t r– w– /	/k r– l– w– /
	/b r– l– /	/d r– w– /	/g r– l– /
ME	/p r– l– /	/t r– w– /	/k r– l– w– /
	/b r– l– /	/d r– w– /	/g r– l– w– /
MnE	/p r– l– w– y–/	/t r– w– y– /	/k r– l– w– y–/
	/b r– l– w– y–/	/d r– w– y–/	/g r– l– w– y–/

2(a)–2(b)

OE	/k n–/
	/g n–/
EME	/k n–/

/g (n–)/

ME /k n– /

/g n–/

MnE — —

— —

/WL– WR–/ CLUSTERS AND /H/

5.9 For purposes of historical study, as opposed to simply descriptive work with Modern English, one more segment of the sequence patterns of consonants should probably be revised in the interests of exactness. Earlier periods of English had /wl– wr–/ clusters, and by the classification thus far established they will have to be described as 3–3 clusters. Since the sequence is invariable, the split into 3 (a) /w/, 3 (b) /r l/ is the obvious solution. Although no instances of */yr– yw–/ or */ry– rw–/ are found within the history of English, 3 (a) may include both /y/ and /w/. The second aspect is the classification of /h/ as a member of the set designated 1 (b): the earlier English clusters /hn– hr– hl–/, the Modern English cluster /hyu–/, as well as /hw–/ in all periods of English make the assignment of /h/ to the full set of spirants the more plausible. On grounds of articulatory features in Modern English, /h/ belongs in a class by itself. On grounds of distribution in clusters throughout the history of the language, it belongs in the group 1 (a–b) constituted entirely of spirants.

Chapter 6

CONSONANT CHANGE: INDIVIDUAL AND SYSTEMIC

PATTERNS OF PHONOLOGICAL CHANGE

6.1 Patterns of English consonants and some differences between earlier and later sets of these phonemes have been described. Our next consideration will be the processes of modification and the selective factors which operated upon them. A preliminary distinction must be drawn, however, so that our consideration of the development of English consonants will not be confused with etymology—tracing the development of words from historically remote to more recent forms.

Changes in the phonological make-up of words can almost always be sorted into patterns, those patterns having been dignified by the term "laws" of sound change; exceptions to these rules are nearly always accountable under patterns of analogy. That Modern English has *books* instead of *beech* as the plural of *book* is not the result of regular phonological change /č/>/ks/, but to the formation of a new, "regular" plural from the singular form *book* + *(e)s*. Regular sound change has been spectacular in English vowels, as we shall see in Chapters 8 and 10; it has also operated in the consonants, as the following preliminary examples will show. Assimilation of one consonant to another gives rise to one of the more obvious patterns of change. When *lefman* was replaced by *lemman* 'lover, loved one,' *wīfman* by *wimman* 'woman,' etc., the regular pattern for these and other words showing identical changes can be represented as /–fm–/>/–m:–/ (/m/ with lengthening), the articulation of /–f–/ having been modified by that of the following /–m–/ until the distinctive features of friction and voicelessness were no longer present, and labiodental articulation no longer intervened between the vowel and the bilabial articulation of /m/. More accurately, the articulation of /–f–/ in conjunction with following /–m–/ came to be modified sufficiently by speakers for some hearers (usually younger ones) not to notice the presence of /f/; their different construing of utterances would then be reflected in their uttering the same words without the features of /f/ but with lengthened /m/ in place of the /–fm–/ of other speakers.

Perpetuation of the new phonemic structuring of the word together with progressive disuse of the older structure of the word constitutes the process of replacement, in this case /–fm–/ > /–m:–/. Partially similar is another assimilative replacement pattern of /–nf–/ and /–np–/ corresponding respectively to later /–mf–/ and /–mp–/, as in *confort* > *comfort* and *nonper* > *noumpere* '(an) umpire'; the first consonant again was assimilated to the second, articulation of /f/ and /p/ being labial and the bilabial nasal /m/ replacing the dental nasal /n/. In the patterns of assimilative replacement just mentioned, the consonant that was assimilated was syllable-final, the assimilation involving articulatory adaptation to the initial consonant of the following syllable. These conditions of position in syllables also obtain for a number of other assimilative changes in English. Old English **ċēapfaru* was replaced by *chaffare* 'commerce' according to the regular pattern /–pf–/ > /–f:–/. The process of assimilative change operates now as in the past: *fifth* occurs in Modern English with /–fθ/, but also with the /f/ assimilated, and *fifths* occurs with /–fθs/, /–θs/, and even /–s/. *Strength* occurs with /–ŋθ/ or /–nθ/ as well as with /–ŋkθ/. The spelling suggests what can otherwise be established, that an earlier form had /–ŋgθ/, and that by assimilation (of voice features) /–k–/ replaces /–g–/ in the shape of the word as it terminates /–ŋkθ/.

Accounting for these patterns of assimilation and some other changes is simplified by descriptions of the kind given for /–nf–/ > /–mf–/. Implied for all the changes, however, are the more accurate conditions of restructuring heard utterances as described for /–fm–/ > /–m:–/, with perpetuation of newer and disuse of older phonemic structures of words.

Articulational adaptation (and phonemic restructuring of words) like that of /–nf–/ > /–mf–/ gave rise to a number of other patterns of phonological change. Old English *spinel* was replaced by Middle English *spindle, þunor* by *þunder* 'thunder'; the reflex of Old English *brēmel* is Middle English *bremble* 'bramble,' *þymel* > *þimble;* Old English *nemne* > Middle English *nempne* '(I) name,' and *ǣmtiġ* > *empty*. In all these instances the change in phonemic shape of the words consists of introduction of a stop consonant with the same position of articulation as that of the nasal consonant it follows; the change occurs at the boundary between heavier and lesser stressed syllables. The voicing or unvoicing of the stop conforms to the existing patterns of final consonant clusters at the time of the change. (*Fifth,* mentioned earlier, also occurs with /–ftθ/.) The close relation of this process of "articulative intrusion" to that of "assimilation" will be apparent.

Many changes consist of "dropping" a consonant, that is, a consonant in an earlier form (normally in a cluster) does not appear in the historically identical form at a later time. Most of these patterns of change are straightforward instances of reduction of consonant clusters to a single consonant. Fully regular was the replacement during Middle English of initial /hn–/, /hr–/, /hl–/ by the voiced consonants /n–/, /r–/, /l–/ alone: Old English *hnutu* > Middle English *nut, hring* > *ring, hlāford* > *laverd* > *lord.* A similar cluster /hw–/ has been replaced in later English in many dialects by /w–/, as in *which, where,* but in other dialects (including most American dialects) /hw–/ still occurs. The initial clusters /wr–/ and /wl–/ have been replaced similarly by /r–/ and /l–/, respectively. The former of these changes took place sufficiently late for the cluster /wr–/ to be reflected in Modern spelling of such words as *write, wring, wry, wrong.* The change /wl–/ > /l–/ was earlier, and most of the several Old English words with this cluster have been lost in English; but *lisp* < *wlips* survives to illustrate the change. For another kind of example, when Old English *swā* corresponds to Middle English *so, swōte* to *sote* "sweet," later /sw–/ corresponds to still later /s–/ as in *sword* or *answer,* the regular change can be represented by /sw–/ > /s–/. The change did not always occur, however, as evident in Old English *swerian* > Middle English *swear;* for these patterns of change, the rule of replacement must be qualified, in this instance by stipulating that the change occurs only before certain vowels.

SYSTEMATIC AND SYSTEMIC CHANGES

6.2 The kinds of changes just described have been numerous in the long course of the history of English. The intrinsic interest they may have is no less important than their indispensability for such practical pursuits as textual editing or facility in reading a variety of early English texts. All these changes are systematic, for they may be generalized under rules of the kind illustrated; wherever a stipulated set of conditions existed, the same change occurred. With a selection of these individual patterns of change it is possible to consider systemic changes —the changes in the characteristics of consonants as they constitute patterns, or systems, within the inventory of phonemes of English. "Systematic" change and "systemic" change are related and consistent, but they are also different. Systemic change finally integrates the smaller-scale formulations, making it possible to comprehend them together with the processes and conditions of still more basic changes.

PHONETIC CHANGE WITHOUT PHONEMIC CHANGE

6.3 Three correlated *phonetic* changes probably occurred regularly between the Middle English and the Modern English periods. In Chaucer's language /t/, /d/, /n/ were probably articulated as dental rather than as alveolar consonants. With a narrow phonetic transcription, the change may be represented thus: [ṱ] > [t], [ḓ] > [d], [ṋ] > [n]. Because the changes are parallel one of the consonants may be used to represent the modification of phonetic attributes of all three.

Variation in articulation is a constant factor in actual speech. For articulation of /t/, the exact point at which the tongue closes with the upper front part of the mouth will vary; the pressure of air built up after this closure will be different each time; the duration of the air stoppage will be relatively shorter or longer; differences will occur in the timing, cessation, or onset of voice relative to the stoppage of air when /t/ has a voiced sound before or after it, and so on. The distribution of the variations—on different occasions, with different speakers, in different phonetic environments—will be random, a characteristic represented by a bell-shaped curve on a graph. Considering only one kind of variation, in location of point of articulation, we can represent the distribution of variations at Time 1 and Time 2 in the diagram that appears in Figure 6A. The vertical line marks the maximum

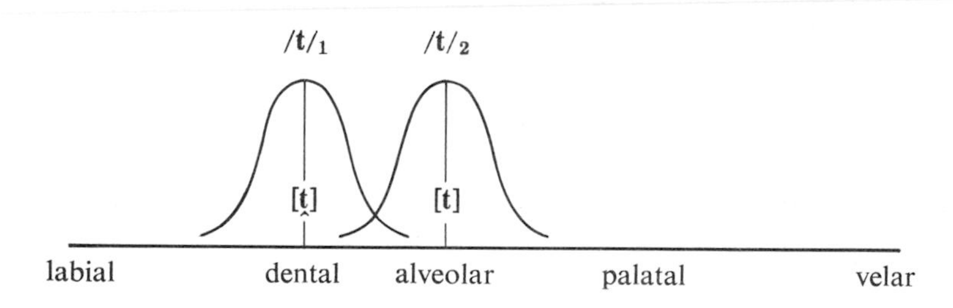

Figure 6A. Phonetic change of /t/ from dental to alveolar articulation during later Middle English; no phonemic change is involved.

frequency of occurrence of a particular variation—the norm of a speech community. The change from dental to alveolar manifestation of /t/ then may be described as a gradual shifting of a speech community's articulatory habits for a persisting phoneme represented by the curve on the left in the diagram to those habits represented by the curve on the right.

This is a simple phonetic change only. Apparently the only distinctive modification in the articulatory norm (represented by the change in the position of maximum frequency—the vertical line) was that of position; all other variations may well have continued without change of distribution. Equally important is the fact that the system of unvoiced stops was not modified phonemically, since the change occurred without overlapping /t/ with other unvoiced stops and without altering their distribution.

PHONEMIC CHANGE

6.4 What will be the effects when a shift in point of articulation (like the one just described) affects some, but not all, of the occurrences of a phoneme? Initially we can only say that the phoneme is manifest by two clearly defined allophones but that the phonemic system remains the same. We have already seen that Modern English /k/ and /g/ have distinct variations, roughly divided as palatal and velar allophones (cf. 3.2); it was pointed out, too, that until late Middle English the language had no /ŋ/ and had instead [n] and [ŋ] as allophones of one phoneme, symbolized above as /n/.

If further changes occur in conjunction with a clear split between allophones of a phoneme, the result may be a phonemic change—a split, with two phonemes of a later time corresponding to one phoneme of an earlier time. A particularly important pair of changes of just this kind occurred in very early Old English: the inherited Germanic /k/ was replaced in Old English by /k k̭/ and /g/ was replaced by /g ĝ/. Some Modern English examples will illustrate some effects of these changes: *drink* and *drench, cool* and *chill* are reflexes of Pre-Old English words with the same /k/ consonant, as are doublet forms such as *church* and *kirk, birk* (especially in place names) and *birch; spring* and *springe,* parallel to *drink* and *drench,* reflect the earlier contrast of consonants in their spellings, when *spring* was phonemically /spring/. The effects of this splitting of both velar stop consonants were not confined to the addition of two phonemes to the inventory of the Old English obstruent system; the effects continued, as we shall see later, in partially determining subsequent modifications of the systems of English consonants. The two processes of split were related and were generally contemporaneous. Because the replacement of earlier /g/ by Old English /g ĝ/ is an extremely complex change, involving more factors than the replacement of /k/ by /k k̭/, we shall trace the conditions of the latter only. Both changes appear in context of English and the other major early Germanic languages, in William

G. Moulton's "The Stops and Spirants of Early Germanic," to which the following is indebted.

By the time the Germanic-speaking Anglo-Saxons began their settlement in England, their speech included two distinct ranges of allophones for /k/ (as well as /g/); on the basis of comparative tests among Germanic languages and reconstructions of early Germanic, it is believed that the allophones must have been very much like those described above for Modern English: a palatal [k̭] conditioned by "palatal," or front, vowels as well as by /j/ (a consonant resembling Modern English [y]), and a velar [k] conditioned by "velar," or back, vowels. The differences in /k/ in Modern English *calls* and *Kells* will illustrate the approximate range of allophones. The /k/ allophones, representing assimilation of /k/ to vowel articulations, at that time never occurred in contrast, never served to distinguish words, even as in Modern English they are merely automatic variants. Sometime after the establishment of the Anglo-Saxon branch of the Germanic languages in England, a limited set of changes occurred in vowels. That set of changes, called "*i*–umlaut," will only be illustrated here. A palatal vowel, such as [o:] (similar to the vowel in Modern English *throat)*, was modified when the following syllable in the same word had [ɪ] or [i:] or [j] (as in Modern English *bit, beet, yes*), and came ultimately to be a palatal vowel [e:] (as in Modern English *state*): velar [o:] > palatal [e:]. Subsequently the [ɪ i: y] that had caused the change of vowel disappeared.

These changes brought about circumstances that produced /k k̲/ in English where there had been only /k/ formerly. For example, the /k/ of prehistoric */ko:ni/ 'bold' had been velar [k]; its later form, after "*i*–umlaut," was /ke:n–/. This later form, spelled in Old English *cēn–*, did not become identical to *cēn* 'torch.' Regular differentiation of spelling emerged only later, but it is clear from some early spellings as well as from later records that the "*k*–sounds" had become different; furthermore, they no longer differed only as automatic assimilations to following vowels, for the vowels of the two words had become the same [e:]. The difference in consonants was also no longer correlated with [ɪ], [i:], or [j] in the following syllable. The differences in the stop consonants were utilized to distinguish two word-roots that had become otherwise identical. Hence there were then two phonemes, here represented for early Old English as /k/ and /k̲/. Only one pair of forms has been used in describing this change, but the split of earlier /k/ into Old English /k k̲/ is attested in several other pairs; the split also occurred elsewhere than at the beginning of words: */strakkjan/ > /strek̲k̲an/ 'stretch,' */banki/ > /benk̲/ 'bench,' etc.

Clearly a phonemic split did occur, and some phonetic changes must also have occurred. There is no reason to suppose that /k/ ever ceased to have two ranges of allophones, palatal [k̭] and velar [k], conditioned by articulation of contiguous sounds; hence the new /k̭/ phoneme (symbolized /č/ in its Middle and Modern English equivalents) must have been manifest as something other than [k̭]. A number of phonetic descriptions have been proposed, but the nature of the evidence precludes any final decision on the precise phonetic characteristics of the sounds manifesting /k̭/. Nevertheless, the circumstances of the phonemic split, together with later evidence, make clear the nature of the difference between the phonetic manifestations of /k/ and /k̭/. Some early spellings, both in runic and roman alphabets, the spelling *cachepol* 'taxgatherer' of a borrowing from French, the new spellings gradually introduced to represent (later) /č/, and Modern English pronunciation—all these point to one conclusion: that /k̭/ was articulated at a point between velar /k/ allophones and /t/ and that its point of articulation was not sufficient to distinguish it from /k/. Some supplementary distinctive feature of articulation must, then, have been developed to distinguish /k̭/ from /k/; that feature is assibilation in Modern English /č/, and may well have been the same in Old English /k̭/.

PHONEMIC CHANGES IN CONSONANT CLUSTERS

6.5 A subsequent important change in the consonant system of English had as its first stage, apparently, a phonetic change in the clustering of /sk/—a change not involving /č/ (</k̭/), since the latter phoneme does not seem to have developed in clusters containing /s/. (Throughout the history of English, down to the present, /č/ has had limited distribution and remains the only unvoiced stop consonant that does not cluster with /s/; see 5.7.) The change of /sk/ to a single articulation [š], as in *shoe, shred,* was probably complete, at least in West Saxon, by about 900. The results of this change can be viewed in one of two ways: first, as the development of a new phoneme, attested in the contrast of *scrincan* ' (to) wither, shrink' and *drincan* ' (to) drink,' or *disc* 'dish' and *diċ* 'ditch,' as /š/ vs. /d/ and /š/ vs. /č/; second as merely a phonetic change in which /sk/ retains its place in the pattern of clusters /sp st sk/, but happened to be articulated as [š] rather than [sk]. On grounds of phonological characteristics it is difficult to argue that [š] can be segmented as /sk/, but on grounds of distribution the form seems to have appeared only as /sk/; otherwise a gap would occur in the symmetrical patterning of clusters of both earlier and later periods. The spelling remained *sc* throughout the period of Old English.

The phonemic ambivalence of [š] was resolved in a subsequent development. The phonetic change of /sk/, [sk] > [š], had occurred in English, but had not occurred in Scandinavian branches of the Germanic languages. By the time the phonetic change was complete, a large number of Scandinavian-Germanic speakers had settled in England. The speech of these "Danes," as the English called them, was still sufficiently similar to that of the English to enable the speakers to communicate with each other in a fairly wide range of circumstances with each group of speakers using their own languages. In the consonant systems of these languages, the most regular and pervasive phonological difference was English [š] corresponding to "Danish" [sk]. Both languages, being closely related, had a large number of cognates —words derived from a common form and still phonetically similar. One of the effects of these circumstances of languages in contact was the adoption of a number of Scandinavian pronunciations of words common to the two languages. Through this process, [sk] clusters came once again to occur in English. The pair *shirt* and *skirt* may represent the effects of English borrowing of "Danish" pronunciation; in the case of this pair, both pronunciations were retained and, with them, the words were differentiated in their meanings. By the time [š] and [sk] were in contrast, differentiating words otherwise identical in phonemic structure, English had a new phoneme /š/.

The emergence of /š/ is particularly interesting both in terms of phonetic change and patterns of consonant clustering. Probably, under the aspect of history, [š] should be regarded as /sk/ in English until replaced by /sk/ of borrowings from Scandinavian dialects. Phonetic considerations of single articulation of [š] and sequence of articulation for [sk] redefined [š] as a single spirant /š/, hence an addition to the inventory of the English obstruent system.

Because English has been conservative in the changes affecting consonants and especially consonant clusters, the effects of the preceding change are still clearly observable in Modern English. The initial cluster /šr–/ is common in English, in native words: *shred, shrink, shrift, shrike, shrine, shroud,* etc.; they are reflexes of early Old English words having normal initial clusters /skr–/. Words having initial clusters with /š/ and any consonant other than /r/ are not common, and are for the most part limited to borrowing, especially in proper names: *Schmidt, shmoo* (a coined word), *schmaltz; Schneider, shnook; Schlitz; Schweppes, schwa; spiel,* etc. When /sk–/ was replaced by /š/, native English clusters consisted of only /šr–/; the gaps in the patterning of common clusters reflect the historical development of English /š/.

The occurrence of /š/ in Modern English is not limited to reflexes of Old English initial /sk–/ and /skr–/. Medial /š/ is a descendant form of Old English *bisceop* 'bishop' and final /š/ from Old English *disc* 'dish,' *fisc* 'fish,' etc. In medial position, in particular, a great number of occurrences of /š/ are attributable to a different process than that of /sk/ > /š/. Many words borrowed during Middle English from French and Latin has /s/ medially followed by /y/ plus vowel, the two phonemes occurring on either side of a syllable boundary. *Issue* will illustrate the circumstances of phonological change: /is: yu/ in Middle English was modified by assimilation of /s/ to following /y/ plus vowel so that in early Modern English [s] > [š], /s/ > /š/. That there are almost no pairs of words in which medial /s/ and /š/ are the sole contrasting elements in Modern English is a consequence of the regularity and comparative recency of this change.

THE SPLIT OF OLD ENGLISH /f þ s/

6.6 Because Old English had no phonemic contrasts within the pairs [f v], [θ ð], [s z], the three spirants have been assigned the symbols /f þ s/ for Old English. During the period of Middle English each of these phonemes split, producing the phonemic pairs that have persisted into Modern English: /f v θ ð s z/. The processes of split for the three pairs were simultaneous in whatever dialect area they took place. In turn, the development of phonemic contrasts between unvoiced and voiced spirants resulted from the loss of distinctive lengthening of consonants. A detailed account of the change is in Hans Kurath's "The Loss of Long Consonants and the Rise of Voiced Fricatives in Middle English," to which the following paragraphs owe a great deal.

The loss of distinctive lengthening of consonants occurred twice, coming at different times in various dialect areas and from remarkably different causes. Phonemic split of the three spirants also occurred at different times in different dialects, but followed from a single pattern of reorganization of distinctive features of consonants. The change from three spirants not distinguished by voicing to six in which voicing was distinctive occurred in intervocalic positions. Old English /f þ s/ were always voiced between a relatively stressed vowel and an unstressed following vowel: [v] in *hōfas* 'hooves' but [f] in *hōf* 'hoof,' [ð] in *āðas* 'oaths' but [θ] in *āð* 'oath,' [z] in *rīsan* '(to) rise' but [s] in *rīs* 'Rise!' (imperative singular). Lengthened consonants did not occur initially in words, and they were not distinctive (they did not contrast with unlengthened consonants) finally in words. Between vowels length of a consonant was distinctive: if *C* is used to represent any one consonant and *V* to represent any vowel, Old English had the contrast /V̆C:V/ vs. /V̆CV/. Phonetically, /–C:–/ was distinguished from /–C–/, in the case of spirants, by two features. Not only did /–C:–/ have longer duration than /–C–/, but /–C:–/ had voiceless articulation while /–C–/ was voiced. Because the contrast no longer exists in Modern English, only make-shift illustration can be offered. In *The play seemed dull* and *The place seemed dull,* continuous articulation of [s] will be longer in the latter sentence in normal utterance. Stop consonants provide another illustration, as with the [k] of *bookcase*. It will be remembered (cf. 3.2) that for stop consonants articulative closure is one of the constant distinguishing factors. In *bookcase,* movement to closure after the vowel identifies the /k/ termination of *book–*, while release of longer-than-normal closure identifies the /k/ that begins *–case*. Without /–k:–/ or any other /–C:–/ instances in Modern English, the lengthened [k:] of *bookcase* is interpreted now as /–k/ plus /k–/, each of the phonemes belonging to a different syllable. Although the illustration using Modern English is necessarily cumbersome and indirect, it may clarify the Old English contrast in which a lengthened consonant /–C:–/ is distinguished by phonetic features of length and concomitant voicelessness from /–C–/ between vowels in the pattern /V̆– –V/.

The contrast between unvoiced and voiced articulation remained the sole distinguishing factor when distinctive lengthening of spirants no longer was present. This contrast had been a second (and probably secondary) factor in distinguishing words; in systemic terms, it became phonemically distinctive. Pairs of spirants came to be distinguished by voicing features whose contrast served to make a difference in the meanings of words that were otherwise phonemically identical.

Once the split of these spirants in intervocalic positions had introduced /f v θ ð s z/, the voiced members of these pairs began to occur in initial as well as final positions as well. Words borrowed from French supplied a number of initial voiced spirants—*vertu* 'virtue,' for example. Unstressed English forms provided *the, than,* and the like. Dialect borrowing accounted for a few more, as in the case of *vat,* a descendant form in southern dialects of Old English *fæt* /fæt/. In final positions, by a process to be explained later (Chapter 16), contrasting pairs such as *safe – save, house* (noun) – *house* (verb), *wreath – wreathe* came into being.

In certain southern dialects only [v ð z] developed separately as the manifestation of /f θ s/ in early Middle English, in word-initial position. Ultimately the phonemic patterns of the spirants reached the same development as that described above; but the process, for example, of introduction of voice-contrasted spirants in word-initial position depended in part on exactly the opposite characteristics of borrowings from French: it was the introduction of words beginning with *unvoiced* spirants that produced contrasts in this position.

THE SPLIT OF /n/ AND A NEW PHONEME /ž/

6.7 Two additional changes in the system of consonants occurred in late Middle English and early Modern English. The earlier change was a split of /n/, yielding /n/ and /ŋ/. Middle English /n/, like Old English /n/, had two ranges of allophones distinct in their articulation: a relatively front articulation [n] that was shifting from dental to alveolar position, as we saw in 6.3; and a relatively back articulation [ŋ] as a velar sound. Velar [ŋ] occurred as an allophone conditioned by a following velar stop in the same syllable; see Figure 6B.

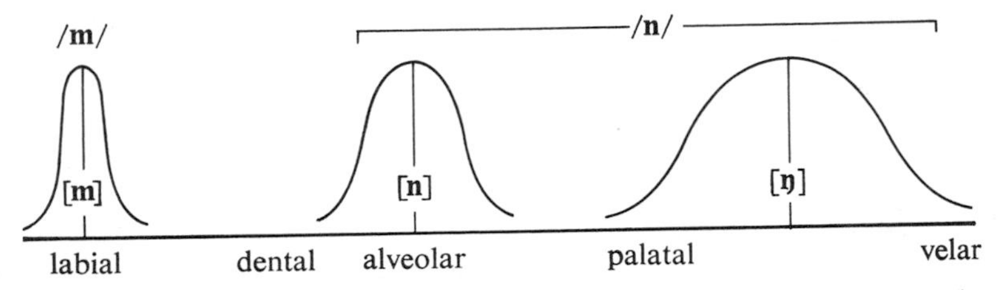

Figure 6B. The phonetics and phonemics of nasal consonants in later Middle English, prior to phonetic split of /n/ to produce /n/ and /ŋ/.

As long as [m] contrasted with [n] and [ŋ] and [n] and [ŋ] did not contrast with each other, there were only two nasal phonemes, which have been represented here as /m n/. A series of phonetic modifications occurred; the changes were consistent wherever the same phonetic conditions obtained. This series is schematically represented in phonetic notation as follows (the symbol *ə* represents a neutral unstressed vowel like that in the final syllable of *Cuba*): [sɪŋgə] > [sɪŋgᵊ] > [sɪŋᵍ] > [sɪŋ] *sing*. Presumably the utterance of [sɪŋᵍ] as a phonetic norm led to a phonemic reinterpretation of the heard utterances so that [ŋ] was construed as distinguishing *sing* from [sɪn] *sin,* or *sung* from *son,* or *king* from *kin,* etc. Progressive use of [ŋ] alone rather than [ŋg] and [ŋᵍ] to distinguish words in pairs like those given led to the split of earlier /n/. A distributional contrast arose in what had been earlier phonetically distinct allophones, with the result that Modern English has two phonemes replacing one earlier phoneme, and the nasals came thus to form the three-member set /m n ŋ/.

The other change is the development of a new phoneme /ž/. Traced through its phonetic history, the origin of this phoneme is unique in English in so far as the phonetic materials in which it developed were present only in words borrowed from French (or in modifications of Latin words). The medial sequence /VziV/ (*V* standing for any vowel) was common among the numerous loan-words: *vision, division, glazier,* etc. English stress patterns were imposed on these sequences so that Anglicized versions were regularly /–V́ziV–/. Subsequently, in the vowel sequence /–iV–/, /i/ was replaced by the articulationally related /y/: the general patterning of English words, syllable sequences, and the like brought about the reinterpretation of the sequence /–iV/ as /–yV–/. Thus three-syllable *vis-i-oun* of Middle English was replaced by /viz–yən/. Assimilation of /–zy–/ at the syllable boundary produced [ž], whose contrast with other medial consonants defined it as a new phoneme /ž/. Both the occurrence and distribution of /ž/ are sharply limited in Modern English; initial and final occurrences—*gendarme* and *rouge*—are ordinarily to be found only in French borrowings and are few in number; in these and similar words a more common English phoneme is often substituted for /ž/.

LOSSES IN THE CONSONANT SYSTEM

6.8 The additions to the consonant system throughout the course of the history of English have now been described. Let us consider next the losses. There have been only two—the unvoiced and voiced palatal-velar spirants /x ǥ/. In most dialects, the loss of /ǥ/ took place in the transition from Old English to Middle English; the loss of /x/ a few hundred years later, belongs chronologically to the transition from Middle English to Modern English. The "fates" of both, nevertheless, have much in common. (Especially in northern and Scottish dialects the loss of /ǥ/ came about in early Modern English, and /x/ has not yet disappeared.) In phonetic terms, the loss of both spirants occurred when one of the distinctive features was replaced by another distinctive feature; the result was a merger of the spirant with one or another of the phonemes already in the language. By substitution of stop for spirant articulation, for example, /ǥ/ > /g/, or /x/ > /k/; or by substitution of glide for spirant articulation /g/ > /w/ or /y/, or /x/ > /y/; or by further drift the consonantal glide was replaced by a related vocalic element to produce a diphthong or lengthened vowel from the original combination of the consonant with a preceding vowel. To add to the complexity of tracing the reflexes of these changes, the changes were subject to different conditionings correlated with other phonetic material in a word, variations in dialect in both place and time, as well as analogical reshaping of words and dialect borrowing.

Some illustrations will clarify the nature of the process by which these spirants disappeared and enable us to proceed to consideration of the systemic change that their disappearance entailed. The variation in changes is exemplified in Modern English *draw* and *drag,* both descendant forms of Old English /drag̃/: in the case of *draw* the series of changes may be represented as /drag̃an/ > /drawən/ > /drawə/ > /drau/ (where /au/ represents a diphthong) > Modern English /drɔ/ *draw;* in different dialectal and developmental circumstances /drag̃an/ > /dragən/ > . . . /dræg/ *drag.* The meanings of these historical doublets have also differentiated. Other examples are Old English *folgian* /folg̃–/ > Middle English *folwe(n)* > Modern English *follow;* Old English *boga* /bog̃a/ > Modern English *bow;* Old English *gōd* /g̃ōd/ > Modern English *good.* A common development of /x/ was "vocalization," that is, loss of spirant articulation and merger with /y/ or its related vowel. *Sigh, high, night, knight, through,* in their *gh* spellings, reflect the occurrence of /x/ in the Middle English forms of these words; in these instances the vocalization of /x/ resulted in lengthening of the preceding vowel. Less common was the change /x/ > /k/, as in Old English *eolh* /eolx/ > Modern English *elk.* Another replacement pattern consisted, somewhat remarkably, of substitution of another spirant for /x/, by which Middle English /laux–/ appears as Modern (American) English /læf/ *laugh,* Middle English /draxt/ or /drauxt/ > Modern English *draft,* and Old English /ġənox/ > Modern English *enough.* A number of occurrences of /x/ in Middle English resulted from the substitution /g̃/ > /x/. An especially interesting example is Old English /dwearg̃–/ > /dwerx/ > Modern English *dwarf,* but at one time or another, in one dialect or another, *dwerk, dwery, dwerowe, dwerwe, dwerth* (and still others) have been descendant forms of the Old English word. Other changes are illustrated by /drouxθ/ > *drought.*

By one process or another, all allophones of /x/ and /g̃/ were replaced in the principal dialects of English by allophones of other phonemes that were then part of the phonemic system of English.

SYSTEMIC EVOLUTION

6.9 Having considered changes in English consonants chiefly as simple additions to or losses from an inventory, we shall examine the evolution of the consonants as they constitute systems or patterned sets. In considering the systemic development we can also rearrange the changes according to the chronological order of their occurrence.

Before the early Old English split of inherited Germanic /k/ and /g/, the obstruent system formed a pattern of the kind represented in Figure 6C.

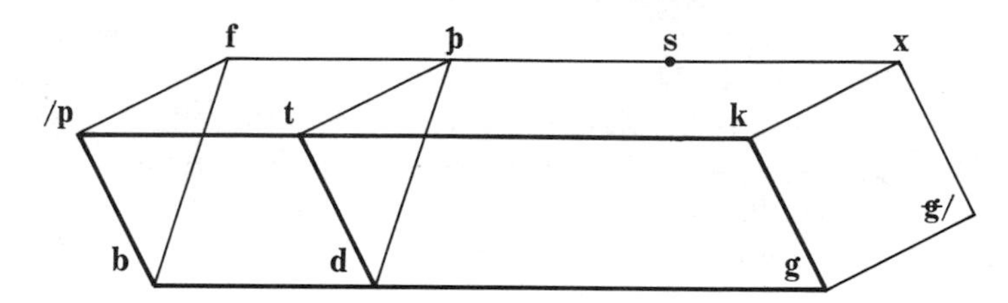

Figure 6C. The obstruent system of pre-Old English before split of /k/ and /g/.

The split producing /k k̭/ and /g ĝ/ modified the system so that its representation must be changed to that in Figure 6D.

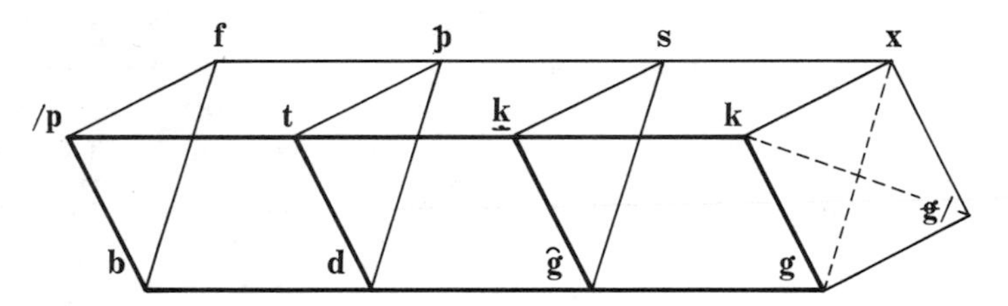

Figure 6D. The obstruent system of Old English.

The lack of symmetry of the palatal-velar set /k g x ǥ/ with the other positional sets was modified by the next change—loss of /ǥ/ by merger with other consonants—to produce full symmetry of pattern, as shown in Figure 6E.

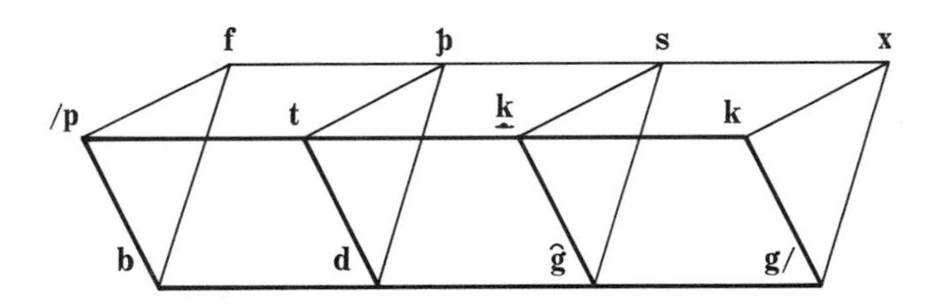

Figure 6E. The obstruent system of late Old English (or early Middle English) after loss of /ǥ/.

The next development was the introduction of /š/. The origin of this change was not like the changes resulting in loss of /ǥ/, nor was it like that which produced Old English /k̭ ĝ/. The obstruent system was complete and symmetrical; the emergence of /š/ had its origin in changes in the clustering patterns of consonants. Introduced through Scandinavian loan-words, the /sk/ clusters took their place in the cluster patterns of /sp st sk/. Because they were distinct from English [š] which had developed from earlier /sk/, the /sk/ clusters displaced [š] from the pattern and redefined it as a new phoneme /š/. With this change were five spirants and four pairs of unvoiced and voiced stops. Diagrammatic representation may be constructed, then, in either of the ways shown in Figure 6F.

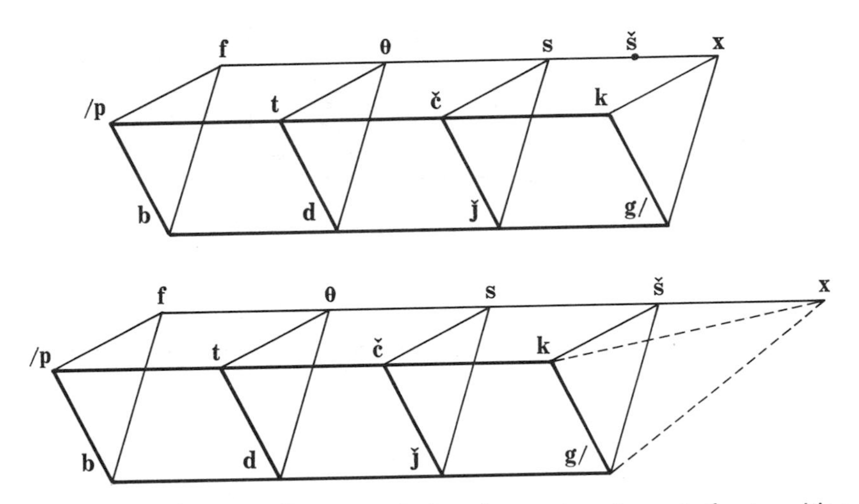

Figure 6F. Alternate diagrams of the obstruent system at the transition from Old English to Middle English. (The symbols /č/ and /ǰ/ replace /k̲/ and /ĝ/, respectively.)

In the first of these diagrams, articulatory similarities are represented by placing /k g x/ in the same plane; in the second, only the general symmetry of the system is taken into account. Choice between these graphic models should depend, perhaps, on considerations of both historical developments and theory of language history. It may be that when /š/ was first added to the system, it was not systemically integrated—as symbolized in the first of these models—and that about five hundred years later an adjustment had come about so that it was /x/ that was not systemically integrated—as symbolized by the second model.

To continue to the next development, the set of splits of the three originally unpaired spirants /f þ s/; at the time of this change /ᵹ/ had disappeared, and /š/ was relatively new and lacked a voiced counterpart. Voicing contrasts were fully established for stop consonants, and were fully established as allophonic variations of the three early

Middle English spirants /f θ s/. Thus, the phonemic splits reshaped the obstruent system by introducing voice-contrasted pairs of spirants parallel to those among the stops. By modifying the latter of the two models in Figure 6F, we may represent the next stage of development by the model in Figure 6G.

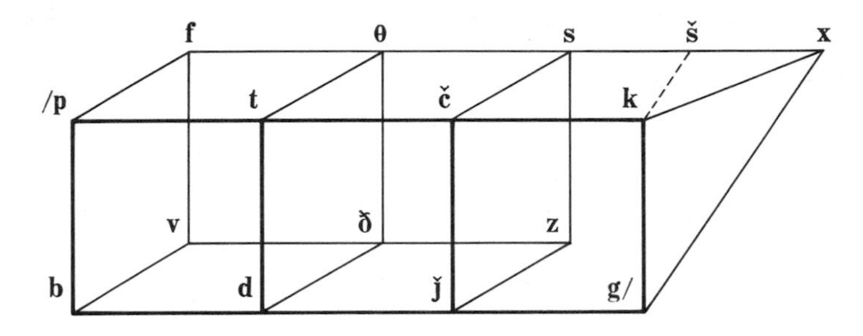

Figure 6G. The obstruent system of Middle English.

As Figure 6H indicates, the loss of /x/ in vocalization or in replacement by /f/ (as in *laugh, enough*) left the obstruent system with a single open position. The position was filled subsequently by

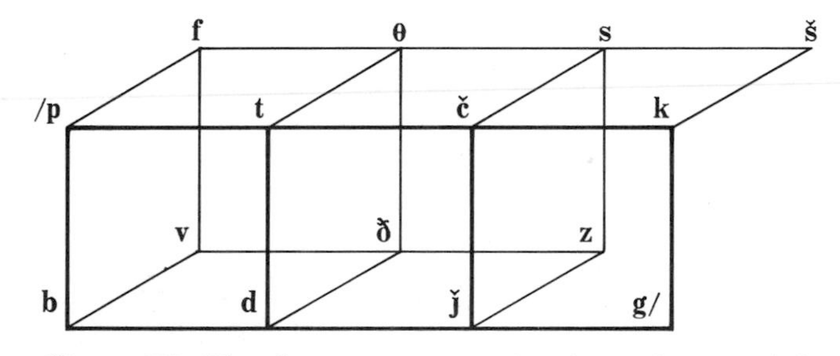

Figure 6H. The obstruent system of early Modern English.

/ž/, the source of which was assimilation of /–zy–/, as we saw in 6.7. This last change occurred in early Modern English and brought the obstruent system into the shape it has had up to the present, represented earlier in Figure 4D.

A SYSTEM OF HABITS

6.10 The split that produced the pairs /k k̲ g ĝ/ was one of the most important in the development of English stops and spirants: the four-position system of contrasts has persisted and has defined the system of sets of distinctive features, thus serving as a selective norm for subsequent changes. The contrast of voicing in the set of stops provided a systematic selection condition for the development of spirants; aside from adjustments to the four-position pattern of contrasts, the changes in spirants have to do principally with the contrast of voiced vs. unvoiced articulation.

The diagrams for the developing obstruent system make the gaps and asymmetries apparent, but they are merely simplified models of a system of shared language habits. For the consonant clusters, described in Chapter 5, the gaps and asymmetries in the systems of language habits should also have been apparent. Again, the dominant characteristics of the systems of clustering appear to have influenced the development of consonant clusters. Some clusters disappear and others emerge; and except for a few highly restricted clusters in borrowed words, all the additions and losses conform to the dominant patterns. Hence, not all the changes need to be described; examples can be used to explicate the changes or to illustrate the selective action of the system. When /y/ < Old English /ġ/ began to appear in clusters (see 5.8), it took its place in the system beside the other glide /w/; when /š/ emerged as a phoneme, its clustering characteristics were consistent with those of other consonants that were articulated as spirants. Again, when /skw–/ and /spl–/ appeared (see 5.6), they conformed to the pattern for initial three-member clusters: *s* + stop + lingual or glide. The initial clusters /hn– fn–/ fell into disuse about the same time, followed by the disuse of /kn– gn–/, leaving finally only /sn–/, still a frequent initial cluster.

On the basis of careful description alone, one cannot fail to realize that an essential aspect of a definition of language is "a system of habits." The systemic aspect of language becomes especially commanding in the study of language history. While language habits of both individuals and communities change, the changes are to a great extent only minor adjustments within a system; the system persists, undergoing gradual modification only in ways that the system itself largely determines.

Chapter 7

VOCALIC UNITS

DISTINCTIONS AMONG VOWELS

7.1 To describe English consonants it was practical to introduce phonemic distinctions immediately and then proceed to a description of the articulation of the various sounds that manifest the phonemes. To describe English vowels it is practical to follow the reverse procedure, that is, to begin with articulatory descriptions of the vocalic features and their sets. The reason for this reversal of procedure lies in the greater phonetic variation within vowel systems, among dialects, and between historical stages of development.

Distinctions among vowel sounds are produced by varying the configurations of the resonance area in which speech sounds are formed —the oral and pharyngeal cavities. One set of distinctions among vowels derives from the height of some portion of the tongue. For the series *sat, set, sit* a portion of the tongue is in progressively higher positions in articulating the vowel; the height of the lower jaw normally varies with tongue height for these vowels and can be readily observed. A parallel series is formed by the vowels of *wrought, wrote, root,* with progressively higher, or closer, articulations, though the actual measures of corresponding lower jaw openings have a smaller range. While the two series are parallel in terms of relative tongue heights, they are obviously different sets of vowels. The difference results from differences in the parts of the mouth in which each series is articulated: for *sat, set, sit* it is the front part of the tongue where height distinguishes the sounds; for *wrought, wrote, root* the back part of the tongue is at various heights with respect to the top of the mouth. For "mapping" purposes, a diagram of the mouth conventionally represents a speaker's left profile (cf. 2.4) in upright position. Thus, the symbols for the vowels of *sat* [æ], *set* [ɛ], *sit* [ɪ], *wrought* [ɔ], *wrote* [o], *root* [u] (when this last word rhymes with *loot*) are placed as in Figure 7A. (*æ* is called "ash," *ɔ* called "open o.")

More high and front than [ɪ] is the vowel of *seat* [i], and higher than [ɛ] is the vowel of *sate* [e]; both are also articulated with greater tenseness of muscles than are [ɪ] and [ɛ]. Less high than [u] is the [ʊ] of *foot* and *book* (in principal American dialects). Between back [ɔ] and front [æ] is the vowel of *hut* [ʌ], in central position. Also with a central articulation but with a very low tongue position is [ɑ],

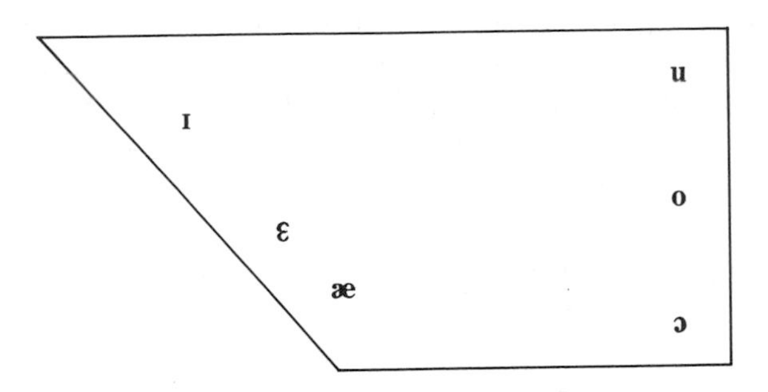

Figure 7A. Vowel chart illustrating three-way contrasts of vowels by height and two-way contrast of front vs. back.

the vowel *in several common dialects* of *lot, not.* All the vowels illustrated thus far are represented in Figure 7B.

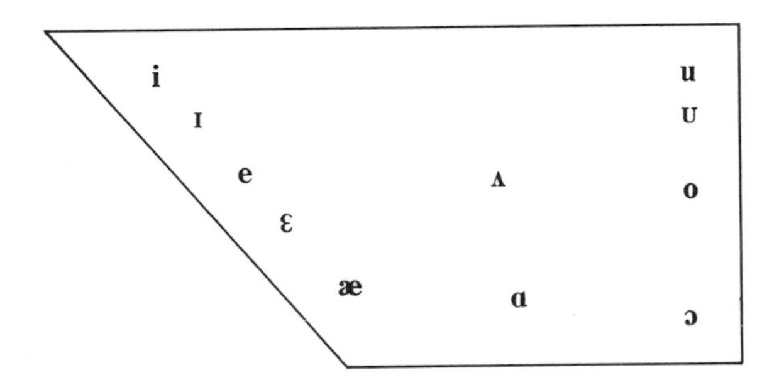

Figure 7B. Vowel chart with additional vowels, including English tense and lax vowels and vowels in central position.

As described above, [æ ɛ ɪ] differ from [ɔ o u] by front vs. back part of the tongue being set at various heights. The lips are rounded for back [ɔ o u] and are not rounded for [æ ɛ ɪ]. For Modern English the rounding or nonrounding of the lips is an automatic adjustment to back vs. front articulation. Front vowels may be formed with lip rounding, of course, and in some periods in the history of English rounded and unrounded front vowels were phonemically distinct. None of these can be illustrated from Modern English, but their articulation can be described on the basis of vowel features already listed. Corresponding to unrounded [i] is rounded [ü], and to [ɪ] is [Ü]; corresponding to [e] is [ø], and to [æ] is [œ].

All the vowel sounds described so far occur, or have occurred, in stressed syllables in English. Two additional vowels occur in nearly all dialects, though the circumstances of their occurrences vary greatly.

The first syllable of *about,* the final syllable in *vista,* or the *a* in *Let's rent a boat* commonly have central articulation (between front and back) and have middle tongue height; the symbol for this sound is [ə] (called "schwa"). Higher than [ə], and also included in unstressed syllables in English, is [ɨ] (called "barred *i*"); in many dialects it occurs in *–ed* syllables of past tense inflection as in *wanted* [wʌntɨd], or in other positions where assimilation to the following consonant produces this higher central vowel, as *runnin'* [rʌnɨn], or *just* in *I jus(t) got home!* [ǰɨst] or [ǰɨs].

DIPHTHONGS

7.2 The vocalic center of many syllables in English is obviously a glide from one vowel articulation to another. The resonant—voiced—part of *pipe, tight, sight,* or of *pout, stout, cow,* or of *soy, toy, choice* is plainly unlike any of the sounds listed so far. The sounds are articulatory (and acoustic) glides, unlike the sequence of relatively separate articulations in such words or phrases as *piano* [piæno], *go in* [go ɪn]. Because they are distinctively glides, and because they distinguish words, and are distributed in syllables in the same way as the simpler vowels, they are regarded as complex vocalic nuclei and classified as diphthongs. Their notation, in phonetic terms, is made by writing in sequence the vowel sounds that may be recognized at the beginning and end of the glides. Generally for American dialects, the diphthongs are these: [aɪ] *pipe,* [aʊ] *pout,* [ɔɪ] *soy.* All these have greater intensity at the beginning than at the end; for this reason they are commonly termed "falling diphthongs."

VOCALIC SOUND AND ACOUSTIC RECORD

7.3 A great many other details and features (such as nasalization) are relevant to the production of vocalic sounds, but these need not be of concern in our examination of English vowel systems and their history. One aspect of vowels must be brought up at this point, though, if we are to make sense of variations in vocalic systems, whether synchronically among dialects or diachronically between successive periods. Quite apart from diphthongs, English vowels are seldom "pure;" they are not sustained in unchanging articulation as they occur in normal speech; neither are they sustained, correlatively, with unchanging acoustic characteristics. This "flow-through" nature of vowels can be demonstrated readily in the results of acoustic analysis. The diagram given in Figure 7C is based on one drawn by Martin Joos in his pioneering study *Acoustic Phonetics.* The grid upon which the vowels are charted represents acoustic factors and not articulational positions. The acoustic data consist of the frequencies (pitch levels) measured in cycles per second of two formants; formants are frequency peaks of harmonic components of relatively simple sounds such as those of voice. For each vocalic sound the acoustic record is plotted with dots representing the acoustic data at intervals of two centisec-

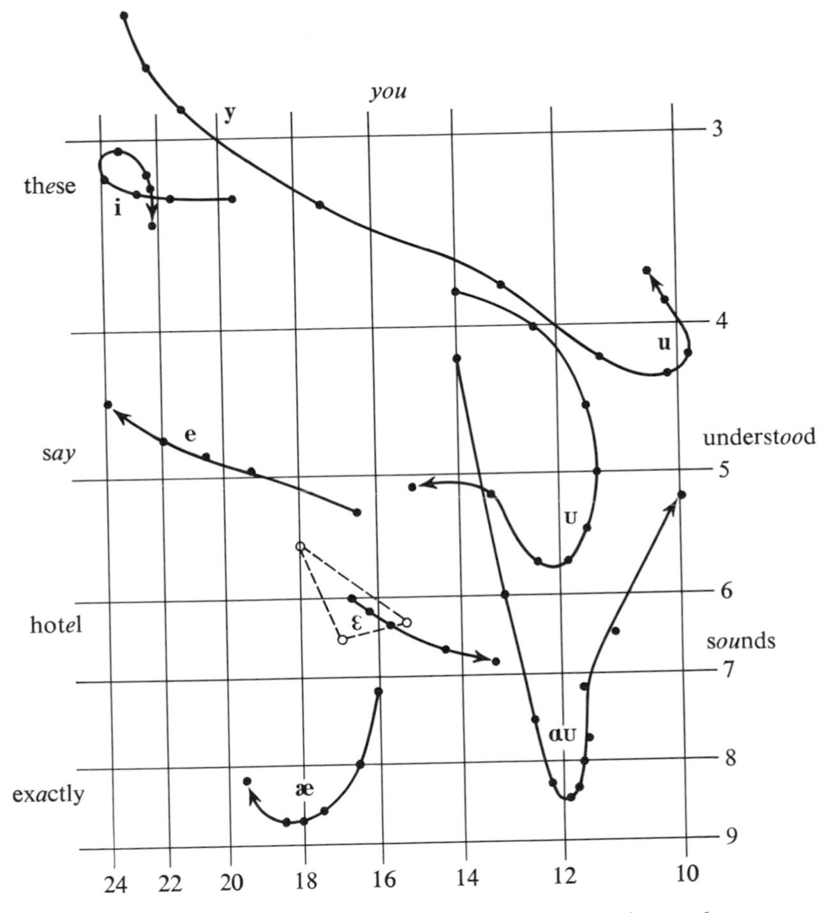

Figure 7C. Charting of acoustic data of vowels in normal speech contexts, based on Martin Joos's Acoustic Phonetics, *p. 52 (Fig. 25); used with permission. The words beside the diagram identify, with italic, the vocalic elements that appear nearest them in the diagram.*

onds; a smooth curve has been drawn to connect the dots, with an arrow pointing to the last dot in the time sequence. The words in which the sounds occurred *in normal speech* are indicated beside the diagram. The chart for acoustic features has been devised so as to match the conventional articulatory representation of vowels. Since acoustic data show that these vowels are not simple sustained ("pure") sounds, it must be inferred that the articulation was a continuous movement rather than a static positioning of the oral articulators.

The plotting of each vowel in Figure 7C is based on only a single utterance of the word containing it. One person uttering the "same" vowels in different phonetic environments would produce slightly different acoustic data. The [ɛ] of *hotel* is clearly influenced by the following [l]. To draw on another of Joos's representations of acoustic data from one person's speech, the variations of [ɪ]–sounds under the influence of phonetic context are as they appear in Figure 7D. (The

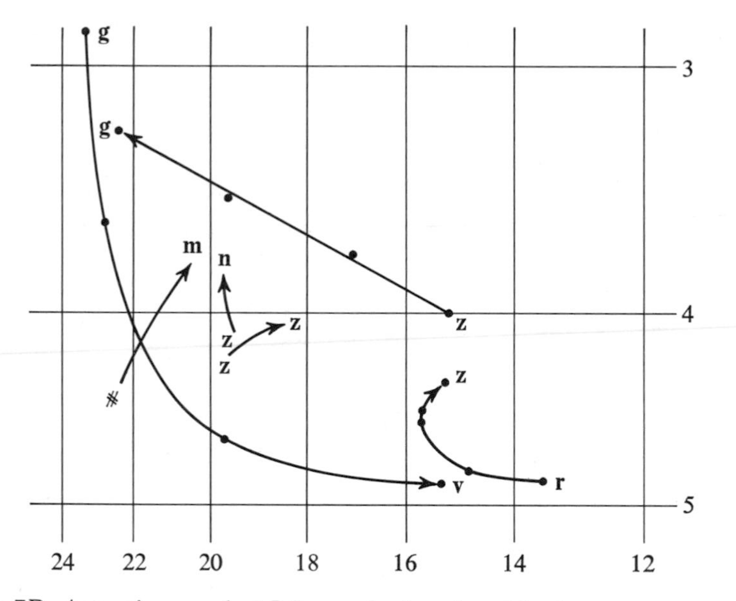

Figure 7D. Acoustic record of [ɪ]*-sounds, based on Martin Joos's* ACOUSTIC PHONETICS, *p. 102 (Figure 35); reprinted by permission. The consonants (or silence, #) preceding and following each* [ɪ] *vowel are marked in the diagram.*

area of this chart in relation to the larger chart of Figure 7C is indicated by the numerical identification of the grid lines.) Aside from the nonfixity of acoustic features (and hence of articulation), these acoustic records are striking because of the "intrusion" of [ɪ] into the [i]–sound characteristics under the influence of [g], and for the fact that the [g——v] curve and the [z——g] curve represent variations in opposite "directions."

Other variations can be observed by comparison of speech samples of different persons. Especially notable is the difference between the acoustic data of normal speech of average women's, men's, and children's voices. The *patterns* of distributions of the various vowels for these voices are nevertheless approximately the same shape for speakers of a single dialect; it is in this respect that different acoustic effects do not interfere with accurate perception of vowels among persons of opposite sex or of different age groups.

DIALECT VARIATIONS IN VOWEL SYSTEMS

7.4 One dialect may be easily noticed to differ from another in the selection of norms of vocalic articulation. Apart from pronunciations of individual words differing as [ˈproˌsɛs] and [ˈpraˌsɛs] *process* or [ɛt] and [et] *ate,* which are endproducts of differing historical developments of individual words, different sounds may make up the vowel systems of two dialects and yet the two vowel systems may be otherwise congruent. There may even be different phonetic manifestations of congruent systems within a restricted geographical area, the differences being correlated with social stratifications. A wide range of variations for the vowel in *bad, dance, ask,* and similar words, and for the stressed vowel in such words as *off, all, chocolate* has been shown to have extensive correlation with varying class status among speakers in an area of New York City. According to William Labov, in "Phonological Correlates of Social Stratification," the vowel widely analyzed as /æ/, for example, occurs with a variation in height ranging from [ɪ], [ɪ:ə] through [æ], [æ:] (slightly raised) to [a:]; five phonetically distinct manifestations of the phoneme effectively index five socioeconomic groups defined by a combination of occupation, education, and family income. (Other socioeconomic and phonetic correlations are found as well with consonant articulation and with alternation of consonants in given words.)

DISTRIBUTIONAL CHARACTERISTICS OF VOWELS

7.5 Besides differences in articulation and acoustic effect, Modern English vowels differ in distributional characteristics. Some vowels do not occur at the end of a syllable, but are always followed by one or more consonants within the syllable; for this reason they are called "checked vowels." While we have words such as *bet* [bɛt], *foot* [fʊt], *cut* [kʌt], there are no words [bɛ], [fʊ], [kʌ] or any that resemble them. For most American speakers [ɪ ɛ æ ʊ ʌ ɑ] do not occur at the ends of words or stressed syllables. The other vocalic units, including diphthongs, may occur at the end of a word, though they may also be followed by one or more consonants in the same syllable: *be* [bi] or *beat* [bit] or *beast* [bist], *bay* [be] or *bail* [bel] or *bailed* [beld], as well as *by* [baɪ], *you* [yu], *so* [so], *flaw* [flɔ], *now* [naʊ]. Their distributional characteristics are indicated by the designation "unchecked" or "free." Full description of these vowels within the classification of checked vs. free may be found in Hans Kurath's *A Phonology and Prosody of Modern English*. In phonetic terms, the latter sets—the free vowels as well as diphthongs—are commonly articulated with glide of a distinct kind. The [e] of *say*, represented in Figure 7C, is a common example of an upward glide; less broad phonetic transcription would appear as [eᴵ]. The upglide tendency is common for all these unchecked vowels; it is usually most noticeable for [oᵘ], as in *snow*, and in [eᴵ]. Nevertheless, even the vowels with high articulation show the same tendency exemplified by the [i] and [u] in Figure 7C.

PHONETIC NOTATION AND SPELLING

7.6 The disparity between phonetic notation and usual spellings for vowels is much greater than that between the notation and usual spellings for consonants. (The phonemic notation for consonants of English, in the preceding chapters, is closely similar to phonetic notation.) The greater disparity between vowel sound and symbol in conventional spelling will imply the difficulty of tracing the history of English vocalic units. Our alphabet has only five letters for vowels (or six, if *y* is counted); obviously there are many more vocalic units than vowel letters. Orthographic tradition has established pairs and patterns of letters to differentiate vowel sounds as well: *fed* and *feed* distinguish [fɛd] and [fid]; *rot, rote, root* distinguish [rɑt], [rot], and [rut] or [rʊt]. There is some overlap, too, as in [bet] spelled *bait* or *bate,* or when [e] is spelled in *say, whey, nation, weigh, straight, strait,* and so on. In Chapter 23 we shall consider some salient aspects of the history of English spelling. For the present it will be sufficient to point out that the evidence in written records from which the history of English vowels and their systems is derived is much less directly accessible than is the evidence for consonants.

It is somewhat reassuring to find that at the beginning of English writing the conventions of representing vowels were comparatively simple. In place of the variety of ways to spell [e], for example, as we have noticed in Modern English orthography, Anglo-Saxon scribes normally wrote *e*. And in place of such bewildering sets of spellings as Modern English *cough, rough, dough, bough,* the earliest writing came close to using a different letter for each phoneme. The weakness of the roman alphabet for writing English was in the representation of vowels. To the set *a æ, e, i, o, u* was added *y*. Even so, *o,* for instance, will represent either of two sounds which will be distinguished with the notation *o* and *ō,* [ɒ] and [o:]; but it will not represent any other sounds when it occurs as the single vowel in a syllable.

FURTHER PROBLEMS IN THE STUDY OF VOWELS

7.7 Before we proceed to the history of English vowels, two further sets of facts need to be introduced; both were relatively insignificant in respect to the development of consonants. The relevance of the first set was noted in the section (6.6) pointing out that the split of spirants into voiced and unvoiced pairs occurred at different times in different dialects and, most remarkably, in one instance as a result of exactly contrary circumstances. Divergence of directions of systemic development, already shown for spirants, is repeated many times over in the development of vowel systems. In one dialect area the changes or the rates of changes may be different from those in other dialect areas. As in the case of spirants, however, convergence of developmental direction has often occurred later. In comparison to vowel systems, the consonant systems of English have maintained extensive uniformity. Our history of the vowels consequently must be much more fragmentary than that of the consonants.

Our historical account of English vowels will also have a major "fault"—a break and dislocation in the line of descent—conditioned by the second set of facts. We have to do here with the nonlinguistic facts of the survival of written texts from which to reconstruct the history. Nearly all the texts of Old English are in the southwestern dialect West Saxon; most early texts—up to the late ninth century—were destroyed or lost as a result of invasion, war, and conquest. Those texts were written principally in the eastern and northern parts of England. The Old English of which we have clear and abundant evidence was written for the most part between 850 and 1050 in southern and western dialect areas. The prominence of the writing done under Wessex-controlled England made it more or less "standard (Old) English." Then came the Norman Conquest. When writing in English again became common enough to leave full evidence of the language and for a new "standard (Middle) English" to emerge, the cultural center had shifted to London and the areas to the north of

London. In effect, the dialects of English continued their generally separate developments, while political and other cultural factors shifted the "linguistic center" of England from one dialect area to quite a different one. A time-map with indication of the prominence of English dialects may be roughly constructed as in Figure 7E.

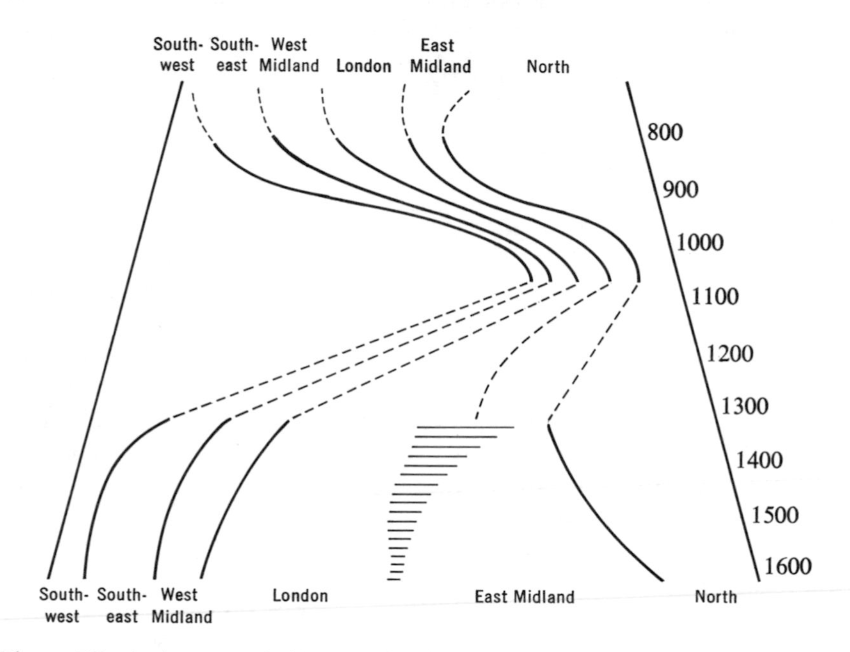

Figure 7E. A time-map indicating the shifts in prominence of the principal Old and Middle English dialects. The break in line of descent between the Norman Conquest and the rise of a new standard dialect in (late) Middle English is registered by broken lines in the center of the map.

Processes of change in the systems and distribution of vowels in English can be carefully studied despite the displacement of linguistic centers—"centers" in terms of both political and cultural prominence and abundance of linguistic records.

Chapter 8

EARLY ENGLISH VOWELS AND VOCALIC CHANGE

PHONETIC RECONSTRUCTIONS

8.1 The phonetics of vowels from earliest English have been reconstructed with great care during the past hundred years of study. Spellings have been analyzed meticulously, changes in spellings have been scrutinized, spellings by writers with different language backgrounds (especially Norman French) have been compared to those of native English writers; rhymes have also been exhaustively studied, and the observations of orthoepists (since the sixteenth century) have been compared and sifted; and so on through the many aspects of historical analysis. The reconstructions may be accepted with confidence, and we shall not take up here the reconstruction of phonetic details of vowels. On the basis of the formulations of phonetic characteristics of the individual vowels we shall proceed directly to the vocalic systems, the changes they have undergone, and a sampling of the changes in the vocalic elements within words.

SHORT AND LONG VOWELS

8.2 Some aspects of (West Saxon) Old English will provide a suitable starting point for study of the vocalic systems. Though the alphabetic system adapted to the writing of Old English was deficient in symbols for vowels, distinction can be made between different vocalic elements that were spelled alike. The grounds for distinguishing them are both contrastive and historical. For example, some pairs of words clearly distinguished in meaning are regularly spelled identically: *hof* 'hoof,' 'dwelling'; *god* 'good,' 'god'; *hol* 'hole,' 'slander'; *dæl* 'deal, portion,' 'dale'; *fæt* '(metal) plate,' 'vessel, cup'; *lim* 'limb,' 'anything sticky'; *æl* 'eel,' 'awl,' and many more. A language may have a number of homophonic word pairs (or sets), such as Modern English *sea, see* or *site, cite, sight*. Not having the weight of tradition and archaism of spelling that we now have, the number of word pairs spelled identically in Old English suggests that at least some of these pairs may not have been homophones.

If a set of words has persisted in the language with minimal change while new spelling conventions have been introduced, then a pair of words with identical spellings at one time which are regularly spelled with different vowel letters at a later time would provide presumptive evidence that the two sets were pronounced differently at both periods. If two Old English words spelled *æl* have Modern English descendant forms *eel* and *awl,* and two others spelled *dæl* have descendant forms *deal* and *dale,* we infer a phonemic difference in the Old English vowels spelled *æ*. The technique of analysis may be complex for certain instances, and the comparisons are normally made at successive, short periods of time: the one-thousand-year interval in the example just given is appropriate only for illustration and not as a serious historical analysis.

For Old English, then, the difference that evidently existed between some pairs of vowels was one that did not motivate writers to invent new symbols to distinguish them. The pair spelled either *þe* or *ðe* (the letters *þ* "thorn," and *ð* "eth" or "crossed *d*," were freely interchangeable) occur frequently and are reconstructed as [θe:] and [θə]; their contrast may be illustrated in this sentence: *Iċ hit eom þe wið þe sprece* 'It is I who [θə] speak to thee [θe:].' Scholars traditionally have marked the difference by writing a macron over the letter representing one of the vowels and leaving the letter for the other unmarked. Thus, *æl* 'eel,' *ǣl* 'awl'; *dæl* 'dale,' *dǣl* 'deal'; *god* 'god,' *gōd* 'good'; *hof* 'dwelling,' *hōf* 'hoof,' etc. The difference between these pairs is designated as a contrast between "long" vowels, as in *sǣd* 'seed,' and "short" vowels, as in *sæd* 'satiated.'

Once this distinction of vowel length is made, the vocalic system of West Saxon is relatively easy to describe. The simple vocalic units con-

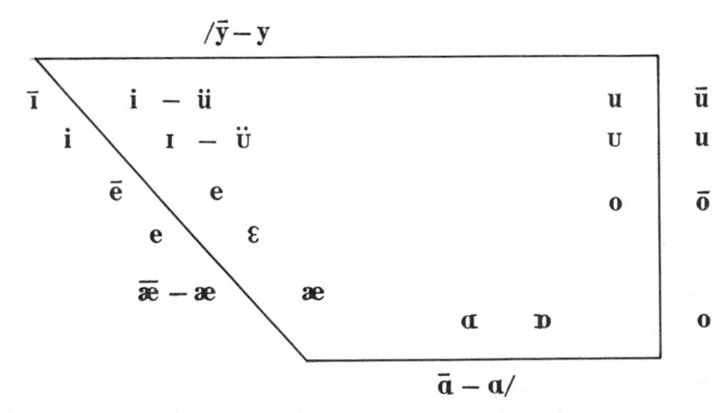

Figure 8A. Vowel chart of simple stressed vocalic units in West Saxon Old English. Phonemic notation appears adjacent to phonetic notation, outside the chart.

sist of two basic sets. The back vowels are all rounded vowel , /u o a/ paired by length with /ū ō ā/. Front vowels are an unbalanced set: the unround /i e æ/ are paired with /ī ē ǣ/, but there are also two rounded front vowels (also paired by length), /y ȳ/. These vowels may be conveniently displayed in systematic form by writing the phonemic notation beside an articulatory (phonetic) diagram for them, as they appear in Figure 8A. Illustrative words are also given in order parallel to that of the vowels in the articulatory chart.

twīn *double thread*	hȳf *hive*		fūl *foul*
twinn *double*	cynn *kin, race*		full *full, entire*
wēste *waste (-land)*			gōd *good*
west *west*		hām *home*	god *god*
dǣl *deal* dæl *dale*		ham *ham*	

Besides the simple vowels are diphthongs, which also pair as "long" and "short." All were "falling" diphthongs, that is, they were stressed at the beginning of the glide. They are given here as they appear in early West Saxon (c. 900), with illustrative words.
/īe/ [iɛ, iə] hīe *they,* tīen *ten,* stīeran *(to) steer*
/ie/ [ɪɛ, ɪə] fierd *army,* siexta *sixth*
/ēo/ [eɒ, eə] hēo *she,* fēond *enemy,* bēo *be, am*
/eo/ [ɛɒ, ɛə] eom *am,* weorc *work,* deorc *dark*
/ēa/ [æɑ:, æə:] hēap *assembly, host,* dēad *dead,* stēap *steep*
/ea/ [æɑ, æə] eart *(thou) art, are,* eald *old,* eall *all*

An additional vowel, occurring only in unstressed syllables, may be listed as /ə/. On grounds of spellings and historical processes of change, this vowel is believed to have been manifest as [ɨ] when it alternated with a front vowel or when conditioned by a following /r/ or /l/, as in *fæder* /fædər/ [ˈfædər] or [ˈfædɨr] 'father.' Otherwise it was apparently manifest as [ə], as in *munuc* /munuk/ [ˈmʊnʊk] or /munək/ [ˈmʊnək] 'monk.'

None of the "long" vowels appears in inflectional suffixes; this fact marks out a major characteristic of the distribution of long vowels because these suffixes are known to have had less than full stress; they are, in fact, known to have had light stress. Short vowels or diphthongs do not ordinarily appear in the final position of word roots consisting of one syllable. Although a number of words occurred with great frequency with short vowels not closed, or checked, by consonants, it seems most probable that the vowels were very lightly stressed—that the short vowels in final position cannot be considered as belonging to the class of stressed syllabics. Thus, when a sequence is analyzed into "words," there often seem to be short vowels that are not checked: *se man* 'the man,' *bi temese* 'along (or by) the Thames' are of this kind. But when the words containing final short vowels occur apart from phrases in which the main stress falls on a following word—when the words in question would take heavier stress in their sentence contexts—these words had "long" vowels: *sē, bī* (and others) instead of *se* and *bi*. Short vowels also occur in "open" position in inflections —*sunu, suna* 'son,' etc. where, again, they had light stress only. In brief, the vowels of Old English that are traditionally called "long" vowels correspond closely in distribution and development to those of Modern English called "free," and the Old English "short" vowels, except as they occurred with light stress, correspond closely to Modern English "checked" vowels.

CHANGES IN VOCALIC SEGMENTS OF WORDS

8.3 In considering consonants, we have seen already that the history of English includes a great many changes in the phonemic make-up of words that do not in themselves either constitute or reflect a change in the system of phonemes. The changes in vocalic elements of words have been more numerous, frequent, and various than the changes involving consonants. It will be worthwhile to illustrate types of changes involving vocalic segments of words before proceeding to the vowels of Middle English: the kinds and nature of change must be distinguished if an account of changes is to proceed clearly.

Gradual, cumulative tendencies in pronunciation resulted in a series of restructurings of words. For some reason, between late Old English and Middle English "short" vowels were replaced by "long" vowels before certain pairs of consonants under specifiable conditions. (The cause, like that for most sound change, is not clearly determined; of the occurrence of the change there is no doubt, and the attendant conditions are fully formulated.) The change took place before /–nd –mb –rd –ld –rθ/, for example, /ċild/ > /ċīld/ 'child' and /feld/ > /fēld/ 'field.' Under other conditions—when a two-syllable form had had an open first syllable bearing principal stress—the reflex of that earlier form had a long vowel instead of the original short one: /a e o/ were replaced respectively by /ā ē ō/. When the change had been completed, the one syllable singular form meaning 'staff' was /staf/, while the plural 'staves' was two-syllable /stāvəs/; Modern English *staff–staves* reflect the effects of this early Middle English change.

A contrary kind of change began at about the same time but continued longer. "Shortening" describes the replacement pattern exemplified by /kēptə/ > /keptə/ 'kept,' /blǣdrə/ > /blædrə/ 'bladder,' /sōftə/ > /softə/ 'soft.' In disyllabic words, syllables not bearing principal stress underwent the same type of change of shortening of vowel: Old English and Middle English pairs are /wī́sdṑm/ > /wī́sdòm/ 'wisdom' and /ā̀rī́san/ > /àrī́san/ '(to) arise.'

These "quantitative" changes of lengthening and shortening did not directly affect the vocalic system of the language: they affected only the phonemic shape of words that persisted during the period of change, words that had historical identity. In addition, the change could not have occurred merely as a gradual lengthening of "short" vowels until they became as long as the corresponding "long" vowels, or vice versa. From what we have seen already about phonemes and reshaping of words, it should be clear that if the process had been one of gradual lengthening on the one hand, and of shortening on the other, the basis for the contrast of "long" and "short" would have disappeared during the process of change. If we regard length vs. non-length of vowels as a binary contrast of distinctive features, the changes will be seen in the same light as consonant changes as they were described in 6.1: the heard utterances were reinterpreted in phonemic terms and the new phonemic shapes of words gradually came to predominate. The gradualness of the process belongs solely to the alternate replacement patterns of "long" and "short" vowels within chronologically persisting words.

QUALITATIVE CHANGES OF VOWELS

8.4 "Qualitative" changes of vowels have also occurred commonly in the history of English words. One of the more conspicuous differences between Old English and Middle English resulted from a change in Old English /ā/. In some dialects it did not change, but in others it was replaced by /ǭ/ "open *o*" (an *o*–sound articulated as a more open vowel than generally in Modern English, and contrasting with "close *o*" /ọ̄/). Within any dialect in which /ā/ > /ǭ/ there was no essential change in the inventory and system of vocalic units. The change is in this respect similar to that of alveolar [t] replacing dental [t̪] (see 6.3).

When a vocalic phoneme was replaced by other, persisting vowels in all words, a systemic change did occur. The history of Old English /ȳ y/ is a case in point. In northern dialects /ȳ/ was replaced by /ī/ and /y/ by /i/; in southern dialects /ȳ/ > /ē/ and /y/ > /e/. The pair /ȳ y/ *merged* with another pair in the respective dialect areas. In systemic terms, the unbalanced set of front vowels described for Old English became (in this respect) a balanced set in Middle English.

In still another set of dialects the merger with /ī i/ or /ē e/ did not occur until somewhat later. In the western regions of England, both Midland and Southern, the rounded, high front vowels persisted; their spelling was altered by a change in writing traditions to *u, ui.* Thus, in the fourteenth century, the differences stemming from diverse developments of Old English /ȳ y/ appear in the following word-sets.

Old English		Middle English		
West Saxon		West (Midland and South)	North	Southeast
/brȳd	'bride'	/brȳdə	/brīdə	brēdə
fȳr	'fire'	fȳr	fīr	fēr
mȳs	'mice'	mȳs	mīs	mēs
kyn(•)	'kin'	kyn	kin	ken
myriġ	'merry'	myriə	míri	méri
syn(•)	'sin'	syn•ə	sin•ə	sen•ə
kys•an/	'(to) kiss'	kys•ə(n)/	kís•ə/	kés•ə(n)/

Typical spelling differences are *fur – fir – fer* and *cusse(n) – kesse(n) – kisse.*

Another set of changes involves diphthongal vocalic elements, both their simplification to simple vowel articulations and their development into vowel with distinctive accompanying glide. If we start again from the Old English system, change in the vocalic system of English included simplification of all diphthongal vocalic elements. Old English /æə/ thus coalesced with /æ/ merely by loss of the centering glide to [ə]; it will be remembered that /æə/ was, like the other diphthongs, a "falling" diphthong, and that reduction to /æ/ was effected when the distinctive lesser-stressed element was no longer distinctively present. To call this kind of change a "loss of drawl" should not be misleading. The Old English pair /eo/ and /ēo/ correspond ultimately to Middle English /e/ and /ē/. For this pair the history is less simple. From a /e/ or /ē/ with a glide to rounding, the front articulation was retained and the lip-rounding was superimposed as another distinctive feature so that the pair of vowels came to have rounded mid-front articulation. The subsequent development was loss of rounding, with mid-front articulation, that is, the articulation for [ɛ] or [e]. The change proceeded at different rates in the various areas of England. The change /eo/ > /e/ was complete in the twelfth century in most areas except the West and South (which does not include Southeast), where the change did not take place until the fourteenth century; and interestingly enough, /ēo/ > /ē/ was a slower change than /eo/ > /e/.

NEW DIPHTHONGS

8.5 The development of new diphthongs is particularly interesting because their sources have been so various and diverse. One source that requires no special commentary here is borrowing. A large number of words borrowed from French during Middle English contained [ɔɪ], and English speakers' retention of that part of the pronunciation established the new diphthong /oy/ in English. But processes of diphthongization were the principal sources of new complex nuclei; these processes have operated repeatedly in English, and they are still in operation, further modifying the system of English sounds.

The best sources of illustration of the processes of diphthongization operating during the transition from Old English to Middle English are "copies" of texts made at intervals great enough to make obvious the direction and scope of linguistic change. It must be understood that exact, graphic copies in which the sequence of letters and spaces is reproduced without change will not reflect changes in the language; "copy" here means approximate reproduction of a sequence of utterances reflecting normal speech at different times. In a manuscript text of the Gospels, written about 1000, *dæge* is the usual spelling for the word 'day'; another manuscript, from 1150–1200, repeats the text word for word, but spells the same word as *daige* or *dayge*. The pronunciation of the earlier forms presumably included the sequence /–æġə/ in which /ġ/ was manifest as a prepalatal spirant with glide; whatever its precise phonetic attributes, it was distinctly consonantal. The vowel-spelling *ai* or *ay* in the later "copy," with retention of the following *g* at the syllable boundary, strongly implies that the vowel of the root syllable in the word had diphthongized, and the *g* represents a consonantlike transition to the next vocalic sound.

The process can be explicated still further. Figures 7C and 7D illustrate the essentially gliding characteristics of vowels as they are assimilated in both onset and termination by the preceding and following sounds. The transition from [æ] in *dæge* to a following [j] (as in *yes*) would involve a glide through some variety of [ɪ]; a very slow pronunciation of the sequence [æjə] is again the most convenient way to observe the glide. The diphthongization of the vocalic nucleus in the word 'day' (and many others) was, in a very simplified sense, a shift in habits of articulating and interpreting the sounds, so that the glide from /æ/ to /ġ/ came to be regarded as significant. The outcome of this set of changes makes the process still clearer. In manuscripts of two hundred years after the *daige, dayge* spellings, the word had come to be spelled *day*. In short, the vowel-consonant sequence /æġ(ə)/ was replaced by a complex vocalic unit—a diphthong—/ay/; /ġ/ was replaced by /y/ by loss of the spirant feature by phonological drift; at the same time redistribution put /y/ in the same class as glide /w/ and postvocalic /y/ came to function as part of the syllable nucleus by the developmental process called "vocalization."

The emergence of /ay/ as a syllable nucleus is but one of several examples of the development of diphthongs in Middle English. Others that involved vocalization of earlier /ġ/ are similar to that in the preceding example: /eġ/ was replaced by /ey/ which later merged with /ay/ as in Old English /weġ/ > Middle English /wey/, /way/ 'way.' /ǣġ/ was replaced in some instances by /ey/ and also merged later with /ay/, as with Old English /grǣġ/ > Middle English /gray/ 'gray–grey.' A related change involving a vowel followed by /ġ/ produced a phonemically simple vowel. In the sequence /iġ/, the glide toward /ġ/, the modification /ġ/ > /y/, and the restructuring such that the /y/ came to function as part of the syllable nucleus produced [i] in words that had not formerly had that vowel. Meanwhile, [i] had persisted into Middle English in other words. Thus, besides Old English /fīf/, /wīs/ > Middle English /fīf/, /wīs/ 'five,' 'wise,' in which /ī/ occurred, Old English /niġən/ > Middle English /nīn(ə)/ 'nine.'

Not only did vowel + /ġ/ produce new diphthongs, but vowel + /w/ also developed new syllable nuclei. The process was similar to that involving /ġ/, with prominent development of a glide from vowel to consonant, and the restructuring by which the glide to the consonant came to be regarded as part of the syllable center. Many of the occurrences of the resultant diphthongs came as well from developments beginning with Old English /ǥ/; it will be recalled that one of the reflexes of /ǥ/ was /w/. For example, Old English /aǥ/ and /aw/ were replaced by Middle English /au/, as in /draǥan/ > /drauən/ 'draw' and /sawol/, /sawəl/ > /saul/ 'soul.' A similar sequence was the Old English /oǥ/ > /ow/ > /ou/, as in /boǥa/ > /bou(ə)/ 'bow.'

PROCESSES OF PHONOLOGICAL CHANGE

8.6 Enough examples of changes have already been given to suggest the variety and range of modifications that the language underwent in its vowel phonology during a period of approximately four hundred years. The preceding illustrations of phonological change were intended to show typical processes by which change in the system of English sounds comes about. We have seen the processes of lengthening and shortening of vowels, the qualitative changes involving merger, addition of a diphthong through linguistic borrowing, and the changes within the language by which new diphthongal vocalic units emerge. The shift in prominent dialects between the Old and Modern periods of the language makes impractical the derivation of the Middle English reflex of West Saxon Old English and the Middle English Midlands dialect that formed the basis of early Standard (Modern) English from its Old English antecedents.

The vocalic system of late Middle English Midlands–London dialect will serve better as the starting point for the next chapter than as the conclusion to the present one: it was but one of the socially and politically equal dialects when it developed; serving as it did as the basis for the principal standard dialects of Modern English, however, it merits special considerations.

Chapter 9

A LATE MIDDLE ENGLISH VOCALIC SYSTEM

PROBLEMS IN FORMULATING CHAUCER'S PHONOLOGY

9.1 The history of English vocalic systems since the fourteenth century—from the time of Chaucer and Henry IV—is not immediately apparent in the typical literary and historical writings belonging to the period from 1400 to the present. Among the dialects of Middle English were several distinct vocalic systems. Change in vocalic elements of words and in the vocalic system has continued from century to century in all the ways illustrated in the preceding chapter for the period prior to 1400. Change of still another major kind has also taken place as we shall see in Chapter 10. Just before the beginning of the period of Modern English the spelling system began to stabilize. Representation of vowels, particularly, came to be traditional rather than reflective of pronunciation. Increasingly spelling of vowel sounds was something one decided on the basis of earlier records and not on the basis of the sounds one heard and uttered. The models of vowel symbolizing, finally, had been established on the bases of conventions of writing Latin and French.

Despite the increasing divergence of speech and writing in respect to vowels, it is possible to reconstruct in detail the phonetic characteristics of Middle, as well as Old and Early Modern English. Shakespeare's pronunciation, for example, has been ascertained both in respect to the vowels and consonants as such, and in respect to the pronunciation of nearly all items in his recorded vocabulary. Chaucer's pronunciation, representing a dominant variety (London–East Midland) of English spoken in London, is well understood even though there are disagreements about some of the details. Descriptions of Middle English phonology based on study of Chaucer's writings may list varying numbers of diphthongs. Apart from differences between phonetic and phonemic descriptions (which need not represent disagreement about a phonological system), significant differences also occur between the various phonetic *or* phonemic formulations. Such disagreements should not, however, raise our doubts about the competence of those who have drawn up differing analyses. The disagreements stem from certain ambiguities in the evidence (the spellings, chiefly), from differences in the purposes the formulations are intended to serve, and from some differences—probably resulting from incompleteness—of theory about historical phonology.

It will be advantageous to approach Chaucer's phonology in terms of the sources of disagreement about its formulation. Spelling is the starting point, together with rhymes, of which Chaucer was regarded as a master. A great number of Chaucer's words are spelled in at least two ways and may appear commonly in three different spellings. The alternation of *i* and *y* may be attributed to habits of writing that were not correlated with differences in pronunciation, the alternation being loosely analogous to varying shapes of *t, r, E, T, W,* etc. that may appear in any individual's handwriting. If *i* and *y* were interchangeable in respect to phonology, it is also clear that either letter represented either of two different sounds. Sets of rhyme words, together with broad lines of historical development of English sounds, show that either letter represented either [i] or [ɪ]: *mile* rhymes with *stile, mille* has the same vowel as *stille.* Modern English preserves a distinction in vowels of the descendant words, such that *mile* and *stile* rhyme, *mill* and *still* rhyme, but *mile* and *mill* do not and obviously have different vowel phonemes. It is clear that Old English had distinctive vowels for /mīl/ 'mile' and /myl(e)n/ 'mill.'

The spellings of some other vowels are yet more ambiguous. On grounds of rhyme and historical lines of development, it can be determined that *e* represented a sound in *hem* 'them' that was different from both the (stressed, root) vowels of *heeth* 'heath' and *swete* 'sweet'; furthermore, the root vowel represented in the latter two words was spelled sometimes *e,* sometimes *ee.* Exactly parallel to *e, ee* spellings are *o, oo* spellings: *other–oother, anon–anoon,* etc. (To complicate matters, *o* also was used quite regularly to represent a sound otherwise represented by *u,* when it was written beside letters made with short downstrokes: /sunə/ *sone* 'son' < Old English /sunu/ *sunu.*) We need not go further into the ambiguities of spellings to appreciate the difficulties that the evidence presents. Careful analyses of the writings by generations of scholars have made clear that *e, ee* spellings together represent three different vowels, *o, oo* spellings three other vowels, and most other vowel letters represent two vowels each.

For the simple vowels the main uncertainty concerns the vowel spelled *u* in such words as *vertu* 'virtue' and *duc* 'duke.' As words borrowed from French, used by speakers generally conversant with French (as Chaucer was), they were probably pronounced with the sound [ü] or [u̇]—rounded high-front or mid-articulation. Others who spoke essentially the same dialect of English probably substituted an English diphthong for this sound in French words, that is, [ɪu] corresponded in these words to the French model with [ü]. Even if the [ʊ̈] were in use by Chaucer and others, the question remains whether to consider it a genuine part of his *English* vocalic system or an anomalous appendage to it; the question is similar to that concerning the spirant [x] in the Modern English speech of those who use it in never more than a few words such as the name *Bach,* words in which an essentially non-English pronunciation is retained.

In the sounds represented by alternate spellings *e, ee,* the vowel of *heeth* had a more "open" articulation than that of the root vowel of *swe(e)te,* that is, it was articulated as a sound closer to [æ]. The two vowels were qualitatively different, with *heeth, dele* 'deal, share' and others rhyming with words that in Old English had had an /ǣ/ vowel: Old English /hǣθ/, /dǣl/ correspond to Middle English *heeth dele.* None of the words that in Old English had had /ǣ/ vowels rhyme in Middle English with words that in Old English had had /ē/ —Old English /fēt/, /mēd/ correspond to Middle English *feet, mede,* and the like. Nor do words with either of these vowels rhyme with words that in Old English had had /e/, as in /bed/, /help–/, Middle English *bed, help–.* Again, the circumstances are parallel for back vowels spelled *o, oo.* It is evident that the assignment of phonetic characteristics is seriously complicated.

If [i] and [ɪ] form a *pair,* how are we to regard the set of *three* "*e*–vowels"? If [u] and [ʊ] form a pair, how are we to regard the set of three "*o*-vowels"? If Modern English and other Germanic languages are any guide, the [i] and [u] vowels were more tense in articulation and probably had normally a longer duration than [ɪ] and [ʊ]. The question is which significant features made these two pairs of vowels phonemically discrete: differences in quality, repre-

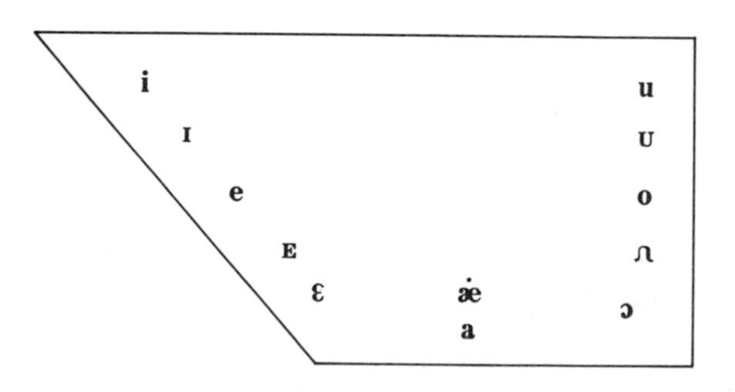

Figure 9A. A tentative reconstruction of simple stressed vocalic units in Chaucer's Middle English dialect; all vocalic differences are registered as solely qualitative.

sented by the different alphabetic symbols [i] and [ɪ]; difference in length (a factor of duration), that may be represented with a diacritic for length in the notation [i:] vs. [ɪ]; or difference of some other kind? If our choice of symbols is to reflect a decision regarding the phonological features on which phonemic contrast was based, should we choose /i ɪ/ or /ī i/ or /iy i/ or some other pair? There would be no problem if it were not for the sets of three that occur with the mid-range front and back vowels. The problem can be clarified by trying to place these vowels in a scheme of articulation. On qualitative grounds we should expect something like the pattern represented in Figure 9A. This pattern looks unlike those that may be derived from traditional descriptions of Chaucer's language. Assuming "long" and "short" distinctions to have been primary for the vowels, we may represent the vowels alternately as they appear in Figure 9B. This

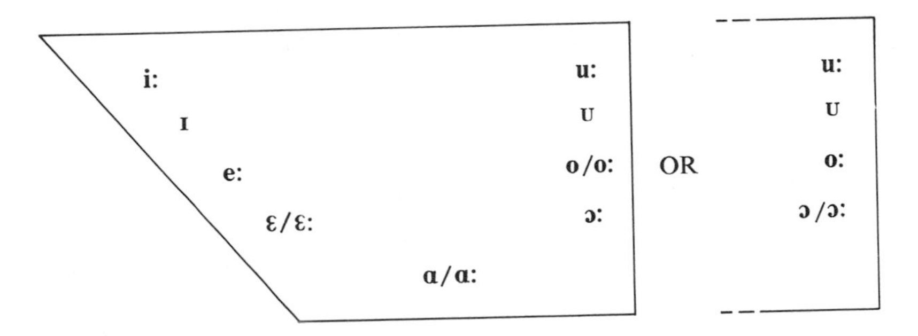

Figure 9B. Another tentative reconstruction of simple stressed vocalic units in Chaucer's Middle English dialect; vocalic differences are registered as partially quantitative and as partially qualitative.

second symbolization implies that two kinds of contrasting features are involved—qualitative and quantitative; for the high vowels [i: ɪ u: ʊ] length is then redundant, and qualitative difference is sufficient; for the mid vowels [e: ɛ: ɛ o: ɔ: ɔ] qualitative difference is not sufficient and, aside from distinguishing [ɛ:] from [e:] just as [e:] is distinguished from [i:] or [ɪ], length is a *necessary* distinguishing feature. The system of stressed vowels of Chaucer's English can be formulated another common way, and we shall turn to it next.

A FORMULATION EMPLOYING SEMIVOWELS

9.2 A system for analyzing stressed vowels of Modern English has been suggested repeatedly as the appropriate model for formulating Middle

English stressed vowels. The various particular formulations that have been offered have not been identical, but the principles they employ are essentially the same. Two notable formulations are those of Robert P. Stockwell in "The Middle English 'Long Close' and 'Long Open' Mid Vowels" and of Jacek Fisiak in *Morphemic Structure of Chaucer's English*. These formulations make use of three symbols /y w h/ that are regarded as representing glide characteristics by which stressed vowels were phonemically distinguished. All three symbols represent off-glides, that is, drift—considered either acoustically or articulationally—of one of three kinds: /y/ represents off-glide toward high

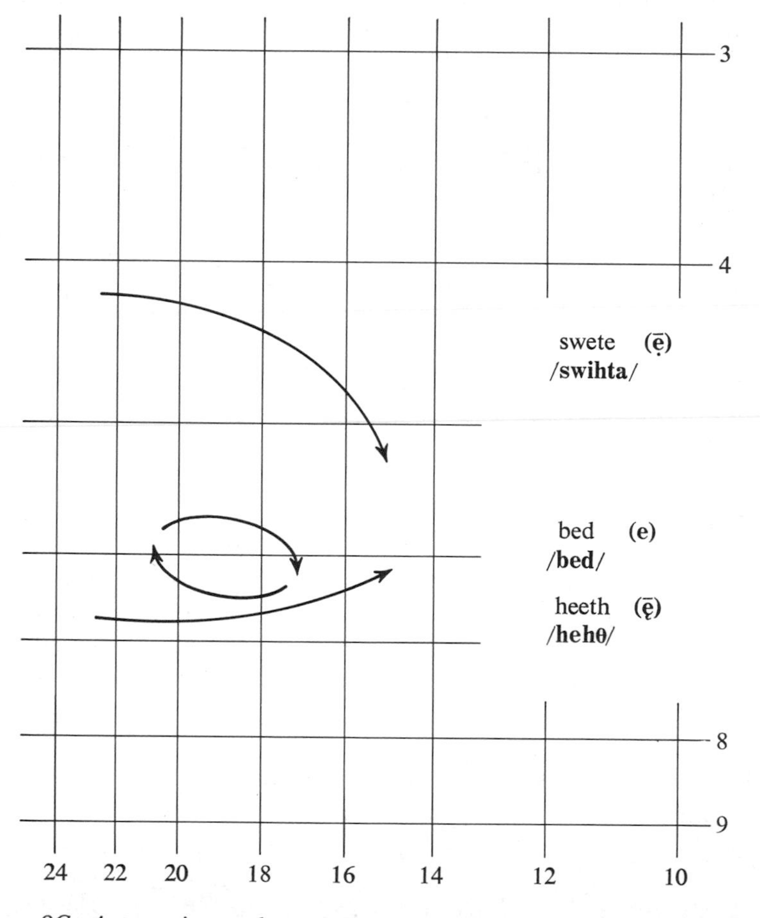

Figure 9C. A tentative and partial third reconstruction of simple stressed vocalic units in Chaucer's Middle English dialect; "long" vowels are assigned distinctive glide features by direction of glide, while "short" vowels lack distinctive guide.

front vocalic sounds, /w/ represents off-glide to high back sounds, and /h/ represents a centering (and/or lengthening) glide. We cannot, of course, recover samples of late fourteenth century London speech. According to some formulations of the phonemics, however, something like the acoustical record represented in Figure 9C presumably would have been produced for the mid front vowels. The "spread" of *swete* and *heeth* vowels may have been greater or lesser, and the length of the lines (length here representing duration) may have been in lesser or greater contrast to the vowel of *bed;* but a pattern resembling the one in the diagram may be postulated. Thus, the stressed vowels in this system of analysis may be distinguished in tabular form in this manner:

/iy/ = ī	*as in* wif/wyf 'wife'
/i/ = i	bidde 'bid, ask'
/ih/ = ẹ̄	feet 'feet'
/e/ = e	bed 'bed'
/eh/ = ę̄	heeth, 'heath'
/ah/ = ā	name 'name'
/a/ = a	bak 'back'
/oh/ = ǭ	boot 'boat'
/o/ = o	on 'on'
/uh/ = ọ̄	boote 'remedy'
/u/ = u	but 'but'
/uw/ = ū	hous 'house'

This method of representing vocalic elements in stressed syllables provides an economical way of representing the diphthongs, the conspicuously gliding syllable nuclei as well:

/iw/	dewe/duwe 'due,' ew 'yew'
/ew/	dew 'dew,' ewe 'ewe'
/ay/	day 'day'
/aw/	sawe 'saying'

/oy/ joye 'joy'

/ow/ growe 'grow'

The notation given here (essentially Stockwell's) was worked out to account for the "lengthening" and "shortening" of stressed vowels during the drift from Old English to Middle English. This notation also is an efficient basis for describing a subsequent major shift in stressed vowels. Having been developed to account for historical changes rather than solely for description of English at one or another time, this is unlike other formulations given and is especially useful in our attempt to arrive at a coherent historical understanding of English vowels. Two main aspects of the formulation, however, need to be considered. First, some of the phonetic implications are questionable, particularly those of the notations for the mid vowels—the same ones that are troublesome to other formulations, as we saw in 9.1. That writers of the dialect used identical spellings for /ih/ and /eh/ (as well as /e/) and identical spellings for /oh/ and /uh/ (as well as /o/) may be questioned, since the principal vocalic elements /i/ and /e/ had regularly different spellings, *i, e;* similarly, /u/ and /o/ were spelled, *u, o.* A principal exception has already been mentioned, attributable to graphic conditionings. That the common off-glide element should lead writers to use identical spellings for vocalic units whose onsets were different—and whose conspicuous onset qualities were regularly differentiated in the spellings of nonglide ("short") vowels—is somewhat unlikely, and is an anomaly among spelling conventions of Middle English. The other aspect of the above formulation to be considered is the assumption on which it rests, that Old English stressed "long" vowels too are best formulated in terms of complex vocalic nuclei consisting of qualitatively specific onset and off-glide. Neither "lengthening" nor "shortening," as we have seen, were processes by which the vocalic *system* was changed prior to the fourteenth century: these processes produced change only in the phonemic makeup of linguistic forms, hence in the specific incidence of any given vowel; any change, by either process, resulted in only a substitution under specifiable conditions of one vowel for another in a persisting linguistic form.

EVIDENCE FROM SPELLING CHANGE

9.3 A formulation of the vocalic system of Chaucer's English—the sample that may stand for the incipient or "proto" standard dialect —will need historically long-range utility. We shall have to deal with a series of related changes by which an [e]–variety of vowel in Chaucer's English was *regularly* replaced by an [i]–variety of vowel, [o] vowels by [u] vowels, [u] vowels by [au] diphthongs, and more of the same pattern. And we shall have to deal with mergers of stressed vocalic elements through which—to illustrate the earliest of them—*heath* and *sweet* came to have the same vowel in Modern English.

As a basis for understanding the phonology and spellings of late Middle English of London–East Midlands and the subsequent major set of modifications which the vocalic system underwent, we shall construct one more formulation of the dialect's stressed vowels. The description will best be undertaken in terms of both phonetics and phonemics. Parallel formulations of sounds and systemic contrasts will enable us to work from all the evidence (especially spellings) for sounds wherever the evidence is clear; where it is not clear, differences between the patterns of phonemic contrasts in consecutive periods of development will enable us to reconstruct the most probable changes by which the different phonemic systems are to be connected.

Especially in their constancy over several hundred years, the spellings seem to indicate clearly the existence of /i e a o u/. One change in spelling conventions, however, the abandoning of the digraph *æ* during the Middle English period, makes it difficult to be sure about the "fate" of Old English /æ/ [æ]. In terms of spelling, the forms persisting from Old English that had been spelled with *æ* occur variously spelled *e, a, ea,* for the most part: *bæð* > *bath, þæt* > *þat* – *that, æppel* > *apple, æfter* > *after* – *efter,* etc. It has often been assumed that Old English /æ/ merged with /a/, as a result of retracting the articulation of [æ] manifesting the /æ/ phonemes. Later English clearly has /æ/, and the evidence of its phonemic identity is fairly early—from the sixteenth and seventeenth centuries; the evidence, interestingly enough, does not appear plainly in the spelling conventions and is in fact only implied by "occasional" spellings, the variants that were not suppressed by full standardization of orthographic conventions. The principal evidence is from sources that had not earlier existed: statements by persons explicitly concerned with the pronunciation of English. (Many of these persons were interested in "correct" pronunciation.)

Two vowels might possibly merge, and later in the history of a language the resultant phoneme might split. In terms of probabilities, it is inconceivable, however, that after the phonemic split a list of words containing stressed /æ/ should closely resemble the list of words that had contained /æ/ before the putative merger of /æ/ and /a/: sample pairs of Old English and Modern English words are /fæst/ > American /fæst/ (British /fast/), /gnæt/ > /næt/, /fæt/ > /væt/,

/stæf/ > American /stæf/ (British /staf/); for reasons given later (10.7) the alternate British and American forms do not lessen the problem. With diphthongal elements the same problem exists. We have already seen that Old English /dæġ/ *dæg* corresponds to Middle English *dai – day*; and in Early Modern English the descendant forms of Old English /fæġən/, /seġl/, /pleġ–/, /æ (ə)l–/, /mæġ–/ and many more like these had come to have identical vowels of *fain, sail, play, ale, may*. To explain how they could have changed in patterns to produce this result, one must assume that [æ] persisted through Middle English; while evidence for the opposition of /æ/ and /a/ is

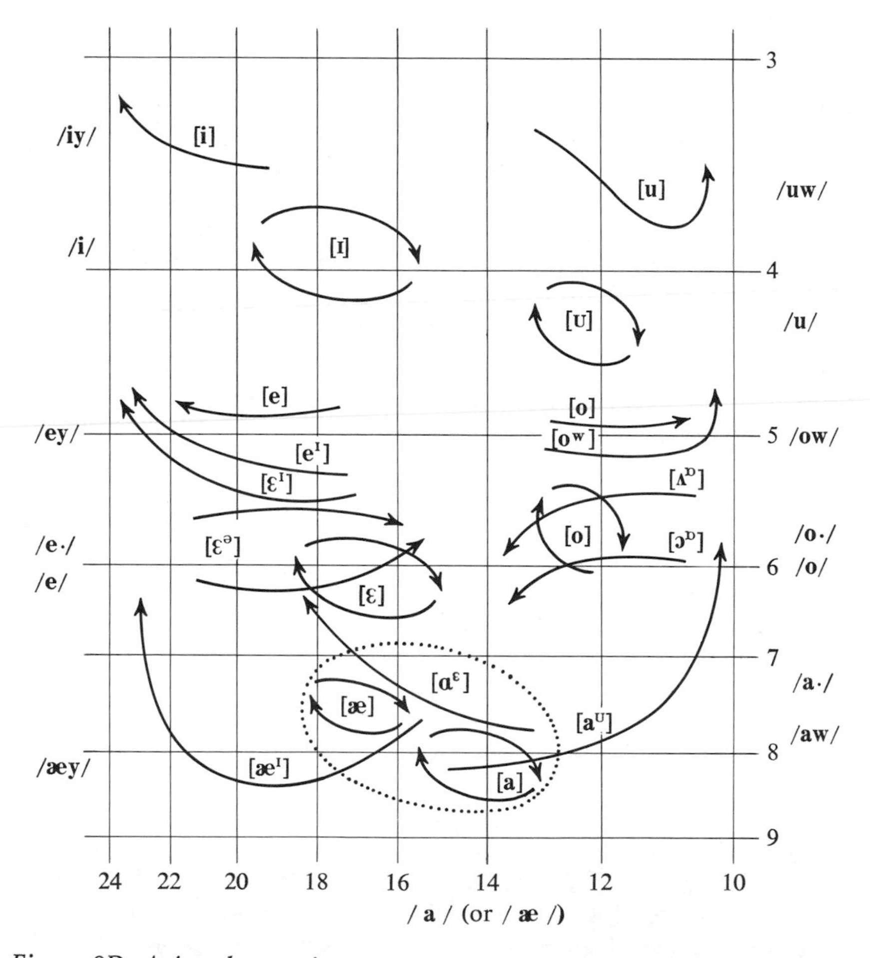

Figure 9D. A fourth tentative reconstruction of vocalic units in Chaucer's Middle English dialect; both simple vowels and diphthongs are registered in hypothetical acoustic charting.

absent in spellings of Chaucerian texts (and others), the historical patterns of development provide strong presumptive evidence that the distribution of [æ] and [ɑ] remained to a great extent unchanged. If no contrasts are known to support the phonemic analysis giving /æ/ vs. /a/, the sounds [æ] and [ɑ] may at least be regarded as distinct allophones, for which either symbol /æ/ or /a/ may be appropriate. At the same time, the inferred continuity of generally consistent distribution of [æ] and [ɑ] in various words, in the absence of phonological conditioning by the phonetic contexts, requires us provisionally to assign quasi-phonemic status to each.

Finally, from the development of spellings and the pattern of systemic change of stressed vowels, inferences can be made about the phonetic characteristics of this major late Middle English dialect. From the spellings *ai, ay,* when the graph *æ* had fallen into disuse, the diphthong may be reconstructed as /æy/, an upgliding relatively low front vowel, in the nature of [æᴵ]. From the alternate spellings *e, ee* of nonrhyming words (apart from those in which the graph *e* represented [ɛ]) and from the previous and subsequent developments of the sounds they represent, we may assume that the vowel represented in *heeth* was [ɛə] or [ɛᵊ], the vowel represented in *swete* was [ɛᴵ]; alternatively, [e] was the norm for closed syllables, and [eᴵ] was the norm for open syllables. The back vowels spelled alternately *o, oo* will have parallel reconstructions. The reconstruction may be clarified by representing it in a vowel chart, shown in Figure 9D. Again it will be emphasized that while the representation here is patterned on the charting of acoustic data of recorded speech, the diagrammatic characteristics are hypotheses about phonetic features of a language system that was in use five hundred or more years ago.

THE RECONSTRUCTION OF CHAUCER'S VOCALIC SYSTEM

9.4 We have examined the late Middle English dialect of Chaucer in a number of ways to arrive at a feasible formulation of the vocalic elements. It is now time to draw together the results of the investigation. To the vocalic units listed in Figure 9D we should add the diphthong acquired by borrowing of frequently used words from French, /oy/ [ɔɪ] *chois* 'choice,' *vois* 'voice,' etc.; and the additional diphthongs developed within English /iw/ [ɪʊ] *dewe – duwe* 'due,' *ew* 'yew,' and /ew/ [ɛʊ] *dew* 'dew,' *ewe* 'ewe.'

By representing the stressed vowels in the manner of a record of acoustic data, three aspects of the vocalic system are given prominence in the graphic details. One is the distinction of the "long" mid vowels, either front or back, by the opposition between the direction of the glide that accompanies each vocalic unit. The vowels commonly designated as "open" *e* and *o,* the /e•/ and /o•/ in Figure 9D, are not distinguished primarily by length (duration) from the "close" *e* and *o,* that is, /ey/ and /ow/. The "open" and "close" varieties of front or back vowels are not much different in the range of sounds with which they are articulated, relative to the high and low vowels by which they are in part defined. They are at the same time distinguished from the "short" vowels /e/ and /o/ either by length or by glide features, or both. The spelling of these sounds represents a development that is normal and as predictable as spelling conventions may be. When [ü Ü] merged with [i ɪ], the graphs *i* and *y,* given the conservativeness of spelling, became interchangeable. With the disuse of the graph *æ,* there were again only five single alphabetic symbols to represent eight vocalic units that were not construed as diphthongs. The graph *a* was the only symbol "naturally" available for the low vowels with which [ɑ] and [æ] had been represented. The graphs *i, y* continued to be used for the distinctive range of high front vowels, as *u* continued to represent high back vowels. That left only *e* and *o* for representing the mid front and mid back vowels, as well as the unstressed vowel [ə]. Any other assignment of the graphs to the vocalic system—as it seems to have existed—can hardly be conceived of, given the traditional nature of English spelling.

The second aspect of the system made prominent in Figure 9D is the difference between "short" and "long" vowels, also called for later English "lax" and "tense" vowels. (For diagrammatic simplicity, the line length has been conspicuously contrasted instead of implying measured duration by dots along each line to mark durational intervals.) Each "short" or "lax" vowel has been represented by a pair of lines; in each pair the arrows are opposed, signifying that the modification during articulation may be toward any other sound. Figure 7D provides the model for this reconstruction. It is to be supposed, moreover, that a stressed short vowel was modified in articulation in every instance of its occurrence by a following consonant. The "short" vowels of Middle English are also distinguished by characteristics of the contexts in which they occur. When stressed they are never "free," that is, they are never both stressed and the final phoneme of a word or separable syllable; instead, a "short" vowel is always "checked" by a following consonant in the syllable in which it is the nucleus. The "long" vowels are "free"; in some instances a syllable in which one occurs is terminated by one or more consonants, but in others the syllable is not thus terminated. For many of their occurrences within a given word element, "long" vowels occurred alternately in closed or open syllables. So long as nouns and verbs (and to a lesser extent, adjectives) commonly had syllable inflections, the vowel in a one-syllable word base could occur in either an open or closed syllable: *bok, bo–kes* 'book(s),' *bon, bo–nes* 'bone(s),' etc. The contrast with short vowels is reflected in spelling conventions as well, as we have already observed in *mile,* 'mile,' *mille* 'mill,' and the like.

The third aspect of the system is the incipience of merger of /a/ and /æ/. Two complex nuclei /aw/ and /a•/ are correlated with [ɑ] and another nucleus /æy/ correlated with [æ], but the phonemic status of [æ] and [ɑ] is not clear from the evidence of the Chaucerian texts; in earlier English these two had been phonemically distinct, and in later English there were also two corresponding phonemes.

With a distributional distinction for a start, with spelling evidence so far as it is explicit, and with a reconstruction of phonetic characteristics based on the various types of evidence, the main features of Chaucer's vocalic system have now been formulated. We are in a position to deal with the most striking set of changes in the history of English vowels—the systematic shift of all the "long" or "tense" free vowels, a shift that constitutes the principal change in the Modern English vocalic system.

Chapter 10

VOCALIC CHANGE FROM MIDDLE TO MODERN ENGLISH

CHANGES IN THE LONG VOWELS

10.1 The "checked," or "short," vowels of Modern English correspond to the "short" vowels of Middle English, for the most part. There is no reason to believe that the [ɛ] of Middle English, for example, has appreciably changed; there is good reason to believe that the Modern English /e/ manifest as [ɛ] is a descendant of Middle English /e/ also manifest as [ɛ]. It is also true that Old English had an /e/ probably manifest as [ɛ]. Furthermore, many words in Modern English have developmental identity in which the base-element vowel has been [ɛ] from the time of Alfred the Great until the present time. Many more words that were also current in Chaucer's language with [ɛ] as the stressed vowel of the base element have persisted into our own time. It would not be appropriate, however, to say that one phoneme /e/ has persisted in the language unchanged. A phoneme is defined as part of a *system* of sounds of a language; if the system has undergone change, any and all parts of it would have participated in the change. Within the subsystem of stressed vowels, the set of "short" or "checked" vowels has had only relatively minor alteration. Within the full system of stressed vowels the alterations have been many. The more basic changes, those which have in turn been partially instrumental in further changes, have occurred in the "long" or "free" set of English vowels.

The changes in the long (or tense) vowels can be simply described in their major aspects. The vowels, both front and back, that were not high front or high back, were raised; the high front [i] and high back [u] were conspicuously diphthongized, with a low-vowel onset. An additional change is often included in the set called the "shift" of vowels—[ɑ] was raised and fronted to [e]. For the most part, these changes occurred between the end of the fourteenth century and the beginning of the seventeenth century; the change [ɑ] > [e] was complete at about the beginning of the eighteenth century. A very closely related change was the merger of the two vowels that had been distinct in Chaucer's *heeth* and *swete.* The vowels were still distinct in Shakespeare's time, and only by the end of the seventeenth century did they merge, participating then in rhymes; for the first time in English *seed* could rhyme with *succeed,* for example, or *mean* with *between.* As may be expected, the merger produced several sets of homonyms: *heel* – *heal, flee* – *flea, deer* – *dear,* etc. Schematically, the fact of the Great Vowel Shift (a name we owe to Otto Jespersen) may be represented thus:

1400	1600	1800
[i:]	[əɪ]	[aɪ]
[e^{I}]	[ɪ:^{i}]	[i:]
[ɛ^{ə}]	[ɪ:ə]	
[ɑ: ~ æ:]	. . . .	[e:]
[ɔ:]	[o:]	[o]
[o:]	[u]	[u]
[u:]	[əʊ]	[aʊ]

The changes may be simply stated in terms of the earlier and later sounds that were the vowels in stressed syllables that persisted in English, but accounting for the changes is less easy. What happened so that *bite* was pronounced [bi:t (ə)] by Chaucer, [bəɪt] by Shakespeare, and [baɪt] by the founders of the American federal government? What was going on so that not only words with stressed [i] later were pronounced regularly with stressed [aɪ], but words with [u] later had [aʊ], those with [e] later had [i], and so on? We may be tempted to say that the shift of all tense vowels resulted from a regular shift in articulation of these vowels. But while the assertion seems true enough, we have added nothing to the statement that the vowels shifted regularly. It is highly probable that the shift was by gradual stages too close to be reflected in any manageable system of alphabetic symbols and diacritic marks. The principal shift, taking place during approximately a two-hundred year period, was probably altogether imperceptible to its speakers. Only when it was well along were the results of the shifting remarked upon by those who wrote about English pronunciation; and then the differences were noticed by comparison of English with other languages traditionally written with the same alphabet. The shift in the qualitative nature of the vowels probably resulted from a drift in the habits of perceiving "long" stressed vocalic units; the drift in perception would be, in turn, a sufficient condition for a gradual modification of articulation. It is not suggested that the differences in perception are to be attributed to physiological differences between earlier and later speakers, or to change in any factor involved in the physical environment that could affect speech sounds. The drift was essentially in the way speakers interpreted what they heard and regarded as linguistically significant. The "regarding" was not done consciously; on the contrary, in the matter of phonology—and in view of the drift apparently not having been noticed—"regarding" refers to the nondeliberate aspects of linguistic habits.

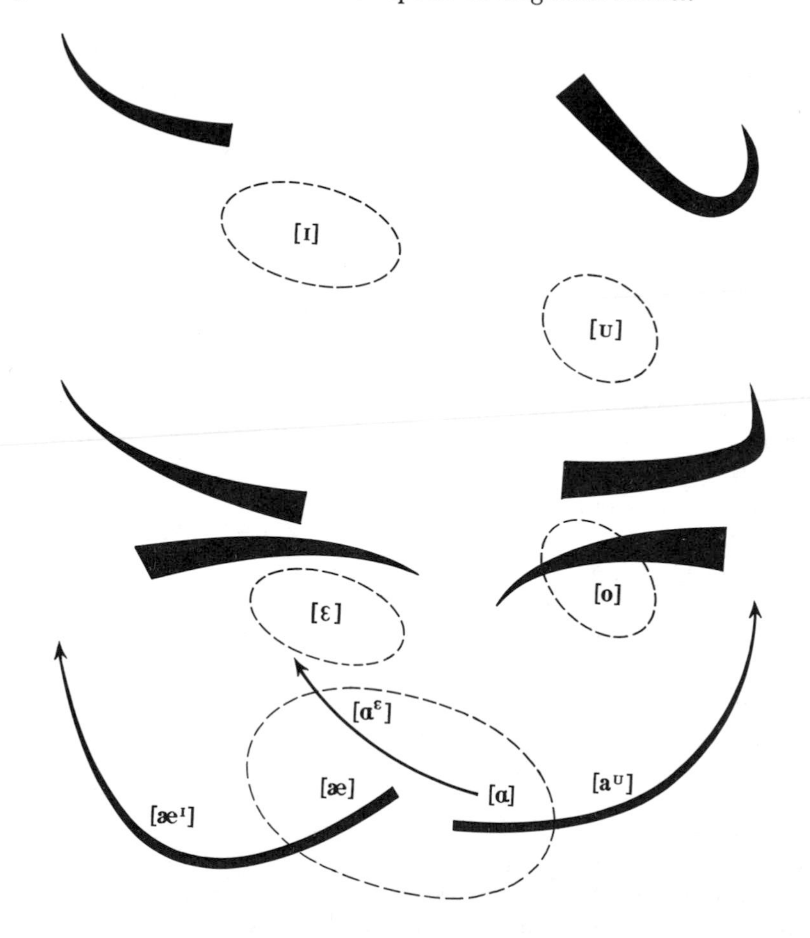

Figure 10A. A simplified and generalized representation of the vocalic units in Chaucer's Middle English dialect; this is in effect a revision of Figure 9D, emphasizing the contrasts that are significant in the systemic relations of the vowels and diphthongs.

PHONETIC "DIFFERENTS" WITH HISTORICAL IDENTITY

10.2 The process of vocalic change may be made more explicit if it is represented graphically. The starting point is the vocalic system represented in 9.3. The insufficiency of symbols of a phonetic alphabet will be immediately apparent, not only for their being too few, but also for their inadequacy in representing details of the glide phenomena on the basis of which the drift can be better explained. Figure 10A displays the same Middle English vocalic system represented in Figure 9D, with the "long" vowels made more prominent and the systemically significant contrasts of vocalic features emphasized by generalizing the phonetic variations of the allophones.

Simplification in representing vowel shift will also be necessary, but the nature of the drift need not be falsified if the change is presented as discrete steps. A most important aspect of the process of the Great Vowel Shift is that it was a systematic process. For expository purposes, we shall select only a pair of phonetic drifts, that of /ey/ and /e•/, remembering that the change is within the entire system of stressed "long" vowels. At the least, all front vowels must be regarded as the system-context for any change among front vowels, and all back vowels regarded as systemically pertinent for any change among back vowels.

Figure 10B represents the change by which vowels spelled alternately *e, ee* were articulated differently at about 1400 and at about 1600.

Part of the simplification for diagrammatic purposes is the use of a single arrow-pattern to generalize all the "same" vowels as they occurred in various phonetic contexts in the speech of various speakers at any given time. The upward glide of the stressed vocalic nucleus, a subphonemic characteristic of the sound, came to be recognized as a differentiating feature by which /ey/ was distinguished from /e/ [ɛ] and from /e•/ [ɛᵊ]. When the glide assumed significance as a distinguishing characteristic of "long close *e*," the vocalic unit admitted of variation of length and of precise sound in its onset so long as its onset was contrastive with other front "long" vowels and diphthongs [i], [æɪ], and so long as alternations between "long" and "short" *e*-vowels remained phonetically related. The selection among these variations statistically favored raised articulation of the onset of the /ey/ units. To use a somewhat loose analogy, the change resembles loss of the initial unstressed syllable of a word when speakers (lacking conservative or corrective influences) substitute *fessor* for *professor, most* for *almost, bout* for *about,* and so on. In these word examples,

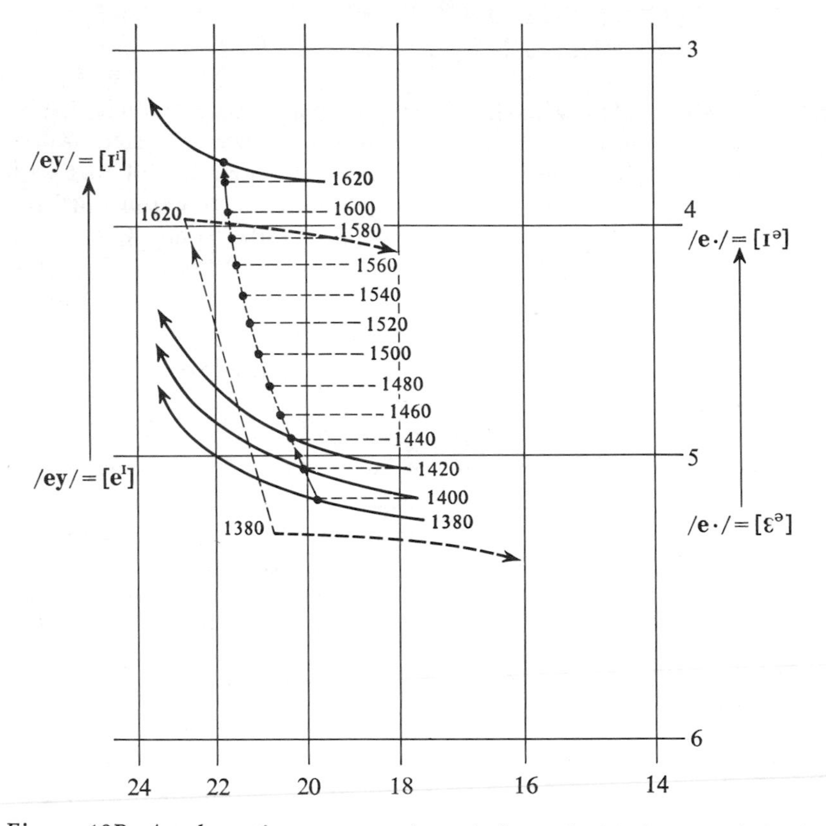

Figure 10B. A schematic representation of the early Modern English shift of the two mid-front "long" vowels, part of "The Great Vowel Shift."

the unstressed syllable is heard as mere noise, that is, it is not recognized for the phonemic shape it has, at least when the shape it has is carefully articulated. As noise, it is disregarded and does not occur when the speaker utters the word himself. Because a stressed vocalic element is not subject to correction with the ease and clarity with which *bout* is corrected to *about*, the raising of the onset of /ey/ was not readily subject to being checked, even if noticed. Moreover, nothing was inherent in the set of vowel phonemes to reverse the tendency to raise the onset. Finally, nothing in the vocalic system stood in the way of progressive raising of the onset of /ey/. While /ey/ has been selected because of its diagrammatic convenience for the single illustration, it will be remembered that all the stressed "long" vocalic nuclei were being shifted similarly, and that the distinctions between stressed vowels remained, no matter what phonetic drifts these vowels were undergoing.

In Figure 10B, the stressed "free" (or "tense," or "long") mid front vowel in Middle English has been represented as /ey/, and its reflex in early Modern English has also been represented as /ey/. The identity of the phonemic representation is valid, for the two are developmentally identical. It becomes cumbersome, however, to represent historically identical but phonetically different vowels within one system of notation: based on phonetic features, /ey/ (1400) was manifest as [e⁽ᴵ⁾], and /ey/ (1620) was manifest as [ɪ⁽ⁱ⁾]. For description of Modern English phonology it is more reasonable to assign a new notation /iy/ for the vowel at the later time and write the results of the shift of the vowel of *feet, swete,* etc. as /ey/ > /iy/. The first representation—/ey/ (1400) > /ey/ (1620)—best represents historical continuity, while the second—/ey/ > /iy/—best represents the correspondences between antecedent and subsequent systems of stressed "long" vowels of English.

SYSTEMIC CHANGE OF THE LONG VOWELS

10.3 We come now to the other principal kind of change in stressed "long" vowels, change being measured from the system of vowels in late Middle English. The entire system of stressed "long" vowels had undergone shift in a set of coordinated changes in phonetic characteristics of the vowels. The upglide of the majority of the vowels was a significant conditioning factor. Two of the vocalic units, /e•/ and /o•/, have been interpreted nevertheless as having centering (or centering and lowering) glides as a concomitant of length. They too participated in the general upward shift of all nonhigh vowels, and their raising seems to be attributable only to the general shift with their systemic correlations to "long" rather than "short" vowels; in contrast, their distinctiveness from diphthongal units /æy/, in the front set, and /aw/, in the back set, could be maintained only by drift of the same kind that was affecting the other vowels.

Upon completion of the major vowel shift a realignment of former vowels and diphthongs also took place. The consequent patterns of front vowels and of back vowels were slightly different, and the "fates" of Middle English /e•/ and /o•/ were correspondingly different. In the front subset the [i]-variety of vowel had replaced the [e]-variety of vowel; in turn, an [e]-variety of vowel had replaced the diphthongal [æɪ], while the [ɑᵋ]-type vowels were approaching merger with new [e]-type vowels. In short, no "opening" existed in the set of front stressed "long" vowels into which the reflex of Middle English /e•/ could naturally move: while vowels may "drift," they do not normally "skip" from one articulation to another that is not positionally adjacent. The upglide characteristic of the other vowels was by then well established. Apparently the centering glide characteristic that had distinguished Middle English /e•/ from /ey/ and later /iə/ from /iy/ ([ɪᵊ] from [ɪⁱ]) was displaced by the feature more common to front "long" vowels—the upglide. The result was the merger of the two units into /iy/. The number of resultant homonyms was not great, and included no pairs of "indispensable" words such as pronouns, verbs of different tenses, prepositions, and the like.

When the major realignment of vowels (and diphthongs) was nearing completion, the situation with respect to back vowels was different. A diphthongal unit /aw/ moved into the low back position generally defined as [ɔ]. Meanwhile, the [o]-variety of vowel had drifted to become an [u]-variety. In this set there was then an "opening," and it was filled by the reflex of /o•/, which was positionally adjacent if not already present. In that [o] position it too lost its centering glide and, assimilating to the dominant pattern, eventually developed an upglide.

CONDITIONING FACTORS OF THE GREAT VOWEL SHIFT

10.4 Three larger contextual matters are related to the process known as the Great Vowel Shift and the attendant development of Middle English /e•/ and /o•/. One has to do with the general shape of the vocalic system; another has to do with the preconditioning of the stressed vowels for the systematic shift they underwent; yet another has to do with changes in the phonetic structure of words resulting from loss of grammatical inflections.

It has been convenient throughout the discussion of vowels to refer to regions in which vowels are articulated, especially to refer to discrete areas of articulation. To use terms like "[i]-variety" of vowels, or to distinguish a mid back vowel from a high back vowel or a low back vowel implies to some extent the notion that a system of vowels must fit a threefold division for height of articulation and a threefold division from front to back. Even the use of alphabetic symbols may condition us to assume that nine vocalic areas, regarded in terms of articulational positions, is somehow an inherent characteristic of human speech. The fact is, of course, that the positions of vowel articulation are continuous and gradual. Instead of three distinctive positional heights, a language may have four. Because continuous gradations in vowel and consonant sounds are not used for linguistic signaling, however, the division into a limited and exact number of areas of articulation is both practical and based on real facts about language. The three height designations for English—high, mid, low—correspond to the phonemic distinctions English has, the distinctions it also has had from its beginning: any front vowel sound is heard as one or another or another, according to a fixed set of distinctions—/æ/, /e/, or /i/, for example, for "short" (or "checked") vowels. In these respects it is legitimate as well as practical to describe a change as, for example, [ɛ] > [ɪ], or /ey/ > /iy/.

Furthermore, the stability of the threefold division according to height of articulation can justify the use of such metaphors as the "gap" or "opening" in a system. If the early Modern English reflexes of Middle English /ey/ and /e•/ had not merged, their distinctiveness could have been maintained (given the phonetic features then present) only by continued difference in direction of the offglides or by a restructuring such that front vowels would have fourfold distinctions by height instead of threefold distinctions. Merger of the two vocalic units represents the least change that the set of habits constituting the "long" (or "free") vowel system could have undergone at the time of the change. On the same grounds, the nonmerger of /ow/ and /o•/ represents the least change in the vowel system after the Great Vowel Shift, for it sustained the threefold division among the back vowels, matched by the threefold division of the front vowels.

A second important contextual matter has to do with preconditioning of the systematic shift of "tense" or "free" vowels. The stressed vowels of Old English were described earlier (8.2) in terms of "long" and "short"; qualitative differences for paired "long" and "short" vowels were listed, as well as distributional differences which for Modern English are described as "free" and "checked." The one exception to qualitative distinctions in the Old English system was for /ǣ/ and /æ/. The data for Old English are too limited to support the kind of precise reconstruction of acoustic or articulatory features that has been made tentatively for Middle English and early Modern English; the limitation lies primarily in lack of a sufficiently dense and extensive record of changes within a single dialect from which to extrapolate the direction of phonetic drift. All the evidence does converge on the conclusion of qualitative *and* quantitative differences between /ē/ and /e/, /ū/ and /u/, and the other paired vowels. Whether there was then distinctive glide articulation of the "long" vowels may be unanswerable. In view of spellings, the likelihood of distinctive glide articulation is not very great. If diphthongal nuclei had two-letter representation and "long" vowels did not, and if later a doubled spelling—*ee, oo, aa,* etc.— represented the reflexes of "long" vowels, any glide articulation of the "long" vowels was presumably not distinctive.

It will also be recalled that English developed a new set of diphthongs in early Middle English. Exept for /oy/, which was introduced by means of borrowing from French, all the other diphthongs had their origin in English. (All the others were also reinforced—were extended in their currency—in words borrowed from Scandinavian or French or both.) With English, /w/, /x/, /ǥ/ > /w/, /ġ/ following a stressed vowel, either long or short, produced diphthongs whose second element was offglide /y/ or /w/: all the new diphthongs had in upglide either toward the front [i]-region or back [u]-region. Given the positions they filled in the stressed vowel system, the new diphthongs established upglide as a differentiating vocalic feature. Some remained prominently diphthongal, as did /oy/ and, for a time, /aw/. At least one, /æy/, filled a gap (mid front) in the vocalic system, and some seem to have joined long vowels in their systemic opposition to short vowels. In short, upglide was introduced into the set of "long," "free" vowels as a result of diphthongal elements produced from vowel-spirant or vowel-glide sequences. When the upglide vocalic units were introduced into this vowel set, their distinctiveness was maintained by a contrast between both upglide and length—/ey/ opposed to /e•/, to use the familiar pair. At this point of development certain positional sets of vowels had a three-way set of contrasts: length, glide (with length), and neither glide nor length—/e•/ vs. /ey/ vs. /e/, and /o•/ vs. /ow/ vs. /o/. All these conditions underlay the subsequent changes associated with the shift of "long" or "tense" vowels and the final alignment of this vocalic system.

The third contextual aspect of the Great Vowel Shift is best treated in connection with changes in unstressed vowels, to which we shall turn next.

CHANGES IN UNSTRESSED VOWELS

10.5 The development of vowels in unstressed syllables in English is as important as it is brief in outline. Old English appears to have had already an unstressed /ə/, manifest as either [ə] or [ɪ]; the two sounds were allophones, with the selection of one or the other determined automatically by the phonetic context. Modern English also has an unstressed /ə/, and it too occurs as either [ə] or [ɨ]. Because this subset of vowels has consisted of only one member throughout the history of English, no changes involving systematic shift or merger has occurred. As a mid central vowel it is positionally of a different order from the front and back vowels.

The history of the unstressed schwa, considered by itself, amounts to a specially remarkable increase in the frequency with which it occurs. This fact implies some principal aspects of its history: it is the vowel that most often replaced any other vowel in words. The replacement by /ə/ has affected countless syllables in word base elements; the regularity and extensiveness of /ə/ replacing other vowels is even more remarkable, though, in inflectional suffixes. Because grammatical inflections occur more frequently than any given word to which they may be affixed, the replacement of any vowel in inflectional suffixes by /ə/ increased the frequency of this "neutral" vowel enormously. When nearly every noun, for example, had a plural form in *–es* /–əs/ and many verbs and adjectives had *–e* /–ə/ inflections, this /ə/ must have been many times over the most frequent vowel in English. The frequency changed considerably when the syllabic inflections were replaced to a great extent (ultimately, almost entirely) by nonsyllabic inflections. Most Modern English nouns have plural forms /–s/ or /–z/, as in *books, logs,* while /–əz/ occurs only after /š č ž ǰ s z/ *dishes, churches, garages, charges, fleeces, sneezes.* While /ə/ had been itself an inflectional suffix, the loss of inflection was at the same time the disuse of word-final /ə/.

The key factor in the history of /ə/, from the point of view of phonology, is that it forms a subset of one member only; it replaced any other vowel in unstressed syllables; and it commonly disappeared from words, especially in inflections. In dealing with the history of English suffix inflections we shall see the role and history of /ə/ in some further detail.

For its relevance to the preconditioning of the Great Vowel Shift, the main point is that the disappearance of /ə/ as an inflectional suffix restructured the "segmental" phonemic makeup of a large number of words. As an inflection in Middle English, /–ə/ had served, among other things, as the present tense first person singular marker for most verbs; this was a circumstance obviously of considerable frequency and prominence. It served also as an adjective inflection, and occasionally (throughout Middle English) as one of the noun inflections. Whenever it followed /y/ or /w/, its presence in effect made the glide phoneme consonantal. When the /ə/ was no longer present as the center of a final syllable, the glide phoneme—always voiced anyway—structured with the preceding vowel. *Growe, knowe, seye, pleye, eye,* and the like came to be /grow/, /know/, /sey/, /pley/, /ey/, even while /growəθ/, /knowəst/ and the like left the glide between vowels, hence consonantal. During the Great Vowel Shift a large number of inflections lost their syllabic quality, throwing even more of the /w/ and /y/ glides into the vocalic portion of the words in which they occurred.

MODIFICATION OF CONSONANT CLUSTERING PATTERNS

10.6 Another consequence of the disappearance of /ə/ in inflectional suffixes was the modification of the clustering patterns of consonants at the ends of words. The patterns were extended both in number of successive consonants and in the combinations that occurred (see 5.5). This aspect of English phonotactics, interesting as it is, cannot appropriately be given fuller discussion here. A few examples may make clear the process by which, with the syncope of /ə/ in the unstressed inflectional syllables, new consonant clusters were developed. Most of the changes resulted from changes involving noun-plural (*–es*) inflections and past-tense (*–ed*) inflections. The unusually long sequence /–mpst/ of *glimpsed* resulted from the change of /glimpsəd/; the /d/ was replaced, by assimilation to unvoiced /–ps–/ by /t/. The sequence /–rld/ became much more frequent when /–əd/ was syncopated, as in /hwirləd/ > /hwʊrld/; about the only source now available for additions to the words having /–rld/ is verbs whose root form terminates in /–rl/. Even the common clusters /–lfs/, /–rvz/, /–rθt/, /–lvz/ in *shelf's, carves, unearthed, selves* result from the loss of /ə/ in syllabic inflections, producing nonsyllabic inflections. Some other aspects of these changes will appear later in our consideration of inflections.

CHANGES IN THE SYSTEM OF SHORT VOWELS

10.7 To conclude this consideration of changes of vowels, we may return to the "short" or "checked" vowels. It was noted at the beginning of this chapter that changes in the short vowels have been minor, by comparison with those of the "long," or "free" vowels. Once more the distinction may be made between changes in the vocalic system and changes in the vowels with which individual words are made up at one or another time in the history of the language. The replacement of any short vowel by /ə/ has already been mentioned. Replacement of "long" vowels by "short" ones has been another frequent type of change. The /i/ of *wick* and *nickname* replaced earlier /iy/; /e/ in *weapon, deaf,* etc. replaced /iə/ < Middle English /e·/; /ʌ/ replaced /uw/ in *dust* and *southern* and many more words. Changes in the system of these vowels have been relatively simple.

Two changes relevant to the "short" vowels collectively have already been implied, being merely the consequences of changes in the "long" vowels. As quantity—that is, longer duration—was supplanted by other features, the defining contrast between "long" and "short" vowels shifted from durational contrasts to two others. One was distributional, so that the distinction between the system of "short" vowels and "long" ones is appropriately described for Modern English by the different set of labels, "checked" and "free." The other was articulational, so that the presence or absence of distinctive glide is a genuine distinguishing opposition between pairs of vowels, such as /i iy/.

The other type of change is in some ways more basic, having to do with the number of "short" vowels, their relationships to each other, and the configuration of the system they formed. There was a split of /u/ early in the Modern English period, by which [ʌ] and [ᴜ] came to be in opposition, that is, they came to be separate phonemes /ʌ/ and /u/. A concomitant of the split was a realignment of the vowel sounds such that allophones of mid and low back vowels were reassigned in many stressed syllables. The differences between typical American and British /rak ∼ rok/, /lak ∼ lok/, /lat ∼ lot/ (*rock, lock, lot*) reflect the differences in the realignment in different dialectal areas during the time of the settlement of the American colonies. Another set of realignments involved the low vowel sounds, and the precise history of this matter remains controversial. Regular differences clearly exist between American and British forms typified by /græs ∼ gras/, /stæf ∼ staf/ (*grass, staff*), but the status of the low "short" vowels in Middle English and again at about 1600, when the colonies were begun, remains unclear. It was argued earlier (9.3) that the reflex of Old English /æ/, if it did not remain distinct from /a/ during Middle English, probably retained at least a quasi-phonemic status. Because [æ] and [ɑ] continued respectively in persisting sets of words, and because in earlier and later periods of English /æ/ and /a/ (American) were separate phonemes, the Middle English [æ] reflex of late Old English /æ/ should be regarded as a relic in early Middle English; during later Middle English the reflex should be regarded as an incipient distinct phoneme /æ/ of Modern English. The change in the system of "short" vowels, between Middle English and Modern English, may therefore be represented as Kurath has analyzed it (*A Phonology and Prosody of Modern English*, pp. 22–23):

Middle English		Modern English			
/i	u	/i	u	/i	u
e	o	e	ʌ	e	ɒ
a/		æ	a	æ	ʌ/
		(American)		(British)	

To take into account a longer stretch of history, the changes between the "rectangular" and "triangular" systems should perhaps be represented in the following form:

Old English		Middle English		Modern English			
/i	u	/i	u	/i	u	/i	u
e	o	e	o	e	ʌ	e	ɒ
æ	a	æ ± a	/	æ	a/	æ	ʌ/
				(American)		(British)	

Ultimately the question of how to formulate the Middle English "short" vowels may be answerable only by analysis of complex factors including the relationship between the developments of "long" and "short" vowels together and of more precise information than has been available heretofore about dialect differences and their mixtures in late Middle English and early Modern English. The historical perspective, with which we have been principally concerned, will be of value in attempts to answer this question in so far as it assists in reconstructing the phonology by establishing the directions and rates of changes in the vocalic system of English.

Chapter 11

TYPES OF FORMAL UNITS

THE VARIETY OF LINGUISTIC FORMS

11.1 The sounds of a language, considered for themselves, do not have meaning. Their history is best comprehended as individual changes that go on within systemic sets. As we turn now to forms, it may be wondered to what extent language units that have meaning also comprise systems and whether their history is importantly systemic or whether their history is more on the order of individual, isolated, nonpatterned change. The fact is that some forms are fully systemic, having meaning by virtue of their distributional characteristics within sets as much as from their convention association with aspects of experience outside language. Differences between *whom* and *who, sits* and *sit* will illustrate the point: inflectional *–m* and *–s* are difficult to assign nonlinguistic meanings to, but they are as much meaningful forms of English as are *who* and *sit*. Other forms such as *–ly, –ness, –able, –dom* or *un–, mis–, a–* can be assigned meanings somewhat more easily. They can be classed in various ways; but even though they are severely limited in number and fall into only a few subclasses, they do not constitute a system or systems in the same sense as do inflectional forms illustrated above. Other forms are words—or stems, as they will be distinguished presently. Most of them are easily assigned meanings, however much we sometimes will argue over the "right" or "best" or "most accurate" definition of one or another of them. *Father, brother, pencil, water, enemy, virtue, ability, tension;* or *sleep, eat, walk, read, understand, choose, metamorphose;* or *green, hot, good, morbid, ambivalent*—nouns, verbs, and adjectives (as well as adverbs) have meanings in their associations with one complex or another of our experience. Some words are not easily defined, it is true: the meaning of *to* and the meaning of *the* are notoriously elusive of definition apart from the structure of the language itself. Be that as it may, "words" are least systemic in the sense stipulated above. Their history, in respect to their meanings as well as their origins, is least systematic of all language units that we have called here "forms."

All the points made briefly in the preceding paragraph will be elaborated upon in succeeding chapters. Our immediate task is to develop another point implied above—the variety of linguistic forms which a language such as English embraces. The necessity for distinguishing among the varieties of forms will perhaps already be partially established: if inflections such as the *–m* of *whom* and the *–s* of *sits* are in some way different from the word-bases *who* and *sit* and if both are different from affixes such as *–able,* those differences must be registered in describing the structure of the language. Equally important for distinguishing types of forms is the fact that the history of any one type differs radically from the histories of the other types.

THE MORPHEME

11.2 The basic *formal* unit of descriptive analysis of language is the morpheme. By design, the term "morpheme" designates a minimal class of linguistic material, providing a basis for more precise analysis than do the broader and sometimes overlapping concepts designated by "word," "inflection," "affix," "compound," "root," "stem," "derivative." These traditional terms nevertheless continue to be useful. The definition of "morpheme" usually consists of both negative and positive statements: negatively, a morpheme is "A linguistic form which bears no partial phonetic-semantic resemblance to any other form," to use Leonard Bloomfield's definition (*Language,* p. 161); positively, it is a formal unit consisting of one or more phonemes and having a meaning. Not only does the term "morpheme" parallel the term "phoneme" in designating minimal units at a different level of language structure, but the technique of analysis on the principle of contrast is common to both phonological and morphological analysis.

For convenience we shall retain the term "form" and alternate it freely with the term "morph." In relation to "morpheme," "morph" (or "form") will designate a segmentable unit of utterance without reference to its having status as a morpheme, nonmorpheme, or morpheme sequence.

It will be apparent already that morphemic elements are not necessarily coextensive with words: *words* is a word, and so is *word,* and there is obviously an additional meaningful element in the morph *words*—something whose meaning may be paraphrased roughly as 'plural, more than one.' The following are also all words:

sleep	write
sleeper	writer
sleeping	writing
sleep-in	write-in

sleeps	writes
slept	wrote

Clearly, elements recur within these words, these morphic bits of utterances. Something like *sleep(–)* and *write(–)* can be isolated (even if the spelling notation is not entirely adequate). Something like *–er, –ing, –in, –s,* can also be isolated, each having the same meaning in the pair of words in which it occurs; *slept* and *wrote* pose more complex problems but, as will be explained in a later chapter, they conform to the same kind of analysis. Morphemic elements are not necessarily to be identified as syllables: *–s,* for instance, does not represent a syllable in *words, sleeps, writes.* In the other direction, *example* has three syllables but cannot be cut into morphemic constituents within English.

FREE AND BOUND MORPHEMES AND ALLOMORPHS

11.3 Through systematic contrastive analysis of the forms of English the morphemes can be identified. Their sorting into types is another aspect of morphological analysis, and the formulation of the permissible patterns of combining morphemes is another. Discussion of sequence-patterns in morpheme combinations may be postponed to the chapters in which they are immediately relevant; a single example will be sufficient here: an inflectional suffix is always in the final position of a fixed morpheme sequence (roughly, in any word) in which it occurs. The sorting can be done for one or another purpose. One purpose sets up the criterion of whether or not a morpheme ever occurs phonologically isolated from others. *Sleep,* in the preceding examples, does occur separately; it is classed as a *free* morpheme. But *–er, –ing, –s* and others never occur in isolation (as represented here by hyphenation) and are classed as *bound* morphemes. In *sleepy, –y* is a bound form, and in *sleepily, –ly* is another; in spelling the corresponding *–y* and *–i–* differ, but the spellings obviously represent the same morpheme.

The phonemic shape of the morpheme spelled alternately *–y* and *–i–* is /iy/ and /i/ or /ə/ respectively, yet the two forms are identifiable as one morpheme, not two. The alternate phonemic materials are identical in meaning and are phonetically related; they are thus classed as "allomorphs"—a term again parallel to the term "allophone" in phonological analysis. The free form *able* /éybəl/ and the bound form –able /–əbəl/, as in *countable,* are allomorphs. A more prominent example of allomorphs in English is the set making up the morpheme affixed to nouns and meaning 'plural, more than one': they have the shapes /–s/, /–z/, /–əz/ in *rats, rags, rashes,* respectively. Because allomorphs differ in phonemic shape, a special notation distinguished by { } is customarily employed to represent a morpheme when there is no intention of specifying its phonemic shape. Thus noun plural inflectional allomorphs /–s/, /–z/, /–əz/ may be generalized as a morpheme and symbolized {–Z}. Verbs have a phonemically identical set of inflections (third-person nonpast forms), and so do possessive-case nouns. Subscripts are therefore used to distinguish noun plural $\{ -Z_1 \}$, noun possessive $\{ -Z_2 \}$, and verb inflection $\{ -Z_3 \}$. Another example already implied is /sliyp–/ ~ /slep–/ in *sleep* and *slept.* When it is required, morphemic notation usually selects one phonemic shape but marks it as generalized by braces, thus { sliyp– } . To avoid implying that one vocalic center is somehow primary, the notation may use *V* to stand for alternate vocalic elements, as { slVp– } . For the morpheme present in both *write* and *wrote* the notation is conveniently given as { r—t– } .

INFLECTIONAL MORPHEMES

11.4 The classification of morphemes as bound and free is a useful broad distinction of morpheme types, but both the description and the history of English require further specification of classes of morphemes. A free morpheme, for example, is defined by its potential occurrence as an isolated unit of utterance: *control* can thus be identified as a free morpheme even when it occurs in *controls, controllable, uncontrollable, tone-control, control ship.* In these occurrences it is not isolated, not actually free, and it is as much to the point to call it a root morpheme: distributionally it is the one that may occur independently and the one to which bound morphemes *–s, –able, un–* (or others) may be affixed, or it is one of two root morphemes that occur as a compound word. Bound morphemes also may be further classified according to additional characteristics. By position relative to a root morpheme the types "prefix" and "suffix" will be familiar; the difference between *write* and *wrote* is sometimes distinguished by calling the vocalic elements /ay/ and /ow/ (morphemic) infixes, though that analysis is not the only one for such morpheme elements. Distributional differences serve to distinguish bound forms further as "inflectional" and "derivational." The *–s* of *controls* is inflectional, but the *–able* /–əbəl/ and *un–* above are derivational. The latter type will be explicated more fully in Chapter 20.

Inflectional morphemes in English are always bound forms. They may be either syllabic—as in *want–ed, wash–es*—or nonsyllabic—as in *want–s, wash–ed*; as syllables they never carry a principal stress in the morpheme sequence constituting a word. Because inflectional morphemes like any others are defined by contrasts, at least two always form a set. In turn, a set is defined by inflectional morphemes that may occur only alternately with a single stem. "Stem" and "inflection" thus are to some extent mutually defining terms: a stem may consist of a root or base morpheme (*cover*), a root plus derivational morpheme (*uncover, coverlet*), a compound of root morphemes (*book-cover*), or even more complex combination of morphemes. A set of inflectional morphemes, together with a stem to which they are affixed, constitutes a paradigm. Syntactic criteria are ordinarily employed as well in defining paradigmatic sets because a stem with a member of one group of inflections may, for example, fill a "noun-position" in a sentence and with one of another group of inflections, fill a "verb-position." Thus, in the frame *He——the book,* the forms *covers* and *covered* will fit; but in the frame *He couldn't find the——*, *covered* will not fit and the *–s* inflection with *cover–* that will also fit here is not the same as the other *–s* in meaning as well as in distribution. In earlier English, when adjectives were also inflected, the syntactic and morphemic contrasts were much more elaborate. Several paradigmatic sets of forms are printed in "blocks" on the page in the next five chapters.

Inflections can also be assigned meanings and rigorously categorized, but the ways and purposes of performing these operations are best taken up as discussion of the various aspects of English morphology requires.

The naming and illustrating of types of forms in these few pages will certainly not have done justice to the complexities of English morphology. The basic distinction between free and bound forms does not, for instance, account for { r—t } with bound morphemes { –ay– } and { –ow– }, in *write* and *wrote;* should we call { r—t } a bound form because it never occurs without another (bound) form? Nor will the simple distinctions in this chapter imply the many sources of interest in the historical morphology of English. The naming and illustrating of types will hopefully facilitate the study of English morphology with its history, in the succeeding chapters.

Chapter 12

PRONOUN MORPHOLOGY AND ITS HISTORY

REFERENTIAL AND CONTEXTUAL DIFFERENCES OF PRONOUNS

12.1 Pronouns will provide the most suitable starting point for the history of English inflectional forms. They retain inflectional differences—case distinction—to a greater extent than do any other classes of English words. Their case inflections more closely resemble the inflections of pronouns of earlier stages of the language than do the inflections of any other class of words resemble their counterparts in Middle and Old English. Pronouns also have gender distinction in their third person singular forms (*he, she, it,* etc.): closely similar distinctions, also labeled gender differences, were characteristic of pronouns and other classes of words throughout the period of Old English. Besides third person pronouns, all other classes of words that could be used to make up noun phrases showed gender distinctions in their suffix inflections. Because pronouns are among the most frequently used words in the language, they exhibit irregularities within paradigmatic sets. Some of the irregularities have been in English from the time of the earliest records of the language, while others have developed during the period of its recorded history. The systems of pronouns and their changes will introduce the chief aspects of the history of inflections of the nounlike sentence elements English speakers have typically used for the past millenium and more.

The forms traditionally labeled "first person" and "second person" —*I, my, mine, me, we, our(s), us; you, your(s)*—have characteristics not shared by "third person" forms; the "third person" forms, in turn, have characteristics exclusive to themselves. The designation—the semantic reference—of first person forms is the speaker, with singular forms, and, with plural forms, the speakers or those included with the actually speaking person. First person forms are defined with respect to a speech context: a participant (to put it in a one-person instance) in a speaking situation uses first person forms to refer to himself while speaking. Choice of first person forms, of course, is not contingent upon the presence, real or imagined, of anyone other than the speaker. Second person forms have as their designation another participant (or other participants) in a speech context: a participant in a speaking situation uses second person pronoun forms to refer to a participant other than himself (or other than those for whom he speaks) while he is speaking.

Put in these terms, first person forms may be said to be those used with self reference by a speaker; second person forms refer, for the speaker, to whomever he addresses his utterance. "Speaker" and "addressee" (or their plurals in any more-than-one reference) are useful terms as alternates to "first" and "second." More important is the point that first and second person pronoun forms designate participants in a speech context. This stipulation holds not only when the participants are people but also when some other participant is only imagined, and when the addressee is nonhuman; an imaginary audience, a deity, an animal, a machine, when it is addressed, has for the speaker at least for the moment the human attribute of understanding his language. Participants in the use of language, in so far as they are perceived by each other, are identified for each other: the referent(s) of *I, me, you, us,* etc. is (are) immediate.

The immediate reference of first and second person pronouns implies another characteristic of these pronouns—they do not have noun or name antecedents to designate their referents. If a noun or name occurs in a speech context with the same reference as one of these forms, it is appositional with that form: *I, Claudius, desire that you, Antonio, should make the voyage as soon as possible.* Third person pronoun forms, on the other hand, do not refer to participants in a speaking situation; their referents are not defined in terms of the situation in which a participant designates himself as speaker or another as addressee of his utterance. Rather, referents of third person forms are known to speaker and addressee by a different set of contextual features. When a noun or name has been expressed and a third person pronoun form is associated with it, the referent of the pronoun has been stipulated by the structure of the linguistic matter, that is, the discourse. *When I saw Claudius, he was reading the passenger list; it did not contain Antonio's name.* In this example *he* and *it* are defined by preceding name and noun forms, *Claudius* and *passenger list.* In *When I got to know him better, I found that Antonio was indeed a shrewd man,* the pronoun *him* is defined by a following name form, *Antonio.* Third person forms are also used when a name or noun does not occur in the linguistic context to define its referent. In these instances the referent is defined for the participants in the speech context by empirical means. That to which the third person form refers is known by both classes of participants, in one way or another: by sight, for example, as with *What do you think makes him act like that?* or by any other means as with *They are in there, but what they might be is a mystery to me.*

The pronoun forms used for reference to participants in linguistic communication have their designations defined by the circumstances of a participant's being either speaker or addressee. These first and second person forms, as we observed, are not alternatives to, or replacements of, nouns or names that may normally occur within the context of their utterance. Thus, while these forms serve in sentences to manifest any part of a sentence that may also be manifest as a noun or name, their occurrence is not regulated by the same rules as are the occurrences of third person forms. The latter are, in an important sense, replacements of nouns or names. It would even be appropriate to call them noun- or name-markers, in that occurrence of a third person form serves semantically to repeat the noun or name without repetition of the noun or name form, or acts as a surrogate for the noun or name. The pronoun signals a semantic recurrence or substitution (with grammatical features required by its place in the phrase or clause structure as well) but does not in itself directly designate those semantic features. *The voyage, with all its hazards, made Antonio suspicious of Claudius' motives;* the "meaning" of *voyage* is marked as recurring by *its,* which also carries the case inflection required by the grammatical context.

Another characteristic of pronoun forms may be connected to the opposition between the self-reference of participants in a speech context and the other-reference established within the context of the utterances or of the other empirical circumstances that may exist. First and second person pronouns are singular and plural—different forms designating 'one' and 'more-than-one'; either singular or plural forms refer to any person, regardless of sex or age or other characteristics, and none of the forms refers to anything that may not participate in linguistic communication. (As implied earlier, in strict terms a participant must be allowed in either a literal or a metaphorical sense.) Third person pronouns are also singular and plural, but unlike first and second person forms, distinctive sets of singular forms refer separately and exclusively to things according to their sex—"masculine" and "feminine"—or to things without regard to sex distinction—"neuter." These "gender" distinctions operate only with the noun- and name-referring pronouns.

Many of the points in the preceding paragraphs about pronouns are obvious; nevertheless, it is important that each of the points be clearly set forth. The details will be justified by the help they will bring in understanding the history of English pronoun forms—a subject somewhat more complex than is that of the pronouns of Modern English.

MORPHOLOGICAL DIFFERENCES OF PRONOUNS

12.2 Our explication of pronouns has dealt so far only with person and gender differences and has established these differences primarily on contextual and referential grounds and secondarily on grounds of different rules of occurrences within sentences. We may turn now to morphological grounds for further explication. That the pronouns of Modern English include genuine inflectional systems appears most clearly in the third person plural forms *they, their(s), them* and the masculine forms (third person singular) *he, his, him.* (For the present we shall set aside *theirs* and any other alternate forms such as *mine* and *ours;* their distribution is governed by syntactic rules separate from rules that concern case inflection.) The plural forms have a single base consisting of /ð–/ with a mid front vowel. The case inflections are suffixes. Two of them are distinctly characterized with /–r/ and /–m/; the first form, *they,* can be distinguished in various ways. We may say that the distinction is (postvocalic) /–y/; or overt inflection is absent in *they* contrasting with /–r/ and /–m/, but because [ɛ] /e/ does not occur as a 'free" vowel—without a following consonant (see 7.5)—the corresponding free vowel [e] /ey/ occurs instead. Absence of overt inflection is conventionally marked as "zero" with the symbol ∅. The three pronouns have a shared referential function signaled by the base element, and they have differing inflectional elements signaling different grammatical functions. Both elements are to be counted as morphemes. The masculine pronouns also have a single base element and three different inflectional elements; the specific identity of the base and the case inflectional forms of *he* are subject to alternate formulations, but the /h–/ of the base is distinctive, as are the /–z/ and /–m/ inflectional morphemes in *his, him.*

With only the forms listed so far, we have two sets of pronouns, each set consisting of a base morpheme and three morphemic contrasts in the inflectional suffix elements. The bases, similar to nouns, differ as /h–/ and /ð–/. The inflections of the two sets are not alike: while /–m/ occurs in each inflectional set, /–z/ and /–r/ are unlike, and we need not choose for these purposes among formulations of *he* and *they*. Tests made by substitution of these forms within linguistic contexts will show, of course, that /–z/ and /–r/ of *his* and *their* belong to a single inflectional category. In setting up categories of inflectional forms, we can then assign typenames and arrange the forms in a system. Traditional names and a conventional ordering of these forms will be sufficient for our purposes. Thus, giving specific types (or categories) adjectival labels, and the general type ("case") a nominal label, the forms so far described may be arranged systemically as follows:

Case	Subjective	he	they	/hi–y	ðe–y
	Possessive	his	their	hi–z	ðe–r
	Objective	him	them	hi–m	ðe–m/

The other pronoun forms cannot be analyzed so as to show a clear symmetry with the masculine (singular) and the plural third person forms. Some do have three distinct members: *I, my (mine), me; we, our(s), us.* In neither of these sets is it possible to isolate a single base element to which inflectional forms are affixed, though with *my* and *me,* /m–/ is obviously a shared element. *You* and *your* present a still different pattern, and in so far as distributional characteristics establish *you* as parallel to both *he* and *him, they* and *them,* the base form /yu–/ seems to be present. *She, her(s)* is another arrangement of forms and is not parallel to any of the other sets in relation of base to inflectional suffix forms. And one more pattern appears in *it, it(s).*

In terms of reference these pronoun forms sort out into three person categories; in terms of meaning and selective function with verb inflections (singular and plural), they sort into two number categories; for singular third person forms they sort into three genders; and the maximum case categories in terms of inflectional variations is three. The generic categories thus represented—person, number, gender, and case—are all that pronouns in English have ever had. The number of specific categories of pronoun forms in the history of English is only slightly different: in very early English there were four cases rather than three, and three numbers rather than two. In its earlier structure, however, the members of both specific and generic categories of pronouns were far more regularly patterned in the sense of having recognizable base elements and in having inflectional elements with parallel sets of distinctions. Probably nothing is more crucial for an understanding of the history of the pronouns of English than is the systemic nature of the entire set of these forms. If the pronouns of Modern English appear more as a congeries than a system, the various changes which individual forms have undergone have their common matrix in the system within which they occurred.

PERSONAL PRONOUNS OF OLD ENGLISH

12.3 From the standpoint of morphology, the pronoun system of English is the more regularly patterned the farther back we go into the history of the language. Even in its earliest recorded form, the system has never had a machinelike simplicity and consistency, but the Old English forms will provide clear illustration of the obvious systemic nature of pronouns. Again it will be advantageous to begin with third person forms. The labels given for specific categories of case will be the traditional ones and will warrant a brief explication. On morphological grounds, "nominative" will be equivalent to the term "subjective" used above for Modern English forms. "Possessive" has been used for modern forms that correspond with the historically identical forms here called "genitive." In place of "objective" we shall use two labels, "dative" and "accusative," for two distinct case categories. The categories are established, again, on morphological grounds just as the one case category "objective" was established earlier for Modern English, as will be clear in the following citations of pronoun forms. The third person pronouns of Old English, using West Saxon forms in their common spellings, were these:

	Singular			Plural
	Masculine	Feminine	Neuter	(No gender distinction)
Nominative	hē	hēo	hit	hīe
Genitive	his	hire	his	hira
Dative	him	hire	him	him
Accusative	hine	hīe	hit	hīe

Phonemic notation (/ē/ represented by spelled *ē*, etc.) very closely parallels the spellings. Phonetic notation will also be helpful in subsequent discussion; the masculine and feminine (singular) forms provide a sufficient sample: [he: hɪs hɪm hɪnə], [he:o hɪre hi:ə]. Like Modern English pronouns, the third person forms in Old English sort into two number classes (singular and plural), and the singular forms sort into three genders. The number categories match those of Modern English—one vs. more-than-one in reference. Similarly, gender categories match those of present-day forms, designating male or female or non-sex-distinguished referent. With plural forms gender distinction does not exist but is obligatory with singular forms.

The entire specific category of third person pronouns has a single base element /h–/, each form having a following front vowel. Further specification of just how much of each form is to be construed as base form and how much as inflection is not practical: among the most frequently occurring words and consisting in many instances of single syllables, pronouns do not admit of segmentation into separate morphemic elements with the clarity and precision of, say, compound nouns such as *gas-light* or noun plural words such as *dish–es, table–s,* or past tense verbs such as *want–ed*. In addition, some forms have identical phonemic makeup. *Him* /him/ occurs as dative case forms of masculine and neuter (singular) and as (common) dative plural; *his* /his/ is the genitive case form of masculine and neuter; *hīe* /hīə/ appears as both nominative and accusative plural and as accusative feminine. Despite these overlaps and the practical indeterminacy of morphemic boundary of base and inflectional elements, there is systemic clarity in that /h–/ can be assigned the significance "third person," and the distinctive elements such as /–s/ and /–m/ and vocalic terminations can be assigned various case significations.

The third person forms of Old English pronouns are distinct from the first and second person forms in several ways, some of which we shall observe in the later considerations of nouns, determinatives, and adjectives. In first and second person pronouns, the category of person is not marked identically in both number categories, as it was (with /h–/) for third person forms. Singular and plural designations are made only in the complete pronoun form in any instance. That person category is not marked identically for the different numbers in first and second person forms will be obvious in the following listing of the typical (West Saxon) forms:

	First Person ("Speaker")		Second Person ("Addressee")	
	Singular	Plural	Singular	Plural
Nominative	iċ	wē	þū	ġē
Genitive	mīn	ūre	þīn	ēower
Dative	mē	ūs	þē	ēow
Accusative	mē (/mec)	ūs (/ūsic)	þē (/þec)	ēow (/ēowiċ)

The dual number forms may also be listed here. The referents of these pronouns are exactly two in number; when used as clause subjects they are always followed by verbs having plural inflections—the same verb inflections that occur in concord with plural nouns, pronouns, and the like. There are no third person dual pronouns.

Dual

First Person	("Speaker")	Second Person ("Addressee")
Nominative	wit 'we-two'	ġit 'you-two'
Genitive	uncer (etc.)	incer (etc.)
Dative	unc	inc
Accusative	unc (/ uncit)	inc (/ incit)

The second person pronouns have a regularity of phonetically consistent base elements approaching that of the third person forms with the difference, as noted, of separate base elements for singular and plural forms. The consistency of singular /þ–/ appears immediately in the spelling. For the plural and dual forms the consistency is less obvious but may be easily explicated. The initial /ġ–/ of *ġē* and *ġit* is approximately a consonantal alternate of /i/; the initial sounds of the other forms are vocalic, either mid or high front vowels. Consonantal and vocalic initial elements vary according to syllable structure of the pronouns. Consistency of the base element of first person dual and plural forms likewise appears if consonantal and vocalic alternate of "*u*–sounds" are considered. Before a vowel of the same syllable the *u* is consonantal; before consonant(s) it is vocalic. The convenience of having symbols to represent the base elements is best served by these: { u– } first person dual and plural, { i– } second person dual and plural, with consonantal varieties assigned a diacritic symbol when necessary making them appear as u̯ and i̯. The singular first person forms have initial /m–/ except in the nominative form. Parallelism of case inflections, such as that of first and second person singular *mīn*, *þīn* and dual *uncer*, *incer* will be clear from the listing of forms already given.

INDEFINITE PRONOMINALS

12.4 The forms we have been considering have been called simply "pronouns," and that part-of-speech label will be adequate if we provide other names for other classes of forms. For the sake of efficiency we can describe an additional class of forms and then consider the history of that class together with the history of (personal) pronouns at the same time.

In addition to the class of personal pronouns, Modern English has the forms *who, whose, whom,* and *what.* Although these are commonly called "interrogative pronouns," the class-name reflects only a syntactic feature, interrogative structure, with which they are often associated. A more satisfactory class-name, especially for these forms throughout the history of English, is "indefinite pronominals."

The set of indefinite pronominals is closely similar to that of third person pronouns. They designate "other" rather than participant(s) within a speech situation. As a class, their differences from third person pronouns may be related to their designative functions. In interrogative constructions they designate persons or things (or whatever may be symbolized by a noun or name) whose identity is not known. *Who is that? Whose ship did Antonio board? For whom did he ask before he embarked? What happened to delay his arrival?* Instead of being defined within the stretch of discourse in which they occur, their occurrence in these constructions calls for definition of that which they designate—that which they mark the place for—in additional discourse. Their relative functions are similar to those of third person pronouns; in relation to syntax they complement the pronouns, occurring in (and serving to identify) subordinate clauses, whereas the corresponding pronouns do not in themselves subordinate clauses. In neither function is number distinguished; one set refers to either singular or plural names, nouns, or pronouns. *It was Claudius who sent instructions, for he knew what to expect on that day.* The relation of these forms to third person pronouns is apparent in their morphological resemblance as well as their "other" designations. The masculine and the indefinite forms match up like this:

Subjective	he	/hiy	who (*and* what)	/huw
Possessive	his	hiz	whose	huwz
Objective	him	him/	whom (*and* what)	huwm/

The relations between indefinite pronominals and third person pronouns are more explicit as well as more systematic, in earlier stages of English. The West Saxon forms for Old English are cited here, with masculine and neuter pronouns for comparison.

Nominative	hē	hwā	hit	hwæt
Genitive	his	hwæs	his	hwæs
Dative	him	hwǣm	him	hwǣm
Accusative	hine	hwone	hit	hwæt

(An additional case form *hwȳ,* from which Modern English *why* has descended, will be omitted here because of its essentially different functions and history; *hwȳ* is the form for the instrumental case, a specific category we shall deal with subsequently.) Clearly, the base elements differ as /h–/ and /hw–/, the pronouns having mid and high front following vowels, the indefinite pronominals having low or back following vowels. The inflectional elements are exactly parallel. There are no additional indefinite forms. Because of their designative functions, plural forms and differentiation of gender as masculine and feminine are not to be expected. The defined reference of pronouns makes sex-gender of first and second person pronouns redundant and gives it a high degree of utility for the third person "other" reference; the undefined reference of the *hw–* pronominals (or *wh–* in Modern English) leaves sex-gender designation of these forms with minimal utility. Without an additional common form for "masculine" or "feminine" or "both," a mandatory distinction parallel to that of pronouns (e.g., *him, her*) would be unworkable. The Old English forms for non-sex-distinguished reference may be designated "neuter" for both pronouns and indefinite pronominals. We have called the *hē*-set "masculine" because of the sex-gender reference contrasting with that of the "feminine" *hēo*-set. The parallel indefinite forms, by reason of their inflectional elements, are often labeled "masculine" and it is explained that masculine forms serve also for feminine forms which are lacking. Because they contrast within the class of *hw–* forms with only neuter, the *hwā*-set would be more usefully designated as "masculine/feminine" for Old English at least. Except for the weight of tradition, even better would be labels more accurately reflecting the contrastive patterns and symmetries of the sets. The singular third person forms occur in three sets with the generic label " (grammatical) gender," but only two of the grammatical genders are associated with sex-gender distinctions. The three grammatical genders belong to a hierarchical pattern rather than to a mere list, thus:

I. Sex-distinguishing vs. Non-sex-distinguishing

II. A. "Masculine" vs.
"Neuter"
B. "Feminine

On this model, the indefinite forms then fall into two simple classes:

"Personal" vs. "Non-Personal"

Terminological problems, however, are not our primary concern here. Working through the relations of the pronoun and indefinite pronominal forms as if to establish an appropriate terminology is merely a means of clarifying the classes of forms, the categories to which they may be assigned, and the relations of the forms considered individually and as sets. We shall turn now to the principal changes within the morphological systems of personal pronouns and indefinite pronominals.

CHANGES IN PRONOUN FORMS

12.5 The changes in the forms we have been considering have been so numerous and varied as to require a deliberate eclecticism as we proceed. Two illustrations will show why this is so. First, the variety of pronoun forms during the period of Middle English may be represented in these lists: feminine nominative pronouns included *sčæ, heo, ho, hue, hi, ȝho, ȝhe, ȝe, sche, she, scho,* and the recorded accusative (merging with dative) plural third person pronouns included *hi, hem, heom, ham, þem, þeim, þaim, theym, his(e)* and others. In Modern English *them* and *'em* are stressed and unstressed allomorphs, respectively, in colloquial speech for most dialects. Isolated dialectal forms still occur for most of the pronouns, such as [šu] beside standard [ši] *she.* Still other variations exist in nonstandard forms that have long and legitimate histories, such as *hisn, theirn, ourn,* and the like. Second, a single kind of morphological change is usually found not to have occurred in most dialects at the same time. The replacement of *h–* by *th–* plural third person pronouns, the replacement of *hit* by *it* and of *his* by *its* must be assigned different dates in different speech communities. To take an extreme example, we shall assign the merger of masculine accusative *hine* with *him* to the period of the twelfth to fourteenth centuries, yet a distinct descendant form of *hine* is /–ən/ in unstressed occurrence continuing in some dialects into the twentieth century.

Eclecticism in formulation of the history of the pronouns and indefinite pronominals must serve more than one interest. We shall want to trace the evolution of the predominant, or standard, modern forms, as well as the evolution of the systems in their various directions whether or not in direct developmental line with the general systems in Modern English. Unless changes are observed in their representative varieties, including other than those eventuating in our own modern standard forms, the incorrect inference may be made that the changes occurred for the purpose of evolving only this portion of

Modern English. While the changes do have a direction, the variety of changes reflect only selective function in the systemic nature of the language and do not reflect a teleological guidance of the cumulative changes.

One of the earliest sets of changes is also one of the simplest to describe. That a number of individual changes occurred together in a set may be seen in the listings given earlier, where four case categories are given for the pronouns and indefinite pronominals of Old English but only three for Modern English. That the change was taking place during the period of Old English is clear from the listing of two forms in some of the accusative categories: *mē* and *mec, ēow* and *ēowiċ*, etc. Further, that the change did not affect all the person categories of pronouns at the same time is apparent from the listings given above; no overlap of dative and accusative forms occurred among the third person pronouns. Where and when precisely the change began is not known, but that the change was systematic there can be no doubt. Every change but one within the person categories conforms to a single pattern—the dative form surviving in all contexts in which either dative or accusative forms had formerly occurred: *hine* (with the exception noted above), *hīe* (feminine), *hīe* (third plural), *hwone, mec, þec, ūsiċ, ēowiċ, uncit, incit*—all were abandoned by English speakers by the end of Middle English, and most had fallen into disuse by the middle of the twelfth century. Both dative and accusative cases were used as object-of-verb cases and as prepositional-object cases. The history of these related changes also reflects the fact that third person pronouns and the indefinite *hw–* forms had a different status from the first and second person pronouns. While the speaker and addressee pronoun sets lost distinctive accusative forms during late Old English, the other two sets lost these case forms subsequently, at varying times up to the end of the fourteenth century.

An exception to the survival of the originally dative form is the neuter *it,* the descendant of Old English accusative *hit*. Contrary to the prevailing trend, dative *him* seems never to have been used where an accusative form would be expected. Exactly parallel in development is another exception, the "neuter" or nonpersonal indefinite pronominal set in which the accusative *hwæt* > *what* came to be the single objective form. The relationships between the set of linguistic habits involving the *hit* and *hwæt* sets were no doubt complicated and probably significant. Despite the overlap of masculine and neuter forms of pronouns and the overlap of personal and nonpersonal forms of the indefinite pronominals, the distinctions in the grammatical genders were unmistakably manifest in the nominative forms *hē* vs. *hit, hwā* vs. *hwæt*. These distinctions were extensively reinforced by other paradigmatic sets that retained grammatical gender while the new "objective" case was becoming established in the pronouns and indefinites. To describe these sets here would be to anticipate parts of the next chapter; suffice it to say here that grammatically "masculine" and "neuter" forms of the very frequently occurring "definite article" or "demonstrative" parallel the grammatical gender distinctions of the forms we are here considering. The selection of *hit* and *hwæt,* then, as the common objective case forms represents two major selective factors. One is the merging of two case categories already complete in first and second person pronouns and, in later Middle English, being extended through other sections of the pronominal forms. The other is the systemic frame of gender distinction that by the time of the change had become solely semantically based. "Gender" distinction was both preserved and clarified by the selection of *hit* and *hwæt.* The resultant sets emerged thus:

Old English		Middle English		Modern English	
hē	hit	hē	(h)it	he	it
his	his	his	his	his	his > its
him	him				
		him	him	him	it
hine	hit				
hwā	hwæt	whō	what	who	what
hwæs	hwæs	whōs	whōs	whose	whose
hwǣm	hwǣm				
		whōm	whōm	whom	what
hwone	hwæt				

Let us pursue the neuter pronouns through their subsequent developments before returning to the other classes. Although the survival of initial /h–/ in *hit,* nominative or objective, reaches into the twentieth century, and *hit* is a common form of the pronoun in the writings of Queen Elizabeth I in the late sixteenth century, the allomorph *it* developed as an unstressed form as early as the twelfth century. *It* and *hit* seem to have been interchangeable, stressed or not, in London at the end of the fourteenth century. At any rate, *it* developed from unstressed occurrences of the pronoun in which the aspirate /h/ was not articulated. The development in no way impaired the system of gender distinctions among pronouns and pronominals.

Differing from *hit* only by absence of the initial aspirate—a common enough phonological modification in English—the systemic modification by which the form lacked the distinctive third person base-element /h–/ was minimal. Once established, however, *it* in both subjective and objective case forms provided a model for change of the neuter *his* to differentiate it from the identical form in the masculine set. Phonological modification of any operative kind would not produce different genitive forms for masculine and neuter; hence the present form *its* developed by analogy. By the end of the sixteenth century *his* was still current as the neuter possessive pronoun, and an uninflected *it* also developed as the possessive form. The historical record is especially thin during this period, for *its* appears commonly and suddenly in the early seventeenth century. Whatever the particulars of its origin and spread, *its* clearly was formed on analogy with nouns which, well before the appearance of *its,* had come almost universally to have *–(e)s* possessive inflections. By the time the neuter pronouns reached their present stage of development, they had lost (in standard dialects) the originally distinctive base element /h–/; their inflections had become altogether unlike those of the other third person pronouns; but at no time did the set diverge from the systemic characteristics of third person pronouns, having throughout their development a distinction from the sex-distinguished masculine and feminine forms and a set of case distinctions congruent with those of the other pronouns. From the point of view of system—considered apart from the particular phonemic shape of the individual members—the pronouns have undergone only one change in respect to morphology, the merger of two case categories.

OTHER CHANGES IN PRONOUNS

12.6 Other changes in the pronouns followed a variety of courses. The history of the dual number pronouns is comprehended by the simplest of principles of linguistic change. Aside from following the trends of change we have already seen for the other pronouns in the period of late Old English, their history can be summed up simply as progressive infrequency of occurrence until finally the forms were no longer used at all by English speakers. By the thirteenth century, dual forms occurred only rarely in the writings that have survived, and by the fourteenth century they had apparently been abandoned altogether. From the surviving evidence it may be inferred that dual pronouns had never been used with frequency approaching that of the other forms. Having referents numbering exactly two, they seem to have been selected only when the duality of reference was to receive special emphasis. *Abram cwæð to Lothe: "Wyt sind gebroðru."* 'Abraham said to Lot: "We-two are the brothers." ' *Da wæron wit twegen on anum olfende.* 'Then we-two twain (*or* two) were on one camel.' Plural forms as well referred to two persons and were in no way restricted in their reference to more-than-one by the place of dual forms in the pronoun system. From the point of view of concord with verb forms, there was no difference between dual and plural forms, both sets requiring a nonsingular verb inflection. When the dual pronouns had become obsolete, the restructuring of the pronoun system was minimal: one number category was lost, but the relationship between singular and plural (that is, nonsingular) was not in itself modified. Since dual pronouns had existed only within the first and second person categories, the loss of these forms affected the "other"—third person—forms not at all.

About the time dual pronouns were becoming obsolete, another change was beginning by which singular vs. nonsingular contrasts in third person pronouns was introduced into the base elements. The binary singular-plural contrast then existed for noun, adjective, and verb inflections as well as in the other person categories of pronouns. The source of the new plural forms was the set of pronouns in the Scandinavian dialects spoken in the north and east of England. The entire set was distinguished by a base element containing *þ–*, later spelled *th–*. Fitted into the phonology of English the forms were variously *þei –ʒre –ʒ – þai, þem – þeʒʒm – þaim,* and possessive *þeir – þere – þeʒʒre – þaier* (to list only some of the spellings). The congruence of case-inflectional elements of these forms with those of *hi – hie, he(o)m, her(e)* will be immediately apparent. Once the entire set had been adopted, third person pronouns were parallel to the first and second person forms in having number distinction in their initial elements.

Substitution of these Scandinavian forms did not generally occur all at once. Chaucer's English provides perhaps the best known illustration: subjective *they* is the regular form, while the possessive and objective forms are consistently *her* and *hem*. The first substitution was that for the nominative form which had become, at various times in many of the dialects, much like that of the masculine (singular) nominative form. Without stress, of course, Middle English *he* and *hi* would easily become indistinguishable; other case forms contrasted more obviously having different consonantal terminations in *his* vs. *her* ('their'), or different checked vowels in *him* vs. *hem – heom – hom* etc.; feminine *hir* generally was kept in contrast to plural *her*. To keep the systemic pattern intact, the borrowing of *þei* was sufficient. (The alternative was an arbitrary creation of a new form keeping /h–/ but employing a clearly contrastive vowel; in such "basic" and frequently occurring forms as pronouns, arbitrary creation of new forms is one of the most nearly impossible alternatives for a natural language.) Sufficient as that change was, however, it did introduce an aberration into the system—/θ–/ in one case patterning with /h–/ in the other cases in the set of plural forms. But once established, it provided a model for extension of the /θ–/ forms, and the possessive and objective /θ–/ forms were ready at hand in their persistent use in regions of England whose social and political importance were increasing. By the end of the fifteenth century, *they, their, them* were established in most dialects. The reflex of *hem* was not displaced altogether: it survives as the common unstressed form /əm/ now widely considered (incorrectly) to be careless pronunciation of *them,* the form customarily written as *'em.*

Those changes which are merely consequences of phonological changes need only be mentioned, since they have little bearing on the history of the system of pronouns. All forms having stressed "long" vowels, of course, underwent phonemic reshaping as part of the "Great Vowel Shift": [me:] > [mi:]; [mi:], [mi:n] > [maɪ], [maɪn]; [u:rə] > [aʊr], etc. The various phonological changes affecting the plural first person forms have obscured the base element *u* which we saw (in 12.3) to have been present in all the case forms. An earlier set of changes affecting the nominative first person singular forms was as follows. The Old English form in West Saxon *iċ* [ɪč], in unstressed occurrences and in those in which the pronoun was not followed immediately and in the same phonological phrase by a vowel, developed an allomorph *ĭ* [ɪ].

Let us restate this in terms of distributional characteristics of the vowel. [ɪ] occurred in either form of the pronoun and, not being a "free" vowel, continued to be "checked" by a consonant. When the pronoun was immediately followed by a word beginning with a vowel, [č] occurred, retaining the older form [ɪč], usually spelled *ich* in Middle English. When the pronoun was immediately succeeded by a word beginning with a consonant, or when the pronoun was unstressed, [ɪ] occurred as a checked vowel or, perhaps, [ɪ] occurred as an unstressed vowel. (The same process was taking place in northern dialects in which the earlier form had been /ik/.) The change so far described belongs to the twelfth and thirteenth centuries. By the fourteenth century a related change had followed. Increasingly, it appears, the pronoun had occurred in a form lacking consonant termination. When its use was extended to contexts in which it occurred before words beginning with a vowel, a "free" vowel was required by the phonological patternings of the language: the "free" phonological correlative of [ɪ] came into use, the *I* [i:] of Chaucer and his contemporaries, the form which underwent the shift of stressed vowels to become the [əɪ] in Shakespeare's London and the [aɪ] of present-day English. In the meantime, the older *ich* (or its dialectal variants) was used less frequently until it disappeared altogether in the main dialects of English. This change, too, had no effect on the systemic structure of the set of English pronouns.

The development of two forms for possessive case pronouns did not alter the overall systemic structure of English pronouns. The phonological conditions by which *mine* and *thine* split to give *my–mine* and *thy – thine* are partially parallel to those that split *iċ, ich* and made possible the eventual development of *I*. Until the end of the period of Old English the genitive–possessive forms of first and second person pronouns had been declined as adjectives, which is to say that to the base forms /mīn–/ and /θīn–/ were joined inflectional forms making up sets for case, number, and grammatical gender. By Middle-English these forms were declined only for number contrasts, for instance, singular /mīn/, plural /mīnə/, and during the period of Middle English these inflectional distinctions were also abandoned. Meanwhile, in early Middle English, the pronouns in their normally lesser stressed positions within noun phrases began to occur without the terminal /–n/ when the following word in the same phonological phrase began with a consonant; when a vowel onset of the next word occurred, the /–n/ was regularly retained: *my lyf, my joye, myn owene lady dere* 'my life, my joy, my own dear lady.' (A following /h–/ also was preceded by an /–n/ form—*myn herte, myn honour* 'my heart,' 'my honor.') The conditions under which this split of forms occurred were specifically those in which the possessive pronoun formed part of a noun phrase; the sequence of words in noun phrases was fixed (in patterns we shall observe in a later chapter), with the pronoun always preceding the noun, or preceding one or more adjectives before the noun, and normally less stressed than the form following it. The other typical conditions under which the possessive forms occurred were not the kind to produce split. The possessive form occurred at the head of a phrase and had, therefore, a higher degree of stress than it did as a constituent part of a noun phrase. As the head of a phrase it normally was not followed immediately by another word; rather, some element of pause, or timing extension, or variation of voice pitch—or all of these—intervened as a marking of the phrase boundary. Some illustration should make the point clear here. Using normal voice modulation and speech timing of Modern English (appropriate enough for this illustration), the following occurrences of *my – mine* will contrast in stress and in relation to the beginning of the following word:

(a) myn owene hóus	'my own hóuse'
my sóne	'my són'
my leve hérte	'my lief (beloved) héart'
(b) They aren bothe myn, if . . .	'They are both míne, if . . .'
an old félawe of mỳn . . .	'an old fríend of mìne . . .'
All this land is myn.	'All this land is míne.'

Because of different conditions of stress and connection to following forms the split into *my – mine, thy – thine* occurred in contexts like those in the (a) group and did not occur in contexts like those in the (b) group. The alternatives of *my* vs. *mine, thy* vs. *thine* continued well into early Modern English, selection of the alternate remaining conditional upon the consonantal or vocalic nature of the initial sound of the following word. As with *ich* vs. *I,* the newer form finally supplanted the older in every occurrence within a phrase of the kind illustrated in (a), above. *Mine* [maɪn] has continued to be the sole form in the "independent" or "disjunctive" positions of the kind illustrated in the (b) set. That *thy* and *thine* are no longer used is the result of changes we shall trace in 12.8.

The development of separate forms *my – mine, thy – thine* in accordance with differences in the syntactic patterns in which the possessive pronouns occurred is paralleled by the development of separate forms for third person possessive pronouns. The processes were different as were also the resultant forms, but the products were systemically equivalent. We have now, congruent with *my* vs. *mine,* the pairs *our – ours, your – yours, her – hers, their – theirs; his,* already ending in a sibilant, did not develop by addition of a sibilant like the others, which would have produced disyllabic [hɪzəz]. Historically, when the possessives occurred in the "independent" position, functioning pronominally rather than attributively, they were joined to a new genitive inflection *–(e)s;* the source of this inflection was presumably the predominant noun inflection for the same case category. Beside *oure* was the independent *oures,* beside *youre* was *youres,* etc. These new formations were not unique, a fact that implies the role of syntactic contrasts and the systemic factors of the set of pronouns as essential selective factors in the development of the paired possessive pronoun forms. The *–(e)s* forms appeared first in northern dialects, where *–(e)s* noun inflections first became fully established. In Midland dialects, of about the fourteenth century, *–(e)n* inflections were joined to all possessive pronouns except *myn* and *thyn,* which already contrasted with *my* and *thy*. Presumably, the source of the Middle English *hisen, hiren, ouren, youren, theiren* was the /–n/ of *myn* and *thyn* construed as genitival inflection and extended analogically to the other pronoun forms. These *–(e)n* forms are obviously equivalent to the *–(e)s* forms, and they have an intrinsic superiority from the point of view of simplicity and consistency within this component of the system of pronouns: with *–(e)n,* all the pairs are matched up phonologically, except for *its* which at the time of the development of the *–(e)n* inflections had not yet replaced neuter possessive *his.* That they did not survive except in regional dialects and that the *–(e)s* forms are now standard can be explained only in terms of social and political history.

THE NOMINATIVE FORM *SHE*

12.7 A set of changes of unusual interest produced the feminine nominative form *she.* The changes involve phonological factors similar to those producing *I* and *my.* The factors illustrate well the selective function of the systemic nature of the pronoun set as well as of the consonants. A representative sample of spelled forms of the pronoun has already been given in 12.5; the variety of pronoun forms with which we must begin represent normal phonological descendants of the Old English forms of the pronoun, that is, those that still conformed to the third person pattern of initial /h–/. In Mercian and Northumbrian dialects of Old English, the forms represented variously as /hīo hīw hīə/ and /hio hiw hiə/ correspond to West Saxon /hēo heo/. The /–ī–/ or /–i–/ element conditioned the initial /h–/ in a way similar to that which we observed earlier for the varieties of /h/ in English: the differences in *h*–sounds of Modern English *he* and *hall* will clarify the variety of sound of the initial consonant; the sound was presumably that symbolized as [ç]. For most dialects, the normal drift of vocalic elements was toward [ö:] (a rounded mid front vowel), which in turn was assigned to one or another of the mid range vowels as the [ö:] was abandoned in the various dialects. The reassignment of the vowel then produced, in some regions, either *hē* or *hō,* two of commonly recorded spelled forms. In those regions in which a [ç–]-variety of /h–/ was retained, the products of phonological change were spelled (typically) *ȝho, ȝhe.*

The systemic nature of the consonants and pronouns operated selectively on these phonological variants—these allomorphs of the feminine nominative pronoun. Because [ç] was not phonemically distinct, it was assigned in some dialects to /h/, as we have seen in the *hē* and *hō* forms. The first of these obviously was identical to the masculine nominative form and prevented any gender distinction in nominative forms, while gender distinction remained operative in other case forms of the singular third person pronouns. These circumstances tended to select the *hō* form, contrasting with masculine *hē* and plural *hī*. But even where *þei* was being adopted, the /–ō/ vowel was incongruent with the nominative (and other case form) front vowels of pronouns. The selective adjustments involved the vocalic element of the forms. Alternatively, the consonantal element could be modified.

The forms beginning with /š–/ evolved first in the Northeast Midlands and adjacent areas—the region with descendant forms of Old English Mercian and Northumbrian dialects. It was in this region that [ç–] forms were predominant and that interaction of Scandinavian and English dialects had earliest developed the new English phoneme /š/ (the process was described in 6.5). Thus a different assignment of [ç–] was possible as a change by allophone from /h–/ to /š–/. And it was there that both *she* – *sche* and *sho* – *scho* evolved. That *sho* /šō/ provided a satisfactory form—both consonantal and vocalic elements differentiating it from *hē*—is attested by its survival into the twentieth century; having undergone normal vowel shift it is recorded as dialectal [šu:]. That *she* became the predominant form is probably to be attributed to the fact that its vowel was identical to that of the masculine nominative form and similar to the vowel of the plural nominative form (and was not, contrary to the system as a whole, a back vowel), while the consonantal element was clearly contrastive. At the outset the different consonantal element was not (in phonetic terms) a phonologically conspicuous departure from the /h–/ element of the other singular third person forms. The utility of the specific form *she*—a nonunique resolution of the systemic flaw in third person pronouns—seems to be attested by its spread throughout all the major dialects by the end of the period of Middle English.

SECOND PERSON PRONOUNS

12.8 Finally, a major set of changes affected second person pronouns. These changes proceeded for the most part from factors unrelated to the system of pronouns and, as will appear shortly, further changes in terms of the systemic structure have also occurred even though they have not been accepted into the major standardized dialects. That Modern English generally has no distinction between singular and plural forms is the consequence of changes beginning in English in the thirteenth century and becoming well established in the fourteenth century. On the model of French and Latin usage, plural forms were used as a mark of respect in addressing a person. For a long time this usage apparently was practiced by the upper classes. By the time it had spread through other social classes, the fact that it distinctly signified respect led to an opposite signification for the singular forms: *thou, thee, thy – thine* conveyed the sense of patronizing, derogation, or inappropriate intimacy on the part of the speaker. As important as any factor in the displacement of singular by plural forms was the social requirement that adolescents use the plural form "of respect" in speaking to their superiors—adults as well as persons of higher social classes. While the two forms were still opposed, the difference in attitude they conveyed when addressed to one person of course afforded new rhetorical possibilities, a fact fully exploited by writers of literature. Because the referent(s) of second person pronouns had definition within a speech context, the loss of efficiency in the pronoun system was not particularly great: by directing one's speech to one person or by directing it variously if others were present, singular-plural specification by choice of pronoun form was contextually redundant. Rhetorical ways could also be used to specify singular reference when a plural form was employed—*You, sir. . .* , for example. When plural forms had come into general use, plurality of reference was specifiable by similar means —*You citizens of Hampshire* and the like. These techniques involved appositional name or noun forms. The outcome of the introduction of plural second person forms for singular reference was eventually the disuse of the singular forms; *thou, thy – thine, thee* became generally obsolete in the eighteenth century.

When the two categories for number persist in nouns and in the first and third person pronouns (as well as in some of the verb inflections) there is reason to expect changes to reintroduce number distinction for second person pronouns. *Youse* is one such new formation that has not spread widely within English. More common are new forms produced as compounds with the pronoun joined to one or another word whose meaning is clearly both plural and inclusive: *you-uns* is such a compound using an unstressed form of *ones,* and the far more successful compound *you-all,* or *y'all,* is self-explaining. A special instance of restoration of number contrast in this group of pronouns is the incorporation of *unu* as the plural pronoun in Jamaican English: it was retained from an African language spoken by the slaves introduced into an English-speaking island colony. Another response to the collapse of number distinction of second person pronouns began in the eighteenth century but has never succeeded in becoming established in standardized dialects. It is the deliberate selection of a singular verb form when *you* is referentially a singular subject of a predicate: *you was* (singular) vs. *you were* (plural). The utility of this innovation, too, is very low, since most verbs no longer differ for second person subjects in singular and plural inflection, and the number category of only subjective pronouns can be indicated (indirectly) in this way. The historically plural subjective form continues to select a plural form of the verb *be,* whether its reference is singular or plural.

The other changes affecting second person forms resulted in the segmental identity of subjective and objective forms. It appears to have occurred almost exclusively within the originally plural set and not to have begun until the use of plural forms with singular reference was becoming common. In the fourteenth century the use of *you* in syntactic positions requiring subjective forms first appears in the surviving texts; at first, *you* is also used in constructions in which the pronoun follows the verb—in questions and imperative constructions. Progressively, *you* was used in place of both *thou* and *thee,* and during the fifteenth century *ye* begins to appear in place of both *ye* (nominative plural and often singular) and *thee* (objective singular only). During the sixteenth and seventeenth centuries *ye* and *you* were kept apart—at least in the dominant dialects—only by careful writers, the translators of the King James (Authorized) Bible being probably the most prominent of them. Otherwise, *ye* and *you* were used with little discrimination in respect to syntactic requirements of nominative vs. objective case forms. Since these forms often occurred with light stress, the analogical force of objective *me* and *thee* was probably in part responsible for the use of *ye* as an objective case form. Although *thou* and *you* did not have identical vowels, [θu:] > [ðəu] > [ðaʊ] beside [yo^u] > [yu:], the similarity was enough to establish some valence of nominative *thou* for nominative *you.* Whatever the particulars of the process, by the time singular *thou* and *thee* were abandoned, *you* was the ordinary form for both nominative and objective case when the historically plural forms came to serve as both singular and plural.

PROBLEMS OF USAGE

12.9 Although usage problems are not strictly within the scope of our present study, one or two of those involving pronouns and indefinite pronominals are interesting as addenda to the historical changes just reviewed. As already implied, the problem of nonstandard *you-all* or of *you is . . .*, *you was . . .* is a response to the systemic factors inherent in the set of pronouns. The spelling of the possessive neuter form also causes problems. Standardized spelling distinguishes *its* (possessive) from the homophonic *it's* (contraction of *it is*). The neuter form is the only one resembling possessive inflection of nouns, always spelled with an apostrophe. Less troublesome but much of the same kind of problem is the spelling of independent possessive forms with an apostrophe, such as *your's, her's;* with these, of course, there are no homophonic contractions to produce confusion. There is also the shibboleth of *who* vs. *whom*. We shall deal later with the replacement of *whom* by *who* (still not approved of by conservative standards). The identity of subjective and objective forms for the nonpersonal, or "neuter," indefinite pronominals causes no difficulty and provides an exact parallel for *who* in both case categories.

Chapter 13

MORPHOLOGICAL HISTORY OF DETERMINATIVES AND SPECIFIERS

DETERMINERS–PRONOMINALS

13.1 Throughout their history morphological classes that fill or participate in the noun-like slots of sentences both differ from and share similarities with the classes of pronouns and indefinite pronominals. As may be expected, they also have some similarities to the two classes of forms we have just considered. One way to make these relations apparent is to list side by side the third person pronouns and another set of forms as they occurred in Old English.

Singular						Plural	
Masculine		Feminine		Neuter		(No gender distinction)	
hē	sē̆	hēo	sēo	hit	þæt	hīe	þā
his	þæs	hire	þǣre	his	þæs	hira	þāra
him	þǣm	hire	þǣre	him	þǣm	him	þǣm
hine	þone	hīe	þā	hit	þæt	hīe	þā
(him)	(þȳ)	(hire)	þǣre		(þȳ)	(him)	(þǣm)

The systemic similarity of this new set of forms to the third person pronouns is thoroughgoing. In their terminal elements—those signaling case, gender, and number differences—they are exactly parallel, if we allow *hīe* and *þā* as parallel in their vocalic termination. With the exception of masculine and feminine nominative forms, the entire set is distinguished from the pronouns in the contrast of initial elements

/h–/ vs. /þ–/. A fifth case category, called "instrumental," has been included; it was becoming obsolete in Old English and was no longer distinct for pronouns, nouns, and adjectives, though it still was distinct for the new forms listed above and for the ones listed in 13.2. The forms have morphological and systemic resemblance to third person pronouns, and are like pronouns in meaning and syntactic use. That they are at the same time a different set of forms—having a base element we may generalize as /þ–/—implies also that they may not be pronouns, as we have thus far used that term. These forms we shall call determiners-pronominals; the appropriateness of the label will appear as we consider their grammatical nature and history.

Here is one kind of use of these forms:

(a) *Sē* þe nys mid mē, hē is ongēn mē.
'*He* (or *that one*) who isn't with me, he is against me.'

(b) *Sē* þe nis agēn ēow, *sē* is for ēow.
'*He* (or *that one*) who isn't against you, *he* (or *that one*) is for you.'

The translations of the *sē* forms will show how Modern English has come to differ from Old English in respect to pronouns and pronominals: *sē* in these sentences can be translated with either *he* or *that one* (or *the one*). In Modern English the only forms specifying gender are singular pronouns; from the listing of forms above, though, it will be clear that both *hē* and *sē* specify "masculine." (The form *þe,* or *ðe,* occurring in both examples is termed a "relative particle"—an undeclined form with something like relative pronoun function; we shall consider it more fully in another place.) The use of *Sē (þe)* in the examples is of course of a special kind, since not only "masculine" persons (or objects) are necessarily implied: *sē* is used as a generalizing form in the same way in which the *hwā*-set is used as a common form for reference to persons without specification of (sex-) gender. Because these forms are gender-distinguishing, grammatically masculine *sē* requires masculine *hē* in grammatical concord, or it requires a masculine form of the *sē*-set in concord. Interestingly enough, *hwā,* in similar constructions also selects masculine *hē*: *Ġif hwā mē lufað, hē hylt mīne sprǣċe* 'If anyone (*or* someone) love me, he holds my speech (*or* word).'

To illustrate other case, number, and gender forms of the determiners-pronominals, as well as their use in different kinds of constructions, the following examples are given:

(c) Ne winne ġē ongēn *þā* ðe ēow yfel dōð.
'Strive you [plural] not against *those* who do you evil.'

(d) . . . þæt sōþe līf on *þām* ðe hē ǣfre libban mæġ. . . .

'. . . the true life in *which* (or the *one* in which) he may ever live. . . .'

(e) . . . ǣlċ *þǣra* . . . þe cwyþ tō̆ mē, Dryhten, Dryhten. . . .
'. . . each of *those* (or *the ones*) . . . who says to me, Lord, Lord. . . .'

These examples, together with the preceding ones, show these forms in a use semantically like that of the third person pronouns. In the examples just given, though, the forms cannot be replaced by (personal) pronouns. This is just one respect in which they differ from the /h–/ forms, and just one reason for calling them "pronominals" rather than "pronouns." Further clarification of their pronominal status can be made by introducing first the other aspect of their distribution and function—the one for which the "determiner" part of their name has been assigned.

In example *(d)*, above, the most common uses of the determiners-pronominals are represented. In the noun phrase *þæt . . . līf* 'the life' (or 'that life'), the neuter determiner-pronominal form is used, and that gender form is obligatory. The reason for the requirement is the grammatical gender (neuter) of the noun *līf*. We shall take up nouns separately in Chapter 15, and it must suffice here to say that in Old English every noun was declined according to one of the three grammatical genders; the grammatical gender was not based on sex distinction of the concept or thing represented by the noun. When a noun occurred in Old English with a determinative form in the same phrase, the recurrence of the meaning of the noun could be marked in an adjacent clause by use of the determiner-pronominal and, in fact, this is a normal facet of sentence construction in Old English. The recurrence of the meaning was never, as a rule, marked by the use of a (personal) pronoun and was never marked by use of an indefinite pronominal; that is, both the following constructions would *not* be "good" or "natural" English: *þæt sōþe līf on him þe* . . . and *þæt sōþe līf on hwǣm þe* . . . 'the true life in the true life which. . . .' In short, the forms we are considering had two principal kinds of function. One was that served by the occurrence of the form within a noun phrase, in which instance it was approximately the equivalent of Modern English *the* or *that – those,* as a determiner or demonstrative. The other was served by the form's occurrence at the head of a clause, not as part of a noun phrase, and commonly followed by the relative particle form *ðe,* in which instance it was pronominal; being a pronominal rather than a noun or pronoun, it also signaled that its clause was not independent. In other words, in a relative pronominal function it had special syntactic as well as referential significance. Like pronouns in

Modern as well as Old English, the relative pronominal use of these forms was governed by rules of agreement (concord) of gender and number with the determined form with which it was linked, but the case form was selected in accordance with the syntactic requirements of the clause in which the pronominal occurred.

SPECIFIERS–PRONOMINALS

13.2 Another set of forms extends the patterns of pronominals. The third person pronouns, the determiners-pronominals, and an additional set we shall call specifiers-pronominals of Old English are as follows:

Singular

Masculine			Feminine			Neuter		
hē	sē	þēs	hēo	sēo	þēos	hit	þæt	þis
his	þæs	þisses	hire	þǣre	þisse (re)	his	þæs	þisses
him	þǣm	þissum	hire	þǣre	þisse (re)	him	þǣm	þissum
hine	þone	þisne	hīe	þā	þās	hit	þæt	þis
(him)	þȳ	þȳs	(hire)	þǣre	þisse (re)	(him)	þȳ	þȳs

Plural

hīe	þā	þās
hira	þāra	þissa (þissera)
him	þǣm	þissum
hīe	þā	þās
(him)	þǣm	þissum

These newly listed forms are roughly equivalent to Modern English *this – these;* the historical connection with present-day forms is most obvious in the singular Old English forms. If the base element of pronouns can be generalized as /h–/ and that of determiners-pronominals as /þ–/, the generalized form of the base element of the specifiers-pronominals may be represented as /þ—s–/.

In their pronominal function, these forms are selected for agreement by gender and number in the same way as forms from the other sets. If the referent is not part of the fuller utterance, the form is determined by the personal or nonpersonal nature of the empirical referent; case-form selection is syntactic. The specifier functions of these forms occur when they participate in noun phrases. They are illustrated in the following examples.

(a) Nimað *þās* þing. 'Take *these* things.'
æfter *þissum* wordum. 'after *these* words.'
on *þissere* nihte. 'on *this* night.'
þæt folc *þis* wundor ġeseah. 'The people beheld *this* wonder.'
Eal *þes* middanġeard, and *þās* windas, and *þās* reġnas. 'All *this* earth, and *these* winds, and *these* rains.'

(b) *þes* is smiðes sunu. '*This* is the carpenter's son.'
Hwanon is *þysum þes* wīsdōm? 'Whence is (*or* for, *or* with respect to) *this* (one) *this* wisdom?'
þes is be þām þe āwriten is . . . 'This (it) is concerning whom is written . . .'

(c) Se hǣlend cwæð, *þis* ġehȳrende . . . 'The Saviour said, hearing *this* [where *þis* 'this' refers to something that had just been said] . . .'
Hwæt is *þis?* Hwæt is *þēos* nīwe lār? 'What is *this?* What is *this* new teaching?'

(d) *þis* lēoht wē habbaþ wið nȳtenu ġemǣne, ac þæt lēoht wē sceolan sēċan ðæt wē mōtan habban mid englum ġemǣne. '*This* light we have in common with animals, but that light we ought to seek that we may have in common with angels.'
þæs ofer-ēode, *þisses* swā mæġ. 'With respect to that, (it) passed over (*or* away); so (it) may with respect to *this.*'
Is *þes* ænga styde unġelīċ swīðe þām ōðrum þe wē ǣr cūðon. '*This* narrow place is exceedingly unlike that (*or* the) other which we knew formerly.'

A fuller list of illustrations has been given because these forms are especially revealing of inherent overlaps among the gender distinctions of the specifiers-pronominals—an overlap we have also observed for the other pronoun and pronominal forms. We have seen that the morphologically masculine pronouns and other pronominals serve generalized reference for *persons* without respect to sex-gender—*Sē þe* 'he who' or *Ġif hwā* 'if anyone'—while neuter forms are retained for objects that are not ordinarily distinguished by sex. In group *(c)*, above, the morphologically neuter form serves generally when not linked to any noun. Even though *þēos lār* is morphologically feminine, the first question, *Hwæt is þis?* utilizes the neuter form. The same selection appears in the (d) group in *þæs ofer–ēode, þisses swā mæġ.*

The specifiers-pronominals, much like their Modern English descendants *this – these,* do not mark a clause in which they occur pronominally as a nonindependent clause. In this respect they resemble pronouns and contrast with determiners-pronominals .

PRONOMINALS IN NOUN PHRASES

13.3 We have now listed the Old English morphological classes apart from adjectives and nouns that belong to the nounlike slots of sentences. Before we proceed to their historical changes, two additional matters require brief exposition. One of these concerns pronominals within noun phrases. Both the specifying and the determinative forms occur in a fixed position: they precede the noun (or nominal) that heads the phrase as well as all adjectival elements that may also occur in the phrase. An exception of a very few forms must be made if *bēgen* 'both,' *eall* 'all,' *healf* 'half' and perhaps *ǣlċ* 'each' are construed as parts of the phrase, for they precede the other forms. Also, they occur with lighter stress than other parts of the phrase. Any of the forms is always in grammatical concord with the noun with which it is structured; the concord includes categories of number, case, and gender. In respect to position in the phrase, however, these forms correspond exactly to their Modern English descendants:

þā þrȳ weras 'the three men'
on þȳs ylcum þrim dagum 'in this same three days'
þæs cynges iunge dohtor ' (of) the king's young daughter'
eall þēos mǣre ġesceaft 'all this glorious creation'
bēgen þā ġebrōþru 'both the brothers'

The other matter is the relationships of these sets as they form a composite set. The group is different from Modern English, as the translations above show in the frequency with which 'the' and 'that' and 'those' have appeared as alternate translations of a determiner-pronominal. A noun phrase in Modern English may have any of the following forms in the fixed position described above: *the, that – those, this – these,* as well as *a* (or *an*) , or a noun phrase may contain none of them. Lacking the "indefinite article" *a – an,* Old English had only two sets from which a form could be selected for this position, while Modern English has three. In contrastive occurrences like those in group *(d)* of section 13.2, /þ—s–/ and /þ–/ forms were opposed as *this* and *that* of Modern English, but a contrast equivalent, say, to *the* and *that* did not occur. As may be inferred from the Old English forms themselves, *the* and *that* of Modern English are reflexes of merely gender-distinguished forms in the earlier single set of determiners-pronominals.

EVOLUTION OF *THE*

13.4 The processes by which the pronominal forms eventuated in *the, this – these, that – those* are by no means clear. Their history is one of rapid and radical change, and the change took place during a period for which written records are especially scarce. By and large, morphological changes occurred first in northern dialects of Old and Middle English, particularly those changes resulting in loss of inflectional forms. Written records from these dialects are few in early Middle English and almost non-existent for Old English. Without a full sequence of evidence from two or three closely related dialects at the least, some of the factors necessary for full coherence of linguistic history can only be supplied by guesswork.

The Peterborough Chronicle is one of the prime exhibits for the changes we are considering. The two passages that follow were written approximately twenty-five years apart, the latter being dated about 1154. The accompanying translations include some constructions not idiomatic for Modern English, since their purpose is that of explication of the older text. No diacritic marks are supplied for these citations, but punctuation is added; the symbol "7" is equivalent to an ampersand.

> [1127.] Đis gear heald se kyng Heanri his hird æt Cristemæsse on Windlesoure. . . . þes ilce Willelm hæfde æror numen ðes eorles dohtor of Angeow to wife, oc hi wæron siððen totwæmde for sibreden: þet wes eall ðurh þone kyng Heanri of Engleland. Siððen þa nam he ðes kynges wifes swuster of France to wife; 7 forþi iæf se kyng him þone eorldom of Flandres. Đes ilce gæres he gæf þone abbotrice of Burch an abbot, Heanri wæs gehaten, of Peitowe, se hæfde his abbotrice Sancte Iohannis of Angeli on hande. . . .
>
> '1127. This year the king Henry held his court at Christmas at Windsor. . . . This same William had earlier taken to wife the daughter of the Earl [i.e., Count] of Anjou, but they were afterwards divorced for (reason of) consanguinity. That was all through [that is, owing to] the king Henry of England. Later then, he took to wife the sister of the king of France, and for that (reason) the king gave him the Earldom [that is, County] of Flanders.

With respect to [that is, in the course of] this same year he gave the abbacy of Burch [that is, Peterborough] to an abbot—Henry he was called, of Poitou—who had in hand [that is, had possession of] his abbacy of St. Jean d'Angely.'

[1135.] On þis gære for se king Henri ouer sæ æt te Lammasse. 7 Ðat oþer dei þa he lai an slep in scip, þa þestrede þe dæi ouer al landes 7 uuard þe sunne suilc als it uuare thre niht ald mone. . . . Wurþen men suiðe ofuundred 7 ofdred, 7 sædon ðat micel þing sculde cumen herefter: sua dide, for þat ilc gear warth þe king ded ðat oþer dæi efter Sancte Andreas massedæi. . . . [1137.] Ðis gære for þe king Stephne ofer sæ to Normandi. . . . Hi suencten suyðe þe uurecce men of þe land mid castelweorkes; þa ðe castles uuaren maked, þa fylden hi mid deoules 7 yuele men. . . .

'1135. In this year the king Henry went across the sea at Lammas (-tide); and the next day when he lay asleep in (the) ship, the day grew dark over all lands and the sun became as (if) it were a three-night-old moon. . . . Men [that is, people] were exceedingly astonished and frightened and said that a great [that is, important] thing should come hereafter; so it did, for that same year the king became dead the second day after St. Andrew's (mass-) day. . . . 1137. This year the king Stephen went across the sea to Normandy. . . . They [the traitors] severely oppressed the wretched people of the land with castle-works [that is, castle-building]; when the castles were made, they filled them with devils and evil men. . . .'

Commentary of these samples must be prefaced by a note that differences in spelling involving *e, æ, i, y* will not permit analysis with all the forms in the same spellings in which they have so far been listed: both dialect area and date of this text are somewhat removed from West Saxon Old English, but the main points will be clear enough. In the sample from the annal for 1127 *se* still occurs for masculine nominative, and *þone* for masculine accusative; *ðes* is equivalent to *ðæs* in *ðes eorles dohtor,* etc.; and *se* is used pronominally in the final clause. In the annals for 1135 and 1137 *se king* occurs in the first line, but *þe king* occurs twice; the use of *th* spelling in place of *þ* is used, too, and the spelling of *the,* though it does not occur in the citations given, would represent the same form. The phrase *þe sunne* corresponds to earlier *sēo sunne* (of West Saxon Old English), marked distinctively as feminine, and it is referred to by the neuter pronoun *it; þe dæi* replaces earlier *se dæg; þe . . . men* and *þe castles* would have been *þā . . . men* and *þā castelas* (masculine) in Old English;

land, historically a neuter form, would not earlier have had again the *þe* form in the phrase it heads. Equally significant is the twice-occurring phrase *Đat oþer dei,* for *þat* corresponds to the neuter *þæt* listed earlier, and *dei* – *dæi* (West Saxon *dæġ*) was historically a "masculine" noun: *þat* (< *þæt*) is obviously no longer in this text a grammatically neuter determiner-pronominal. These two short passages from the language of the Peterborough Chronicle suggest some of the inferences to be drawn. By 1154, the scribes' language had only a few relics of the systems of determiners-pronominals and specifiers-pronominals that had existed in West Saxon only 150 years earlier: *þe,* equivalent to *the,* was almost completely established. The Modern English opposition between *the (þe)* and *that (þat)* was at least in its incipient stages. Grammatical gender distinctions consequently were nearly gone, replaced by "natural" gender, and number distinction for *þe (the)* was already lost. Finally, the changes summarized here did not occur within a mere quarter of a century. Although the evidence in these passages is not full enough to demonstrate it, the earlier passage was written in partial imitation of the "classical" language of earlier chronicle entries. The language of these earlier entries had already become archaic, and the dialect remote; this accounts for archaic elements such as *se* and *þone.* In the later passage, the imitation of the archaic language was almost altogether abandoned.

While the Peterborough Chronicle provides some of the best evidence of the change from essentially Old to nearly Modern English morphology of pronominals, this document would not be adequate to represent the full range of changes and their processes even if it had been continued into the sixteenth century. The document shows how the simplification of the morphological sets occurred in one region and at one time. In other regions, and particularly at later times, other processes of change operated. Several of the possible explanations for the changes are more than hypothetical, for the forms and patterns they would produce are attested in surviving written records of English.

In a noun phrase, the pronominals occurred in a fixed and thus fully predictable position, and with light stress. The particular form within any of the morphological sets was selected in concord with the noun or nominal of the phrase. The case, gender, and number significations were therefore entirely redundant. For the set headed by *se, sēo, þæt,* the form *þe* could occur in place of any of the forms without lessening the clarity of the structure. For this reason, replacement of the nominative masculine and feminine *se* and *sēo* by analogy with the other forms would be unobtrusive. Also, the unstressed *þe* [θə] substituted for any of the other forms when unstressed would be unobtrusive because in its initial element, *þe* has phonological resemblance to the others; hence no essential grammatical signal would be lost thereby. Ultimately *þe* did replace all the members of the Old English set of determiners-pronominals. However, some other possible distributions of and distinctions among forms might—and did—occur. For example, singular–plural distinction, operative in the inflections of nouns, pronouns, verbs, adjectives (commonly) as well as the reflexes of *þes – þēos – þis,* was retained for a while in some dialects as *þe* singular, *þā* plural. In at least one dialect, *þe* did not generalize as the single form: *þat* was the common singular form, with plural *þā.* In one process, a singular distinction similar to the one made for pronouns and indefinite pronominals produced *þe* for nouns designating animate objects opposed systemically to *þat* for nouns designating inanimate objects. Elsewhere *þe* came to be the generalized form before words that began with one or more consonants, while *þat* was generalized before words with vocalic initial elements: the forms alternated according to strictly phonological circumstances.

The evolution of these forms and sets is still more complex than the preceding paragraph suggests, however, for we have considered them only in their occurrences within noun phrases. In their pronominal functions their position in a *clause* was fixed, but they were not fixed as "satellites" of a noun; the forms occurred separately, so that case or gender or number specification would be signaled if at all by the pronominal form only. It will be recalled that a form *þe* was already well established as a relative particle occurring either alone or with one of the pronominals. If the pronominal function were not dissociated from the demonstrative–determiner function, and the generalization of the *se – sēo – þæt* forms were producing *þe,* a new redundancy in the iteration *þe þe* would develop. The generalization of *þe* within noun phrases reinforced the earlier relative *þe* and brought the relative-pronominal use of the determiners-pronominals to a dead end—a merger with a segmentally identical form. The consequences of this change are highly important to the development of relative pronoun forms. For the evolution of the determiners-pronominals, the change meant only that the pronominal function of these forms came to an end and that singular–plural distinctions of the residual forms were of that much less utility and hence the more likely to disappear.

EVOLUTION OF *THIS–THESE, THAT–THOSE*

13.5 The contributing factors to the emergence of *this – these* and *that – those* were in part coextensive with those producing the single form *the.* The selection of *this*—the phonologically correspondent form to neuter nominative and accusative *þis* of Old English—probably does not represent specifically the selection of the neuter specifier-pronominal as much as it represents a reduction of the entire set of forms to the base–element /þ—s/ and a phonological selection of /–i–/ as the unstressed vowel; this front vowel accommodated the consonant articulatory features of the generalized form. In both singular and plural the specifiers-pronominals had not been so restricted in their occurrence as had been the determiners-pronominals: the former had commonly occurred as pronominals, as illustrated in groups *(b)* and *(c)* in 13.2. Like other sets of forms, they generalized case and gender forms, but still kept the most extensively used of all the distinctions in English morphology, that of singular vs. plural. As forms standing alone as sentence subjects, specifier-pronominals conformed to the "sentence–slot" requirements of distinguishing singular and plural in concord with verbs. As pronominals with number-distinguished referents, they also kept number distinctions.

The plural form *þēs(e)* in Middle English from which Modern English *these* derives directly, arose in the Midlands; its source has been variously explained but may be finally irrecoverable. It is not a phonological descendant form of the earlier nominative–accusative plural *þās,* and the nature of language systemic change for singular forms such as *þēs, þēos* (which could produce *þēs(e)* by phonological change) makes unlikely the reassignment to plural designation. The earlier plural *þās* had become partially associated with the emerging *þat* 'that' as its plural. Pending the discovery of fuller historical evidence, we can only construct tentative explanation. The general collapse of the gender and case inflections among these and the related sets of forms tended to leave only the base element intact—/þ–/ for the determiners-pronominals, /þ—s-/ for the specifiers-pronominals. Number inflection could be made from the residual segments in only two ways: contrast of vowel or addition of suffix. (These were the only two ways of creating number distinction in accordance with existing number distinction devices in English.) The Midlands form *þēs* and other dialectal forms *þǖs* and *þō̄s* represent the first of these ways. Later forms *þēse, þise, þǖse, þō̄se* also developed, the final *–e* being a plural inflectional suffix on the analogy of the plural suffix then in use with adjectives. Another plural form in northern dialects, *þir(e) – þeir(e),* etc. was probably adapted from a related Scandinavian form. By the time *þēs(e)* had spread widely among the dialects, the loss of final unstressed /–ə/ was well under way and the dominance of Midlands dialects was increasing sufficiently to make survival of other forms as the general plural unlikely. Whatever may have brought *these* in as the regular plural counterpart to *this,* probably the most significant aspect of the entire history of this set of forms is this: in all dialects, the systemic change was identical—loss of gender and case distinctions within the set, but retention of number distinction.

With respect to *that – those,* the history has a different beginning, but the final stages are much like those for *this – these.* We have already seen the principal stages in development of a separate set in which *þat* (= *that*) came into opposition with emerging *þe* (= *the*) and the existing *þ—s* (> *this – these*): phonologically contrasting forms *þe* and *þat* were assigned different functions so that the earlier determiners-pronominals split into two sets. The *þe*-set, becoming essentially the determiner—"definite article"—that it is in Modern English, no longer had pronominal function and soon lost singular-plural contrasting forms; it was reduced to a set consisting of one member only. The *þat*–set, retaining a demonstrative function as well as a pronominal function (reinforced by an earlier relative form *þæt(te)),* required singular-plural distinction of forms in so far as it remained consistent with the number-distinguishing contrasts of nouns, pronouns, and pronominals other than the indefinite ones. At early stages the plural remained *þā* or its equivalent through phonological (and spelling) change—hence *þā, þō, thō;* their descendants did not die out in some dialects. Another form *þōs* also developed as plural beside singular *þat.* Apparently this development was in part a reassignment of the specifier-pronominal plural *þās – þōs,* having already a plural designation and a termination in /—s/; this termination by that time was becoming general as the plural inflection for nouns. In the principal dialects *þōs* supplanted *þō* by the middle of the sixteenth century. Again, the systemic results of change were identical, whatever the particular forms utilized to make up the set.

THE INDEFINITE ARTICLE

13.6 The indefinite article *a – an* also belongs to the set of forms including *the, that, this*—a set defined by the structure of noun phrases. The ancestral form in Old English was a cardinal numeral with the base form *ān* 'one.' To the base were added inflectional suffixes of the set used also for adjectives; these suffixes signified distinctions of grammatical gender, case, and number. The principal adjectival inflectional forms are worth listing at this point.

Singular

	Masculine	Feminine	Neuter
Nominative	ān	ān	ān
Genitive	ānes	ānre	ānes
Dative	ānum	ānre	ānum
Accusative	ānne, ǣnne	ānne	ān

Plural

	Masculine	Feminine	Neuter
Nominative	ānne	ānne, –a	ān
Genitive	ānra	ānra	ānra
Dative	ānum	ānum	ānum
Accusative	ānne	ānne, –a	ān

(Also, the form *āna* was used adverbially in the sense 'alone.') We shall entirely anticipate the history of adjective and noun inflections by simply stating that all adjective inflections ultimately fell into disuse by late Middle English and that in early Middle English *–s* plurals of nouns were well established. Thus, the numeral occurs in Modern English as adjectival *one* without inflection and with plural *ones* as a noun (*the machine failed to print the* ones *correctly*). Other usages from Old English to the present include nominalization, as in *ēower ān* 'one of you' or *se ān þe* 'the one who'; despite the semantic restrictions in terms of numbers, the form has also been used throughout the history of English with plural inflection, falling somewhere between pronominal and nominal status: *ānra ġehwylċe* 'each of the ones.'

The development of *a – an* may be symbolized by the contrast between *the one person I know who . . .* and *a person I know who. . . .* Though earlier serving as numeral forms, *a – an* belong to the same syntactically defined class as *the*. In terms of loss of inflections the history of the single base form (with two allomorphs *a – an*) closely resembles the history of *the*: only the base form remains. In terms of other attendant factors its history is different. The base form had at the outset an individualizing function by virtue of the central semantic association with numerical 'one.' The form *sum* had a partially similar function that may be indicated by translation as '(a) certain (one – ones).' The *ān* forms for some reason became more frequent than *sum* forms in this function by late Old English. Perhaps as important as any factor was the difference in distribution of these forms, accompanied by differences in degrees of stress with which they occurred. We have already cited as typical *se ān (þe)* 'the one (who),' in which *ān* would have had stress equal to that of an ordinary noun in a noun phrase; under these circumstances the form developed as *one*. Also common had been the phrase structure in which *ān* occurred without the preceding determiner-pronominal, as in *ān bōc* 'a book' or 'one book,' according to the probabilities defined by the context and the emphasis of *ān*. As a form with which numerical count could be expressed, *ān* would presumably have kept the prominence of stress and distinctness (as a numeral) with which other numerals were uttered in identically structured phrases. As a form also with individualizing function, it would presumably have drifted to the same stress and distinctness (in this instance "indistinctness" is a more appropriate term) of functionally similar *þe* 'the' and the like. By the time the case and gender inflections were leveled to Ø (and number categories were semantically incompatible with the form in its individualizing function), difference in degree of stress and correlative length of vowel was the one available means to signal explicitly whether enumerative or individualizing function was intended. Under these circumstances the base form split phonemically, producing the prototypes of Modern English *a* – *an* and *one(s)*. The differentiation of *a* and *an* was a phonological one, similar in part to that by which *thy* – *thine* and *my* – *mine* originally split (see 12.6). It is not adequate to say that *ān* lost stress and inflections and resulted in /ə ∼ ən ∼ n̩ ∼ æn/: its split of form probably derives essentially (though not entirely) from the shift of one of its typical occurrences to the position and stress of the emerging definite article. With those features of position and stress, it developed as the indefinite article.

A brief postscript is in order to emphasize that our concern here is principally with morphological history. Another function of the indefinite article was not clearly established at the time *a* – *an* developed as a new morphological set—the generalizing function illustrated in *A man has to be always on the alert.* Distribution and frequency of the indefinite article have not been considered in their own right, for these matters belong to the area of syntax.

Chapter 14

HISTORY OF ADJECTIVE MORPHOLOGY

USE OF THE NOTATION –∅

14.1 In respect to morphology, much of the history of adjectives in English follows the same course and nearly the same chronology as that of the forms we have already examined. The processes for adjectives may seem simpler because when the inflectional suffixes are abstracted from early adjective words, the base of root element still appears to be a word; however, little difference exists between the morphemic analysis of /þ–/ or /þ—s–/ plus their inflections and that of /dēad–/ 'dead' plus its inflections.

If Modern English adjectives were said to have inflection, it would be necessary to say simply that any and all inflections are –∅, that is, empty, or not overt. ("Compared" forms such as *sorrier – sorriest, bigger – biggest, better – best* will be taken up separately, with the affixed typical forms *–er* and *–est* analyzed as something other than inflectional morphemes.) From the vantage point of Modern English and with the purpose only of describing the morphology of adjectives, the attribution of –∅ inflection(s) is pointless. Nothing except good linguistic sense prevents us from construing *dead* in *Antonio wished to see him dead* as having masculine –∅, objective –∅, singular –∅. English adjectives have never had three successive inflectional suffixes, but the notation –∅ will have two useful functions in working through the history of adjective morphology. One will be in representing a change consisting of the disuse of an inflectional suffix form, as in *–e* > –∅. The other will be to mark the absence of an overt form within a paradigmatic set in which overt forms appear in some but not all categories, as in *god–e* vs. *god–∅*. By these means we can avoid the misleading metaphors based on paradigmatic lists, such as 'Old English dative plural adjective added *–um* to the nominative masculine singlar form.'

OLD ENGLISH ADJECTIVES

14.2 In the period of Old English, adjectives were inflected for the same categories as were the pronominals—case, (grammatical) gender, and number. Case inflections were selected by syntactic factors that most commonly included concord with a noun with which the adjective was related, either attributively or predicatively; in nominal use of an adjective form, syntax alone selected case inflection: *būton hē ġebinde ǣrest þone strangan* 'unless he first bind up the strong (one – man). Number inflections were selected similarly, except that in nominal use the number category was semantically based: *Læt þā dēade byrigan hyra dēadan* 'Let the dead [plural] bury their dead.' Gender inflections were selected in most occurrences by the grammatical gender of the syntactically related noun—the adjective was inflected in concord with the noun. Adjectives were like the pronominals in that a base form cannot be said to "belong to" or "have" a grammatical gender in the sense that Old English nouns can be said to "belong to" or "have" a grammatical gender. In addition, the three grammatical categories for adjective inflections were manifest in either of two sets of inflectional forms. In this respect the morphological class of adjectives is altogether unlike the forms we have thus far observed and also unlike the nouns, which we shall observe in Chapter 15. Choice between the alternate systems of inflections was obligatory and based primarily on syntactic factors. The most frequent and representative structure in which selection was made from the "weak" or "definite" set of inflections consisted of a determiner or specifier form preceding the adjective: to the examples given at the beginning of this paragraph may be added *þæs gōdan gōdnes* 'the goodness of the good' and *on þissum lǣnan līfe* 'in this transitory life.' Selection from the "strong" or "indefinite" set typically accompanied lack of a determiner or specifier (or genitive-inflected pronoun) before the adjective. The contrast between the two sets is illustrated in the following quotation, as will be clear from the occurrence of determiner forms and from the listing of inflectional suffixes given below.

> . . . ǣlċ gōd trēow byrþ gōde wæstmas ond ǣlċ yfel trēow byrþ yfele wæstmas. Ne mæġ þæt gōde trēow beran yfele wæstmas, ne þæt yfele trēow gōde wæstmas. Ǣlċ trēow þe ne byrþ gōdne wæstm, sȳ hit forcorfen. . . .
>
> '. . . each good tree bears good fruits and each bad [*or* evil] tree bears evil fruits. The good tree may not bear evil fruits, nor may the bad tree bear good fruits. Each tree which does not bear good fruit, it is cut down. . . .'

Some differences existed between the inflections for different classes of adjectives—each adjective, ordinarily, belonging to only one class—but these differences have little relevance to the principal processes by which adjective morphology evolved in English. The listing here is representative of Old English adjective inflections of the indefinite and definite paradigmatic sets.

Indefinite:

	Singular		
	Masculine	Feminine	Neuter
Nominative	blind–Ø	blind–Ø	blind–Ø
Genitive	blind–es	blind–re	blind–es
Dative	blind–um	blind–re	blind–um
Accusative	blind–ne	blind-e	blind–Ø
(Instrumental)	blind–e		blind–e
	Plural		
Nominative	blind–e	blind–e, –a	blind–Ø
Genitive		blind–ra (all genders)	
Dative		blind–um (all genders)	
Accusative	blind–e	blind–e, –a	blind–Ø

Definite:

	Singular			Plural
	Masculine	Feminine	Neuter	No gender distinction
Nominative	blind–a	blind–e	blind–e	blind–an
Genitive		blind–an (all genders)		blind–ra, –ena
Dative		blind–an (all genders)		blind–um
Accusative	blind-an	blind–an	blind–e	blind–an

The inflectional elements of the adjectives inflected with the indefinite set of forms closely resemble the corresponding elements we have already reviewed for /þ—s–/; they also resemble the inflections of the numerically predominant classes of nouns, as may be seen by referring to the listings in Chapter 15. The set of definite inflections are unlike any we have dealt with thus far, but are very much like those of "weak" or "*n*–stem" nouns.

EVOLUTION OF ADJECTIVE MORPHOLOGY

14.3 The history of adjective morphology is much like the history of Modern English *the* in that the changes by which case, number, and gender inflections were replaced by –Ø are not simply attributable to phonological change. Very early adjective inflections were subject to the same trends of phonological change as were the sounds in unstressed syllables of other kinds. The vowels in the inflections, being unstressed (or, under weak stress) neutralized to /ə/; a final /–m/ was often replaced by /–n/. These changes would obviously bring about still further segmental identity among inflections, especially those of the definite set. However, with the number of identical inflections in the stage of English represented in the listing of forms, the distinctions were regularly kept. After the sound changes during the transition between the periods of Old and Middle English still more forms were homophonous so that one would expect from the set of forms considered by itself, that the development would have taken a different course than the one that did come about. Rather than the loss of adjective inflection, the extension of *–en* /ən/ (< *–an*) to all or most of the intersecting categories would seem to be more probable; the result would then have been a common inflection signifying "definite" (or "weak") in syntactic terms in opposition to the set of "indefinite" (or "strong") inflections.

Furthermore, for the indefinite set listed above, phonological changes simply will not account for the loss of the forms. The *–es* inflection, for example, is phonologically identical to the *–es* genitive inflection of a class of nouns that not only was retained, but was also generalized for other classes of nouns. It is not probable, therefore, that the loss of adjective inflection can be attributed either to simple phonological change or to "confusion" resulting from changes produced by phonological change. We must look to other factors to account for this major aspect of the morphological history of English adjectives.

Adjectives had closely defined characteristics of occurrence. Within noun phrase constructions they preceded the noun and in turn were preceded by a determinative or specifying form (if any). Occasionally, one of two paired adjectives occurred following the noun, always immediately and linked by a coordinate conjunction. A predicative occurrence was signaled by position in relation to one of a small class of verbs serving as the predicate of the clause. Word order and syntactic boundary markers (described in a later chapter) together with lexical context were sufficient to define an adjective and its place in the structure of the utterance in which it occurred; with these structural signals the grammatical signals of the inflections were redundant. As to why adjective inflections began to change radically when they did is not easily answered. The general simultaneity of the major changes in determiners-pronominals, specifier-pronominals, the "indefinite article," and the adjectives, however, should repay serious study. The main point about the loss of adjective inflection is that it appears to have been the abandonment and *not* the decay—phonological or otherwise—of a set of grammatical inflections that were redundant.

A subordinate segment of the history of these inflectional forms is that of the early Middle English intermediary stage between distinctive forms for gender, case, and number and the total replacement of the forms by –Ø. The middle stage is again much like that of the forms considered in the preceding chapter. From the pattern of syllabic suffix inflection that was generally operative in English there emerged a contrast of –Ø vs. *–e* /–ə/—a contrast that is about as minimal as the English phonological system may have. The contrast was overt only with the adjective morphemes of one syllable terminated with a consonant (and a very few other morphemes). The contrast was utilized in the following way. In constructions that continued the Old English selection of the definite set of inflections, singular and plural were distinguished as –Ø and *–e,* respectively. For "indefinite constructions" both singular and plural markers were identical, as *–e.* In tabular form:

	Indefinite:	Definite:
Singular	god, strong	gode, stronge
Plural	gode, stronge	gode, stronge

Any distinction made within a set is for number categories of singular and plural. It will be recalled that the evolution of *the* included a similar stage, and that the evolution of *that – those* and *this – these* stopped at the same stage. By late Middle English the minimal set of inflectional forms disappeared in the merger of *–e* with Ø, and no further systemic change of adjective inflection has occurred.

COMPARISON OF ADJECTIVES

14.4 The topic of comparison of adjectives is both different from and related to morphology and derivation, but it is most conveniently taken up at this point. Clearly, the signification of *–(e)r* and *–(e)st* in *larger* and *largest* is not like any of the kinds represented in the grammatical inflections already listed, nor do these forms constitute a set at all resembling others. A particularly important point from the standpoint of Modern English, is that the presence or absence of either of these affixed forms does not give—by "derivation"—a different part of speech: *large, larger, largest* are all adjectives, without grammatical differentiation. Because the affixed forms are used only for comparison they may be called "comparative morphemes," but their further characteristics are most easily explicated by their history.

In preceding sections we have discussed only uncompared adjectives (usually called, unfortunately, adjectives in the "positive" degree). We have seen that their history in respect to morphology is the loss of all inflectional variations. Forms such as *larger* and *largest* also have no inflections in Modern English. In Old English adjective forms in the "comparative" and "superlative" degree had the same suffix inflections for case, number, and gender as did the uncompared forms. The only important restriction was that the "definite" set was used exclusively with comparative degree forms. The inflectional suffixes were affixed in their usual, final position; the comparative morphemes were affixed to the adjective base form. Representative instances are the following:

(a) Se eorl wæs æðele. 'The earl was noble.'
(b) of æðele ġebyrde. 'of noble birth – lineage.'
(c) on mōde æðelra þonne on ġebyrdum. 'in mind nobler than in birth.'
(d) of ðām æðelestan cynne. 'of the noblest race.'

Despite the persistent formulations that state, for example, that the comparative adjective in Old English is formed by "adding" *–ra* to the positive degree (i.e., those forms with *–Ø* inflection), it is obvious that *æðelra* in *(c)* consists of a grammatical inflection *–a,* an adjective base *æðel–*, and a comparative morpheme represented here as *–r–*. Similarly, *æðelestan* in *(d)* may be cut into three morphemes to include *–est–* as the representation of the morpheme of superlative degree. Nearly all adjectives of Old English conform to the pattern explicated here. Explication of the contrasts inherent in structure of adjective words may be served by representing the combinations of forms thus:

	Morphemes					Adjective
	Base		Comparative		Grammatical	Words
Uncompared	æðel(e)	+	–Ø–	+	{ Ø, es, re, an, etc.; a, e, an, etc.	æðele, etc.

Comparative	æðel(e)	+	–r–	+	a, e, an, etc.	æðelra, etc.
Superlative	æðel(e)	+	–est–	+	{Ø, es, re, an, etc.; a, e, an, etc.}	æðelesta, etc.

Some qualification must be added. The vowel of the superlative morpheme varies in accordance with a number of factors, though none of them affects the subsequent course of development. For more precise formulation, using *V* to stand for any vowel, the superlative form can be represented /–Vst–/. In some forms the vowel had already been lost, as in *strengsta* 'strongest.' And as we may expect in any stage of the language there are "irregular" comparisons or, more technically, forms in suppletive relation. The inventory of these forms has remained remarkably constant, the irregular sets in Old English consisting of these four (listed with typical spellings in nominative singular masculine inflection):

Uncompared	Comparative	Superlative
miċel 'much, great'	māra 'more'	mǣst 'most'
gōd 'good'	bettra, sēlra } 'better'	betst, sēlest } 'best'
yfel 'evil, bad'	wiersa 'worse'	wierrest 'worst'
lȳtel 'little'	lǣssa 'less'	lǣst 'least'

Middle English had the same inventory:

muchel, mikel	mōre	mēst, mōst
gōd	better	best
ēvel, ill, badde	werse	werst
litel, līte	lesse, lasse	lēst(e)

A few irregularities resulted from a phonological change (called "i-umlaut") in early Old English; the change affected the stressed vowel of the base morpheme in adjectives having a particular phonemic makeup of the comparative and superlative morphemes, producing sets typified by these examples:

Uncompared	Comparative	Superlative
eald 'old'	ieldra 'elder, older'	ieldest 'eldest, oldest'
lang 'long'	lengra 'longer'	lengest 'longest'.

These two examples imply the subsequent history of the "mutation" comparisons. Analogical reformation has generally restored the regularity of a single base form, as in the case of *lang* 'long.' Nothing perhaps shows more clearly the systemic independence of morphemes in their historical development than reformations of this kind. With the compared forms of *eald* 'old' a reformation also occurred; the "mutation" forms have also survived, however, chiefly in attributive function in stereotyped constructions—*the older brother, the eldest son*—or in specialized meanings, as *an elder of the church.*

A small number of exceptions or irregularities, particularly those that occur with words of specially high frequency or in stereotyped constructions of specialized contexts, do not lessen the significance of the systemic pattern of adjectives either in descriptions of morphology or in pattern of development. Throughout its history, English adjective comparison has hardly changed at all in terms of its morphology, since all one-word comparisons still make use of /–r–/ and /–Vst–/; only phonological adjustments have occurred with these morphemes. The loss of morphemes of grammatical inflections, it should be clear, was entirely independent of the history of comparative morphemes. The mode of marking comparison, however, changed greatly. In Old English adjectives of all kinds, no matter how many syllables in their base element, were compared in the way illustrated above; in Modern English periphrastic marking of comparison is the rule for all but a limited set of forms—that is, comparison marked by *more* and *most* in conjunction with the base element. The morphemes *–(e)r, –(e)st* affixed to the base have been replaced except with one-syllable base forms and a small list of other adjectives: *loud – louder – loudest,* and the like; and two-syllable bases, typically those ending in *–y* such as *lucky – luckier – luckiest.* Phrasal comparison such as *more anxious, more complete, most desirable, most fitting* continues the comparative marking with /–r–/ and /–Vst–/ even though the construction is radically modified. The comparative signals occur in the separate words *more, most* in free forms rather than in bound forms and occur in advance of the adjective (base) rather than as a postposed affix to the base. These observations bring us through the intergrading between morphology and syntax. The morphemic material of adjective comparison has changed but little, while the syntactic aspects of comparison are still in noticeable historical transition.

Chapter 15

HISTORY OF NOUN MORPHOLOGY

DIFFERENCES OF NOUNS FROM OTHER FORMS

15.1 Nouns make up the remaining class of forms that fill or partially fill what we have loosely called the nounlike slots of sentences. As would be expected nouns are similar in some respects throughout their history to the other forms we have been considering; their similarity during the evolution of English implies that their morphological history will be similar to that of the other forms, too. Conversely, differences at any time and through historical time are to be expected as well.

The similarities of nouns to the other forms are implied by their syntactic characteristics: nouns, pronouns, or indefinite pronominals are the classes of forms that typically occur as subjects or objects of predicates or as objects of prepositions. In the earlier history of English some major classes of nouns were also similar to the other forms in terms of the inflectional morphemes with which they occurred.

The differences from pronouns, pronominals, and adjectives (and, in Modern English, the definite and indefinite articles) are perhaps best indicated by the nature of the classes each set of forms constitutes. Pronouns, for example, make up a very limited set of forms. Except for additional forms to distinguish, say, feminine possessive and objective cases or to restore number and case distinctions to the second person set of forms, addition or deletion with respect to the set would reconstitute the system. As the system now exists there are contrasts of two numbers and three persons, each with its case inflections; the persistent pattern throughout the history of English clarifies the primacy of person distinctions: none of the changes in pronouns have modified the three-person system. Furthermore, the signification of each of the person-sets is defined in relation to the rest of the set which in turn is a map of the prominent aspects of any speech context—the speaker, the addressee, or the "other"; singularity or nonsingularity, of course, is stipulated for any of these (except Modern Standard usage for second person forms). Unlike the pronouns are the nouns of English. They make up a very large set. Additions to or deletions from the set do not reconstitute the system in any significant way. The crucial difference, already implied, is that the signification of any noun is not exactly defined relationally in respect to all other nouns. Let us phrase this in nontechnical terms appropriate to characterizing a natural language. The universe of speaking can be dissected and accounted for fully in a simple way—the person speaking, the one to whom he speaks, and someone else neither speaking nor being addressed. In so far as it is "mapped" by nouns, the universe of experience is not that simply dissected, and many aspects of that universe may not—in the practical business of using language—be related to other aspects. Each word has an associative, explicit relationship to others in many subsets of nouns: *father, mother, brother, sister*; *king* and *queen*; *air, water, earth*; *heaven* and *hell; hero* and *coward*; *iron, silver, gold, aluminum, chromium,* etc. Such nouns as *radish, kindness, diversity, elephant, fuselage, asteroid, warmth,* etc. do not in any persisting way form subsets—that is, the meaning of any one is not related practically to the meaning of any of the others. The pronouns, in short, constitute a closed system, while the nouns constitute an open system.

Other differences of nouns and forms examined in the preceding chapters include the following. The designations of pronouns and pronominals are defined contextually in terms of the utterances in which they occur or in terms of the circumstances of speaking. On distributional grounds, *a – an, the, this – these, that – those* and possessive pronouns form a set different from nouns. Although adjectives no longer have grammatical inflections, nouns still have number and case inflection. The /wh–/ structure of nouns, such as *whelp* or *whistle,* is not used to signal interrogative utterance, as in /wh–/ of *what* and *who* (as well as *where, when,* etc.) .

These reasons imply certain expectations about the history of noun morphology in relation to the morphological history of other forms. The pronouns and all but the indefinite pronominals now formally distinguish singular and plural; before ceasing to function pronominally, what have been called the determinative-pronominals also had formal distinction for the two number categories. All the forms, including adjectives, had at one time a set of inflectional forms for four grammatical cases (or five, partially complete for a few sets) . For all except the first and second person pronouns, which were different in referential and formal ways already examined, the other forms had inflectional sets that distinguished gender, on one basis or another. If the nouns of Old English had grammatical inflections, a plausible inference would be that the inflections marked two numbers, four (or five) cases, and three genders. The syntactic grounds for distinction between the definite and indefinite sets of adjective inflections do not offer a basis for confidence in inferring similar sets of inflections for nouns, although they do not rule out the possibility of similar sets serving some distinguishing purpose. If these inferences are accurate, we should expect that the history of noun morphology may have followed a course and a chronology similar to the history of the other forms. Let us turn back to the morphology of Old English nouns and follow the history through to Modern English.

OLD ENGLISH NOUNS

15.2 The nouns of Old English constitute several more classes than those of Modern English when they are grouped according to the sets of inflectional morphemes with which they occur. Most of the classes are much larger in Old English. The largest single class may be represented by the paradigm for *cyning* 'king.' In terms of number of items in the lexicon, this class accounts for slightly more than one-third of the nouns of Old English. About one-tenth of the nouns belong to a class represented by *nama* 'name'; this is the ancestral class of the *–(e)n* plural class of Modern English, to which belongs only one member *ox – oxen.* The two paradigms are listed here side by side.

	Singular		Plural	
Nominative	cyning–Ø	nama–Ø	cyning–as	nam–an
Genitive	cyning–es	nam–an	cyning–a	nam–ena
Dative	cyning–e	nam–an	cyning–um	nam–um
Accusative	cyning–Ø	nam–an	cyning–as	nam–an

Lack of similarity between the sets of inflectional morphemes of these two classes fully distinguishes them and offers no grounds for linking the classes in any significant way. Still other classes, based on paradigmatic grouping, consist of a rather small proportion of the inventory of nouns; each class, however, contains words that occur with considerable frequency. Four of them are represented here by *sunu* 'son,' *rīdend* 'rider,' *fōt* 'foot,' and *lēode* 'people.'

	Singular				Plural			
Nominative	sunu	rīdend	fōt	lēode	suna	rīdend	fēt	lēode
Genitive	suna	rīdendes	fōtes	lēodes	suna	rīdendra	fōta	lēoda
Dative	suna	rīdende	fēt	lēode	sunum	rīdendum	fōtum	lēodum
Accusative	sunu	rīdend	fōt	lēode	suna	rīdend	fēt	lēode

Some partial similarities are to be found here, particularly in the *–es* genitive inflections for *cyning–, rīdend–, fōt–,* and *lēode–,* and all the classes here represented have dative plural *–um* inflection. Even so, on the basis of these sets of inflections no way of grouping these classes into one larger form class is apparent.

All the classes represented so far do have a common characteristic, nevertheless, on the basis of which they are all assigned to a single class. They do not require the occurrence of a determiner-pronominal or other form in the same phrase in which they occur; but if another such form does occur, it will always belong to one specific grammatical gender; or, if it is linked with one of the forms used pronominally, the pronominal form will always be selected from a specific grammatical gender. For example, *cyning, sunu, fōt* always occur as singular subjects; and if accompanied by a determinative, that form will always be *se* and will never be *sēo* or *þæt.* Because *se* is labeled "masculine" for reasons we have taken up earlier, all the classes of nouns selecting masculine forms are also called "masculine." The following citation provides good illustration of the patterning: *þe-læs hē þē sylle þām dēman and se dēma þām bydele ond se bydel þē sende on cwertern* 'lest he give you (over) to the judge and the judge (give you over) to the beadle [that is, warrant officer] and the beadle send you to prison.' To assign these various morphological classes to a single larger class "masculine" is to set up a selective category; at the same time, the sets of inflections contain no common element to which any label can be assigned.

Other morphologically defined classes of nouns belong to the selective category "feminine." They are typified by the following paradigms of *fæhðu* 'strife,' *dǣd* 'deed,' *dohtor* 'daughter,' *bōc* 'book,' *heorte* 'heart.'

Singular

Nominative	(sēo)	fæhðu	dǣd	dohtor	bōc	heorte
Genitive	(þǣre)	fæhðe	dǣde	dohtor	bōce	heortan
Dative	(þǣre)	fæhðe	dǣde	dehter	bēċ	heortan
Accusative	(þā)	fæhðe	dǣde	dohtor	bōc	heortan

Plural

Nominative	(þā)	fæhða	dǣde	dohtor	bēċ	heortan
Genitive	(þāra)	fæhða	dǣda	dohtra	bōca	heortena

Dative	(þǣm)	fæhðum	dǣdum	dohtrum	bōcum	heortum
Accusative	(þā)	fæhða	dǣde	dohtor	bēċ	heortan

The remaining classes belong to the selective category "neuter"; they are illustrated with paradigms of *land* 'land,' *rīċe* 'kingdom,' *ēaġe* 'eye,' *ǣġ* 'egg.'

		Singular			
Nominative	(þæt)	land	rīċe	ēaġe	ǣġ
Genitive	(þæs)	landes	rīċes	ēagan	ǣġes
Dative	(þǣm)	lande	rīċe	ēagan	ǣġe
Accusative	(þæt)	land	rīċe	ēaġe	ǣġ
		Plural			
Nominative	(þā)	land	rīcu	ēagan	ǣgru
Genitive	(þāra)	landa	rīca	ēagena	ǣgra
Dative	(þǣm)	landum	ricum	ēagum	ǣgrum
Accusative	(þā)	land	rīcu	ēagan	ǣgru

The selective categories of "feminine" and "neuter" nouns are much like the "masculine" category in having one class dominant in number of constituent items. About one-fourth of Old English nouns belong to the feminine class(es) represented here by *fæhðu* and *dǣd,* and a limited number belong to each of the other classes. About one-fourth of the nouns belong to the neuter class(es) represented here by *land* and *rīċe*; there are very few nouns within the other neuter classes.

GRAMMATICAL GENDER OF NOUNS

15.3 With the noun classes before us, the distinction between "sex gender" and "grammatical gender" should be made once more. At no stage of English is gender distinction made for the first and second person pronouns, for such distinction is redundant. (Redundancy does not, however, preclude such distinction in any language.) With the forms we have called indefinite pronominals, *hwā* > *who, hwæt* > *what,* etc., gender distinction is inherently impractical and English has always had only personal vs. nonpersonal contrasts for these forms. The third person singular pronouns are distinguished as three gender classes, with the distinction associated with the sex of the person immediately referred to by a form or with the nondesignation of the sex of the person (or thing) referred to by the form. The determiners-pronominals and specifiers-pronominals of Old English were distributionally distinct from the pronouns; instead of having immediate referents or reference to persons named, their referents were nouns whenever they functioned pronominally. Resemblance between them and the third person pronoun forms in terms of phonological and systemic features was the basis for labeling them with the gender terms of pronouns. Because they are selected by nouns, the only way in which categories of sex distinctions suggested by the gender names could be appropriate would be the attribution of sex-distinguished characteristics to all things designated by nouns. That state of affairs has never existed in the use of English. A number of "masculine" nouns did in fact refer to males: *se man* 'the man,' *ðeġn* 'thane, (male) servant, freeman,' *cyning* 'king,' *cniht* '(> knight) boy, youth,' *cocc* 'cock, male bird,' and so on. Many "feminine" and "neuter" nouns designated female and non-sex-distinguished referents, respectively. More terms than not, however, were anomalous rather than significatory with respect to sex gender of their referents, as may be expected when the range of things designated by nouns is considered. As a matter of historical fact, the large classes of nouns in Old English belonged to one "gender" class or another on the basis of the type of phonological shape of the base form they had and had had long since. Only pronouns had "natural" gender in their association with referents; nouns belonged to selective categories and their pronominal substitutes or determinative or specifying attributives and adjectives formally resembled the pronouns: nouns had distributional characteristics such that "grammatical" in the term "grammatical gender" in effect cancels any significance of sex distinction in the gender label of the three selective categories.

The preceding paragraph may seem to be a laboring of the obvious, but the importance of making clear the nature of grammatical gender cannot be overemphasized. The nature of certain changes in the morphology of nouns of English will be properly understood only if the types of gender and their bases are fully distinguished.

INFLECTIONAL MORPHEMES OF NOUNS

15.4 If we may set aside the selective attributes of the nouns of Old English and return to the sets of inflectional morphemes, another feature of Old English nouns can be explicated. This feature is essential to comprehension of changes that have transformed the morphology of nouns for tenth century speakers of English into that for twentieth century speakers. For any of the morphological classes of nouns, the inflections signal both case and number. While both grammatical categories are represented in any inflectional suffix, they are not represented separately. To use a technical term, the inflections are syncretic. Some illustration may prove helpful. The inflections for the major class of masculine nouns, given above with the base form *cyning–*, are abstracted here:

	Singular	Plural
Nominative	–Ø	–as
Genitive	–es	–a
Dative	–e	–um
Accusative	–Ø	–as

If case and number were separately represented, there should be some way to stipulate which phonemic material manifests the plural morpheme, which manifests "dative," and so on. Provisionally we might stipulate "back vowel"—*a, u,* in this set—as "plural" in contrast to nonback vowel—*e* (and Ø)—as "singular." Case is clearly not represented in both singular and plural by any common element, however, and we can hardly set up even provisional number morphemes for other sets of noun inflections. Certainly there is no basis for asserting that the various sets of inflectional suffixes of nouns systematically represent a case inflection and a number inflection in sequence. Consequently it may be predicted that if significant changes should occur in noun inflection, a general pattern of change will not be simply the loss or modification of one or the other of the inflectional categories of number and case.

From these considerations still another explication may follow. The concept of grammatical case has to do with either morphological or syntactic features of a nominal element or with both these features. Case has reference to nothing outside the utterances of a language; nothing in a speaker's nonlinguistic experience differs, for example, when the forms *he* and *him* are used, nor for speakers of Old English, was there presumably any difference when *cyning* and *cyninge* were used. The same person is referred to by either pronoun form or by either noun form, and no difference with respect to that person is represented by nominative vs. dative–objective inflection affixed to the pronoun or noun. If the term "meaning" is used to refer to the association by the speaker of morphemic material in an inflection with something in the utterance—something in exclusively linguistic experience—the meaning for convenience is stipulated as a specifically grammatical meaning. For the morpheme *cyning–* the meaning is an association between the speech form and a person with specifiable social attributes; a kind of meaning inhering in the association of a linguistic form with some aspects of a speaker's nonlinguistic experience may then be termed referential meaning. The base morpheme of *cyning–e* is said to have referential meaning, and the grammatical case "dative" of the inflection is said to have grammatical meaning.

The categories of number in English inflections may have both grammatical and referential meaning. Plural inflection with a noun in the subject function of a sentence is associated with a plural inflection of the finite verb form in the same clause; in Modern English this pattern of association is regularly distinct only with forms of the verb *(to) be: Antonio's followers were eager for him to return.* A plural inflected noun is referred to by a plural pronoun form: *Antonio's followers. . . . They.* A plural noun selects a plural determinative or specifying form: *These followers, . . . those opponents.* The reference of a plural inflected noun also has to do with experience of a nonlinguistic kind in so far as speakers distinguish between the one and more-than-one characteristic of the referent(s) symbolized by nouns. For nouns, pronouns, and pronominals of English, number categories of the forms have both kinds of meaning.

EVOLUTION OF NOUN MORPHOLOGY

15.5 The evolution of noun morphology from that of Old English to that which is operative in Modern English was essentially completed in the period of Middle English. In some dialects it had been completed in the twelfth century, and perhaps earlier, though the paucity of records makes exact determination difficult. Nouns in Modern English have inflectional sets distinguishing two numbers, singular and plural, and two cases, commonly called nominative (or subject) and possessive. (Both the last two labels will be considered presently.) Typical paradigms, using ordinary spelling and the apostrophe, are these:

Singular				Plural			
boy	hat	wife	horse	boys	hats	wives	horses
boy's	hat's	wife's	horse's	boys'	hats'	wives'	horses'

Some relics of earlier inflection patterns survive—*ox* – *ox's* – *oxen* – *oxen's* (a one-member class); *child* – *child's* – *children* – *children's* (having historically a double plural); *foot* – *foot's* – *feet* – *feet's* and a few other "umlaut-plural" instances; *wife* etc. (above) and a few others with morphophonemic alternation in the base form but otherwise like the main class of nouns. Other special instances are typified by *penny,* plural *pence* (but also *pennies* in a different set of contexts). In a few special classes the number categories are represented by the inflections in the language from which the base form was borrowed into English: listing only singular and plural nonpossessive forms, *alumnus, alumni; alumna, alumnæ; basis, bases; die, dice; focus, foci; cherub, cherubim; phenomenon, phenomena,* etc. The variety of exceptions tell nothing about the principal aspects of English noun morphology and tell only a little about the history of noun morphology. These relics and borrowings tell us a great deal more about the general culture of English-speaking peoples than they do about the language and its history. We shall set them aside, therefore, as inconsequential to an accurate understanding of the major features and trends in the history of noun classes in English. We shall turn to the development of the case and number forms that define almost all English nouns as belonging to one form class characterized by two cases and two numbers, and falling into three selective gender classes based on referential meaning.

What happened in the course of change from the complex noun inflection of Old English to the relatively simple noun inflection of Modern English? Aspects of the systemic change can be enumerated easily enough. To reconstruct the principal processes is somewhat more difficult, for the exact chronology of particular changes has not been recovered in sufficient detail. Our reconstruction of the process must therefore be tentative.

Many contrasts among inflections that signified (in part) grammatical case were abandoned. Inflectional /–a/ and /–e/ were replaced by (written) *–e,* presumably /–ə/; inflectional /–as/ and /–es/ were replaced by (written) *–es,* variously /–əs –is –es/ as allomorphs; inflectional /–an/ and /–um/ were replaced by (written) *–en,* variously /–ən –in –en/; the final vowel of base forms, as in *sunu* 'son,' was replaced by /ə/ with the result that noun bases that had terminated in *e* or any other vowel came to have uniformly a terminal /ə/. Base-final /ə/ was phonemically identical to inflectional /–ə/; constituting as it did an additional syllable and having regularly only a light stress, the base-final element resembled inflectional /–ə/ and apparently came to be regarded in many instances as quasi-inflectional. This systemic anomaly was compounded by the increasing incidence of contrasts between /–ə/ and Ø, the least prominent of all contrasts in terms of English phonology: presence or absence of /–ə/—that is, the difference between /–ə/ and –Ø—came to depend in part on the phonemic shape of the base form. In all, the marking of grammatical case, especially as it was signified by the vocalic elements in inflections, was sharply reduced.

The progressive abandonment of distinctions is obviously similar to the "leveling" of adjective inflections and the reduction of the specifier-pronominal sets to two forms (singular and plural) and of the determiner-pronominal set to one form only–*the*. The abandonment of distinctions was pragmatically workable because of the redundancy of case signification in the inflections to syntactic features of word order patterns and overt signaling such as that inherent in prepositions. The relative lack of stress together with the suffix position of the inflections left open the way for phonemic change of the inflectional vowels to /ə/. The conditions of change were much like those under which case (and gender) distinctions were dropped in the abandonment of inflectional sets for the other components of noun phrases.

The abandonment of distinctions differentiating grammatical case proceeded a little less rapidly with nouns than it did with the other form classes used as constituents of noun phrases; also, it obviously did not proceed so far, since two cases remained when the sequence of changes had been completed. The end product of the changes for nouns may be viewed as something between the morphology of pronouns and that of the other forms we have considered: pronouns retained three case inflections, nouns retained two, and adjectives and the new article and demonstratives emerged with only one case form. Among the various factors contributing to retention of objective case inflection for pronouns were the nonsyllabic nature of the grammatical inflections, the high frequency of occurrence of pronouns, and the absence of formal subclasses. We have already considered the circumstances attendant to the loss of all case distinctions for adjectives and other forms. For nouns, the retention of two case forms was apparently conditioned in part by syntactic factors. The two cases retained for nouns are possessive (< genitive of Old English) and another for which various labels may be appropriate. A principal difference in function and distribution of possessive-inflected forms may be indicated by saying that they are noun-related, in some sense such as the following. A possessive-inflected noun form does not occur as subject or object of a predicate; if it occurs within a noun phrase (in any syntactic function) the possessive form is adjectival: in terms of word order, it precedes the noun that heads the phrase and in terms of meaning it is attributive. Coming as it does before a noun, it is subject to stress patterns characteristic of adjectives. The possessive inflection in the singular (though not in the plural) also serves to differentiate the syntactically adjectival characteristic of a form from the occurrence of a noun-base in a compound; there may be accompanying contrast of stress features: Modern English *the pâper's wéight* vs. *the páper-wèight.* Nouns without possessive inflection, are not noun-related in the sense just described. Thus, in terms of the surviving noun inflections for case, the categories are oriented to syntax in a simple twofold distinction of noun-related (or adjectival characteristics) vs. non-noun-related (or "normal" noun characteristics).

That three case categories were not retained for nouns, as they were for pronouns, brings up a second aspect of the evolution of noun morphology. For the dominant classes of nouns the overt inflections were syllabic; but the nominative and accusative forms for some of the classes had –Ø. Inflections signifying dative-singular, for many classes, had consisted only of a vowel and the tendency was for any vowel to be replaced by /–ə/; dative-plural inflections, for all classes, tended to be replaced by /–ən/, a form not restricted to dative-plural distribution in the inflectional sets. By and large, the phonetic prominence was slight in any of the originally nominative and accusative (and later dative) case forms. There was little from which to make—or keep—the objective case inflection operative.

At the same time, some of the inflections in the dominant classes of nouns had phonetic prominence, particularly those having the shape /–əs/ and /–ən/. The /–əs/ inflection in particular also had prominence in its recurrence in both subject and object functions in plural-inflected nouns of the largest single class of Old English nouns. This inflection had prominence in the special genitive-possessive—or noun-related—function in singular possessive-inflected nouns of the largest combination of classes of nouns, the principal masculine and neuter classes of Old English. In terms of frequency of occurrence, number of base forms to which they were affixed, phonetic distinctness, and syntactic prominence, the /–əs/ inflections would appear to have had an inherent potential of survival that the other inflections lacked.

Still another factor contributed to their survival and generalization. Noun inflections of Old English were syncretic—each inflection signaling case and number, but without distinctive phonemic components to signal these categories separately. Case signification constituted only "grammatical meaning" while number signification constituted both "grammatical meaning" and "referential meaning." Grammatical case of nouns was identified by syntactic features quite independently of inflectional features. The only category of the noun inflections that had had concord with another element of a sentence was that of number: at the least, a noun-subject and the finite verb form were both either singular or plural. Thus, the factors of both referential meaning and concord of noun (subject) with predicate would tend to preserve number in noun inflections.

We have now accounted for two principal selective factors in the changes in noun morphology. One concerns the grammatical categories likely to be lost or retained and the other concerns the inflectional materials that persisted. As the changes began, the case significance of the inflections (except for possessive) for nouns was minimized along with other components of noun phrases; number significance, however, was not minimized. At least for the major classes of nouns, the most prominent inflectional syllable was /–əs/. For the largest single class of nouns this syllable had signaled plural and either subjective or objective case. With case significance diminished and 'plural' meaning preserved, the latter meaning became predominant. With that increasing limitation of meaning and the obscuring of meaning 'plural' in other inflectional syllables, some further adjustment was required. That adjustment was achieved principally by replacement of any inflectional syllable less distinctly signaling 'plural' by the /–əs/ syllable that more distinctly signaled 'plural.' As /–əs/ replaced all other inflectional syllables for the plural set of inflections of a class of nouns, it became a new morpheme (more precisely, a dominant allomorph) signifying 'plural' only.

The evolution of *–(e)s* /–əs/ as a distinctly plural allomorph occurred earliest in the northern dialects of English, was complete in the mid-twelfth century in Midlands dialects, and was fully advanced in southern dialects by the end of the period of Middle English. One other development must be mentioned in this connection—the evolution of *–(e)n* /–ən/ as another distinctly plural morpheme (or, strictly, allomorph). Its circumstances and stages almost exactly correspond to those of /–əs/. Plural /–ən/ developed in southern dialects, where /–əs/ also developed, though /–əs/ emerged somewhat later in these dialects than in the northern ones. For social as well as linguistic reasons /–ən/ was in turn replaced by /–əs/, and since the fifteenth century English has had only one major class of nouns defined in part by the "*s*–plural."

The evolution of possessive *–(e)s* /–əs/ is enough like that of plural *–(e)s* /–əs/ that it need only be outlined. The /–əs/ morpheme was the inflection for genitive-singular of the major classes of both "masculine" and "neuter" nouns and had the same kind of syllabic and phonetic prominence. Genitive-inflected nouns had a distinct status, described above, so that genitive (> possessive) grammatical meaning would tend to persist. The singular possessive /–əs/ then would remain fixed; its homophony with the plural /–əs/ in simultaneous development precluded systemic conflict that would have developed if separate plural and possessive inflections had had to be affixed to nouns for possessive plural inflection: the system of noun suffixes contained no examples of successive morphemes for the case and number significations. Thus /–əs/ developed as a distinctly possessive-case morpheme. In systemic terms—whatever the historical sequence—it followed the number inflection: if number inflection was Ø, as in singular nouns of the two major classes, /–əs/ was in practical terms affixed to the base; if the number inflection was /–əs/, the possessive inflection was Ø, or in practical terms, case and number were syncretically manifested in the syllable /–əs/.

To this account of the evolution of noun inflections we should append a brief mention of the subsequent developments in the phonological shapes of the inflections themselves. When the new and essentially Modern morphology of nouns came into being the overt inflections—possessive and plural—normally had the phonemic shape /–əs/; they were syllabic and they terminated in /s/, and at that early time the final /s/ was always the unvoiced allophone [s]. (/z/ had not developed when /–əs/ was being generalized for the two inflections.) After /s/ split to produce the pair /s z/, the inflections tended to lose their syllabic status—that is, the unstressed /ə/ in the final syllable was syncopated, or replaced by Ø. In all circumstances in which clustering patterns of consonants in word-final positions permitted it, the sibilant then immediately followed the final consonant; phonological assimilation then selected /s/ or /z/ as the manifestation of the inflectional element. Because /z/, a relatively new phoneme, was not utilized otherwise for noun inflection, there was no systemic factor to prevent or modify the assimilation. In all circumstances in which the base form of the noun terminated in a vowel, the change /–ə/ > Ø brought the sibilant into the same syllable as the termination of the noun base form and assimilation of the consonant to vocalic articulation produced /z/ in every instance. Where clustering patterns of consonants precluded /s/ or /z/ in word-final clusters, the inflection remained syllabic; in these circumstances, however, the voiced sibilant regularly replaced the unvoiced one, that is, /–əs/ > /–əz/.

For Modern English /s z əz/ are usually distinguished as three allomorphs of the plural or possessive morphemes; the morpheme notation {–Z} is usually assigned, with the plural and possessive forms marked with subscripts, thus: { $-Z_1$ } for plural, { $-Z_2$ } for possessive. The selection of allomorphs conforms to purely phonological rules that may be schematized as follows.

/–z/ is affixed to base forms ending in voiced sounds, except for sibilants (/z ž/) and assibiliated stops (/ǰ/): it occurs following /b d g v ð m n ŋ r l/ and any vowel.

/–s/ is affixed to base forms ending in unvoiced sounds, except sibilants /s š/ and assibilated stops (/č/): it occurs with /p t k f θ/.

/–əz/ is affixed to base forms ending in /s z š ž č ǰ/.

Some nouns have alternate base forms before { $-Z_1$ } and { $-Z_2$ } inflections; the example *wife's* vs. *wives'* was mentioned earlier. The phonemic alternation of /f ∼ v/, /s ∼ z/, /θ ∼ ð/ *knife's – knives, house – houses, path – paths* will be recognized as a survival of phonetic alternation that was only allophonic before the split of /f þ s/ into /f v θ ð s z/. Less than two dozen words show this alternation in Modern English.

EMERGENCE OF A SINGLE MAJOR CLASS OF NOUNS

15.6 Several factors contributed to the emergence of a single major class of nouns. The extension of /–əs/ plural inflections from "masculine" to "neuter" major classes was relatively unhindered by speech habits in so far as the nominative and accusative neuter plural forms had had the same Ø inflections as the singular case forms; if any overt inflection were left, it was only /–ə/. The extension to neuter nouns began very early, perhaps before the major change was under way, simply as analogical extension from the largest single class of nouns. The dominance of /–əs/ genitive or possessive inflection and /–əs/ plural inflection began initially in the number of forms in the two classes and, correlatively, the frequency with which the inflections occurred. Concomitant with the development of the /–əs/ as distinctly case and as distinctly number morphemes, the specifiers-pronominals and determiners-pronominals were undergoing the changes that left no more than number distinction. Contrastive sets constituting gender categories merged with Ø. As this change occurred, nouns came no longer to have grammatical gender, since that gender attribute had been only a selective gender, for all practical purposes. The reinforcing of distinctions among noun classes by grammatical gender was thus removed. Then, with a great number of the inflections being manifest as /–ə/ and with the other drifts observed already in connection with nouns, the replacement of any other plural inflection by /–əs/ could occur unobtrusively; similarly the replacement of possessive inflections by /–əs/. Finally, the collapse of grammatical gender of nouns apparently made the generalizing of plural /–əs/ and possessive /–əs/ systemically feasible and unobtrusive—"natural" as we are wont to say. The merger of the Old English subclasses of nouns into a single major class proceeded rapidly, particularly with only Ø or vocalic inflections in most of the earlier sets in the categories in which /–əs/ was becoming established. That merger was completed during Middle English when the new system of noun inflections was employed for all but a few nouns. That only one major class existed is best reflected in the fact that all nouns added to the lexicon of English from the time of early Middle English have appeared with only the one set of inflections.

DEVELOPMENT OF "NATURAL" GENDER OF NOUNS

15.7 The evolution of noun morphology went its own way conditioned by factors we have been examining. The changes in pronominals and pronouns went their own ways as well, subject to conditionings partially apposite to nouns. During these changes in morphology, sentence construction continued to include the use of noun-substitute words. In earlier stages these words were the relative particle *þe* or the pronominals; with the latter, nouns in part derived their grammatical gender. By the time the pronominals began to lose their "gender" distinctions, the noun-substitute or noun-referring words had begun to include pronoun forms. (First and second person pronouns were not involved, of course.) Third person pronouns resembled the pronominals formally and systemically (cf. Chapter 13), and were the only set of forms available to serve as noun-referring sentence elements. Their distributional difference from the pronominals had the obvious concomitant of the difference in their meanings whereby gender forms were selected on the basis of sex characteristics of their (then) personal referents. The meaning of any of the singular forms, in other words, was in part referential. Replacement of the pronominals by the pronouns as the noun-referring forms in sentences therefore involved a matching of selective rules of pronouns based on sex characteristics of the referent to the characteristics of that which the noun represented. The matching amounted to establishing what is called simply "natural gender" of nouns, that is, any noun designating something not regarded specifically as male or female is considered "neuter" and is referred to by selection of the base *it–*, and similarly for the other gender categories. Thus, *man, boy, soldier, butler, king,* etc. are consistently referred to by masculine third person pronouns (and personal indefinites); *woman, girl, maid, spinster, queen,* etc. are referred to by feminine third person pronouns (and personal indefinites); *person, friend, classmate, assistant,* etc. are referred to by either masculine or feminine pronouns (and personal indefinites); *table, window, reason, weight, paradox, story,* etc. are referred to by *it* (and nonpersonal indefinites); and various alternates of masculine or feminine with neuter pronouns occur for such nouns as *bull, cow, baby, infant, rooster, ship,* and the like. The "gender" of nouns after the establishment of "natural" gender was still a selective category, since noun gender of Middle and Modern English consists of only a pattern of pronoun substitution. From a selective and inflectional system, noun gender had become an analytical, semantically based system.

Chapter 16

HISTORY OF VERB MORPHOLOGY

AN AGGREGATE OF SYSTEMIC SETS

16.1 The remaining major class of English words characterized by sets of inflectional morphemes is that of verbs. In the usual sentence structure, verbs make up one of the two elemental constituents of most utterances. In the last four chapters we have been studying classes that constitute or participate in the other major constituent of most utterances—pronouns and nouns and the attributive classes. Several form classes are defined by inflectional sets for the nounlike parts of sentences. Only one class of forms is identified by its morphological system in the verblike part of sentences. Throughout the history of English only the one class has been identified. Accordingly, the systemic changes in verb inflectional forms cannot be expected to show direct effects of changes in other form classes: the conditions of change will be primarily within the class, inherent in the relations of subclasses of verbs to each other.

Another general aspect of verb words throughout their history in English is that with some of the inflections the morph specifically operates as a predicative word—specifically fills the verb-slot of a sentence—while with other inflections the morph has distributional and other features resembling those of other parts of speech. The latter group of morphs includes participles that have affinities with adjectives *(The growing tree)* and gerunds (or gerundives) and infinitives that have affinities with nouns *(Leaving was sad. To come was enjoyable).*

When every difference within the sets of verb inflections is taken into account, the number of subclasses of verbs in Modern English amounts to more than fifty; about three-fifths of these classes consist of only one member each. When all the differences in the base form within a paradigm are taken into account, the number of classes based on those differences is again very large. Consequently, any formulation of verb morphology for Modern English becomes extremely complex when the differences in the forms are all subsumed under a single analytical scheme. The complexity of such formulation is much greater than that for nouns; it is also much greater than a formulation of pronouns would be if it included (as available formulations do not) all the dialectal variants. Describing English verb forms under one synchronic scheme would be impractical for our purposes. (Two principal analyses of this kind are those by Bernard Bloch, "English Verb Inflection," and Alphonse G. Juilland and James Macris *The English Verb System.*) Furthermore, there is some question whether a single scheme of verb morphology provides an appropriate model of the systemic speech habits of the speakers' language that includes a large number and variety of verb-inflection sets. To encompass all the facts within a single system is something different from regarding the facts as systematically arranged. We may say that speakers of English have multiple systems of verb inflection, and differences among these systems need not imply a single supersystem from which each separate system is derived. It is rather in features such as the categories of inflectional forms that the singleness of system inheres. In all likelihood the affixing of inflections to base forms syntactically defined as "verb" also unifies the variations that verb-words exhibit. The unity of the sets of inflections, in short, does not appear to be an intrinsic characteristic of morphology per se.

For these reasons the morphology of English verbs will be dealt with as an aggregate of systemic sets rather than as a single inflectional system. In practice we distinguish between a set of inflections that is dominant in frequency of occurrence and number of base forms to which the inflections are affixed, and a set of one or only a few members that are specially learned and maintained. The obvious illustration is the *–ed* type of past tense inflection, for the first, belonging to a set most widely used and extended to all new verbs that are devised; for the second, the paradigm *grow – grew – grown* represents a pattern of limited use, one that is often replaced in undisciplined speech (and "slips of the tongue") by the dominant pattern; the extreme examples are those of *(to) be* and *(to) go,* with suppletive forms making up the paradigmatic sets. Besides our practical distinctions, the history of English verb inflection also points to an aggregate system rather than to a logical and derivative verb-inflection system.

FINITE FORMS OF OLD ENGLISH CONSONANTAL VERBS

16.2 The morphological features of verbs in Modern English reflect the evolutionary processes perhaps more than is true for any other form class. Nevertheless, the changes verbs have undergone have been of such systemic consequence that attempting to explicate the phylogeny of verb morphology from the ontogeny of Modern English is impractical: particularly in respect to loss of features, the changes have put the morphology of Old English verbs beyond the practical capacities of the method of internal reconstruction. Again our procedure will be to begin with the forms in Old English and trace the principal changes by which verb inflection of Modern English eventuated.

Two major divisions of verb inflection have been characteristic of English throughout its history. Some verbs (to use Modern English examples) form paradigmatic sets on the basis of suffix inflection for tense—*walk* – *walked, want* – *wanted, pay* – *paid;* for these the suffixes are respectively /–t/, /–əd/, and /–d/. Others form sets on the basis of alternation of the vowel in the base syllable—*sing* – *sang, win* – *won, steal* – *stole, give* – *gave,* etc. Some are not so obviously classifiable, such as the one-shape sets like *put, set, cut,* or such other sets as *buy* – *bought, catch* – *caught, have* – *had,* but they too are assignable to one of the two major groups of verbs. The same basis of division of nearly all verbs into two classes applies to Old English forms. (The twofold division, characteristic of all Germanic languages, is exclusive to the Germanic branch of Indo-European languages, having been fully established long before English had become differentiated as a language in its own right.) The traditional names for the divisions are "weak verbs" to designate those with suffix inflection and "strong verbs" for those with vowel alternation within the base. Preferable terms, for their being more linguistically descriptive, are "consonantal" and "vocalic", respectively, and it is these terms that we shall use. The categories of these inflections involve tense.

Until well into Modern English, verbs also regularly had sets of number and person inflections; Shakespearean and Authorized (King James) Biblical locutions such as *thou seest, he asketh* will recall these inflections in early Modern English. Number and person inflections occurred with both consonantal and vocalic verbs.

Differentiated person inflections occurred (with rare exceptions) only with inflections making up one category of mood—that of the "indicative." For subjunctive and imperative mood categories, inflections distinguished only number categories singular and nonsingular (plural).

The inflectional forms categorically described so far belonged to verb words that constituted or were always present in sentence predications—that is, the words commonly called "finite" verb forms. Only one such form is found in any verb phrase in Old, Middle, and

Modern English: *He was here* has only one verb word, a finite form; *He was found,* with two verb words again has only one finite form *was; He was hoping to have finished planting by Saturday,* with several verb words in a series still has only one finite form *was,* whose form is selected in concord with the sentence subject. (With so-called "compound predicates" more than one finite form occurs with a single subject, but in strict terms each finite form occasions a separate verb phrase.) Other suffixed forms in Old English were not thus distributed, were not used as "finite" verbs. These other forms made up the infinitive and participle verb words.

We shall consider first the verb inflections of the "finite" forms. It was mentioned above that number and person inflections occurred in Old English with both consonantal and vocalic verbs. Implied in this observation is the fact that inflection for tense was separate from inflection for number and person (for indicative sets of forms). The morphemic makeup of finite verbs has its clearest illustration with consonantal verbs, of which the partial paradigms of *frem(m)–, ner(i)–,* and *dem–* are representative. The forms cited are West Saxon.

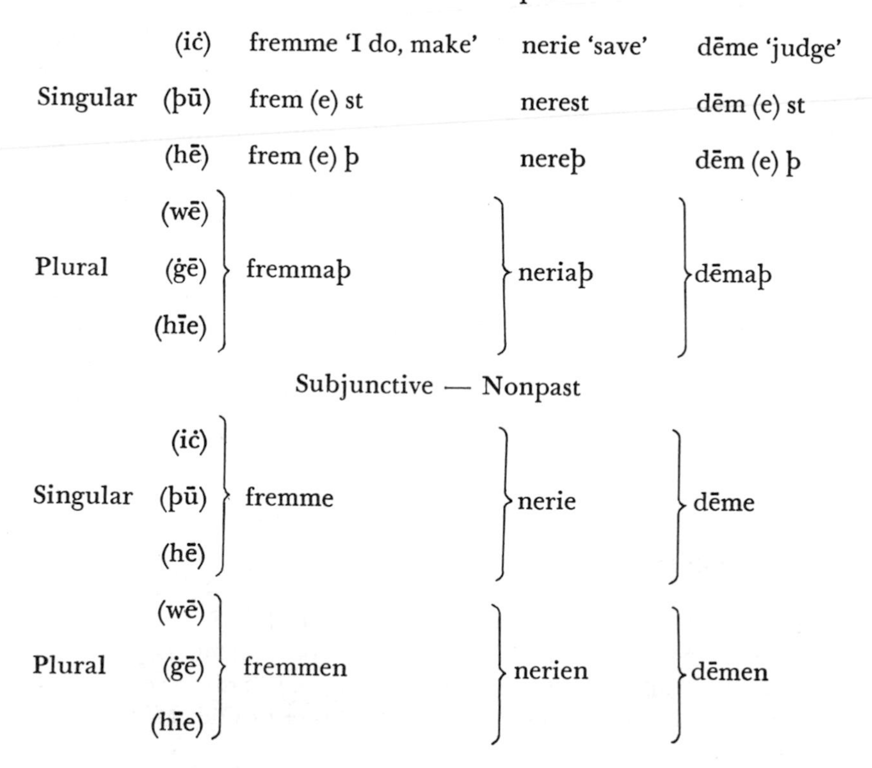

Indicative — Nonpast

	(iċ)	fremme 'I do, make'	nerie 'save'	dēme 'judge'
Singular	(þū)	frem (e) st	nerest	dēm (e) st
	(hē)	frem (e) þ	nereþ	dēm (e) þ
Plural	(wē) (ġē) (hīe)	fremmaþ	neriaþ	dēmaþ

Subjunctive — Nonpast

Singular	(iċ) (þū) (hē)	fremme	nerie	dēme
Plural	(wē) (ġē) (hīe)	fremmen	nerien	dēmen

Imperative — Nonpast

Singular	(þū)	freme	nere	dēm
Plural	(ġē)	fremmaþ	neriaþ	dēmaþ

Indicative — Past

	(iċ)	fremede	nerede	dēmde
Singular	(þū)	fremedest	neredest	dēmdest
	(hē)	fremede	nerede	dēmde
Plural	(wē, etc.)	fremedon	neredon	dēmdon

Subjunctive — Past

Singular	(iċ, etc.)	fremede	nerede	dēmde
Plural	(wē, etc.)	fremeden	nereden	dēmden

(The variations in length of consonants terminating base forms—the *m* vs. *mm*—the presence or absence of *–i–* after the base form, and other features have their own historical backgrounds that are of great interest, but those backgrounds take us farther back into the history of English than we have occasion to go here.) The listings of verb words make apparent that suffixes belonging to categories of tense are separate from those of number and person. In addition, the inflectional suffixes occur sequentially, and the sequence is specifically that of (base +) tense morpheme + number (and person) morpheme. In the forms listed, the past tense morpheme consists of /–d–/ with or without a vowel preceding it; that is, in Old English the past tense morph of weak verbs may be syllabic or nonsyllabic. Absence of past tense inflection distinguishes the 'present' forms. The term "nonpast" is preferable to "present," on grounds of morphology and in the absence of the simple meaning 'present times' for morphs lacking the /–d–/ inflection. No other inflectional forms belong to the general category of tense. Old English, as well as Modern English, in common with the other Germanic languages has only two specific tense categories: past and nonpast. (The two-tense system is consistent for both vocalic and consonantal verbs.) The final inflections sort into several sets. Three mood categories are thus distinguished, and in each of them two number categories are thus distinguished. In the indicative-mood set person categories are further distinguished in the singular forms. In the forms cited mood, number, and person categories are for most practical purposes syncretically manifested.

FINITE FORMS OF OLD ENGLISH VOCALIC VERBS

16.3 With a set of consonantal verb forms as a model, the same systemic features can be seen in vocalic verbs. Some typical forms in West Saxon Old English, representing the same categories as those illustrated for consonantal verbs, are given for the three verbs *drīfan, drincan,* and *faran* (cited by the infinitive forms).

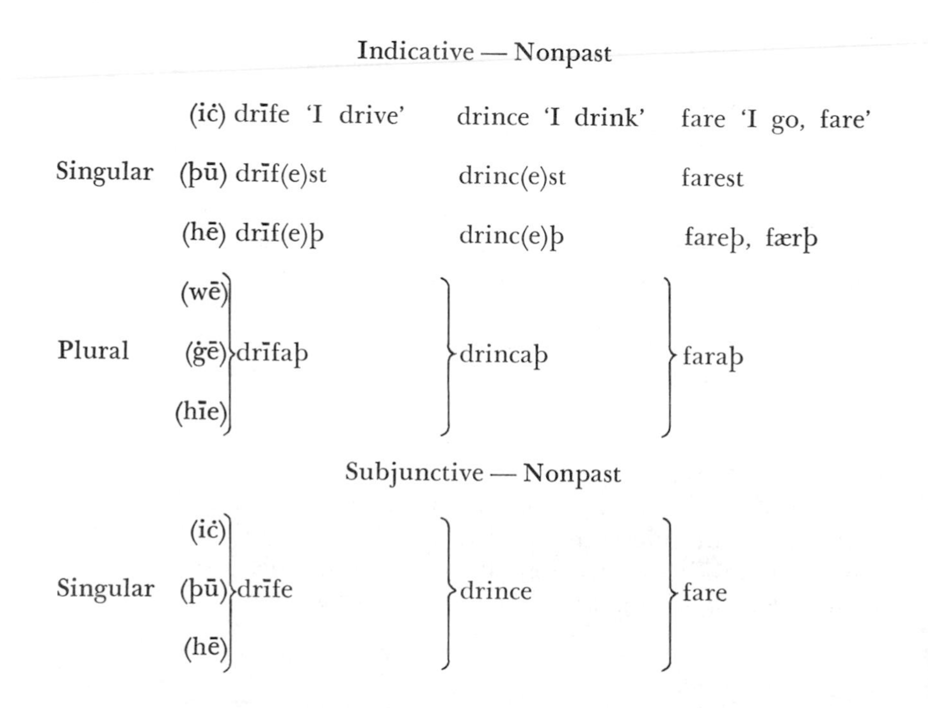

Indicative — Nonpast

Singular	(iċ)	drīfe 'I drive'	drince 'I drink'	fare 'I go, fare'
	(þū)	drīf(e)st	drinc(e)st	farest
	(hē)	drīf(e)þ	drinc(e)þ	fareþ, færþ
Plural	(wē) (ġē) (hīe)	drīfaþ	drincaþ	faraþ

Subjunctive — Nonpast

Singular	(iċ) (þū) (hē)	drīfe	drince	fare

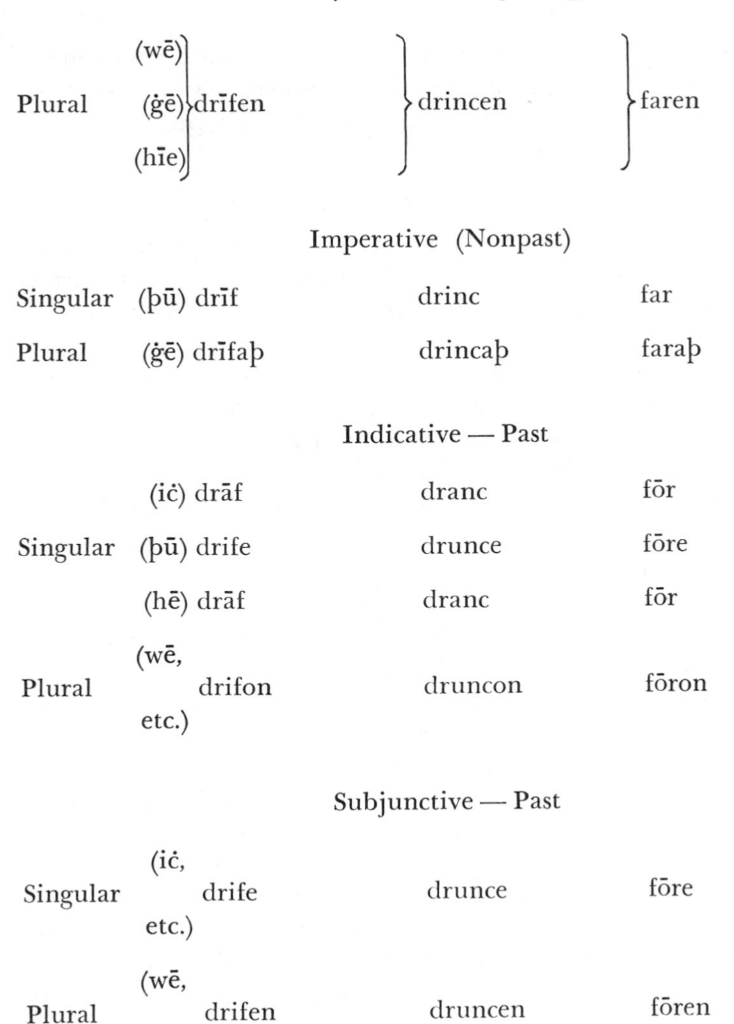

Plural	(wē) (ġē) (hīe)	drīfen	drincen	faren

Imperative (Nonpast)

Singular	(þū)	drīf	drinc	far
Plural	(ġē)	drīfaþ	drincaþ	faraþ

Indicative — Past

	(iċ)	drāf	dranc	fōr
Singular	(þū)	drife	drunce	fōre
	(hē)	drāf	dranc	fōr
Plural	(wē, etc.)	drifon	druncon	fōron

Subjunctive — Past

Singular	(iċ, etc.)	drife	drunce	fōre
Plural	(wē, etc.)	drifen	druncen	fōren

Several similarities in the inflectional forms of vocalic and consonantal verbs will be apparent, especially for subjunctive and imperative sets. Some differences appear, too, especially in the past indicative sets. The vowels involved in the alternation distinguishing past from nonpast form different patterns themselves—even as in Modern English *drive – drove* and *drink – drank* are exactly parallel but have different vocalic alternations. The alternation of vowels within the base syllable to reflect inflectional categories has been variously described, for example, as a suffix in nonsequential order and as an infix. We shall be less interested in the precise descriptive rationale of the vocalic verb inflection for tense than in the general nature of differences between tense inflection patterns for vocalic and consonantal verb types.

NONFINITE FORMS OF OLD ENGLISH VERBS

16.4 The nonfinite verb words require only brief description and illustration. The infinitive inflection in Old English is marked uniformly for both consonantal and vocalic verb types by *–an* affixed to the (nonpast) base form: *fremman, nerian, dēman, drīfan, drincan, faran;* they never occur with past inflection and, as the distinguishing factor that marks infinitive morphs as nonfinite, they do not occur with number or person inflections. To the infinitive suffix may be affixed, however, one other suffix, *–ne,* which occurs only when the infinitive word is preceded by a separate prepositional word *tō* 'to, for the purpose of': *(hrædest) tō secganne* 'to say [it] (quickly, *or* briefly).' The anterior history of the inflected infinitive is a special subject in itself. For the main directions in the history of English as a separate language the important observation is that the use of *tō* + (base) + *an–ne* was increasing during Old English in locutions to express purpose and causality and to adapt verb-expressed notions to grammatical requirements of substantive, or nounlike, form. That is, an infinitive phrase may appear in the "noun-slot" of a sentence, as in 'To see the truth hurts some people' or, in Old English, *þæt sōð tō gesēonne dereð summum monnum.* Besides the infinitive morphs were the participial morphs. The "present" participle was marked by *–and–, –end–,* or more broadly, *–Vnd–* affixed to the nonpast base form; the "passive" participle is marked much the same way as past tense forms, as the illustrations will show. The participles are in turn inflected as adjectives—in syntactically adjectival occurrences; they lack adjective inflectional suffixes when they are syntactically verbal.

Infinitive	Inflected Infinitive	Present Participle	Passive Participle
fremman	(tō) fremmanne	fremmende	(ge–) fremed
nerian	(tō) nerianne	neriende	(ge–) nered
dēman	(tō) dēmanne	dēmende	(ge–) dēmed
drīfan	(tō) drīfanne	drīfende	drifen
drincan	(tō) drincanne	drincende	druncen
faran	(tō) faranne	farende	faren

In sum, the morphological aspects of verbs in Old English manifest systems involving the following categories. Tenses are past and nonpast, and they are separately marked (except for a few verbs) in one of two ways—suffix vs. ∅ or alternation of vowel in the base form. The two syntactically defined categories are finite and nonfinite. Finite verb words include base form, tense marking, and number-indicating inflection, in that order; the final inflectional forms also make up sets distinguished for mood—indicative, subjunctive, imperative. Within the set of forms distinguished as indicative, the final inflections also signify three person categories (with both past and nonpast forms) that match up with the three person categories of pronouns, together with pronominals and nouns (and names) selecting the same verb inflections as do third person pronouns.

CLASSES OF CONSONANTAL VERBS

16.5 In dealing with particulars of the major verb categories, it will be necessary to be highly selective. The illustrative forms given above for verbs distinguished by tense inflection by suffix—the consonantal type of verbs—were all selected from one subclass, the class traditionally called "Class I." (The numerical designation "I" is based simply on this class having the largest number of members.) Another class, "III," consisted of four verbs; by convention they are cited by infinitive forms: *habban* '(to) have,' *libban* '(to) live,' *secgan* '(to) say,' *hycgan* '(to) think.' The last of these has become obsolete, but the other three of the four have persisted with minimal change of meaning. "Class II" consisted of a fairly large number of verbs a great many of which have become obsolete but many of which survive as common, "basic" items in the lexicon of Modern English. The principal differences among these classes appear in the indicative (finite) forms and in the passive participle. Once again, West Saxon examples are given.

	Class I		Class II	Class III	
Nonpast Indicative					
Singular 1st	nerie	dēme	lufie	hæbbe	secge
2nd	nerest	dēm(e)st	lufast	hæfst	sæġst
3rd	nereþ	dēm(e)þ	lufaþ	hæfþ	sæġþ
Plural					
(1st, 2nd, 3rd)	neriaþ	dēmaþ	lufiaþ	hæbbaþ	secgaþ

	Class I		Class II	Class III	
Past Indicative					
Singular 1st	nerede	dēmde	lufode	hæfde	sæġde
2nd	neredest	dēmdest	lufodest	hæfdest	sæġdest
3rd	nerede	dēmde	lufode	hæfde	sæġde
Plural					
(1st, 2nd, 3rd)	neredon	dēmdon	lufodon	hæfdon	sæġdon
Passive Participle					
	(ge–)nered	(ge–)dēmde	(ge–)lufod	(ge–)hæfd	(ge–)sæġd

The principal differences among these subclasses are the following. The vowel of the past tense morpheme is /e/ or /ə/ for Class I, /o/ for Class II. In the nonpast forms the spelled *i* before the number-person inflections represents a consonant in Class I and a vowel in Class II: /nerġə/ etc. and /lufiə/ etc. Also in the nonpast forms the vowel of the number-person inflections in two singular forms differs as /e/ and /a/. In Class III the final consonant and the vowel of the base varies, so that the base element must be represented as having distinct allomorphs. The differences among these subclasses are not of especially prominent kinds. The past-tense morpheme, when it is syllabic, is a lesser-stressed syllable than the base form, and the difference in vowels is thereby minimized. The difference in vowels in the number-person inflections, when they are syllabic, is also minimized by the lesser stress of the inflectional syllable. Both types of inflection, furthermore, have nonsyllabic forms. The difference between /–ġ–/ and /–i–/ is essentially that of consonantal and vocalic articulation of otherwise identical, distinctive features. The differences in the base forms in Class III are phonemic alternations that involve minimal differences in the system of consonants and are alternations found elsewhere in Old English. Finally, the common elements in all these sets diminish the prominence of differences: all first person singular past and nonpast forms have final inflections that are only vocalic —/–ə/; all second person singular past and nonpast forms have final inflections that terminate in /–st/; all third person singular forms terminate in /–þ/ in the nonpast set and in /–ə/ in the past set; all plural past forms terminate in /–on/. In the examples given, all past forms are marked by /–d–/. In sum, the points of difference in the inflectional system have balancing points of identity: if **lufest*, for example, were substituted for *lufast,* the sound would still be construed only as second person singular nonpast inflection of /luf–/ 'lov(e)–.'

Classes II and III of the consonantal verbs exhibit almost no internal variations in the inflections; with only four members in Class III, each member having frequent occurrence, the likelihood of variants developing was slight; Class II characteristically had a vowel /o/ in the past tense inflection that was not subject to syncope—the loss of a vowel between consonants. Class I has several variations. Those involving the past tense morpheme are the only ones we shall consider here.

The variations may be accounted for, as they are in many of the grammars of Old English, by reconstructing their history. More to our purpose will be to refer the variants to phonological rules, especially those having to do with clusterings of consonants and with syllable structure of words. For simplicity, only third person singular word forms with past and nonpast inflection will be cited. The forms of /frem(•)–/, /ner(ġ)–/ were given above. For these the past tense morpheme is /–ed/ or, probably, /–əd/. The forms of /dēm–/ were also given; the past tense morpheme is /–d/.That there was always a number-person inflection following the past tense morpheme and the final inflection was always syllabic made the syllable division variable. After a "long" base form such as that of /dēm–/ containing a "long" vowel, syncope of the unstressed vowel of the past tense morpheme was normal; in syllabic structure *dēmde* was presumably *dēm–de.* The same omission of the unstressed vowel before /d/ also occurs with base forms terminating in two consonants: nonpast *bærneþ* 'burns,' past *bærnde* 'burned' and others. Syllabically, it is *bærn–de,* not *bærnd–e.* The base form is also considered to be "long."

Another variation occurs with "long" base forms which, as /dēm–/ and /bærn–/, phonologically select a past tense morpheme without a vowel. Those forms terminating in a voiceless consonant condition the consonant of the past tense morpheme with the result that /t/, the unvoiced counterpart of /d/, occurs; the process is that of assimilation. Examples are *cēpeþ* 'keeps' and *cēpte* 'kept,' *scierpeþ* 'sharpens, (makes) sharp' and *scierpte* 'sharpened, (made) sharp.'

Another type of variation reflects another set of phonological conditions. The past tense suffix morpheme, as the examples above illustrate, may be syllabic or nonsyllabic and may contain either the voiced or unvoiced dental stop consonant. What shape did the past tense verbs have when the base form terminated in a dental stop consonant? If the nonsyllabic morpheme having an unvoiced dental stop consonant were affixed to the "long" base *sett–* /set•–/ 'set,' the past tense form would be **settte*. The morphological patterns of language, however, did not take priority over the phonological ones; the only contrast of length for consonants was a binary one—lengthened vs. nonlengthened—and the usual past tense of /set•–/ was *sette*. By the same conditions, the past tense form of /mēt–/ 'meet' was *mētte* 'met.' Similarly, base elements terminating in a voiced dental stop showed nonpast and past forms such as these: *lǣdeþ* 'leads' and *lǣdde* 'led,' *fēdeþ* 'feeds' and *fēdde* 'fed.' The same conditions obtained for those base forms terminating in two consonants, of which the second was a dental stop: for /wend–/, (*wend(e)þ* >) *went* 'turns' and *wende* 'turned,' (*send(e)þ* >) *sent* 'sends' and *sende* 'sent.'

Finally, variations related to syllable division and clustering of consonants occurred as follows. The base /cys•–/, terminating in a voiceless consonant, selected /t/ in the past tense morpheme, but beside the nonpast form *cysseþ* 'kisses' is the past form *cyste* 'kissed.' At the syllable boundary—that is, in the final position in a syllable—a lengthened consonant (written as doubled letters) does not occur. Several of the circumstances of variation are represented in /þyrst–/ and /wēst–/: (*þyrst(e)þ* >) *þyrst* 'thirsts' for nonpast and *þyrste* 'thirsted' for past, and (*wēst(e)þ* >) *wēst* 'lay waste' for nonpast and *wēste* 'laid waste' for past.

The past tense morpheme thus had the following allomorphs for Class I consonantal type verbs: /–əd– –d– –t– ∅/; when the base form terminated in a nonlengthened dental consonant, /–d–/ or /–t–/ was replaced by lengthening of the /–d–/ or /–t–/ already present in the word.

The allomorphs of the inflectional morpheme of the passive participle forms were segmentally identical to those of the past tense of finite verb forms. It will be recalled that the past tense morpheme in finite verb forms was regularly followed by an inflectional morpheme containing a vowel. Hence the distribution of the allomorphs often differed between the past tense forms and the passive participle forms of a paradigmatic set. The most convenient way to illustrate the various differences is to list three typical forms of the verbs already cited.

Finite		Nonfinite
3rd Sing. Nonpast	3rd Sing. Past	Passive Participle
fremeð	fremede	(ge–) fremed
nereð	nerede	nered
dēm(e)þ	dēmde	dēmed
bærneþ	bærnde	bærned
cēpeþ	cēpte	cēped
scierpeþ	scierpte	scierped
setteþ > sett	sette	seted, sett
mēteþ > mētt	mētte	mēted, mētt
fēdeþ	fēdde	fēded, fēdd
wendeþ > went	wende	wended, wend
sendeþ > sent	sende	sended, send
cysseþ	cyste	cyssed
þyrsteþ > þyrst	þyrste	þyrsted
wēsteþ > wēst	wēste	wēsted

DEVELOPMENT OF FINITE INFLECTIONS OF CONSONANTAL VERBS

16.6 Many of the developments we are to trace occurred very early in some dialects (usually Northern) and very late in others. Some of the inflections that were obsolete by the end of Middle English persisted in smaller dialects into and sometimes through the nineteenth century, particularly in England. At any time, in fact, the uniformity of the historical development of English that necessarily appears in a general accounting such as the present one should be gauged by the actual diversity of usages that are recorded in dialect grammars and atlases. When we turn our attention to processes of change, we can deal only selectively and broadly. Once we have reconstructed the processes of change, the history of the inflections of any particular verb cannot be deduced automatically from either the Old English or the Modern English forms. The "passing over" of a verb from one type to another and from one class to another has gone on at all times in the history of the language. In Modern English, in the speech of linguistically uninhibited people, *thunk* and *brang* are past tense forms corresponding to nonpast *think* and *bring*; *come* substitutes for *came* (with historical justification of one kind); *laid* replaces *lay*, *het* corresponds paradigmatically to *heated*, as does *rid* to *rode*; *broadcast* and *broadcasted* alternate as past tense forms. During Old English, a number of consonantal type verbs changed inflections from those of Class I to Class II and vice versa. Middle English showed perhaps more indeterminateness of verb classes and specific forms within dialects, and it certainly showed great diversity among dialects.

All these qualifications do not invalidate the analysis of principal systemic changes. The "passing over" of a verb from one paradigmatic pattern to another, in fact, attests to the primacy of systemic features of morphology rather than undermining it. "Analogical change" affects words individually or in groups, but analogical change is ultimately a consequence of alternate systemic patterns.

With these preliminary reminders, let us turn now to the principal developments of the consonantal type of verbs. The number-person inflections (the finite-form inflections) underwent changes which were substantially independent of the tense inflections: they separately made up inflectional sets of categories unlike the tense categories. The illustrative sets of forms in Old English that have been given were typically West Saxon. The corresponding Middle English dialects were the generally southern or southwestern ones. By late Middle English, number-person inflection of consonantal verbs in the latter dialect group were alike for all verbs that earlier had constituted three subclasses. Generally, the differences we examined earlier had disappeared, and the non-past indicative inflections were singular *–e*, *–es(t)*, *–eþ* (or *–eth* in the newer spelling) for the three person categories and *–eþ* (= *–eth*) for the common plural; the imperative inflections were Ø and *–eþ* for singular and plural, respectively. The past tense inflections were these: indicative *–e*, *–est*, *–e* singular for the three person categories, *–e(n)* for the common plural; subjunctive *–(e)* singular and *–e(n)* plural. The differences among the earlier three subclasses were not especially prominent, as we saw, and the merger of the various inflectional vowels into a common /ə/ was the principal factor by which a common, or single, class of consonantal verbs developed; analogy did most of the rest of the leveling of differences. When the minor differences had been eliminated, the major distinctions remained, and the number-person inflections in this dialect group of Middle English are about the same as those in the corresponding Old English dialect. In systemic terms almost no change took place, except in the merging of the subclasses. The same categories of inflections remained and the conspicuous phonological aspects of the various inflections showed little change.

Further change in number-person inflections of verbs in southern dialects is probably to be attributed much more to influence of speech in other dialects than it is to further internal development. When the general features of inflections had reached the stage of development just described, different sets of changes in other large dialect areas had produced different features of the inflectional system. In the Midlands (especially the culturally influential eastern and southern areas, and London) the inflections were typically as follows. The indicative nonpast forms were similar to those of southern dialects, singular *–e, –es(t), –eþ,* but the plural was *–en,* later *–e(n)*; subjunctive singular *–e,* plural *–en,* later *–e(n)*; imperative singular *–e,* plural *–eþ*; indicative past forms were singular Ø except sometimes *–e* for second person inflection; plural was *–en,* later *–e(n)*; subjunctive past, like southern dialects, had *–e* and *–en,* later *–e(n),* singular and plural, respectively. The most conspicuous difference from southern dialects is the *–e(n)* plural generalized for both past and nonpast inflections. In effect, the development represented the emergence of a single plural inflection for finite verb forms.

Northern dialects had even more radical development. All the past forms had Ø inflection for number and person, both indicative and subjunctive. To restate the matter in descriptive rather than historical terms, mood, number, and person were absent as inflectional categories for consonantal verbs with past tense inflection in northern dialects of Middle English. In this respect, northern dialects of Middle English had become essentially Modern English. Nonpast forms show a development of a different kind. From the period of Old English the northern dialects had already alternate singular inflections *–es* complementing both second person *–est* and third person *–eþ,* and the common plural inflection *–as* complementing *–aþ*; these occurred in indicative inflections. Subsequently, *–es* came to be the normal form for singular second and third person inflection; somewhat like the generalizing of /þ–/ for nominative singular of determiners-pronominals, *–es* was generalized then to first person singular forms. The contrast of singular *–es* vs. plural *–as* subsequently disappeared as *–as* merged with *–es,* and all nonpast consonantal type verbs had a single inflection *–es.* At this stage person and number inflection for indicative verbs no longer existed. Number distinction nevertheless remained in the imperatives, with singular Ø vs. plural *–es*. A subjunctive set remained partially with singular *–e* vs. plural *–en,* both inflections alternating with Ø. The systemic imbalance will be apparent: an indicative set without number or person distinctions, an imperative set with number distinction for some verbs and some contexts, but not all.

Subsequent history of person-number inflection and the differentiation of inflectional sets into indicative, imperative, and subjunctive is to be traced, in large measure, in the complex shifts of centers of cultural, linguistic dominance and the consequent dialect mixing. The history must also take into account the emergence of a standard dialect, beginning about 1400 or just after—the time at which inflections had reached the stage of development we have so far observed. In addition, the inflections for number and person, and their sets constituting three mood categories, became thoroughly consistent for both vocalic and consonantal types of verbs. Let us therefore suspend our accounting of the later history of these inflections until we have considered the history of the vocalic verbs up to the same point in the historical continuum.

DEVELOPMENT OF PAST TENSE INFLECTIONS OF CONSONANTAL VERBS

16.7 Developments affecting the past tense inflectional morpheme of the consonantal verbs require only brief description, given the analysis already made for the subclasses of these verbs in Old English and the allomorphs of the inflection. One development is especially significant. When the Old English Class II inflection /–od–/ was replaced by /əd–/, the past tense inflection was subject to the same conditions of syncope, consonant clustering, and syllable patterning that had established the variety of allomorphs for Class I past tense inflections (cf. 16.4). The replacement of /–od–/ by /əd–/ is usually explained as a "weakening" of the /o/ in unstressed position. The explanation may well be accurate, but is probably not complete. Replacement of various unstressed vowels by /ə/ did constitute a regular pattern of phonological change, especially in inflectional syllables, but the correspondences between Class I and Class II consonantal verb inflection were also of the kind to occasion analogical change. In other words, the more prominent similarities in the /–d–/ element of the inflectional morphs were very likely sufficient to produce analogically inflected forms of originally Class II verbs in the pattern of Class I without an intermediary stage of "weakened" /–od–/ > /–əd/. Once the contrast between /–od–/ and the allomorphs of originally Class I verbs disappeared, the past tense inflection of consonantal verbs had one morpheme with a set of allomorphs which were only phonologically conditioned.

While number (and person) inflections persisted for past tense verbs, the phonological selection of allomorphs remained much as it had been for Class I verbs of Old English. As soon as the finite inflections were abandoned (early in the North, late in the South), the selection of allomorphs began to take on the appearance of the pattern operative in Modern English inflections. If we have before us the main patternings of present-day past tense suffix allomorphs, the developments between Middle English will be more readily inferred. It should not be surprising that the patternings follow principles much like those of plural and possessive inflections of nouns (see 15.5, end).

/–d/ is affixed to base forms ending in voiced sounds, except for the alveolar (formerly dental) stop consonant /d/; it occurs following /b g ǰ v ð z ž m n ŋ l r/ and any vowel.

/–t/ is affixed to base forms ending in unvoiced sounds, except for alveolar (formerly dental) stop consonant /t/; it occurs following /p k č f θ s š/.

/–ed/ is affixed to base forms ending in alveolar (formerly dental) stop consonants /t d/.

The principal changes between Middle and Modern English have consisted mainly of progressive loss of syllabic inflection except after base forms terminating in an alveolar stop. The frequent syllabic inflections in Chaucer's English may be familiar: *hoped* 'hoped,' *loked* 'looked,' *lerned* 'learned' and the like were two-syllable words. The less frequent syllabic inflection of verbs in Renaissance verse may also be familiar; but the commonness with which poets could select—and even alternate—syllabic and nonsyllabic inflection is still a better representation of the historical trend in the sixteenth and seventeenth centuries: *wisht* – *wished, ask't* – *asked, look't* – *looked,* and the like. The regular substitution of nonsyllabic inflection for syllabic inflection of all verbs except those whose base forms terminate in /t/ or /d/ has become established, with phonological accommodation of the dental stop suffix to the clustering patterns of consonants—the patterns already operative in Old English and present in the inflection of its Class I consonantal verbs.

The passive participle inflectional suffix has followed almost exactly the case course of historical development. A very few differences, such as the contrasting finite and nonfinite forms *learned* and *learnèd, cursed* and *cursèd* must be listed separately for descriptions of Modern English.

The descendants of other inflectional patterns of consonantal verbs remain for brief notice. The ∅ inflection persists for one verb listed earlier for Old English in the Modern English *set,* as well as for several other verbs—*put, cut,* etc. Those verbs which in Old English had past tense inflection manifest as lengthening of a /d/ or /t/ terminating the base form have descended into Modern English, for the most part, with a different contrast between past and nonpast forms. Length of consonants, it will be recalled, lost its significance during Middle English. Before that phonological change, however, presence of lengthened consonants conditioned a change in a preceding long vowel: the examples of *fēdde* and *mētte,* given earlier, were replaced in early Middle English by *fĕdde* and *mĕtte,* whence Modern English past *fed, met,* beside nonpast *feed, meet.*

TENSE INFLECTION OF OLD ENGLISH VOCALIC VERBS

16.8 The vocalic (or "strong") verbs have remained radically different from the consonantal (or "weak") verbs throughout the history of English. While the latter type has marked past and nonpast tenses and the passive participle by presence or absence of a suffix containing a dental (later alveolar) stop consonant (or its phonological reflex) , the former type has marked these distinctions by differences in the vocalic element in the stressed base syllable. The vocalic type of verbs, furthermore, has always included more subclasses, for each series of vowel alternations constitutes a separate set of markings of the "principal parts": *freeze – froze, ride – rode, sink – sank,* etc. are only three of corresponding pairs of nonpast and past forms. Other differences occur as well. Similarities between vocalic and consonantal verb types are also important to the proper understanding of the vocalic English verbs and their history. The inflectional categories are identical for both types of verbs, and have been throughout the history of the language. The morphological differences have not been associated with other differences such as the opposition of transitive and intransitive. The independence of the base element, the tense-marking element, and the number- and person-marking element is apparent in both synchrontic and diachronic analysis of verbs. We shall begin with earlier verb forms and trace the changes through which the morphology of Modern English verbs has evolved.

The morphemic makeup of verb words and the inflectional categories of vocalic verbs are illustrated in the paradigms of finite forms of the verbs *beran* '(to) bear,' *scrīfan* '(to) decree, shrive,' and *climban* '(to) climb.'

Indicative — Nonpast

	(iċ) bere 'I bear'	scrīfe 'I decree, shrive'	climbe 'I climb'
Singular	(þū) berest birst	scrīf(e)st	climb(e)st
	(hē) bereþ birþ	scrīf(e)þ	climb(e)þ
Plural	(wē) (ġē) (hīe) beraþ	scrīfaþ	climbaþ

Subjunctive — Nonpast

Singular	(iċ) (þū) (hē) bere	scrīfe	climbe
Plural	(wē) (ġē) (hīe) beren	scrīfen	climben

Imperative — Nonpast

Singular	(þū) ber	scrīf	climb
Plural	(ġē) beraþ	scrīfaþ	climbaþ

Indicative — Past

	(iċ) bær	scrāf	clamb
Singular	(þū) bǣre	scrife	clumbe
	(hē) bær	scrāf	clamb

Plural	(wē, bǣron etc.)	scrifon	clumbon

Subjunctive — Past

Singular	(iċ, bǣre etc.)	scrife	clumbe
Plural	wē, bǣren etc.)	scrifen	clumben

The number and person inflections are alike for these verbs, and the sets they make up to distinguish the three moods are also alike. Although these three verbs belong to different subclasses (/e∼æ∼ǣ, ī∼ā∼i, i∼a∼u/), the subclass distinction is made only in the alternation of base element vowels. The same is true of all the other subclasses. In short, the entire group of vocalic verbs is inflected for person, number, and mood with a single set of suffix elements.

The suffix inflections, furthermore, are identical for nonpast forms to those of the largest class (Class I) of consonantal verbs; it will be recalled, too, that the differences in these inflections from those of other classes of consonantal verbs are minimal. Differences between the inflections of past vocalic and consonantal verbs must be noted. Singular past indicative forms have *–e* for second person inflection, Ø for first and third person inflection. Plural indicative inflections of past tense verbs are identical to those of consonantal verbs, and the inflections of both major types of verbs are the same in imperative and subjunctive forms.

A principal difference in inflection of the two types of verbs obviously lies in the marking of past tense. The pattern for the vocalic verbs is that of alternate vowels marking past tense, these vowels in turn alternating with a vowel of nonpast forms: in the past tense first and third person singular forms have one vowel, second person singular and all plural forms have another, in the indicative set; in the subjunctive set only one of these vowels appears in both singular and plural inflected forms—the one used also for plural and second person singular forms. How this state of affairs came to be is a matter beyond the scope of our present concern. The pattern obtained for all subclasses of strong verbs, and was rigorously established. The systemic implications, then, deserve particular attention. Vowel alternation in the base element always distinguished past from nonpast. However, alternate vowels—not a single vowel—signaled the meaning 'past.' The two "past" vowels were not distributed consistently with any of the inflectional categories manifest in the suffix inflections or their patterns: that is, the alternation of /ā ∼ i/ of *scr—f–*, for example, corresponded neither to the number categories of singular and plural, nor to the person categories, nor to the categories of mood. The alternation of vowels for past tense inflection, in short, did not represent different meanings, and it did not reinforce any systemic distinctions in a consistent way.

For the nonfinite forms, the characteristics may be briefly stated. The infinitive and present participle of a vocalic verb were marked in the same manner as the same forms of consonantal verbs. Thus, the infinitive had the suffix *–an* joined to the nonpast base element: *ber–an, scrīf–an, climb–an,* etc. The inflected infinitive appeared as *ber–an–ne,* that is, *beranne, scrīfanne, climbanne.* The present participles of these verbs are *berende, scrīfende, climbende.* The passive participle, however, was marked in the same way as tense, by vowel alternation. For the three verbs serving as illustration, the base alternants of the four "principal parts" may now be listed:

Nonpast	Past		Passive Participle
ber–	bær–	bǣr–	bor(en)–
scrīf–	scrāf–	scrif–	scrif(en)–
climb–	clamb–	clumb–	clumb(en)–

DEVELOPMENT OF TENSE INFLECTION OF VOCALIC VERBS

16.9 The Middle English developments in number and person inflections for vocalic verbs (and the sets in which they combined to mark mood of verb forms) were identical to those of consonantal verbs, to the extent the inflections had been identical in Old English. In the respects that these inflections had differed in Old English, the Middle English inflections also differed. In those dialects in which morphological change proceeded at a conservative rate, the past tense forms showed the same pattern as did the Old English forms, with only phonological and orthographic modifications of the individual forms. One set of past tense forms will provide sufficient illustration:

(I)	bar 'bore'	(we)	
(thou)	bęre	(ye)	bęren
(he)	bar	(they)	

Changes began to occur in the past tense forms, however, at an early date of Middle English in northern dialects. In any of the dialects, one of the changes was the replacement of the vowel of (singular) second person base forms by the vowel of the (singular) first and third person forms. In effect, this change by itself established a "singular base—past" contrasting with a "plural base—past," so that the number categories were marked consistently by both suffix number inflection and base vowel. The change, still considered by itself, made a new consistency as well in contrasting of indicative and subjunctive, in the past singular forms. The fuller systemic consistency thus produced was not the most significant of the changes, however, and was actually only a minor modification of the morphology of vocalic verbs.

The principal change occurred in the loss of vowel alternation for marking of past tense forms. Whereas four "principal parts" had been the pattern of vocalic verbs in Old English, the changes that occurred during Middle English produced a pattern of three "principal parts" for Modern English. While the change was a simple one in respect to the systemic aspects of vocalic verb morphology, the attendant factors, the particular changes, and the patterns of change were extradordinary diverse. Two subclasses of vocalic verbs in Old English had in fact only one vowel in past tense forms; those verbs traditionally labeled Class VI and Class VII had principal parts illustrated by the following forms:

	Nonpast	Past	Passive Participle
VI	far– 'go, fare'	fōr–	far(en)–
VIIa	lǣt– 'let'	lēt–	lǣt(en)–
VIIb	feall– 'fall'	fēoll–	feall(en)–

In some of the earlier sets the generally "plural" past forms had the same vowel as did the passive participle, while in some of the sets the vowels were different. In none of the sets was the vowel of the generally "singular" past tense forms identical to that of either the nonpast forms or the passive participle, and phonological changes in Middle English did not as a rule cause any of the differences to disappear. When one base element vowel came to serve in place of alternate vowels, past tense forms would seemingly manifest the Middle English reflex of the vowel of the originally plural forms—if duplication or reinforcement were the bases of selection. The fact is that the selective factors seem to have been as various as were the materials. Particularly in northern dialects, where the change operated earliest and most rapidly, the vowel of (singular) first and third person forms replaced the vowel of the other past tense forms in the indicative set; the same vowel also replaced the alternate "past" vowel in subjunctive forms. It was in these same dialects that number and person inflections were abandoned for past tense forms at about the same time. In these dialects, then, a systemic restructuring occurred that can be described as the establishment of a (single) past tense marking and disappearance of morphological distinctions for number, person, and mood for past tense forms. In those dialects where the radical restructuring of several aspects of the morphology did not take place almost simultaneously, a greater variety of changes occurred. For many verbs the single past tense vowel marking was the reflex of the earlier subjunctive and generally plural indicative forms, and for others it was the reflex of the generally singular indicative forms. In some instances the vowel of a given verb was one in one dialect and the other in another. The variety of changes—always complicated by dialect mixture—was further increased by partial resemblances between the various patterns of vowel alternation. The complexities of the developments can be appreciated fully only by special study of Middle English, but they may be broadly indicated by the Modern English reflexes of some of the verbs. Today, in American English, *swung* is the Standard past tense form, while *swang* is regarded as archaic or nonstandard; yet *swam* is Standard and *swum* is nonstandard as past tense; *flung* (not *flang*) is the general past tense form for a verb entering Middle English as a borrowing from Scandinavian dialects spoken in England; *sang* is Standard past tense, *sung* is not: these verbs belonged originally to a single subclass—the same class as *climb–*, cited above—and out of the variety of developments of past tense forms standard dialects of Modern English preserve one or another form without regard for consistency of historical development; past tense *clumb* is historically more "correct" than *climbed.*

Perhaps the best way to summarize and characterize the changes in past tense inflection of vocalic verbs is this: a single selective principle operated—ultimately producing a single "past tense" vowel alternate—but it operated on a variety of materials under differing and changing circumstances.

NONFINITE FORMS

16.10 The nonfinite forms of both major types of verbs had differed in Old English in the passive participle. Otherwise, the infinitive had been marked always by *–an* affixed to the base element (nonpast), the present participle by *–ende* (occasionally *–ande*). The developments in Middle English, broadly stated, were the following. Like other inflections, the *–an* of the infinitive was replaced by *–en* /ən/, which was in turn replaced by *–e(n)* /–ə(n)/, and in turn, /–ə/∼Ø; ultimately those forms defined syntactically and historically as infinitives had Ø inflection. The inflected infinitive, not frequent even in Old English, was replaced by other forms. Once again, these changes occurred earliest in northern dialects and were complete in southern dialects only by the end of the period of Middle English. The present participle did not merge with Ø. There were dialectal differentiations of phonological developments, such that northern dialects had *–and(e)*, west Midlands and Southern *–inde* – *–ende*, and east and north Midlands usually *–ende; –and* also occurred in southern dialects apparently in imitation of the French present participle inflection that appeared in England as *–ant* – *–aunt* as in *accordant, conversaunt*. The major change, from the point of view of subsequent developments, was the replacement of *–nd–* inflections by those having *–ng–*. The new inflection *–ing(e)* originated in southern or south Midlands dialects. The circumstances and selective factors for this new form remain only tentatively formulated. Clearly, the new form would not have been evolved by any of the patterns of phonological change generally operative at the time. It may well be that the distinctness of the participial present inflection from other nonfinite inflections was reduced in the trends of change in less-stressed suffix elements in southern dialects; if so, preservation of the systemic relations among nonfinite forms required introduction of new phonologically distinguishing features in one of the inflections: linguistic changes are by nature irreversible. The /–ən/ shape of the infinitive inflection, especially in view of the same shape of other inflections for other than verb words, had little possibility for modification. As long as it continued as an alternate to (probably) /–n(•)/, the /–nd–/ shape did offer a possibility for modification. Replacement of /–nd–/ by /–ng–/ involved substitution of one voiced stop for another (/g/ > /d/) and an allophonic substitution that was phonetically prominent, [ŋ] > [n]. Such a modification of the present participle inflection represents deliberate change for the purpose of keeping the system of nonfinite forms from changing. There was also probably a model for the particular change in the set of nouns that were formed from verb base elements by affixing /–ing–/ (and /–ung–/), a fairly common feature in Old and Middle English; if *grēt–* 'greet' were a common verb and *grēting* were a common noun, for example, syntax would distinguish participial and nominal forms *grēting* more dependably than it would distinguish participial and infinitive forms *grēt-en.* Once developed, the *–ing(e)* participial inflection spread through the other dialects and became fully established for standard dialects of Modern English.

NUMBER AND PERSON INFLECTIONS

16.11 We have now considered the main lines of development of nonfinite inflections and the tensemarking inflections to the point at which the morphology of verbs in Modern English is approximated. At varying rates of development, the principal dialects arrived at essentially the same systemic features. We must return now to the number and person inflections. At about 1400, a considerable variety of developments had taken place, and the major dialect areas had inflectional patterns that differed systemically and in respect to the particular inflections that signaled number or person, or both, for one or more moods. A standard dialect began to emerge about that time. The general drift toward loss of inflectional /–ə(n)/ continued in those areas where it had not already disappeared. The differences between number and person inflections of vocalic and consonantal verbs in past tense continued to produce analogical extensions (and irregularities), with *–est* attached to second person vocalic verbs, and *–e* substituted for *–est.* No single, dominant, or consistent pattern of inflections signified number or person for both past and nonpast forms, nor was mood distinguished in a consistent and distinctive way. The eventual result for the dialects from which the standard dialect emerged was a mixture of inflectional patterns that had been stable in only two respects: ∅ inflections and third person singular inflection of nonpast verbs, the one generally described as *–s* inflection. Thus, all past tense verb words now lack overt inflection; in person, number, and mood past tense forms no longer have inflectional categories. Only one overt inflection, *–(e)s,* occurs for nonpast verbs. Its origin is in the dialects described earlier in which *–es* was fully established, but its distribution in Modern English is different. The systemic status of *–es* is anomalous, for the form occurs only in conjunction with singular noun subjects or third person singular pronouns or the pronominals. The form is gender-related, for it is correlated with the only gender-indicating category in the morphology of Modern English. It is anomalous as the only overt inflection of finite forms apart from tense inflection (and apart from the special case of the verb *be*). It is also anomalous in being replaced by Ø in some nonstandard constructions such as *he do, he don't.* Nevertheless, the inflection *–(e)s* shows no signs of being abandoned in Modern English.

Subjunctive and imperative inflections also came to be uniformly Ø in standard Modern English. The only morphological distinction between moods that remained in Modern English was the opposition between indicative *–(e)s* and subjunctive Ø with singular third person subjects, for nonpast verbs: *If he think it best* vs. *He thinks it best.* The distinction hardly exists, however, except in carefully schooled usage that preserves the archaic subjunctive Ø inflection. With rare exceptions such as these, Modern English verbs may be said no longer to have morphological distinction of mood.

The *–(e)s* verb inflection resembles the plural and possessive inflections of nouns in its set of allomorphs and in the distribution of the allomorphs by phonological criteria (cf. 15.5, end).

SPECIAL VERBS

16.12 Our consideration of the two major types of verbs has proceeded mainly in terms of the sets of their inflectional characteristics; citation of particular verb base elements has been only to improve the illustrations. Being bound forms, inflections have never occurred without the base forms, and all the major verb subclasses have been in part defined by the sets of bases to which one or another set of inflections has been affixed. In so far as they are major types of verbs with a large number of member base-forms, the "autonomy" of the inflectional systems has been nearly complete. Borrowing, derivation, invention and the like have added thousands of consonantal verbs, but these additions have not in the least affected the morphology of this principal type of verbs. With the verb types to which we now turn, the relation of the morphological aspects to the set of base elements is different. The "conjugations" of *be* or *ought,* for example, represent in a very important sense inflectional sets that are not autonomous. The systems exist for specific, limited sets of verbs, some of the sets consisting of only one member. These are the verbs, obviously, that have an unusually high frequency of occurrence. They are also verbs which, for the most part, have special characteristics of distribution with respect to other verbal forms within sentences. Throughout the history of English they have apparently been learned, perpetuated, and modified as separate items in the verbal system. Their morphology, viewed synchronically at any time or diachronically through any stretch of time, marks them as constituting largely independent subsystems of verb words. Accordingly, we can deal with them briefly, and we must handle them mostly as small packages of related facts. Only the more prominent sets will be mentioned.

The history of the set represented by the nonpast base *go–* offers perhaps the best starting point for these "special" verbs. The morphological history is compressed in paradigmatic sets.

	Old English (West Saxon)	**Middle English (Midlands)**	**Modern English (Standard)**
NONPAST			
Indicative			
Singular 1st person	(iċ) gā	(I) gǭ	(I) go
2nd person	(þū) gǣst	(thou) gǭst	(you) go
3rd person	(hē) gǣþ	(hē) gǭþ	(he) goes
Plural	(wē, etc.) gāþ	(wē, etc.) gǭn	(we, etc.) go
Subjunctive			
Singular	gā	gǭ	go(es)
Plural	gān	gǭ(n)	go
Imperative			
Singular 2nd person	gā	gǭ	go
Plural 2nd person	gāþ	gǭþ	go

	Old English (West Saxon)	Middle English (Midlands)	Modern English (Standard)
PAST			
Indicative			
Singular 1st person	(iċ) ēode	(I) yede – wente	(I) went
2nd person	(þū) ēodest	(thou) yedest – wentest	(you) went
3rd person	(hē) ēode	(hē) yede – wente	(he) went
Plural	(wē, etc.) ēodon	(we, etc.) yede(n) – wente(n)	(we, etc.) went
Subjunctive			
Singular	ēode	yede – wente	went
Plural	ēoden	yede(n) – wente(n)	
Infinitive	gān	gǭ(n)	go
Present Participle	––––	gǭende – gǭinge	going
Past Participle	gān	(y–) gǭn	gone

In most respects the developmental patterns are the same as those for the larger classes of verbs: number and person inflections have been essentially "normal" at each stage of English, and the nonfinite forms show many of the usual developments. Among the differences, the principal one is the relation of the base element for nonpast and past forms. Throughout the history of English different bases occur within the paradigm—*ēod–* in Old English, *went* in Modern English; the past and nonpast bases are said to be in suppletion. The special interest in this verb is the change of the past tense base element during Middle English while the suppletive pattern persisted. Why *went–* should have replaced (Middle English) *yed–* is a matter not readily explainable. How the replacement could occur is plain enough. The consonantal type of verb *wend–* (nonpast base) in Old English meant 'go, walk' and specifically implied 'go on foot'; the stereotyped phrase *ryde or gon* 'ride or go (on foot)' in Middle English displays the specific meaning that continued from Old English. The past tense of this consonantal verb had developed a form *went–* in Middle English and it was this that replaced *yed–*. In so far as *wend* is retained in English, it continues as a normal consonantal verb with past tense *wended,* past participle *wended.*

The verb paradigm labeled *(to) be* is another set of forms in suppletion, even more varied in its base elements but not having had replacement of one of its base elements by another. Again the forms are displayed so as to provide a compressed morphological history.

	Old English (West Saxon)	**Middle English (East Midlands)**	**Modern English (Standard)**
	NONPAST		
	Indicative		
Singular			
1st person	(iċ) eom – bēo	(I) am, em	(I) am
2nd person	(þū) eart – bist	(thōu) art – bēst	(you) are
3rd person	(hē) is – biþ	(hē) is – bēþ	(he) is
Plural	(wē, etc.) sindon, sint – bēoþ	(wē, etc.) aren – bēoþ, bēn, bē	(we, etc.) are
	Subjunctive		
Singular	sīe – bēo	bē	(be)
Plural	sīen – bēon	bēn	(be)
	Imperative		
Singular	bēo – wes	bē	be
Plural	bēoþ – wesaþ	bēþ	be

	Old English (West Saxon)		Middle English (Midlands)	Modern English (Standard)
		PAST		
		Indicative		
Singular				
1st person	(iċ)	wæs	was	was
2nd person	(þū)	wǣre	wēre – wast	were
3rd person	(hē)	wæs	was	was
Plural	(wē, etc.)	wǣron	wēre(n)	were
		Subjunctive		
Singular		wǣre	wēre	(were)
Plural		wǣren	wēre(n)	
Infinitive		bēon – wesan	bēn, bē	be
Present Participle		bēonde – wesende	bēing	being
Past Participle		-----	(y–)bē(n)	been

The distinctly number and person inflections occurring as suffixes have followed the main lines of historical change while nonsuffix inflections for the grammatical categories have an independent history. The special nature of this verb is reflected in its preservation of an alternation of consonant—*was* vs. *were*—that developed long before English developed as a separate language. The same alternation had appeared on some other Old English verbs, with the base element of past tense forms (and others) differing in singular first and third person from the others: *ċēas – curon* 'chose,' *lēas – luron* 'lost,' *frēas – fruron* 'froze,' etc. For all but *(to) be,* the alternation disappeared by early Modern English with replacement of the *–r–* forms of the bases by analogy with the *–s–* forms.

Two other verbs—*will* and *do*—are also special but their morphological history need not be set down here in paradigmatic form. The special characters of *will, do, be, go* may be traced back into the earliest stages of Indo–European languages; only these four verbs in English continue a special category of the earliest known ancestral language to which English is related.

Another special category of verbs is called preterite-present. The name implies a developmental factor that sets these verbs apart. At an early stage of development in the Germanic languages some past tense verb forms were assigned special functions as a result of which they shifted from designating 'past' to 'nonpast' meaning; as could be predicted, new 'past' forms were also developed. The original verb paradigms had been of the vocalic type; the new paradigms were of the consonantal type. We shall not trace the intricacies of this prior development, but only illustrate the consequent development in English. Several of the preterite-present verbs of Old English have fallen into disuse. Those that have survived have developed still more special functions as the principal Modern English examples will imply: *can, may, shall, must, ought.* The morphology of these verbs in Modern English shows even fewer forms than verbs of the major classes: *must* and *ought,* in fact, have only one form. The morphological history is again compressed as parallel paradigms of two of these verbs, *can* and *must.* The alignment of forms is only partially satisfactory since it sets up categories with the Old English verbs that are inapplicable to the morphological descendants in Modern English. Participles have been omitted even though Old English had, for example, a passive participle *cūþ;* a Modern English reflex of this form appears in the adjective (with negating prefix) *uncouth.* The Modern English verbs do not occur as infinitives (historically or syntactically). Also, *must* (like *ought*) can no longer be said to have a past tense category, these two having partially repeated the earlier process of becoming preterite-present verbs.

	Old English (West Saxon)	Middle English (Midlands)	Modern English (Standard)
		NONPAST	
		Indicative	
Singular			
1st person	(iċ) cann; mōt	(I) can; mōt	(I) (can; must)
2nd person	(þū) canst; mōst	(thōu) canst; mōst	(you) (can; must)
3rd person	(hē) cann; mōt	(hē) can; mōt	(he) (can; must)
Plural	(wē, cunnon; mōton etc.)	(wē, cunnen; mōte(n) etc.)	(we, etc.) (can; must)
		Subjunctive	
Singular	cunne; mōte	cunne	(can; must)
Plural	cunnen; mōten	cunne(n)	(can; must)
		PAST	
		Indicative	
Singular			
(3rd person)	cūþe; mōste	couþe — coude; mōste	(could; – –)
Plural	cūþon; mōston	mōste(n)	(could; – –)
		Subjunctive	
Singular	cūþe		(could; – –)
Plural	cūþen		(could; – –)
Infinitive	cunnan	cunnen	(– – – – –)

The morphological history of preterite-present verbs gives way in significance to the syntactic history in which they participate. For the most part they have become a special class of "modal" verbs which we shall consider in a subsequent chapter. One final observation is in order, however. A few verbs have come to belong to more than one class. *Will,* in Modern English, is a verb morphologically (and distributed syntactically) like *can, may,* etc.: the only nonpast form belongs to an otherwise "defective" paradigm. *Will* is another verb—it belongs to another class—in which it carries specifically the meaning '(to) express volition'; this verb has an *-s* inflection for a nonpast form, *he wills that they proceed,* it has the past tense form *willed* (as opposed to *would*), and it has a full paradigm of the consonantal type. *Need* occurs as a "normal" verb (*needs, needed,* etc.) and with the "defective" morphology of preterite-present verbs that have come to make up part of the "modal" set of verbs: *he need not go, he need eat only what he wishes.* The second verb is particularly interesting for having replaced an earlier preterite-present verb, Old English *þurfan,* Middle English *tharf,* etc., with almost the same meaning. By and large, morphologically distinct pairs of verbs with some identical forms are rare. In terms of morphology (apart from distinct syntactic attributes such as "intransitive" and "transitive"), related verbs develop morphological distinctions. Modern English "causative" verbs provide the chief examples. New verbs of the consonantal type developed expressing the cause of an action expressed by another verb, the other (earlier) verb being a vocalic type: *set* and *sit, drench* and *drink, fell* and *fall, raise* and *rise, lay* and *lie.*

Chapter 17

WORD SETS: FORMAL AND INFORMAL

QUASI–PARADIGMATIC SETS

17.1 In this short chapter we shall consider a sample of the patternings of forms that lie in between the paradigmatic patterns of English inflections and the open system of the vocabulary at large. These borderline sets will provide a transition from the morphology to the lexicon of the language. We shall continue the study of forms, or morphs, in English, but shift from morphs whose meanings are in some important measure linked with the structure of the language itself to those whose meaning is essentially independent of the structure of English. To recall examples from Chapter 11, the present chapter will concern aspects of English that lie in the middleground between inflectional morphemes such as the *–m* of *whom* or the *–s* of *sits* and "words" such as *brother, pencil, water, virtue, morbid, ambivalent, from, and,* as well as such bound morphemes (other than inflections) as the *–th* of *ninth, –er* of *sleeper,* and *dis–* of *disenchanted.*

In Chapters 12 and 13 we observed systemic and functional relations of several sets of forms: third person pronouns (*he,* etc.), indefinite pronominals (*who, what,* etc.), determiners-pronominals (Modern English *the* only), and specifiers-pronominals (*that, this,* etc.). The symmetrical correspondences of these sets were extensive in Old English, most obviously in their obligatory inflectional forms, and in Modern English the relations among the sets may still be observed, although they are now less elaborate and complete. It was possible to isolate initial elements /h–/, /hw–/, /þ–/ for the respective Old English sets; the same notation is nearly adequate for the Modern English reflexes of these forms. In some sense, /h–/, /hw–/, and /þ–/ represent broadly a contrastive set of forms for any period of English.

The relations of these forms, in their designative and inflectional features, brings them together as a set partially resembling paradigmatic sets of inflectional forms. If it were possible to segment the initial consonantal elements from both another morphemic element *and* the suffix inflections that occur with them, the initial elements might reasonably be considered as inflectional too. These pronouns and pronominals would then be analyzed as initial inflection + base form + suffix inflection. The same set of contrasts occurs among other forms as well. The following are examples given with Old English and Modern English forms paired:

hēr	here	hwǣr	where	þǣr	there
hider	hither	hwider	whither	þider	thither
heonan	hence	hwonan	whence	þonan	thence

Other forms make up partial sets in the same pattern:

hwanne	when	þonne	then
hwilċ	which		
hwæðer	whether		
hū	how		

The correspondence to pronouns and pronominals is clear when we list some of the forms similarly:

him	him	hwām	whom	þǣm	the
hit	it	hwæt	what	þes	this
hēr	here	hwǣr	where	þǣr	there
etc.		etc.		etc.	

Despite their traditional denomination as adverbs (and adverbial conjunctions and the like) the forms *here, there, where, hither, when,* etc. may be better described as some kind of pronominal forms. The sets they form, their resemblance to pronouns and pronominals in their initial consonantal elements, and even certain of their syntactic attributes would appear to outweigh the semantic criteria by which they are classified as adverbs: the fact that they express a notion of 'when, where, how, or why'—or however the meaning-based definition of adverbs may be given—is less informative about their place in the structure of English than are the facts of their shapes and patternings. Labeling of these additional forms incorporating *h–, wh–* and *th–* is a task best left to specialists in terminology, but we may provisionally assign some descriptive labels. The sets headed by Modern English *here, hither, hence* all designate something in respect to place. If we called these sets 'pronominals of place,' *here, where, there* may be informally defined as forms referring to 'place at,' *hither, whither, thither* as 'place to,' and *hence, whence, thence* as 'place from.' *When* and *then* may be termed 'pronominals of time'; alone they make up an imperfect set, but with *now* construed as a suppletive form (roughly similar to the verb forms *go* and *went*) the set is completed. In parallel fashion, *whether* may be provisionally labeled as 'pronominal of alternates,' usually—and historically—for binary alternates and commonly for yes–no alternates: *He couldn't decide whether to go or not.* Another 'pronominal of alternates' is *which,* partially overlapping with *whether,* but more commonly used with options of any number and not usually used in connection with yes–no alternatives. Like *whether, which* was historically an adjectival inflected only as a 'strong' adjective closely similar to pronoun inflection, as we have seen. To describe *how* as a 'pronominal of means' follows the descriptive manner already established. If we add *why* to the set, it may be termed a 'pronominal of reason or cause.'

With this somewhat different analysis of *h–, wh–,* and *th–* forms, let us examine the nature of the sets they constitute. It was said earlier that if the initial elements of the forms could be segmented, they might then be classified as initial inflections. A double problem is involved: whether the initial consonantal elements are in fact morphemic; if so, whether they are to be classified as inflections. The latter of these questions can be answered with some definiteness, but any answer to the former one must remain tentative. Clearly, the *h–, wh–,* and *th–* (in the Modern English words) form sets, but to call them inflections implies that these initial consonantal elements have grammatical characteristics of the same order as those of pronoun, noun, and verb inflections or, in earlier English, those of adjective inflections. They seem to lack inflectional characteristics of case, number, and gender in not being subject to rules of grammatical concord. The categories of mood for verbs can be associated only in tenuous and imperfect ways with the *h–, wh–, th–* elements; the categories of tense inflection come only a little closer to corresponding if we associate past inflection (nonpresent) with *th–,* nonpast (present) with *h–,* leaving *wh–* unmatched. One more inflectional pattern may be considered—that of person of pronouns. It will be recalled from Chapter 12 that the three person categories segment the universe of discourse into 'speaker,' 'addressee,' and 'other.' If we conceive of the speaker category as having the attribute of immediacy, we may associate it with the nonpronoun *h–* forms *here, hither, hence* (and the suppletive form *now*) as designating immediacy of place and time. Correspondingly, 'addressee' may be assigned an attribute of stipulated identity different from the immediacy of 'speaker' but defined by its relation—'other'—to the speaker; *th–* forms *there, thither, thence, then,* as well as *the, this, that,* etc. may also be said to stipulate identity that is not immediate, not the here-and-now-or-speaker but defined in relation to the form designating immediacy. And the *wh–* forms correspond to the indefinite marking of person, thing, place, time, cause, or alternate.

The relations between the set of *h–, wh–,* and *th–* pronominals and the set of person categories of pronouns are obviously tenuous; they have, as well, the awkwardness of the correspondence of *h–* forms of pronouns with the *th–* forms of the adverblike pronominals. If this is the best we can do, the group of *h–, wh–, th–* pronominals should not be regarded as inflectionally related, even though it comes almost as close on morphological grounds to inflectional status as does the three-person set of pronouns. The question of the morphemic status of these initial consonantal elements then does not appear to be crucial. Clearly, we have some related sets of forms with definable patterns of contrasts. The sets are not quite like those involving inflectional morphemes that we group and regard as paradigmatic sets. For the convenience of considering the *h–, wh–, th–* pronominal sets in relation to other groupings of morphs, let us refer to them as quasi-paradigmatic sets.

SETS WITH AMBIVALENT CHARACTERISTICS

17.2 To leave the *h–, wh–, th–* sets in a quasi-paradigmatic status is not to evade the question of their place in the structure of English. If they were the only sets that proved intractible in thoroughgoing disposition of structural aspects of English into major, airtight divisions, we should not be content until they had been securely fixed as either inflectional or not, with a prior clear decision as to the morphemic status of these consonantal elements of the relevant morphs. To recognize that they are not the only sets with ambivalent characteristics we need only recall the morphic elements that occur in the comparison of adjectives, for example. The /–r/ and /–st/ of *slower, slowest,* of *bigger, biggest,* and the like are clearly morphemic, but the question of whether to regard them as inflections remains. Some other ostensible sets, different from the morphemes of comparison, may also be considered.

The forms designating the cardinal points of the compass provide a simple and limited case in point. If we pair the forms *north, south* and *east, west,* /–θ/ obviously recurs in the first pair and /–st/

in the second. (The Old English forms were essentially the same—*norþ, sūþ, ēast, west.*) Since the forms making up each pair designate the converse of each other in respect to terrestrial directions, perhaps we should regard /–st/ as a morpheme whose meaning is 'terrestrial direction on an axis parallel to the path of the sun,' and /–θ/ as a morpheme meaning 'terrestrial direction on an axis at right angles to the path of the sun.' If we should decide tentatively to assign these elements morphemic status, it would be necessary to ask whether /–θ/ and /–st/ are derivational forms or inflectional forms. They do not seem to signal—to "mean"—anything in relation to the structure of utterances, and if the meanings assigned informally to them are approximately right, we should have to conclude that these final consonantal elements are not inflectional. Before we can conclude anything about the recurring consonantal elements in the forms, the legitimacy of their morphemic status has to be settled. Unless we can regard the initial elements *nor–* and *sou–* and *ea–* and *we–* as morphemic (even with very special status like that of the unique element *cran–* in *cranberry*), the terminal voiceless consonants in *north, south, east, west* cannot be assigned morphemic status. To educe a scheme for integrating these ostensible sets into paradigmatic formulation would require even more ingenuity than that for associating *h–, wh–, th–* sets with person categories of pronouns. In short, the morphs designating cardinal points of the compass form sets of some sort, they are nevertheless probably not even quasi-paradigmatic; in any event, their significance as structure points in English would remain practically negligible.

ABSENCE OF MORPHOLOGICAL PATTERNING

17.3 Lest the groups of forms we have considered thus far be regarded as having no structural significance at all in their recurrent initial or final elements, other groups will show, by contrast, a clear absence of morphological patterning. One such group may be represented by *flap, flop, fling, flounce, flump, flurp, flounder, fluster, flurry.* Recurrence of initial consonants does not provide for the assignment of morphemic status to /fl–/, and certainly there is no way of setting it in partial contrast to other recurring elements. At best, we can recognize some degree of sound symbolism in /fl–/, but not much more can be claimed. A better example of sound symbolism is a group with initial /sl–/: *slip, slide, slush, slurp, slime, slick.* Another is /sn–/ forms: *snake, snoop, snooty, snout, sneer, snarl, snide.* We may add still another group with /bl–/: *blow, blop, blab, blurt, blurb, blast,* etc.

That these groups share some sound symbolism—/bl–/ signifying something like violent exhalation, /sl–/ signifying moistness and messiness, etc.—still that is about all that can be said. There are always exceptions, as well: *blue, bland,* and many others, *slow, slay, sleep, slat.* Also, there is no system to pairings or groupings such as *flop – blop* (and *cop, stop, fop,* etc.) or *snoop – sloop* and others. Elements in any language have fortuitous recurrences or symbolisms of the kind just illustrated. With such instances as the /sn–/, /sl–/, /bl–/, /fl–/ groups, we have something clearly beyond the bounds of morphology and system.

NUMERAL SYSTEM

17.4 A further kind of patterning will illustrate another principle of grouping. The patterns do not reflect morphological patternings on the order of inflections, although some of them in one way or another have affinities with morphological sets. The prime example lies in a most conservative portion of the language—the numeral system and certain forms closely associated with it. English has always had a numeral system based in its overall set of forms on the decimal system. Also built into it is a system based on twelve (the duodecimal system), as the following list will illustrate. Residual in Old English, the sexagesimal system (counting by sixties) is evident in the numeral words standing for the decades from 10 to 60 and from 70 to 120. Among several aspects of numerals that we shall not pursue is the fact that the decades, *hund(red),* and *þusend* of Old English were regularly nouns but came during Middle English to be adjectives.

Old English		Middle English	Modern English
ān	/ān	ǭn	one
twā, twēġen (etc.)	twā	twǭ	two
þrīe	þrīə	þrē	three
fēower	fēowər	fǫur(e)	four
fīf	fīf	fīf, fīve	five
siex, syx	si(ə)ks	six	six

Old English		Middle English	Modern English
seofon	seofan	seven(e)	seven
eahta	æəxta	eiȝte	eight
nigon	niġon	niȝen(e), nīne	nine
tīen	tīən	ten(e)	ten
endlefan	endlefan	en(d)lev(ne)	eleven
twelf	twelf	twelf, twelve	twelve
þrēotīene	þrēotīənə/	þrittēne	thirteen
fēowertīene	etc.	fourtēne	fourteen
. . . .		. . . . .	. . . . .
twēntiġ		twenti	twenty
þrītiġ		þretti, þritti	thirty
fēowertiġ		fourti	forty
fīftiġ		fifti	fifty
siextiġ		sixti	sixty
hund-seofontiġ		seventi	seventy
hund-eahtiġ		eiȝ(te)ti	eighty
hund-nigontiġ		niȝenti, nīn(e)ti	ninety
hund-tēontiġ, hund, hundred		hundred, hundreþ	hundred
hund-ændlæftiġ		hundred and ten	hundred and ten
hund-twelftiġ, hund-twēntiġ		hundred and twenti	hundred and twenty
. . . .		. . . . .	. . . . .
þūsend		þousend	thousand

With respect to systemic grouping of forms, the adjectives signifying count are of great interest. Let us observe first the ordinal numerals.

Old English	Middle English	Modern English
forma, fyrmest, fyr(e)st, ærest	first – ferst, etc.	first
ōþer; æfterra	oþer; secounde	second
þridda – ðirda	þridde – þirde	third
fēorþa	fourþe – ferþe	fourth
fīfta	fifte	fifth
siexta	sixte	sixth
seofoþa	seveþe, sevenþe	seventh
eahtoþa	eiȝteþe	eighth
nigoþa	niȝeþe, nīnþe	ninth
tēoþa	tēþe, tenþe	tenth
en(d)leofta	ellefte, ellevende	eleventh
twelfta	twelfte	twelfth
þrēotēoþa	þrettēþe, þrettenþe	thirteenth
etc.	etc.	etc.

The series is longer than needed for our immediate purpose in order to show in addition the operation of analogical reformation of some of the forms, such as those corresponding to *seventh, ninth,* and *tenth*. In these the cardinal forms *seven, nin, ten(e)* came to be the base of the ordinal forms. Of primary interest is the fact that the ordinal numeral forms *first* and *second* in Modern English, and their equivalents in earlier eras of English, have a different relation to the ordinal numeral forms than those beginning with *third* in the sequence. All ordinals from *third* onwards have as their base an obvious allomorph of the cardinal numeral. The two ordinals corresponding to the cardinals *one* and *two,* furthermore, are unlike. Using terminology of Romance language resources, we may describe these dispositions of terms by saying that singularity or unit, duality, and plurality (more than two) are represented in different relations of numerically matched cardinal and ordinal numeral forms. A systemic characteristic in the set of terms is implied by the one innovation in the historical pattern. The form *ōþer* 'other' was displaced in part by a Latin-derived form, *second*—the only major change in the linguistically conservative set of number words. If singularity, duality, and plurality had not somehow been systemically dominant, we should expect the Middle English equivalent of **twoth (two + th)* to have developed: but that form is not attested.

In Modern English, adjectival forms other than ordinal numerals signifying count include *all, both,* and *half.* These forms constitute a special set by virtue of their characteristic distribution within noun phrases. They are the only forms that regularly precede a determinative form in Modern English if one of them occurs within the phrase: *all the large black books, both the brothers, half the students. Both* denominates exactly two and *all* denominates more than two, while absence of either form (and absence of any numeral form) implies unity. These are the forms used with an integral count. For fractional count, the one form that does not include an allomorph of the corresponding cardinal numeral is *half;* the remaining fractional forms—*one-third, two-thirds, five-sevenths,* etc.—are derivational. Schematically, the sets may be represented in the following manner.

Numerals		Non–numerals	
Cardinal	Ordinal	Collective	Fractional
one	first	——	——
two	second	both	half
three, four . . .	third, fourth . . .	all	–third(s), –fourth(s) . . .

With these we may observe in passing the adverbial *once, twice, thrice,* noting too that no numerals beyond *three* occur within this pattern of derivation.

These patterns of count forms have affinity especially with early English pronoun morphology; the pronouns had three categories—singular, dual, and plural. Dual pronouns—those whose referents were exactly two in number—fell into disuse in early Middle English. However, at any time in the history of the language, number categories of pronouns were made up of suppletive sets, for example Old

English *þū* 'thou,' *ġit* 'you–two,' *ġē* 'ye, you (plural)'; correspondingly, the forms we have been examining form suppletive sets in numerical categories approximately congruent with number categories of pronouns.

Clearly, with the number-words we have to do with sets that are neither inflectional nor derivational. The groupings of morphs have similarities to structural features of the language but are not integral to the structure. The groupings are more nearly congruent with structural features than are other conceptually related groups of forms that will be illustrated next.

CONCEPTUALLY RELATED SETS

17.5 The forms *father, mother, brother, sister* exhaustively stipulate the possible types of members distinguished by sex in a single parent-offspring generation. For this set each member clearly consists of a single morpheme; the recurrent /–ər/ cannot be segmented as a separate morpheme, hence the set is not formed on the basis or inflectional or derivational elements. The set rests entirely on a conceptual basis in Modern English. (The shared /–ər/ is a normal phonological reflex of unstressed /–or/ in Old English, at which stage of the language's development all these forms belonged to a single small subclass of nouns: *fæder, mōdor, brōþor, sweostor;* the class included one more member, *dohtor* 'daughter.') The set and its constituent forms in Modern English are developmentally identical to those of Old English and earlier language history, as well. However, some terms for less direct genetic relationships do not have developmental identity, while the set of relationships has been modified only slightly in the ways in which they are regarded socially (and modified not at all, of course, genetically). *Uncle* replaces the Middle English reflex *em* of Old English *ēam. Aunt* replaces the Middle English reflex of Old English *faðu,* a term that designated specifically a father's sister, a relationship now expressed by the latinate phrase *paternal aunt; mōddrie – mōdriġe* in Old English designated a mother's sister, now designated by *maternal aunt. Stepfather, stepmother, stepson, stepdaughter* match exactly the Old English compound terms with *stēop–* and the corresponding kinship form. The *foster–* terms such as *foster-father* also have Old English counterparts in *fōster–,* as in *fōstor-fæder.* Old English *āþum* 'son-in-law, sister's husband' has not survived.

There are many other conceptually related sets: *old – young, large – small, king – queen, first – last, rich – poor, strong – weak, right – left, full – empty,* for example. They do not exhibit common morphemic elements, however, much less common inflectional elements. In so far as these sets may be said to form systems, the systemic relations among the members are something other than those of the structure of the language. To consider them as sets, we should have to leave behind the study of the language for a study of socially ordered ways of regarding aspects of experience reflected in, but not integral to, the language itself.

Chapter 18

STUDY OF THE ENGLISH LEXICON

A COLLECTION OF ELEMENTS

18.1 The phonology and morphology of English are characterized by rather precise and pervasive systems. The syntax and prosody will also be seen to be highly organized. That the words *set, pattern, system, systemic, systematic* have been used so often in the preceding chapters follows directly from the nature of speech sounds and inflections in our language. The history of these aspects of English has with good reason been referred to several times as an evolution—the modification of systems as they persist in time.

If the phonological and morphological elements of the language exist and change within relatively tight systems, the lexical elements exist more as a collection than as a closed system. English at all times has had "abstract" and "concrete" nouns, has had adjectives conveying favorable and unfavorable attitudes or signifying "good" and "bad" qualities, has had verbs classifiable as designating action or state of being, and so on. Although we can thus categorize words of the language, we cannot assert that the lexicon is systemic or systematic in any sense that is also applicable to those elements we have already considered. The kinship terms mentioned at the end of the preceding chapter will have made this point clear.

The history of words, singly or in groups, also differs from the history of sounds and grammatical forms. Rather than a study of the evolution of systems, resembling paleontology, historical lexicography comes much closer to resembling social history and biography. Each "word," or stem, as well as each derivational form has its history apart from the changes in sounds with which it is manifest and the fixed combinations it enters into with other morphemes. The changes in meaning—in reference to things outside the language structure—can be sorted into broad types, as we shall see in Chapter 22, just as biographies can be categorized as dealing with rise or decline, achievement or failure, of the subject person; or as they can be sorted into types such as biographies of military heroes, martyrs, thinkers, humanitarians, tyrants, and the like. Biography is considered good only when it recounts the individuality, the uniqueness, of its subject within a more familiar pattern to which a life history may be assigned. No matter how many biographies we have read, the next one we read will be different. Similarly, no matter how many etymologies we may learn, we may expect the next word to have its own history, which usually will be in some way unlike any particular etymology we have read before.

To attempt anything like a comprehensive survey of etymologies of English words is impractical; the best resources are etymological and historical dictionaries. Given our purposes here, there is little point to assembling a collection of case histories of notable words in the language, entertaining as such a collection may be; a number of books, some of which have attained the status of modest classics, are readily accessible and to be recommended. Instead of lists and collections of lexical data, this and the following chapters will deal with the vocabulary of English more briefly, centering on the persisting aspects and patterns of modification of the English lexicon.

DEVICES OF NEGATION

18.2 An ideal procedure in studying the lexicon of English is that of comparing utterances differing in time and place of origin but purporting to be equivalent. Translations of a single text provide this kind of data. Two texts and a third in the Modern English glossing will serve as an example:

> Hēt hē him his seax ārǣċan tō scrēadiġenne ǣnne æppel. (Ælfric, c. 1000)
>
> He badd himm brinngenn ænne cnif, an apell forr to shrædenn. (Orm, c. 1200)

'He bade him hand (to him) his (*or* a) knife, to pare an apple.' The pronouns remain constant, as does the word *apple; shred (scrēad–, shræd–)* has changed meaning so that *pare* is the Modern English equivalent; *knife – cnif* replaces *seax, bade – badd* replaces *hēt,* and so on. The three translations of a single text given in 1.2 provide another sample. This procedure is impractical, however, because of the limited number and uneven chronological distribution of suitable texts. Moreover, lexical history has been developed as the study of individual words (as they are listed in dictionaries), not as the study of the lexical items with which a meaning or sentence concept is expressed.

The lexicon of English can be described in both its synchronic and diachronic aspects by several other important means. These ways are not mutually exclusive, and they do not lend themselves to hierarchical ordering. To examine additions to the vocabulary borrowed from other languages requires that we consider words both as they have come into English and the subsequent effects of their presence in the language. These effects are evident in the processes of derivation and compounding and the like. To consider additions to the vocabulary through derivation or compounding may bring up matters of syntax as well as certain aspects of borrowing. Semantic categories, sources of vocabulary, morphemic structure of words are all subjects with different inherent structures; hence only one subject can be pursued at a time.

Some ways in which the study of vocabulary items may intergrade with morphological, syntactic, semantic, phonological, and still other factors are well illustrated in the devices of negation in English. Let us take first a simple aspect—the development of the form *not.* It is a free form in Modern English, unlike the inflections, but is not a reference-signaling term; it denotes a logical conception, as opposed to an empirical conception such as that signaled by most ordinary nouns, pronouns, verbs, and adjectives. Its function is to negate a word, as *not burn,* or phrase, as *not on the way out,* or clause, as *That's not going to be finished today.* The form derives historically as the coalescence of two separate forms, *āwiht* 'aught, anything' or, adverbially, 'at all, by any means' and an earlier negating particle *ne;* the two forms regularly occurred in the collocation *ne āwiht. Ā–wiht,* furthermore, was originally a compound form made from *ā* 'ever, always' and *wiht* 'creature, wight, thing.' The coalescence of the negating particle with *āwiht* was in the nature of negative contractions typified by Modern English *isn't* (*is* + *not*), *doesn't* (*does* + *not*). Part of the story of this form involves the pairing of *āwiht* and *ne āwiht* > *nāht* (in Old English) that may be understood from their descendent forms *aught* and *naught.* A by-form of this development is *nought.* The three phonemes of Middle and Modern English *not* correspond to the three separate original forms *ne* + *ā* + *wiht* which combined by compounding and coalescence.

The development of *not* as a general purpose negative particle is not comprehended in merely the etymology of the form. Syntactic structures are also relevant, as are some poorly understood "principles of negation" that apparently form part of the psychological aspects of language use. Some data are clear and fully attested. The principal mode of negation in the earliest eras of English involved use of a general purpose negative particle *ne;* it was used prior to the development of *not.* Regularly it preceded the element it negated: Old English *nǣfre* 'never' is a coalesced form of *ne* + *ǣfre* 'not + ever,' *nā* 'no, not at all' reflects its origin *ne* + *ā* 'not + ever, always,' *nān* < *ne* + *ān* 'not + one; none'; *ne* preceding the finite verb negated the verb (or verb phrase) and often coalesced with the very common verbs with initial vowel, *w*, or *h*, so that *ne wæs* 'was not' and *næs* 'wasn't,' *nis* 'isn't,' *ne wǣre* 'were not,' *nǣre* 'weren't,' *ne wolde* 'would not,' *nolde* 'wouldn't' and others were altogether normal; *ne* preceding a clause negated the entire clause, and *ne . . . ne . . .* occurred correlatively with about the same function as Modern English *neither . . . nor. . . .* In clauses redundant negative elements were fully established: *iċ nāht singan ne cuðe* literally 'I didn't know how to sing nothing– (not–) at–all'; *ne þurfan ġē nōht besorgian* 'You needn't (not–) at–all be anxious.' Even triple negation, though less usual, was not abnormal or ungrammatical.

In the last example may be seen the pattern in which *not* (< *nōht, nāht*) began to develop towards its present nature. The finite verb form *þurfan* was negated by *ne*, with the negation of the clause indicated by the negated verb placed at the beginning. *Nōht* followed the construction of verb plus pronoun-subject but preceded the infinitive *(besorgian)* that completed the predication; *nōht* had adverbial status as a coalesced phrase, reinforcing or perhaps emphasizing the negation. Typically, negativization of a clause was achieved by negating the finite verb, and the adverbial reinforcement was positioned by the verb or within a verb phrase. The forms like *nōht*, however, never preceded a negated finite verb form, since the position of *ne* was rigidly fixed immediately preceding the form it negated. Greatly simplified and schematized is the following abstract of the course of evolution of negation of predicates in English (the examples are Jespersen's, from *Negation in English and Other Languages*):

Iċ ne secge.
I ne seye not.
I say not.
I do not say.
(I don't say.)

Particularly interesting in this developmental pattern is the return of the negative particle to a position preceding the principal verb word: *ne secge* and *(do) not say* are closely parallel. How this should have come to be is a complex matter involving syntactic features and probably some psychological factors. A few factors, however, may be mentioned. *Not* replaced the particle *ne* in verb negation and in some other functions as well. Modern English examples will suggest the historical factors. Compare "I don't want to challenge the principle", "I want not to challenge the principle (but to . . .)," "I want to challenge not the principle (but the . . .)." In short, *not*, like *ne* earlier, has many negating uses and regularly precedes the specific part of the sentence that is specifically to be negated. A sentence in early Modern English beginning *I say not* . . . leaves the negative particle positionally ambiguous: "I say not to him that . . ." vs. "I say not that . . ." will illustrate the point. Certainly, the risk of misunderstanding in this ambiguity was not great; for other speech factors of stress and grouping of sentence parts were available to obviate any misconstruing of what element was to be negated. (We shall consider these other speech factors that complement syntax in later chapters.) Using punctuation to indicate differences in way of speaking these sentences we may distinguish "I say not, to him, that . . . ," "I say, not to him, that . . . ," or "I say not, that . . . ," "I say, not that . . . ." The development of auxiliary verbs during approximately the same periods as the development of the patterns *I ne seye not* and *I say not* provided the materials to which to attach the negative particle so that it would precede the semantically prominent verb. Apparently the positional ambiguity of *not* in the pattern *I say not* was an important factor in the return of the negator to a position preceding the prominent, that is, nonauxiliary, verb form. Another equally important factor was the attachment of the negating element by position to the finite verb form, the form inflected for grammatical signaling.

OTHER NEGATING DEVICES

18.3 Among other devices of negation a most common one is that of affixing a negating morpheme to a word. The prefix *un–* has been in English from the beginning of its history. Through heavy borrowing of Latin or Latin-derived words during the periods of Middle and Modern English, the prefixes *in–, ir–, il–, im–* also indicate negation of the forms to which they attach: *incessant, irresistible, illiterate, immediate;* they were allomorphs in the source language, phonetically conditioned by assimilation to the following consonant that stood initially in the root form. Historically they are cognate with English negative *un–*. They cannot be claimed in English to be simply allomorphs of English *un–,* even though for most words they are distributed as allomorphs: in some instances they contrast and must therefore be designated as different morphemes. There are differences, for example, between *unartistic* as applied to a child's not having artistic skills and *inartistic* as applied to an adult's having produced a thing not considered artistic. The history of the English lexicon contains many examples of shifts in the use of these related negating prefixes, putting the lexical resources of borrowing and derivation into a most complex web of interrelations: *impossible* and *unpossible, inglorious* and *unglorious* and many more pairs have occurred in the language.

Furthermore, negativization cannot be fully described in English without taking into account many other factors as well. The prefix *a(n)–* 'not, without' got into English with borrowings of Greek words: *anarchy, amorphous, anacoluthon, amoral.* Much the same force of the negative prefixes is conveyed by the suffix *–less,* which has been present and employed continuously in all periods of English. Paired words denoting contrary circumstances also imply the negation: *failure* is the negative of *success; negative* and *positive, plus* and *minus, yes* and *no, absent* and *present, exclude* and *include,* and many more are words with each member of the pair signifying the negative of the other member. If negation of *right* is now expressed by a paired word *wrong,* it was expressed in Old English by *unriht* (= *unright*); *wrong,* at least as a negative of *right,* developed as a borrowing from a Scandinavian language. Understatement may carry negation without utilizing words denoting negation: *I hardly think so,* for example, especially when spoken as irony is clearly negative. Some distributional factors make up part of the nature of the use of *un–* in negativization. In Modern English *un–* attaches to adjectives and adverbs —both root forms and derived forms—with relatively few restrictions as in *unkind, unfair;* it contrasts partially with some fixed phrases made with *non–,* a prefix in English but a negating adverb in Latin, from which it was borrowed. With the introduction of *non–* about half way through the recorded history of English, the meaning and distribution of *un–* was modified. English *un–* does not attach freely to nouns consisting of a single root or a compound of root forms. It combines readily with participial adjectives: *unneeded, uneaten, unbeaten, uncut,* and the like. These distributional characteristics have persisted throughout the history of English, though a great number of individual words have undergone change.

THE MANY FACETS OF THE LEXICON

18.4 In sum, the lexicon of English is a congeries of items having a wide variety of facets of disparate natures. To take but one example, the morphemic makeup of words—the patterns of fixed combinations of forms—is one facet, but to consider any more than the abstract patterns of these combinations in English we need to reach variously into the history of borrowing from other languages, into syntax, into phonology, or other topics. Indeed, for the modern vocabulary of technology, the morphemic patterns of words in source languages for English vocabulary is often relevant. For giving order to the following exposition, we shall nevertheless have to deal with one facet at a time, and it is with borrowing that we shall begin.

Chapter 19

LEXICAL RESOURCES: BORROWING

CONDITIONS OF BORROWING

19.1 That the lexicon of English is extremely mixed in its origins has long been anathema to some, a cause for celebration by others, and a matter of unconcern to most speakers of the language. During the renaissance the task of "enriching" the language—in effect, the introduction of countless words, mostly from Latin—was carried on by some with serious dedication only to be opposed by others with a contempt symbolized by the term *inkhornism* they applied to bookish and bombastic words thus brought into English. During the nineteenth century the relearning of Old English inspired many to wish to see English "purified" of foreign words, returning the language to its "Saxon" splendor. Nevertheless, words from many languages had been "borrowed" into English and a great many of them were retained. By the time of early Modern English—about the time of world exploration, colonization, increased learning, and the beginning of modern science—the wide contact of speakers of English with other languages began to bring words from the most diverse sources into the language at a rapid rate. The precedent for borrowing had become well established before the merits and demerits of the process had become an issue: English had permanently incorporated seven thousand or more words from French during the period of Middle English.

Both the process and the attendant conditions of borrowing preclude the incorporation of most lexical elements except nouns, verbs, and adjectives. The nature of foreign borrowing (as opposed to dialect borrowing) normally consists simply of the use of a morpheme or morpheme combination within discourse that is substantially in another language. In strict terms, of course, borrowing occurs between idiolects—one person using a form he learns from another person, even when both speak the "same" language; dialect borrowing also occurs, and is in effect a statistical abstraction of the process represented by idiolect borrowing. By and large, "borrowing" by a language is understood to mean incorporation by a significant segment of the speech population of lexical elements native to a different language. Thus, a borrowing by English denotes the incorporation of lexical elements of foreign origin into the speech system of a segment of the English-speaking peoples.

The characterization of borrowing in the preceding paragraph is made somewhat laborious, not so much to establish the meaning of the fairly familiar term, but to clarify the reason for lexical borrowing being so rigidly limited to stems and especially to certain classes of words. Seldom is a sentence borrowed by a language. Except for exclamations—a very special category of sentences—only a few short sentences can be said to have come into English from foreign sources: *Veni, vidi, vici; Che sera sera; C'est la guerre.* The latter two are not far removed from exclamations. Borrowed phrases, other than a few like *etcetera,* seldom occur except within the jargon of trades, professions (especially law), or other special groupings of speakers. Many phrases, nevertheless, have come to constitute single words in English: a *post mortem* (compound word), for example, or a compound word consisting of the names of letters, such as *A.M., P.M., A.D., B.C., Q.E.D.* Sentences and phrases can be translated as long as generally equivalent terms and syntactic patterns can hold these terms in generally equivalent constructions. Except for very short sentences or phrases that recur with considerable frequency, constructions of this order will not often be understood in the context of discourse in a different language: translation will be required if normal (understood) discourse is to occur. If, however, a foreign word stem is used in an English sentence, most of the utterance including probably all its structure will be understood, and any incompleteness of normal comprehension can be made good by giving a definition (verbal, ostensive, or otherwise) of the non-English word. For the semantically important lexical element to be used in an English sentence, an item of an inflectional form class will occur with its English rather than foreign inflection: the inflection is part of the structural machinery of the English sentence.

The other-language elements adopted by English have always been almost entirely stems. Derivational morphemes, such as *–able,* have ultimately a foreign source but, as we shall see in the next chapter, these morphemes normally can be considered derivational within English only after they are no longer borrowings in any pragmatic sense. Inflectional morphemes are not borrowed either, as a rule, and historically foreign inflections ordinarily form only restricted allomorphs of the inflectional forms of the language; some examples, for nouns, were cited in 15.5. Foreign lexical elements, furthermore, are rarely found in the classes conjunctions and prepositions, or in the auxiliary verbs, or in the nouns, verbs, and adjectives most commonly used.

Sputnik provides a versatile example not only of the linguistic aspects of borrowing, but of some nonlinguistic ones as well. When the Soviet Union launched the first man-made object and established its orbital movement around the earth, there was no word in general currency in English for precisely this kind of object; the spectacular and unexpected nature of the achievement—together with its political implications—created a need for a term to describe a man-made object orbiting the earth through technological means. The name of the first object of this kind was (in English) *Sputnik I*. When only one such object was in existence calling it by its Russian name was appropriate for speakers of English. Though a unique object with a name that included numerical designation, the uniqueness was obviously only temporary: *sputnik* came into English essentially as both name and noun.

Probably no word has entered English so suddenly—that is, no word has become part of the lexicon of a great majority of speakers in so short a time. The period required for assimilation of the word into English is measured in hours, not years or decades. The suddenness is attributable to the means and extensiveness of electronic communication, the significance of the object designated by the term, and the lack of an English word for just that sort of object. However, its introduction into English reflects normal aspects of lexical borrowing. The pronunciation was in normal English phonology; pronunciation also varied, as may be observed by examining the pronunciation sections of entries in dictionaries that list the word. In respect to its morphological characteristics, the term entered English (as a noun) only as a stem. Pluralization was ordinary English—*sputniks*.

The name and noun *sputnik* entered English in 1957 as an item in the lexicon of most speakers except small children. That ten years later it should be unknown to a large proportion of speakers born since that year reflects some other aspects of borrowing and assimilation that are also pertinent. Partly for political and general cultural reasons and partly for linguistic reasons the term declined rapidly in use. Political rivalry between English-speaking and Russian-speaking nations created the need for English-speaking peoples to have a non-Russian term to designate the same type of object created by Americans. The fact that the original term was a name for a unique object *(Sputnik I)* made the establishment of an alternate, non-Russian term the easier. Furthermore, the orbiting objects had not become numerous or commonplace enough for their individual names not to be prominent. While as a noun the pluralized form *sputniks* occurred, subsequent establishment of an alternate term already in English changed the status of the borrowed term: it reverted to naming one Russian-built orbiting object or (as a noun) one of a few such objects originally thus named with numerical designation. The general name, in English, for all such objects subsequently became *satellite*—a term accurately translating *sputnik*. A major linguistic reason for the displacement of the borrowed Russian word was the paucity in English of other words from the same source language, especially words with partial resemblance to it. Although as a noun *sputnik* will probably remain displaced, analogical creations within English—such as *peacenik* and *beatnik*—have become fairly common.

OLD ENGLISH AND EARLY MIDDLE ENGLISH BORROWINGS

19.2 The meteoric career of the borrowed *sputnik* is not matched elsewhere in the history of English and is rarely even approximated among the tens of thousands of borrowings in English. Words have entered (and dropped out of) the language at rates conditioned extensively by the prevalent modes of communication in which they were used. An average audience of less than a dozen people and an audience of perhaps ten million, and repetition at intervals of days or months as opposed to repetition at intervals of hours account for the great difference between the introduction and assimilation of most words in English and the one spectacular instance of borrowing in 1957. The difference between propagation of a new word by speech and by writing also makes a difference in borrowing, as much in the kind of words concerned as in the rate of adoption. These fairly obvious factors of numbers of speakers, frequency and conditions of speaking situations, and the differences between vocal and written use of the language comprehend the most significant particular facets of the history of borrowing in English. To speak of the hospitality or the aversion of a language in respect to borrowing is merely to use metaphors, harmless enough in themselves, but likely to lead to misapprehension of the real factors when they are construed literally.

Borrowing during the period of Old English and well into the period of Middle English was not extensive. Speakers of Germanic dialects in England—the dialects becoming differentiated as the separate, English language—had little occasion, need, or means to adopt words from other languages. Their Germanic dialects were sufficiently similar for ordinary communication on a variety of subjects. The speakers' linguistic contacts outside of England were primarily with speakers of other Germanic dialects (in the regions of modern Sweden, Holland, Denmark, the Frisian Islands, northwestern Germany). Within England the speakers had minimal linguistic contact with non-English speakers. The romanized Celts were a politically subordinate people, a large number of whom were compelled to live in regions not controlled by the Anglo-Saxons. Even when they lived in the same regions, agricultural as well as other factors kept them effectively separated linguistically from English-speakers: Anglo-Saxons preferred to farm river valleys, while the native people preferred higher, sandy soils. Aside from place-names—*London* being the prime example—and a few topographical terms, almost no words entered English from the languages of the roman Celts; and place-names, important as they are for many historical purposes, are only peripheral lexical items in the development of a language.

Nevertheless, there came to be an influential group of people in England who regularly used the Latin language: the primary definition of the group was not linguistic, and the influence was of a specific kind only—the clergy in whose hands were the spread and administration of Christianity. A number of words were incorporated into English from Latin in the generations that saw the conversion of Anglo-Saxons to Christianity; most were to the religion on the same order as topographical and place-names were to geography: *angel, pope, deacon, psalm, disciple, priest, mass, minster,* and the like (cited here in their Modern English forms). That these were fully assimilated into the language is attested by their subsequent phonological history—undergoing phonological change identical to that of native English words—and by the variety of derivatives and compounds in which they appear. Here is but one example:

mynster	'monastery, minster'
mynster–bōc	'minster–book'
mynster–clūse	'minster–close'
mynster–fæder	'abbot'
mynster–hām	'minster–home, i.e., monastery'
mynster–land	'land owned by a monastery'
mynster–līċ	'monastic'
mynster–līf	'monastic life'
mynster–prēost	'priest of a minster'
mynster–munuc	'monk who lives in a monastery'
mynster–prafost	'provost of a minster'
mynster–stede	'monastic building (Cf. *homestead*)'

(The morphs *abbot, preost, munuc,* and *prafost* were themselves Old English borrowings from Latin.) Besides the many Latin-derived words for Christian concepts, church officials, parts of liturgy, and the like, a few other Latin words were incorporated into English—as diverse as *plante, –ian* 'plant' and *fers* 'verse.' A good many terms were introduced, not as borrowing in the strict sense, but as translation of Latin terms: *mildheortness* (Modern English cognates *mild–heart–ness*) renders *misericordia, þryness* 'three-ness, trinity' renders *trinitas, godspell* (> *gospel*) renders *evangelium.*

By the end of the Old English period another type and source of borrowing became significant, with much different conditions and effects. The widespread settlement of Scandinavian peoples in northeastern regions of England, after generations of raiding and smaller settlements, established a variety of Germanic dialects in England somewhat different from those of the Anglo-Saxons. In earlier chapters we have seen some ultimate effects of "Norse" language on the phonology of English and on the inflectional system of the language. It was from the "Danes" (as the Anglo-Saxons called Scandinavians generally) that the pronoun forms *they, their, them* came; as we saw, these forms are lexical borrowings conditioned by morphological more than semantic features. The verb form *are* is likewise of Scandinavian origin. The preposition *till* owes its place in English to the Scandinavian dialects. For a great many words the term "borrowing" is only partially appropriate, since it is the phonemic shape that is owed to the other language rather than the presence of the lexical item in English: *bask, boon, stack, cast, sky, gate, egg, law* are typical examples whose historical relationships to English forms is best traced in such sources as the *Oxford English Dictionary.* Well more than a thousand place-names in England are Scandinavian. The influence of Scandinavian dialects on the English language reflects the circumstances of the linguistic contact. The peoples of the two language groups spoke dialects almost different enough to be classed as separate languages, yet similar enough to permit some communication and the ready development of communication with nearly full comprehension. Principal words were cognates in the two languages and the grammatical systems had considerable congruity. The borrowing entailed spoken communication almost exclusively. These circumstances go a long way toward accounting for the relatively small number of borrowings of nouns, verbs, and adjectives beside the large number of place-names, unequalled borrowing of pronoun forms, and the adoption of the semiforeign forms of words cognate to native English ones. The paucity of linguistic records of the first four hundred years of Scandinavian and English linguistic contact in England leaves much of the history beyond recovery.

MIDDLE ENGLISH BORROWINGS FROM FRENCH

19.3 Much better documented, for both the inventory of lexical items and the conditions under which borrowing occurred, is the levy on French that occurred during the period of Middle English. The two languages were dissimilar enough so that distinguishing historically between English and French forms, making the "internal reconstruction" of the borrowing, is a practical procedure. (It should be added, however, that a good number of words cannot be distinguished as French or Latin in language origin, since many words had similar forms in the two languages, and many of them were probably borrowed in their forms in both languages, usually with the French form finally dominating.) Historical records are extensive for the social, political, economic, geographic, and general cultural relations of English and French speakers for the period in which the extensive borrowing took place. The circumstances of linguistic contact between speakers of English and speakers of French produced borrowing of an unprecedented number of lexical items, with a negligible number of place-names and no items in the classes of pronouns, prepositions, and conjunctions.

The single rule of England and portions of (modern) France following the Norman Conquest entailed several significant conditions of linguistic influence. While French-speaking nobility were but a small minority of the population, French was instituted for law, some of the schooling, a share of church affairs not carried on in Latin; French merchants had special privileges; French literature was dominant, and so on. French had both prestige and practical importance for the English, it was encountered by most classes of people to some extent, and it was present in both speech and writing. Borrowing of French terms did not proceed much more rapidly in the century after the Conquest than before it, however, the non-English language remaining essentially a second language of Britain. To cite but one social factor keeping the languages apart, the French merchants brought into major English cities tended to live within restricted areas —in social and linguistic enclaves. Subsequent political and social changes produced extensive bilingualism for both native speakers of English and native speakers of French; but for the majority of speakers, English was the native and predominant language, and their bilingualism was apparently restricted to understanding some of the second language but speaking it in only limited and imperfect ways. The bilingualism of both French and English speakers, however qualified, was nevertheless of crucial significance.

Between 1250 and 1400 the rate of appearance of French words in English increased strikingly. The social history, well presented in brief, comprehensive form in Albert C. Baugh's *A History of the English Language,* may be epitomized by saying that it was more and more the case that speakers of English incorporated French words into their utterances (and writings) with confidence that they should be understood. If we keep in mind the varieties of linguistic experience that existed, the understanding of a French word in an English sentence by both French and English speakers would tend to increase the rate of borrowing. We have to rely on written records to trace the trends and incidence of borrowing; these records suggest, however, that understanding by English speakers of French words incorporated into English sentences commonly proceeded from familiarity with French rather than by definition of the incorporated term. Fourteenth century biblical translation, sermons, and literary narratives seldom gloss a French word. In the following quotation from Chaucer's *Parson's Tale,* a number of French-derived words occur without gloss; curiously enough, it is a native word *(wanhope)* that is glossed by an originally French word:

> Thanne shaltow [= shalt thou] understonde whiche thynges *destourben penaunce;* and this is in foure *maneres,* that is, drede, shame, hope, and wanhope, that is, *desperacion.* And for to speke first of drede; for which he weneth that he may *suffre* no *penaunce;* ther-agayns is *remedie* for to thynke that bodily *penaunce* is but short and litel at *regard* of the *payne* of helle, that is so *cruel* and so long that it lasteth withouten ende.

Of the nine different French-derived words in this passage, at least half are first recorded in English at about 1300; *desperacion* is recorded only from Chaucer's own times. The words that occur from about 1225 are cited typically in historical dictionaries from *Ancrene Riwle;* in that earlier text, however, many French terms are glossed with English ones: *Consence, þet is skiles ȝettunge* 'Consent, that is reason's acquiescence,' *desperaunce, that is in unhope and in unbileave forto beon iboruwen* 'despair, that is lack of hope and lack of belief in being redeemed.' Except in special instances, a written text, translation or not, is not a likely place to find glossing as an integral part of the text: writers then as now, presumably, tended to choose those words they should expect their audiences to understand immediately. Near absence of paired words—one borrowed and one native—of defining clauses, and of other hints concerned with lexical familiarity suggest nevertheless that the borrowing proceeded under the conditions described above.

That French words were borrowed for the most familiar as well as the unfamiliar concepts is both a major aspect of this phase of borrowing and another indication of the extensive bilingualism of both native English speakers and French speakers; that French words should have displaced native English words is of special significance—the example of *wanhope* > *despair* is by no means unique. Commonplace are such words as *face, age, arm, large, poor, reason, country, river, uncle, war, save, pay, nice, gay, use, please, dance, change, waste.* The use of French over a long period for law introduced dozens of terms such as *bar, bail, judge, heir, property,* besides the more technical terms still characteristic of jargon of the legal profession. *Government* is a French word, and to government affairs belong such borrowed terms as *tax, state, court.* Names of foods and domestic equipment, names of social classes, personal traits, diseases—for these subject areas and many more the French language was the source of thousands of lexical items in English. The word *language* came into English from French, as *langage,* in turn related to Latin *lingua* 'Tongue.'

The phonology and morphology of Anglo-French did not offer any serious obstacle to extensive borrowing. The sounds of French spoken in England formed different sets and patterns, but to a great extent they "matched up" with those of English. We have seen already the relation of voiced spirants to the evolving system of English spirants and stops. The most prominent mismatching, the diphthongal /oy/ that had no English equivalent, led to introduction of the diphthong into English via the French words that contained it. Noun morphology, to take only one example, coincided sufficiently with that of English at that period to enable ready incorporation of French stems in English sentences. Grammatically neuter and feminine nouns had only number-contrasting inflection, singular Ø opposed to plural *–s.* The well developed contrasts of singular Ø vs. plural /–əs/ in Middle English leaves somewhat ambiguous the matter of whether English adopted French words complete with number inflection. In some instances the French plural-inflected forms do seem to have been taken into English, for such spellings as *vestemenz, marchauntz* 'vestments,' 'merchants' indicate termination in [ts], the plural morpheme being shaped thus /–s/ rather than normal English /–əs/. Even so, any word that is recorded in a form like that in the examples just given is also recorded with suffix spellings in *–es, –ys,* and the like, indicating that English pluralization of the French stems was also normal and in most instances apparently dominant. Somewhat different was the pattern of inflection of French grammatically masculine nouns. These nouns retained subject-object case inflection as well as number inflection in French, but already in the thirteenth century had begun "passing over" into the major morphological class comprising feminine and neuter nouns. Typical paradigms are the following for *murs* 'wall' and *bers* 'baron':

	Singular		Plural	
Subject	murs	bers	mur	baron
Object	mur	baron	murs	barons

From the partial resemblances between paradigmatic patterns like these and the pattern of the dominant class of Middle English nouns, it has been inferred that speakers of Middle English adopted the accusative case forms of Old French masculine nouns. The inference, thus formulated, enables one to predict accurately the English form of borrowing from French, with only a few inevitable exceptions. That the formulation is misleading, however, may not only be guessed from the nature of lexical borrowing, but from proposing an alternate formulation equally utilitarian but altogether implausible. Let us place English and French paradigms of this kind side by side:

	Singular			Plural	
Subject	murs	Subject	name	mur	names
Object	mur	Possessive	names	murs	

A fuller correspondence is registered if we should say that the French object-case form became the English subject-case form, and the French subject-case form became the English possessive-case form, in the singular; in the plural, the object-case forms became English subject-case and possessive-case forms, and the French subject-case form may have reinforced the singular subject case in English. ("Subject-case" is better called "nonpossessive" for the English example.) Obviously, this accounting for the borrowed lexical items is as untenable as it is elaborate. The example of *bers, baron,* etc., given above, is more informative: of the morphs in the paradigm of the term meaning 'baron' the stem *baron–* was abstracted, contrary to the French model, but in accordance with the normal morphological structure of English words. Whatever the case in the source language, in instances like these English borrowed the lexical items as (English) stems.

The point about stem borrowing as the essential procedure in morphologically simple words can be illustrated with another word brought into English through French, during the period of Middle English. The present-day stem *admiral* entered English from both French *amiral* and *admiral;* the source was the Arabic form that has also given English *ameer, amir, emir* (variant spellings). Misunderstanding of the Arabic structure, however, made of the construction *amir al*—— 'commander of ——' a single word stem, *amiral.* The stem was influenced analogically in Latinized *amiralis* by *admirari* 'to wonder at,' hence the second shape *admiral–*, the source of Modern English *admiral.*

BORROWING OF LATIN FORMS

19.4 The next major source of foreign word stems in English, in the chronology of the language, was Latin. Some Latin forms had been brought into English throughout its early history, and a few words like *cheese, wine, street* had been borrowed in pre-English Germanic dialects. The extensive borrowing from French during Middle English established a very large number of words in English that were cognate with Latin words, French being a Romance language closely related to Latin. Direct borrowing from Latin on a large scale began after the period of wholesale importation of French morphs. This borrowing dates from about 1500, reaching its most prominent—and controversial—development during the English renaissance, and has continued right on through most of the period of Modern English.

Latin had been the principal language of advanced learning all through the early history of English, but from the renaissance the mainstream of Latin borrowings arose. The renewed learning was in Latin. French had ceased to be for English speakers a second language, whether for commerce, literature, or more ordinary affairs. Literacy began to increase significantly at about the same time. Schools taught Latin, for it was in Latin that the principal learning in law, theology, medicine, and literature was to be found. Formal education made latinists of all who had a nominal term of schooling. The increase in literacy and education was accelerated notably by the full establishment of printing in the sixteenth century. In short, the community of users of Latin as a second language took on a size and activeness and cultural significance it had not had before.

Borrowing of Latin words thus proceeded by two means—by incorporation of foreign terms into spoken English and by the use of these terms in written English. For many of the terms there was a genuine need, since the new learning made use of many concepts foreign to the speakers of English and for which, consequently, they had no items in their English lexical inventory. For many there was no particular need, and only the arrogance of education or the notion of the superiority of Latin or other such notions of prestige of the learned vocabulary induced individuals to chose a Latin-derived word when an English one was available. Whatever the motivation, a person introducing Latin words into English sentences could expect his readers or hearers to understand him, or if he were not understood, it was only for lack of his audience's fitness for learned discourse.

Under these circumstances two common aspects of borrowing emerged for the first time in the history of the English lexicon. One was the deliberateness of introduction of foreign lexical items by individuals, primarily through their writings; and the writings were now reproduced rapidly in many copies by printing. The other was the evolution of a stratum of vocabulary now generally called "learned" as opposed to "popular." Many Latin-derived words passed into the "popular" vocabulary, either directly or indirectly—*recipe, item, fact, anticipate, exact, contradictory,* for example. The steady influx of Latin elements (and their recombinations and derivations in English) reflects the advancement of learning, of knowledge, that has steadily continued for English-speaking peoples since the renaissance: it is in the "learned" vocabulary that Latin has come to be as important a lexical source in Modern English as French had been for the lexicon of ordinary affairs in late Middle English. About one-fourth of the lexicon of Latin has been incorporated into English, according to the calculations by Greenough and Kittredge (*Words and Their Ways in English Speech,* p. 106).

GREEK AS A SOURCE OF ENGLISH WORDS

19.5 The remaining major foreign language source of English words is Greek. Unlike the other major sources, Greek was never a spoken-language source for English, even as Latin was to some extent. Greek continued as a language from the time English emerged as a separate language, but it was the classical, not a contemporary form of Greek upon which English drew. We noted that the nature of contact with Latin changed from about 1500, making right the conditions for importation of a remarkably large block of the lexical inventory of that language. Latin had had a continuous tradition of use as a learned language, but Greek had not for northern Europeans: it was revived by scholars within the period of Modern English. Much of Greek learning as well as many Greek words had made their way into English culture through Latin by 1600, and more came rapidly into English after that time. Some words from this source have become common in English: *crisis, encyclopedia, biography, atlas,* and the like, as well as very old borrowings such as *church* and *devil.* But Greek did not have the nearly universal status within schooling that Latin had for centuries (well into the nineteenth century, or longer), and it had not been familiarized and mixed with another language to the extent that Latin had with French. To note an illuminating fact, Greek texts were translated to a greater extent than Latin ones were into English before the twentieth century.

The remoteness, the lack of intimacy of contact of English and classical Greek is one factor that made it ultimately a prime source for new words in English. That Greek was used in much the same way in French and English and other European languages was another factor: *telegraph* derives from Modern French *télégraphe* a compound made in French from Greek morphs; *telescope* has its origin in Italian *telescopio* (Galileo's term) and Modern Latin *telescopium,* based on a Greek stem; *telepathy* was coined in English in 1882 (by F. W. Myers). A word adopted from Greek or coined from Greek morphs in any of the modern European languages is immediately adaptable in recognizable orthographic form to the other languages in which the Greek lexical resources have been exploited. Another factor by which Greek has come to be a prime lexical resource is that the morphological structure of compound and derived word stems is similar to that of the modern European languages. Finally, a nonlinguistic factor of greatest importance is the relatively sudden emergence of modern science and technology principally among speakers of European languages, creating an unprecedented demand for terminology that could not be supplied from native language resources if two practical conditions were to be met: a consistency, a fixity of meaning of constituent morphemes of the complex terminology, and an immediate intelligibility of the terminology for speakers of Romance and Germanic languages alike. That the new terminology could have been made up for the most part from native resources is attested by German—*Fernsprecher* and *Wasserstoff* being loan translations corresponding to Greek-derived *telephone* and *hydrogen*—and more recently by Japanese *denwa* literally 'lightning speech' corresponding to *telephone, dempoo* literally 'lightning report' corresponding to *telegraph.* That some principal languages in which science and technology developed could utilize the resources of the Greek lexicon when the sudden expansion of the sciences began at once facilitated the interchange and advancement of science and reinforced the tendencies in English (and other languages) to incorporate Greek-derived words into the vocabulary. Thence many of the learned words of science have passed into popular lexicon—*psychology, psychopath(ology), thermometer, thermostat, gyroscope, sclerosis, hysterical.* The etymological histories of *aeronautics, astronaut,* and *cosmonaut* reflect the diverse sources of similar coinages. Apparently on their way to popular status are even the words *phoneme* and *morpheme,* although *sememe, grapheme, lexeme, prosodeme* and others may never leave the status of learned words only. One need only turn to the technical and scientific journals —or to advanced college textbooks in the sciences—to appreciate the exploitation of classical Greek for the new lexical items occasioned by the nature and products of modern science.

MINOR SOURCES OF ENGLISH LEXICON

19.6 It is not appropriate here to sample the many and various foreign sources of English words that make up minor aspects of the English lexicon. Almost every language with which English speakers have had sustained acquaintance especially since the era of exploration and colonization—in the period of Modern English—has provided some new words. Most of the languages from which statistically minor additions to English have come have either not had extensive literature (American Indian, Polynesian, etc.) or, as in the case of Chinese and Japanese, have had writing systems that very few English speakers have learned. The borrowings, consequently, have been through speech—indeed they often reflect "mistakes" of the kind illustrated above with *admiral*. The romance of words is seldom more engaging than in these exotic borrowings, for with so many instances they belong to believe-it-or-not lore. Fascinating as these may be, they add almost nothing to understanding of borrowing as a lexical resource for English.

Chapter 20

LEXICAL RESOURCES: FUNCTIONAL SHIFT AND DERIVATION

PROCESS OF FUNCTIONAL SHIFT

20.1 Other languages are not the only lexical resources upon which English has drawn, even though borrowing from them constitutes the most conspicuous source of new words. From within English itself have come uncounted innovations in vocabulary. Two of the "internal" lexical resources are "functional shift" and "derivation." The former concerns the relation between, say, the paradigmatic group *(a) telephone, (the) telephones, (the) telephone's location* and the group *(to) telephone, telephoning, (he) telephones, telephoned.* The latter concerns such relations of forms exemplified in the group *pronounce, pronounceable, pronounceableness, unpronounceable, mispronounce, pronunciation, pronouncement,* and the like, involving "derivational" as opposed to "inflectional" morphemes in combination with base forms. Clearly, the study of these two lexical resources concerns groups of forms related by recurrence of base elements without reference to differences among inflectional morphemes that may occur within a paradigmatic set.

The process of functional shift and the resulting circumstances involve two main factors—one morphological and the other syntactic. The latter requires only brief and informal accounting for our purposes here. Syntactic factors in functional shift have their most obvious manifestation in Modern English in word order. "The *tile* was broken." "The *tile* floor had been covered over." "He plans to *tile* the floor on Saturday." Sentence positions define the part of speech of *tile* in each instance, as may be seen if the italicized word is replaced by a blank, a slot to be filled. The italicized words in the three sentences cannot be said to be the same, except for their identity of phonemic structure: they are different words, the difference being broadly described by saying that in the first *tile* is a noun, in the second *tile* is an adjective, and in the third *tile* is a verb. In Modern English, with few inflections in the principal form-classes, many such sets of sentences can be found in which phonemically identical forms are defined by their differing distributions in larger constructions (such as sentences) to be different forms. Sets of forms like these are also differentiated within small constructions too, if we consider their occurrences within "words." The noun *tile* may occur with plural /–z/ but not with past-tense /–d/, or the adjective *tile* may not occur with any overt inflection. In other words, $tile_1$ may combine with noun inflections, $tile_2$ may combine with adjective inflections (of which none remain in Modern English), and $tile_3$ may combine with verb inflections; the coincidence of lack of overt inflection (Ø) within the Modern English separate sets of noun, verb, and adjective inflections should not obscure the morphological factor by which *tile* (a noun) can be distinguished from *tile* (a verb), and so on. Distinctions of this kind are no more difficult when phonemically identical forms occur as one or more "parts of speech" that lack inflections. A single example should suffice: "He fell *down*"; "He dropped the glass *down* the shaft"; "The team had one *down* to go"; "He *downed* his opponent within five minutes"; "He went up the *down* ramp." Words said to be related by functional shift are thus marked by the following characteristics: the base morphemes or stems resemble each other both phonetically and in respect to meaning; they belong to different parts of speech as defined distributionally in larger constructions; and any inflectional morphemes with which the stems may occur define the words as belonging to different form-classes.

The process of functional shift in English is simply that of using a stem in a syntactic function it has not had before, with such inflectional affixes of a different set as may be required. Regarded as an occurrence in a time continuum, a functional shift constitutes a change in the language such as the addition of a verb to the lexicon. If at one time, for example, English had a noun with the stem *pump–* but no verb with a stem both phonetically and semantically related, and then *pump–* occurred with related meaning as a verb stem, the verb is said to be a new word in the language, produced by functional shift. By its nature this kind of innovation in the language is created by principles of analogy, best illustrated by a set of correspondences. If English had only a noun with the stem *pump–* but already had a number of pairs of nouns and verbs with related stems, a pattern like the following abstraction of the resemblances could readily occur to a speaker:

Noun	Verb
answer, –s, –'s	answer, –s, –ed, –ing
love (etc.)	love (etc.)
wonder (etc.)	wonder (etc.)
pump	———

To "invent" the verb *pump–* would then be an easy, almost automatic action, though not necessarily an inevitable one. The same kind of pattern in other speakers' awareness of the language would make the innovation immediately understandable, probably unobtrusive, and perhaps unnoticed.

TYPES OF FUNCTIONAL SHIFT

20.2 The process of functional shift has been a common lexical resource throughout the history of English. More occurrences of shift can be found in records of earlier English than can be inferred from Modern English forms alone. From *mæsse* 'mass (a service of the church)' was derived by functional shift the verb *mæssian* '(to) say mass,' for example; only the noun survives in Modern English. The process of shift has operated in fundamentally the same way and with generally the same classes of words from pre-Old English times to the present. The patterns by which morphemes combine in words have not undergone any significant change; such patterns constitute an extremely conservative structural aspect of a language. Most particularly, inflections for all classes of words in English are not only suffixes, but they are word-final suffixes as well: no base element or derivational form follows an inflectional form in a word. Apparently the reduction in number of inflectional suffixes for the various form classes has not had any major effect on the "ease" or frequency of occurrences of functional shift. That the process appears to occur more frequently now than in the records of the past is probably to be attributed in part to changes in attitudes to language, but even more to the remarkable acceleration in the development of the lexicon. Differences in the effects of this process and in some of the aspects of it are nevertheless of some interest, and it is these that we shall briefly consider next.

In earlier chapters some illustrations have already been introduced in other connections. The split of spirant phonemes into pairs distinguished by voicing features is reflected in such related, "shifted" pairs as these:

Noun	Verb
house /haus/	house /hauz/
advice	advise
sheath	sheathe
teeth	teethe
wreath	wreathe
strife	strive
grief	grieve
thief	thieve
shelf	shelve

The relation between members of these noun-verb pairs is apparent in respect to both meaning and phonological structure; the difference in the final consonants of any pair represents an alternation of a single phonemic unit that developed independently of the functional shift itself. Much like these pairs are such others as *bath – bathe, wake – watch* with both vowel and final consonants in alternation in the two forms. An identical pattern of morphophonemic alternation is found in a few singular-plural contrasts in nouns—*staff – staves* (an alternation likely to be lost because of the newer "regular" plural *staffs*). Adjective-noun-verb sets of a similar kind include *safe* (adjective and noun) and *save.*

From early replacements of one vowel by another under certain conditioning, some pairs of words reflecting functional shift have had alternate vowels throughout the recorded history of English. Modern English examples, with both noun-verb and adjective-verb pairs, are the following:

blood	bleed
doom	deem
gold	gild
full	fill
whole – hale	heal

Still others are embedded in words that survive only with derivational affixes; one instance is *comb* and *unkempt* (participial adjective). The phonological relationship of the base forms of these two words is much less obvious; several phonological changes have occurred, making the underlying functional shift apparent only with historical analysis. At an earlier time the phonemic shape of the noun was /kamb–/ or /komb–/, while the verb stem was /kemb–/—showing an alternation of vowel similar to the kind illustrated just above. Originally, the difference had been only in the post-base elements, the base forms having been alike as in the example of *pump–*, noun and verb. Phonological changes in the participial form followed the normal course; so did phonological changes in the noun base. The Modern English verb *(to) comb* /kowm–/, however, is not a phonological descendent of Old English /kemb–/. It is, rather, a reformation on the model of the phonemic structure of the noun base. We have to do here with a special circumstance in functional shift. Instead of addition to the lexicon where no phonetically and semantically related item had existed previously, the innovation of *comb–* as a verb provided a new form—a new phonemic shape—for the verb corresponding to the noun *comb*. At the time *cemb–* and *comb–* existed side-by-side, they constituted allomorphs in one sense. The eventual disuse of *cemb–* resulted in a change called "analogical leveling," by which the analogically formed base displaced the historically "shifted" form that had come to differ from the noun form through phonological change. We have seen similar instances involving inflectional forms in the preceding chapters.

Alternate stress patterns may also appear in words reflecting functional shift. Whether of native English origin or borrowed, generally the words are etymologically compounds or coalesced phrases. One may be *upsét* or he may *upsét* a plan, but the result is referred to as an *úpset*. The elements of *lay off* are separable—*(to) lay off fifteen men*, or *lay fifteen men off their jobs*—in which instances the stress on each element is syntactically determined; the noun *láy-off*, on the other hand, always has greater relative stress on the first element. Patterns are similar with *(to) foul things úp* and *a fóul-up*, and the thousands of instances like them in Modern English. Borrowed words provide a number of instances; in most of the pairs, adjustments of the vowels reflect presence of stress in one or the other of the syllables: *rebél* /rəbél/ (verb), *rébel* /rébəl/ (noun). With shifted stress either regularly present or optional, depending on dialect and date, are *import, insult, increase, discourse, absent, transfer, protest, recoil, convict, castrate, convert, project, repeat,* and others.

SHIFT OF VERBS FROM INTRANSITIVE TO TRANSITIVE

20.3 Another pattern of functional shift has been present during all stages in the history of English. It produces none of the divergent phonemic structures or stress placements of the kinds illustrated above; neither is it manifest in different form-classes of the original and the "shifted" forms—that is, the resultant forms are not different "parts of speech" from the point of view of inflection. Lack of these prominent markings of shift has caused the process and patterns of functional shift from intransitive to transitive verbs commonly to be overlooked.

Development of a transitive verb on the model of an intransitive one, like the other patterns of functional shift, comes about through using a stem in a syntactic function in which it previously had not occurred. (At no time in English has there been a distinction in the suffix inflection of transitive and intransitive verbs.) The differences in syntactic function are in the requirement or lack of a direct object —a distributional contrast sufficient to establish the difference in the two types of verbs. A great many pairs of verbs are identical in phonemic shape of their stems and in form-class features and approximately the same in meaning, differing only in their distributional characters; these are the ones normally listed in dictionaries under one headword with classifications of both "transitive" and "intransitive." Only a few exist in Modern English as intransitive only, *last, exist, elope, recur, secede,* for example. Old English had a larger number of intransitive verbs without transitive counterparts. Some that have persisted in English and have served as a basis for functionally shifted transitive verbs are *būgan* '(to) bow, bend,' *strīdan* '(to) stride,' *strutian* '(to) stand out stiffly' (>Modern English *strut*), *climban* '(to) climb,' *famġian*' '(to) foam.' Verbs that have been borrowed by English as solely intransitive have also commonly developed transitive counterparts as well: *accrue, travel, pace, jazz.*

The factors relevant to this type of functional shift are set forth with copious illustration in F. Th. Visser's *An Historical Syntax of the English Language,* Part I. That "transitivation" is a characteristic process during the whole of the history of the language also makes it noteworthy. The process has involved several of the other major changes in English. One factor was the loss of an initial morpheme *ġe–* by which a number of transitive and intransitive verbs were distinguished; an unaccented bound form, it went from *ġe–* /ġə–/ through /i–/ to Ø, and was for all practical purposes gone from the language by the beginning of Modern English. Old English, however, included a number of words paired like *winnan,* intransitive '(to) struggle, toil, win' and *ge-winnan,* transitive '(to) obtain by struggle, toil, (to) gain, conquer.' Merger of accusative and dative categories of inflections for both nouns and pronouns removed formal distinctions between direct object and indirect object so that a construction such as *He answered the question* appears to have a transitive verb. Both development of passive constructions and replacement of inflectional syntactic signaling by phrasal expressions were contributory, but these last factors require more lengthy explication than is justified here.

VERB WORDS DERIVED FROM NOUNS

20.4 The most frequent pattern of shift in English has always been that of verb words being derived from noun words. Particularly in Modern English has this direction of shift become so prominent that it is only modest exaggeration of the tendency to say that in the jargon of many businesses, trades, and technologies almost any noun can be "shifted" to produce a new verb. To consider a recent trade name, from *Xerox,* a noun and name, a verb *(to) xerox* was formed almost immediately. The reverse process is less common, but in unconservative speech the shift from verb to noun is common enough: give it a *try,* give it a *go,* have a *say,* have a good *think.* Other shifts are less common. Indeed, it is as informative for our purposes to notice the kinds of limitations on functional shifts as it is to extend the illustrations already given. *Visible* is a familiar adjective: *a visible planet, the clock was visible.* The adjective can be converted into a verb: *When will it visible again? Ask them to visible it back; He visibled the clock.* The verb "works," of course, but it is not in the standard lexicon and, we may guess, will never be. (The negative derived form *invisible* is equally familiar and common and even more unlikely to be shifted.) Prepositions and adverbs are seldom converted into nouns, verbs, or adjectives, although there are a few instances: *He has his ups and downs; They upped the price; He neared the edge of the road.* Such forms participate in functional shift more commonly when they have become embedded in compounds—*(to) foul up* and *a foul-up,* (*to*) *run down* (*a list*). and *a run-down.* But as members of compounds these forms are no longer (on syntactic grounds as well as morphological grounds) prepositions and adverbs. The limitations on the types of functional shift reflect something about the grammatical structure of the language, but even more do they imply that other processes operate in the language by which new lexical items are made with base forms already in the language. The one most closely related to functional shift is that of derivation, to which we shall turn next.

DERIVED FORMS

20.5 Derived forms are to be distinguished as words containing a stem and a bound affix morpheme that is not a grammatical morpheme. (A few exceptions or borderline cases, nearly all of which are best recognized as archaic formations, are illustrated below.) In English the derivational affixes occur, alone or in sequence, next to the stem in the morpheme sequence. They may be either prefixed or suffixed; any derivational suffix precedes any inflectional suffix(es) that may also occur in the sequence.

Ordinarily, a derived form in English belongs to the same form-class as the underlying form when the derivation involves a prefix: *tie – untie, read – reread, happy – unhappy, final – semifinal,* and so on. The prefix *ġe–* in Old English has been mentioned above. There are some exceptions, notably *en–* by which verbs are derived from adjectives, as *enable, endear, enfeeble,* and *be–* in such instances as *bedevil, bejewel, bedwarf.* Derivation involving a suffix supplies one of the important means of extending the lexicon by creating distinctly marked special categories of substantive, attributive, or predicative words in correspondence to stems already in the language. A simple example is the derived form *dancer,* with the suffix *–er* signifying not only noun class but also a noun denoting that by which the dance is done; to use the grammatical label, *–er* is an agentive suffix; another noun *dance* and the verb *(to) dance* stand in a relation of functional shift. Derived forms in English belong more often than not to a form-class different from that of the underlying form—*boy* (noun), *boyish* (adjective), *boyishness* (noun), *boyishly* (adverb). The principal instances of derived forms and underlying forms belonging to the same class involve designation of special classes corresponding to some aspect of the grammatical system. Masculine vs. feminine categories, for example, are reflected in *actor – actress, count – countess,* and (historically) *weaver – webster,* and others.

Throughout the history of English, derivation has been a common lexical resource. The history of English derivation, however, concerns too many factors and obviously embraces too many items for anything like a comprehensive survey of that history to be attempted here. Only some of the salient aspects will be mentioned. Probably most important is that the morphemic structure of words involving derivation has not altered at all: the brief characterization given in the preceding two paragraphs with Modern English illustrations is apposite to all periods of English. A number of the bound derivational forms have perisisted in English not only in derived words from earlier eras, but as forms entering into new derivational morpheme sequences: *–ness, –y, un–, –ing* (the last used for deriving abstract nouns) enter into new combinations now as freely as they did in Old English. A number of derivational forms have either been lost altogether or have persisted only in words derived long since. The verbal prefix *ā–* of Old English served both as an intensifier and as an indicator of perfective aspect of the action denoted by the underlying verb form, as *āfyllan* '(to) fill up, fill full,' *āsingan* '(to) sing (a song) to the end.' *To–* and *for–* as intensive and perfective prefixes have been lost except in rare archaic formations such as *forlorn,* originally a participial adjective meaning 'utterly, altogether lost.' These are but three derivational bound forms in extensive use in Old English that have since disappeared, and a look at a listing of such forms in a grammar of Old English will reveal how many more have also been lost.

Change in derivational morphemes within English provides one of the more curious aspects of the history. Modern English *–hood,* as in *boyhood, statehood, falsehood, likelihood,* has had continuous development from Old English, in which it had the shape *–hād.* In Old English, however, its status was ambivalent, for there was also a common stem *hād,* one range of meanings of which was substantially that of the putative bound form *–hād;* in effect, *–hād* appears to have originated as a common second root member of compound words. There is no evidence, however, to indicate that it was otherwise differentiated as a bound allomorph, on the order of *–able* /əbel/ corresponding to *able* /éybəl/ in Modern English. Ultimately, the root *hād* disappeared and the morpheme persisted solely as a bound derivational form. A split, during Middle English, produced allomorphs of the derivational morpheme that appear in Modern English as *–hood* and *–head.* The suffix *–isc,* present notably in earlier *Englisc* 'English' has a different history of change. Phonetically it has hardly been modified at all. Semantically, though, it has both maintained its meaning in such instances as *Polish, Danish,* and developed pejorative and approximate meanings—*babyish, fortyish.*

Perhaps the most curious of all the strands of history of derivation in English is that of the most common adverb derivatives. From adjectives as their underlying forms, adverbs were freely and frequently derived by suffixation of *–e* /–ə/ in Old English: *ġeorn* 'eager,' *ġeorne* 'eagerly'; *fæst* 'firm, fast, secure,' *fæste* 'firmly, fast, securely.' The underlying form of many of the adverbs thus derived was in turn a derived form—an adjective derived by suffixation of *–līc*. Like *–hād,* that form had ambivalent status as a bound derivational affix, for there were both noun and adjective morphemes, *ġe–līc* with corresponding meaning 'like (–ness), same (–ness).' Unlike *hād* and *–hād, līc* and *–līc* have both survived into Modern English, as *like* and *–ly, –like*. The history of adverb-deriving *–e* paralleled that of inflectional *–e,* as they both fell into disuse under the same trends of phonological change. If the morphological history of adjectives is recalled, the subsequent development will be immediately apparent: by late Middle English, adjectives were without inflections and derived adverbs were without the earlier overt derivational suffix. The adjective form *fast,* for example, was segmentally identical to the adverb form *fast*. Still later developments reflect the prominence of derivational *–līc, –līce* > *–ly* both for the number of adjectives and adverbs thus derived and the frequency of occurrence of the derived forms. The loss of the one all-purpose adverb-deriving suffix *–e* was made good by construing the later *–ly* as an adverbial derivative morpheme, certain overlaps and inconsistencies notwithstanding. That the consequences of the historical merger of *–līc* and *–līċe* and the shift of *–ly* to adverbial derivative function have not yet been systematically sorted is fully apparent in the shibboleth of *slow* vs. *slowly,* the failure of **fastly* to develop beside *fast,* the segmental identity of *kindly* (adjective) and *kindly* (adverb) and many more such matters.

THE AUTONOMY OF MORPHEMES

20.6 The autonomy of morphemes, as opposed to words, is attested in the history of derivation in English just as it is in the history of English inflections. Historically regarded, the words *statehood* and *falsehood,* mentioned above, must be considered hybrids, since *state* and *false* are borrowed roots. The point will be clear: any stem incorporated into English may serve as an underlying form of derivation. Derivational affixes from other languages may come to be freely combinable with different stems than those with which they entered English in derivative words; and they may also combine with stems of native morphemic stock. The suffix *–able* is borrowed and is one of the most productive now present in English; it appears in words with native underlying forms, such as *eatable, drinkable, sinkable, thinkable*. There is nothing bizarre about this historical hybridism, for the process and rules of derivation in English have been followed and the concepts of "native" and "borrowed" are apposite only to historical study. The presence of a number of words incorporating *–able,* especially when pairs such as *agree – agreeable, count – countable* were both present in English, would lead to the same segmenting of the suffix morpheme that operated to keep alive any other derivational suffix distinct in the language. Speakers analyze the linguistic materials they encounter. To mention again a curious aspect of lexical modification, the process commonly called "back formation" reflects morphemic habits of speakers without regard to history. The undoing of a derivative, so to speak, occurs occasionally. While we have the word *inevitable,* its contrary is not the same less the prefix *in–*, that is, we do not refer to events as **evitable;* yet *edit* and *burgle* and *enthuse* and *diagnose* and others are products of the same process that would produce **evitable,* and they are fully established in English whether all of them have the blessing of "correctness" or not. Another fairly rare occurrence that nevertheless reflects the autonomy of morphemes is the splitting off of *–ism* to produce a new nonbound form *ism,* pluralized normally as *isms.* For the most part the creation of free morphemes on the model of derivational morphemes is limited to humorous utterances, as in the aphoristic "Orthodoxy is my doxy, heterodoxy is your doxy."

The occasions of derivation, the motivations of speakers to make new derivative combinations of morphemes, is a matter we shall not take up here. Suffice it to say that the resources of derivation have not prevented development of a number of suppletive pairs in English—*eye – oculur, moon – lunar, English – anglicize*—reflecting mixed motivations for borrowing and derivation with more regard for filling gaps in the lexicon than for building it on the simplest and most systematic principles.

Chapter 21

LEXICAL RESOURCES: COMPOUNDING

IDENTIFICATION OF COMPOUNDS

21.1 Compounding, like derivation and functional shift, has been a common "internal" lexical resource throughout the history of English. During the period of Old English it supplied new stems to a far greater extent than did borrowing; in the period of Middle English borrowing was the more important means of supplementing the lexicon; in Modern English compounding has again become increasingly a major resource. The characteristics of compounding, again like those of the other modes of expanding the lexicon, have nevertheless remained almost constant throughout the entire history of the language.

Up to this point it has been practical to proceed without closely defining the criteria by which morphemes or morpheme sequences are classed as "words" as opposed to sequences of words; the borderline between morphology and syntax of English has not perforce been a crucial concern. The reasons will be apparent: the inflectional, derivational, and root morphemes, in whatever combinations they occur, are recognizable as fixed combinations. Particularly our phonological habits and morphological habits—reinforced by writing habits—mark the combinations of these types of morphemes as words in the ordinary sense. By the same linguistic rules compounds are identified. But because of the strong influence of writing (or reading) habits, the nature of compounds is easily and commonly confused: writing conventions and linguistic structures at the morphological level are quite inconsistent, manifesting numerous contradictions. *Cannot* is a British convention of writing, while *can not* is an American convention: does British English therefore have a compound word corresponding to two uncompounded morphemes in American English? If *bedroom* is a compound, why should we not regard *dining room, living room, recreation room* as compounds also? Do we have both uncompounded *in so far* and compounded *insofar*? Does the compound *nevertheless* correspond to *never the less* in the same way that *insofar* corresponds to *in so far?* Are there any grounds for considering *telephone operator* and *steam shovel operator* to be compounds, despite the convention of writing the roots with intervening space? These examples will imply the necessity of explicating the concept of "word" in English more fully than we have done thus far.

CHARACTERISTICS OF WORD UNITS

21.2 English words, including compounds, are marked by morphological and phonological characteristics. For the classes of words of most interest to us in respect to compounding—nouns, verbs, and adjectives—a principal aspect of morphological structure is defined by the position of inflectional morphemes: inflections in English occur only finally in fixed sequences of morphemes. The possibility of their occurrence in a morpheme sequence thus becomes a test of whether the sequence consists of one such structure or perhaps more than one. (For adjectives the test is overt for Old English and parts of Middle English, implicit for Modern English.) For derivatives the test is obvious: /prins/ + /–əs/ + /–əz/ *princesses* has a fixed sequence, and the plural-inflecting morpheme /–əz/ cannot occur at any other position; any following morphemes cannot belong to the same word to which inflectional /–əz/ does. The euphemistic *unmentionables* is defined as a completed sequence of root and derivative forms by the plural inflection /–z/. The potential of inflectional suffixation rather than the particular presence or absence of the inflection, of course, constitutes the test. For compounds the test works the same way. *Toothpick* is pluralized only by terminal /–s/, not by the plural form *teeth. Sundown* is pluralized only as /sʌn/ + /daun/ + /–z/, never as /sʌn/ + /–z/ + /daun/ **suns-down; grownup* (noun) can be pluralized only as *grownups*. The examples of *dining room, living room,* given above, may be tested in the same way: it is two (or more) *dining rooms,* not **dinings room*. Even compounds incorporating a plural first element, such as *salesgirl,* is pluralized as *salesgirls*. Examples of verb compounds conform to the same test: *overcrowd* has past inflection *overcrowded,* not **overedcrowd; blue-pencil* will not have a past tense **blued-pencil*. The test of potential of inflection can be supplemented in some instances by a contrast between a syntactic order of morphemes and their order within a morphological structure. The sequence *cast out* may be varied inflectionally as *(he) casts out;* the compound *outcast* has syntactic and morphological characteristics of a noun—plural *outcasts*—rather than the characteristics of a verb phrase: both the order of the root morphemes and the position of the inflection contrast in this pair.

Phonological tests of the unity or multiplicity of word-units in a morpheme sequence are equally important, and they are especially useful for Modern English sequences of adjective and noun roots, since adjectives no longer are inflected. To take first an example in which the contrast between a sequence of words and a single compound word is reflected in writing conventions, we may consider how *(a) blue book* and *(a) bluebook* differ. Contrastive stress patterns may differentiate the two sequences as syntactic or morphological: marking relatively heavier stress with <´> and lesser stress with <^> and still lesser stress with<`>, the contrast /blûw búk/ *blue book* and /blúw bùk/ *bluebook* is clear. Not always, however, will /blúw bùk/ necessarily signify a compound. The pattern /blúw bùk/ or /blúw bûk/ also serves another contrastive purpose, as in the question "Is it the *blue* book that you want?" Still another phonological factor distinguishes *(a) blue book* [*not a red one*] from *(a) bluebook* if ambiguity arises. The potential of pause between the forms or prolongation of the first element as part of normal utterance can signify the word sequence, while a prominent pause or prolongation is inadmissable within the compound. An experiment in which timing was varied at the boundaries between three root forms *light, house, keeper* (in that order) has been reported by Dwight L. Bolinger in "Disjuncture as a Cue to Constructs": a relatively long interval between the first two roots, with a shorter interval between the latter two, with intensity (or stress-level) equalized for the three root morphemes, is construed by hearers as *light housekeeper;* the reversal of relative length of interval between adjacent roots in construed as *lighthouse-keeper.* This test is particularly useful for compounds whose stress patterns have no ready, clear contrasts with noncompound sequences: *sky-blue, grass-green, worldly-wise, self-made, all-knowing.*

A morphophonemic factor will also be useful in distinguishing some compounds from derivative formations, especially for those derivatives that were compounds in earlier stages of English. By the tests outlined so far the following are clearly compounds: *payday, May Day, working day, shopping day, birthday; Mother's Day* and *Father's Day* also meet the tests despite the possessive inflection of the first element—the compound having been made with the adjectivally inflected form. What, though, is the nature of *Monday, Tuesday,* etc., or of *Holiday*? The spellings reflect the etymologies of these words, all of them having at one time been compounds. But the second element *–day* in the names of the days of the week is normally not /dey/, but /diy/; the first element in *holiday* is not /howliy/ but /hali/ or /halə/. For these words, one element is a bound allomorph of *day* or *holy,* that is, it occurs only in conjunction with a root and never as a separable unit in a free syntactic construction. An extensive set of compounds and formerly-compound derivatives exist in English with *–man*: in compounds the allomorph /mæn/ occurs, in derivatives the allomorph /mən/ occurs. *Lead man* /líyd mæ̀n/ is a compound, as are *white man, red man, weather man, fixit man,* and many more; *seaman* /síymən/ is a derivative, formerly a compound, as are *policeman, clergyman, horseman, shipman, fisherman, rifleman,* and many more. *Mailman* and *postman* provide a notable contrastive pair. The historical changes by which root forms drift into nonroot status have shifted morpheme sequences from compound to derivative structure. In this connection the examples of *–hood* < Old English *hād* and *–ly* < Old English *–līc, –līce* may be recalled. That a number of instances in Modern English may be analyzed variously as derivatives and compounds signals the transitional state of development rather than a confusion of the speakers of the language.

COMPOUND LEXICAL ITEMS

21.3 Compound lexical items, then, are specifically those in which a stem consists of two (or more) root morphemes. Compounding is the production of new stems by fixing root morphemes in their free allomorphic variants into a sequence that (with few exceptions) admits of neither variation nor interruption. The two-root stem is, and has always been in English, numerically the most common pattern. More-than-two-root compounds commonly are phrases "frozen" into the shape of a word. *Do–it–yourself* is a comparatively recent phrasal compound: the verb element cannot (except humorously) appear in the past inflectional form *did,* nor can the other two elements be varied; nor can the constituent compound be modified to, say, *myself;* on the other hand the phrasal compound, like any other word unit, is susceptible to derivational modification— *(he's a) do–it–yourselfer;* others are *man–in–the–street, dog–in–the–manger. Ne'er–do–well, devil–may–care* are older compounds of this kind. Similar to these but growing out of different compounding requirements are such modern coinages as *foot–pound–second.* Phrasal compounds have been made with two members as well; from the sequence *on* + noun have come a number of words, for example, that have the preposition now reduced to /ə–/ *a–*: *afire, aloft, asleep, aboard, asunder.*

For the more common two-member compounds, the patterns by which the constituent morphemes combine may be described briefly. It must be said, first, that semantic criteria do not provide a practical set of combining patterns. The first element *fire–*, for example, appears in *fireplace,* designating what the place contains (or is designed to contain); a *fireman* (now a derivative but formerly a compound) is one whose special concern is fire(s); a *firehose* does not contain fire; a *fireball* consists of fire; *firewood* is wood used as fuel for fire; a *firearm* is an instrument from which a missile is "fired," that is, propelled by an explosive; a *firebreak* is a cleared strip of land for preventing spread of fire; and so on. A *horse doctor* is one who "doctors" horses, a *foot doctor* is one who gives medical attention to feet, but the semantic pattern does not extend to *man doctor* and *woman doctor*. Semantic patterns do occur within sets of compounds, but the relationships between the root morphemes are semantically associational and not formal and systematic.

Formal patterns can be set up on the basis of the form-class to which the constituent root morphemes can be referred. The number of possible patterns and their stipulation is then simply a matter of all the possible combinations of adjective + adjective, adjective + noun, etc. Some of the combining patterns have never been very productive— noun + verb, for example, as in *sideswipe*. The most productive classes have involved nouns in the patterns noun + noun, noun + adjective, and adjective + noun. Illustrations from Modern English are so readily to be found that none need be listed here. The productivity of noun + noun in Old English and Modern English may be illustrated, however, by the following partial list of Old English forms that happen to be preserved in written records, together with a companion list that will appear in any standard dictionary with the headword beginning *sea(–).*

sǣ–ǣl	'sea–eel'
sǣ–ælfen	'sea–elf, naiad'
sǣ–bāt	'ship, sea–boat'
sǣ–beorg	'cliff by the sea'
sǣ–burg	'seaport town'
sǣ–ċeaster	'seaport town'
sǣ–ċeosol	'sea–sand, shingle'
sǣ–ċir	'sea–ebbing'
sǣ–clif	'sea–cliff'

sǣ–col	'sea–coal, jet'
sǣ–cyning	'sea–king'
sǣ–dēor	'sea–monster'
sǣ–draca	'sea–dragon'
sǣ–fisc	'sea–fish'
sǣ–flōd	'tide, inundation'
sǣ–lāf	'sea–leavings, jetsam'
sǣ–land	'sea–land, coast'
sǣ–mann	'seaman, pirate, viking'
sǣ–mearh	'sea–horse, ship'
sǣ–net	'sea–net, net for sea–fishing'
sǣ–scell	'seashell'
sǣ–snæġl	'sea–snail'
sǣ–strand	'sea–strand, foreshore'
sǣ–wæter	'sea–water'
sǣ–weard	' (sea–) coast–guard'
sǣ–wiht	'sea–creature, marine animal'

The stipulation that compounds contain two (or more) root morphemes does not exclude derivational elements in compounds. Each instance has its own history, of course, and dominant patterns and processes are involved in compounding and derivation. From a strictly analytic point of view, the derivational formation *do–it–yourselfer,* given above, consists of a stem and an agentive derivative affix; the "outer layer" is detachable, and the stem is a chronologically prior as well as analytically simpler lexical unit. Compounds, however, are also made with a member consisting of root morpheme plus derivative affix with no underlying or prior stem lacking the affix. *Cupbearer* is not a direct derivative of a compound *(to) *cupbear; fruit–bearing (tree)* is not a derivative of *(to) *fruit–bear. A fender–bender* (a coinage denoting a minor automobile accident) does not derive from *(to)*

**fender–bend*. These compounds, made with derivationally composed elements, seem to be constructed in the same way as compounds consisting of root morphemes only. Normally a derivational construction will be the second element in a two-root compound in English.

"VERB–ADVERB" COMBINATIONS

21.4 While the nature of compounds can be explicated and illustrated fairly readily, another type of morpheme sequence partially resembles that of compounds but cannot be brought fully under the definition of compounds. This sequence is specially interesting as a link between morphological structures and syntactic structures and is important for being one of the most productive structural patterns in Modern English. In 20.2 the examples of *láy-off, úpset, fóul-up* were mentioned and treated as nouns and as compounds, with their verbal counterparts contrasted in their alternate stress patterns. Typically these pairs were made from native English morphemes, and they parallel alternate stress patterns in borrowed words such as *rebél* (verb) and *rébel* (noun). Our concern here is specifically the verbal sequences of the type *lay off,* meaning to cease or to terminate employment. Most of the constructions of this type do not conform to the stipulation for compounds that the sequence of root morphemes does not admit of interruption: *They laid him off at the end of the season; He fouled things up badly*. Whether they are to be construed as a kind of compound having discontinuous structure or be given some other designation, they are of interest as a lexical source of the language. Let us consider some of the characteristics of constructions of this type.

First, the element that may be listed by itself as the preposition (or adverb) — *up, off,* etc.—occurs after the verb morpheme with which it is associated. (Otherwise there is a clear pattern of compounding: *upgrade, underestimate, overprice.)* Next, the prepositionlike morpheme may occur without an object: *He threw up* ('vomited'); *He really fouled up that time* (i.e., on that occasion); *He spouted off about his big chance; She was hired to live in on weekdays.* Many of these have nominal or adjectival counterparts that are structurally compound: *It was a foul–up; She had a live–in job;* etc. Some occur in more varied constructions: *He said he would stand by me through thick and thin; He was on stand–by duty; He was a good stand–by.* When constructions like these are followed by an object, syntactically regarded, the object appears to be not that of a preposition but that of the verb and the prepositionlike form in combination: *He never failed to stand by me through all those years of trouble.* But this should be contrasted with the following: *He wanted to stand by* ('next to') *me while we watched the parade.* In the first of this pair of sentences *by* ordinarily has greater stress than *by* in the second sentence; there is potential of pause only after *by* in the first sentence but before the *by* in the second; and, obviously, the semantic meanings of *stánd by me* and *stand bý me* are different.

Of still more importance are two other aspects of these constructions. One aspect is brought out by instances in which a combination of this type is correlated with a single verb word: *He pledged to keep and watch over the place until his friend returned; He teased and chased after the girls; They approved of and welcomed the new neighbor; He caught on and kept quiet about it.* Clearly, the two-element predicates function as units by both semantic and syntactic tests. The other aspect is the deployment of the two forms in question as they appear in corresponding active-voice and passive-voice constructions.

The committee objected to the proposal.
(The committee turned down the proposal.)
The proposal was objected to by the committee.
(The proposal was turned down by the committee.)
(It got a turn-down.)
They didn't believe in it.
It wasn't believed in (by them).
Let's look over the place /Let's look the place over.
The place was looked over.
(It got a good looking-over.)

Again the two morphs appear to function as a unit, even though there is no requirement that they be regarded as fixed phrases in the nature of compounds rather than as free phrases: they may be discontinuous—*look* the place *over;* the inflection occurs with the verb-form element of the phrase, never at the end of the phrase—the construction **look-overed (the place)* being un-English. Yet *They looked over the wall and saw a garden* shows a clearly contrasting use of *look* + *over.*

The common recourse is to call sequences of the type illustrated here "verb-adverb combinations." Their contrastive relations in terms of major stress position, semantics, or position of potential pause have been overlooked in most grammars of English until the past few years. Their status appears to be much like that of compounds, but they clearly do not fulfill all the requirements of compounded stems described earlier in this chapter. These "verb-adverb" combinations are generally treated as lexical units by modern lexicographers. The productiveness of the type in recent English is nowhere better attested than in dictionaries of slang; a good single example is the list under the heading *–up*—called a "suffix word"—in the *Dictionary of American Slang,* compiled by Harold Wentworth and Stuart Berg Flexner.

Probably the ambivalent nature of these combinations is best comprehended by and referred to their history in English. Sometimes they do not conform to many well established patterns of derivation, compounding, and/or syntax. While their history is somewhat obscured by lack of clear evidence of placement of stress, of contrastive citations, and of specific lexical definitions, their relative newness to the language is clear. Apparently the evolution of passive constructions provided for the rapid increase in productiveness of the pattern, but this is a problem we cannot take up here. Possibly the presence of a large number of words of French and Latin derivation provided a model for expansion of the following type: a place may be *inhabited,* or it may be *lived in;* one may *inspect* something or *look into* it; one may either *subtract* or *take away,* and so on. The loss of certain prefixes conveying perfective aspect may also have affected the historical development, as is illustrated in the verb-adverb translations of the following Old English examples: *ā–heawan* '(to) cut off' beside *heawan* '(to) cut, hew'; *ā–hebban* '(to) lift up' beside *hebban* '(to raise, heave'; *ġe–sittan* '(to) inhabit, live in' beside *sittan* '(to) sit'; *ġe–sceran* '(to) cut through' beside *sceran* '(to) cut, shear.' Loss of the prefixes, by phonological change, did away with contrastive patterns of the kinds illustrated; the resultant gap in the lexicon was filled in part by the combinations represented in the translations given. All the factors that appear to be separately and collectively contributory to the new combination have been present in force only since the beginning of Middle English—the time at which the new pattern began to emerge.

Chapter 22

MEANING CHANGE

"MEANING" DEFINED

22.1 Compared to the other topics we have dealt with so far in the study of the English language, meaning and change of meaning are topics both broader in scope and different in kind. Up to this point our concern with meaning has been not so much *what* is the meaning of a form, but *whether* the meaning of one morpheme is essentially the same as or essentially different from the meaning of another form regardless of the phonemic identity of or difference between the forms. We have attended mainly to units of expression, their identity, and their structure. "Meaning" ordinarily refers to the experiences, feelings, ideas, attitudes, fantasies, and the like that are conventionally associated with symbols, and we have confined our study to linguistic symbols. At one extreme, meaning of linguistic symbols takes in a great part of the culture of the speech group using those symbols. At the other extreme, the meaning of a form can be efficiently defined as the totality of the associations of that form with other linguistic materials—that is, the totality of the contexts in which it occurs. Practically, we can do no better than regard the meaning of a form as an alternate linguistic expression that a group of speakers of a given language consider equivalent in reference: the meaning is a verbal definition that is conventionally assignable to a form. Change in meaning has to do with difference in "content" or definition which is associated with a morpheme or morpheme combination and designated as its meaning.

The preceding stipulations about meaning apply primarily to "content-words"—generally those formally defined as nouns, verbs, adjectives, and adverbs. Or, to specify more closely, the study of meaning—the area of semantics—traditionally concerns symbolic associations with stems of the form classes having the largest number of items. In observing the traditional limits of semantics for this chapter we are thus setting aside derivational and inflectional morphemes, the "form-words" making up the classes of prepositions and conjunctions, and the "substitute-words" comprising the pronouns and pronominals. The meanings and change of meanings of many of these forms have made up part of the description already provided for them. In treating of nonlinguistic associations of stems, semantics concerns only what was distinguished earlier (15.4) as referential—as opposed to grammatical—meaning, and is limited to segmental morphemes, usually stems.

The nature and complexity of semantic change is best shown, probably, by explication of the traditional categories used to classify changes of meaning. We shall proceed more formally than usual, leaving the details of the examples to be supplied from historical dictionaries and leaving further examples to be supplied from the many books on words and meanings; for the latter, *Words and Their Ways in English* may be specially mentioned for its long-standing influence and popularity.

CATEGORIES OF MEANING CHANGE

22.2 *Narrowing* and *widening.* These terms, or their alternates *specialization* and *generalization,* name categories characterizing the extent or range of the meanings associated with a word. The range may be defined numerically or, more commonly, in terms of diversity among the objects, experiences, etc. with which a word is associated; it is sometimes called the "area" of meaning. We can formulate the criteria for classifying this kind of change as follows. If at one time T_1 a word has a given range R_1 of associations ("contents"), and if at a later time T_2 the word has had continuous existence but has a different range R_2 of associations: then if R_1 is more diverse (and its members more numerous) than R_2, but R_2 consists of members of R_1, the meaning is said to have narrowed; whereas if R_2 is more diverse (and its members more numerous) and contains members of R_1, the meaning is said to have widened. The change in the first case is thus named *narrowing,* in the second case *widening. Go* has generalized or widened in meaning from a verb signifying '(to) advance (especially on foot)'; *get* has retained the sense '(to) obtain' but has also taken on the characteristics of an auxiliary verb. *Hand* has a wide variety of meanings, in *hired hand, on the other hand, a clock hand, a hand of bananas,* etc. that it did not have earlier. The etymologies of *stick* (noun), *undertaker, wanton, doctor* will illustrate narrowing of reference.

While *specialization* and *generalization* commonly name the same categories of change as do the terms *narrowing* and *widening,* the former sometimes may also refer to a rhetorical aspect of words which are placed in those categories. For example, a word whose meaning has been generalized should be considered more comprehensive, or more abstract, or less specific in regard to its associated content, hence useful only when comprehensive, abstract, or general designation is desired. *Thing* and *meat* are native English examples, *circumstance* a borrowed one.

Elevation (amelioration) and *degeneration (pejoration).* These terms name categories, not of range of meanings, but of attitudes of users of particular words to those elements of content with which the expressions are associated. Frequently the attitude toward the meaning "content" is also taken to the expression with which it is associated. We can formulate the criteria for classifying changes of these kinds as follows. If at one time T_1 the referent of a term has directed to it one attitude A_1 among those who use the term, and if at a later time T_2 its referent has a different attitude A_2 directed to it: then if A_1 has been favorable (in the nature of awe, admiration, respect, pleasure, security), but A_2 is unfavorable (often the opposite of A_1), it is said that the word has undergone degenerative (pejorative) change; whereas if A_1 has been unfavorable but A_2 is favorable, it is said to have undergone elevative (ameliorative) change. Degeneration is illustrated in the history of the meaning of *wench, lewd, cunning, counterfeit.* Elevation is illustrated by *knight, enthusiasm, Puritan, fond.*

Weakening and *strengthening.* These terms are applied to categories based on changes in the meaning content of an expression when that content is regarded as having shifted in the degree of seriousness, dignity, specificity, and the like with which it is is viewed. *Soon* meant 'at once, immediately' until weakened; *twit* and *yelp* have lost all the "dignity" they once had. Plainly, these kinds of changes may be concatenated with elevation or degeneration, or with narrowing or widening, or perhaps with combinations of them. Their formulation can be carried out in the manner of the preceding kinds of change.

Radiation, divergence, concatenation. While the preceding terms name the results of comparisons of meanings of a word at two different times and imply processes of change, the three terms under consideration here name patterns described by two or more changes, when these changes are associated with a single word and are considered in relation to each other. *Radiation,* of which the meanings of *head* are a good example, names a pattern by which widening or generalization have occurred with related meanings developing from a common "core" meaning. Often, different spellings develop to distinguish the two meanings, as in the case of *flour* and *flower. Divergence* in some cases seems to be equivalent to radiation, but it more frequently refers to a process by which meanings which at one time were considered as separate but similar (hence not properly a single, core meaning) develop at a later time into meanings regarded as less similar, or distinct. *Concatenation* refers to the pattern of several successive changes of one or more of the kinds already mentioned. To trace *cardinal* and *virtue* from their original pre-English meanings to present-day English meanings will illustrate this pattern. The Latin source of *virtue,* for example, denoted warlike prowess; as the term developed in English it progressed through meaning 'fortitude,' 'power or capacity,' 'noble, admirable power,' 'moral integrity.' Formulation of these categories, then, can be made on the following model. When two or more changes in the associations of content with an expression occur, then (a) if several meanings appear to have developed from a core meaning, we call the pattern of change described by these changes *radiation;* or (b) if two or more meanings appear to have developed from two (or more) meanings associated with an expression and if the earlier meanings seem to be more similar than the later meanings, the pattern is that of *divergence;* or (c) if there appear to be several successive changes in the meaning attached to a word, we call the pattern of succession *concatenation.* Radiation and divergence are patterns of changes viewed as occurring between two points in time; concatenation is a pattern of changes viewed as occurring within a span marked by three or more successive points in time. The first two patterns may be "enlarged" if the second point in time is put still later, while the third pattern may be "lengthened" in a greater scope of time. The results of radiation and divergence will presumably be classified as widening, extension, etc., and any one of the changes forming part of the pattern of radiation, divergence, or concatenation may belong to one of the first three pairs of categories listed above.

Figures of speech: metaphor, synechdoche, metonomy, synaesthesia. These several types of figures of speech name categories of still another sort: the relations among differing contents when those relations are viewed as conforming to one of the several specified rhetorical processes or types of association. For example, if the difference in content associated with a word at two different times is such that the earlier content is considered to be associated with the later content as cause, effect, container, or the like, it is said that the word has undergone change by metonomy. A simple example is *He keeps a fine table,* in which *table* incorporates the food served on it.

Euphemism. This term does not refer to changes in range of content associated with a word; nor does it refer to changes in attitude to the content (though attitude to content functions in the rise of euphemism); nor to a pattern described by two or more changes; nor to a specific rhetorical relation noticed as existing between two successive "contents." These other kinds of change, however they differ among themselves, are not considered as change in expression; in fact, they assume persistence of an expression. Euphemism is the opposite to these. It is the expression—the word, usually—with a particular content that changes. This radical difference between euphemism and the other categories indicates that euphemism is not properly classed with the others we have listed as a kind of semantic change, though traditionally it is thus classed. Without questioning the usefulness of the category *euphemism* for other purposes, we may notice briefly the relation of semantic changes occurring concomitantly with euphemistic change. Apparently the substitution of one word for another, with the new one associated deliberately with the content of the former one, is thought to be a way of modifying some aspect of the content itself. If so, the change in content, if it occurs, is probably the result of assimilation of an "undesirable" content to another, "desirable" content, or the assimilation of accompanying attitudes—the assimilation achieved by the agency of word substitution. The result, then, is the extension of the range of meanings of an expression (or modification of the attitude to the content associated with it) to include a meaning (or attitude) formerly associated with another word (or its content). As a result, the word or expression to which the content has deliberately been reassigned may have its range of meanings undergo semantic changes of the kinds listed above.

COMPLEXITIES OF SEMANTIC HISTORY

22.3 Explication of these traditional categories of semantic change underlines both their usefulness and their limitations. As names for recurring patterns or processes of meaning change, they constitute a significant check-list; separately they label generalizations of the observations of historical semantics. However, because several of them are not mutually exclusive categories, they cannot be organized into a single, consistent system of classification. None of them explains semantic changes, nor together do they present a model from which causes can be inferred and explanations constructed.

The complexity of the semantic history a stem may have can be illustrated by a relatively recent addition to the English lexicon, the form *jazz*. While the word is listed in the specialized *Dictionary of Americanisms* and the Wentworth and Flexner *Dictionary of American Slang*, it appears also in standard desk dictionaries both British and American. Generally, current dictionaries do not label the form as slang; even the *Pocket Oxford Dictionary* does not mark noun and verb uses as slang, even though adjectives have been thus labeled. *Jazz* appears to be thoroughly established in the lexicon of English.

Origins of *jazz* and its meanings prior to the twentieth century are obscure. However, within the time in which its meanings have been recorded, the semantic changes seem to have been somewhat as follows. As a regional (Southern United States) class taboo word before 1900 *jazz* referred to copulation, sex, a woman considered solely as a sexual object. Apparently this range of meaning preceded another range: animation, enthusiasm, enthusiasm and a fast tempo or rhythm, frenzy; if so, the word—still a regional, class word—had its meaning generalized. Another range of meaning is related to music: the only original American type of music, primarily emotive and suitable for dancing, based on ragtime, characterized by syncopation and prominent rhythms with variations of themes and melodies, and mainly improvisational in development. Historical evidence shows that the music is a later development than the word applied to it, so that the word, by extension, developed a specialized meaning when associated with a particular type of music. When the musical type spread in popularity and appeal and developed many distinctive forms, the word *jazz* spread from regional to national distribution. In so far as its national usage was associated with only a type of music, its meaning was no longer taboo: this represents elevation of the word. In so far as its national meaning was confined to music, it underwent narrowing. Moreover, from the point of view of those speakers (mostly associated with jazz up to, say, 1940) who associated the term with its earlier meanings, the additional meanings (for music) represent radiation, as well as elevation and narrowing. Perhaps the early, basic change of meaning—in extension to a type of music—should be classified as change by metonomy. Again, for those who remained regionally limited in their lexicon, the word probably underwent no change at all for fifty years or more. In respect to the proliferation of types of music called *jazz* the term generalized or widened, collectively referring to such subsequent specific forms as "Dixieland" (a term referring to the general type of earlier music which had earlier been called *jazz),* the "back-alley or low-down dirty," the "slurred gutbucket," the "swinging," "bop," "cool," "progressive," etc.

Out of the music-range of meanings have developed subsequent, associated meanings: 'lies, exaggeration; insincerity,' 'nonsense, idle talk,' and the like. Also from music-meanings, apparently, have been derived adjectival meanings recorded in British dictionaries (but not specifically American ones), 'discordant,' 'loud in color,' 'rude,' 'burlesque.'

PROBLEMS OF WRITING SEMANTIC HISTORY

22.4 Besides illustrating the traditional categories of semantic change and their relations, the meanings of *jazz* may be used to illustrate the problems of ascertaining and specifying the conditions and extent of a word's use for the writing of its semantic history. If, for instance, evidence at one time should have been drawn from a regional, class dialect, then at a later time from national general usage, and still later from, say, a prominent individual's usage, changes of meaning for *jazz* would probably be described as, successively, specialization and elevation, then further specialization. If, however, our evidence were confined to regional, class dialect throughout the same time span, the change probably would be described as widening with partial elevation (that is, elevation of some meanings but not others), or it might appear that no change had occurred. On the basis of early, regional dialect, then national general usage, and still later national general usage, the changes are those of extension to specialized meaning, then generalization. Changes of meaning within trades groups, professions, social strata, and the like, as well as shifts of a word and its meanings in the styles and registers of various groups, affect descriptions of semantic change in the same way, depending on whether these specialized meanings are taken into account or not, all or some of them, and if not all, which ones.

Traditional categorization of semantic changes is oriented to the practical task of sorting and stops short of serving the requirements of ascertaining causes and processes of the changes. By its very nature, the direct correlation of language stems and nonlinguistic circumstances can never produce more than approximative formulation of either meaning or change of meaning of linguistic forms.

Chapter 23

SPELLING

MATCHING WRITING UNITS TO LANGUAGE UNITS

23.1 Although not itself part of a natural language, spelling is perhaps the most important of the paralinguistic subjects, especially for historical study. Except for sound recordings in the last few decades spelling provides the only close record we have of earlier sounds of English, and it has during the past three centuries come to be a significant influence on our language. Spelling has been brought into our consideration of English and its history at several points already: the reconstruction of phonology of earlier stages of English (4.1 – 4.2); sound change reflected in spelling change (Chapter 6 and 8.3); spelling of vowels in Old and Middle English (7.6, 8.2, 9.1 et seq.); the shift of stressed vowels in early Modern English (9.4); the allomorphs of inflectional morphemes (especially Chapters 12, 14–16); and the writing of compounds (Chapter 21). It is a subject that appropriately and traditionally has a place in the study of English, albeit that place need not be a large one. The nature of English and its spelling is such that it is best taken up in the light of both phonology and morphology.

Because English has always been written normally in alphabetic symbols, the association between spelling and language tends to be almost exclusively between alphabetic symbols and segmental units of sound: spelling is regarded almost solely as an adjunct of phonology. Thus the study of spelling resolves itself for the most part into a consideration of the completeness, the accuracy, and the simplicity with which vowels and consonants are matched to discrete letter-symbols. Depending on one's interests, investigation may consider either the representation of sounds by letters or the accuracy of signaling of sounds by the writing symbols. The practical interests of most orthographers and educators and spelling reformers have led to proposals for changing spelling to match speech in instances where the two are inconsistent. The practical necessity of linguistic study has led to development of special and augmented sets of symbols. The study of English spelling may be better served, however, by considering the morphology of English as well. The relations of morphological structures to spelling may well be more basic to the study of spelling than are the relations of spelling to phonetic features of actual utterances of normal speech. Important and obvious as is the correspondence of graphic units—"graphemes"—and phonological units, it is with the correspondence of morphological and graphic features that we shall begin.

The pragmatic nature of writing is reflected in the requirement of segmenting the utterance to be recorded into pragmatically manageable units. Conventions of breaking utterances into "write-able" blocks were, of course, established prior to the writing of English; historically, the conventions—alphabetic and otherwise—of writing Latin were adapted to the writing of English. In practice, the units are those marked generally by leaving space between series of letters in linear sequence. Details of these conventions have varied to some extent in the history of English writing, but the underlying principles have not changed appreciably. As we saw in Chapter 21, Modern English conventions include the types *bedroom* as well as *living room* as compounds; hyphenation is now used as another way of indicating the boundary of a segment of utterance— *part-of-speech-designation,* for example. *Stepfather* is now written without spacing between the constituent morphemes, but writers of Old English commonly did space the corresponding elements, as *steop fæder,* even though the sequence constituted a compound stem then as now. The principles of segmenting utterances for purposes of writing have been in the nature of rules of thumb, hence cannot be cast in simple and consistent formulation, but they are generally as follows, for English. Any single segment will contain no more than one stem. A stem without inflectional or derivational bound forms morphologically structured with it will constitute a distinct segment—a unit—of the utterance for writing purposes, hence its representation will be bounded by spacing. Prepositions, conjunctions, and "articles" thus normally are spaced unless they are construed in speech to be clitics, as in Old English writing *inenglisc* 'in English' is typical or in Modern English deliberate spelling to represent a particular mode of utterance produces *(I don't) wanta,* beside conventional *want to.* In earlier Modern English conventions, especially those for writing verse, *th' arm,* for example, signified that /ðə/ was not to be given syllabic status for metrical purposes. Stems of the major form classes constitute the basis of spacing. Further, any bound morpheme will not constitute a segment to be separated by spacing from the stem with which it is morphologically structured. This principle is most fully observed in suffix morphemes, both derivational and inflectional. In early English writing a prefixed morpheme, however, was not so regularly represented in juxtaposition to the writing of the stem, being written either with some spacing or, later, with a hyphen when separated from the writing of the stem. For compounded stems, the writing of the two root morphemes has generally been variable throughout the history of English, as the examples near the beginning of this paragraph indicate. Hyphenation of the spellings of the constituent roots is a relatively recent innovation.

These broad principles reflect patterns of morphological structuring that we have observed in connection with derivation, compounding, and borrowing. The basic unit of segmentation of utterances for writing is approximately that of the "word"—the morpheme or morpheme sequence that may take a single prominent stress and may be uttered separately without contradicting patterns of normal speech flow. The ambivalent conventions of writing compounds follows naturally from the underlying principle, for the first root morpheme of a compound has much the same utterance characteristics in a compound as the same morpheme has apart from its occurrence in a compound stem. There are two main negative implications of the principles of segmenting utterances for writing. One is that syllables do not constitute the immediate criterion for breaking up the utterance sequence; the inconsistency between syllabic structures—a purely phonological matter—and morphological structures—a matter of constructions that are significant and meaningful—points to the primacy of morphological structures in the segmentation of utterances. The inherent unsuitability of syllabic units serving as the basis for writing will be obvious: [ðə in hɛr ənt ʌn sut ə bɪl ə ti əv sɪl læ bɪk yu nəts] etc. The other negative implication is that writing conventions have not provided for recording directly the sounds of particular utterances, in which morphemic elements may be obscured by the phonetic modifications within a syntactic structure. To take an extreme example, the following dialogue represents a common enough sequence of utterances. [ˈǰi ˈčɛt]? [ˌnɑˈčet]. [ˌyəˈwʌnə]? [yæə]. [ˌlɛsˈko]. Standard writing conventions render the dialogue thus: *Did you eat yet? Not yet. (Do) you want to? Yeah. Let's go.*

Morphographs have always been used in writing English, but they have always been employed only as auxiliary devices. The ampersand ⟨ & ⟩ represents *and,* the numeral digits have one-symbol writing as well as spelled representation, the symbols of mathematics, such as ⟨=⟩, ⟨÷⟩, ⟨+⟩, stand for words, and abbreviations are conventional shortenings of spelled forms by which the full phonological representation of a word is signaled by a portion of it. The writing of typical or continuous speech, however, has never been carried out in English with these symbols.

RELATION OF SPELLING TO PHONOLOGY

23.2 With morphological structure of the order of words as the practical unit for writing conventions, the representation of those units takes on, for English, some significant restrictions. The graphemic units of alphabetic writing are correlated directly with sounds, not morphemes, but the sounds to which they are matched are only those that make up the morphological structure as it may occur in isolated utterance. Not only, then, does spelling conventionally disregard the phonetic actualities of particular sentence utterances in respect to the string of vowels and consonants, it further disregards the features of pitch contours, degrees of stress, and types of pause or other timing factors that are concomitant, in normal sentence-length utterances, with the vowels and consonants that make them up. Each morphological structure is represented as if it were uttered by itself, and because each is thus represented, the features other than vowels and consonants are disregarded. (The concomitant features will be taken up later under the heading of prosody.) For these reasons, spelling is essentially the representation of the sequence of vowel and consonant sounds that occur in segments of utterances practically equivalent to words.

Two tendencies are operative in the writing of a segment of utterance. One is to work out, whether deliberately and slowly or not, the sequence of constituent sounds of just that segment that is being written. The other is to recall and conform to spellings previously encountered for the same segment. It is the first of these that brings about change of spelling to fit differences—dialectal or chronological—in pronunciation of words; the second acts as a conservative factor by which standardized spelling can exist and by which, with enough changes in speech, spelling and speech can become seriously mismatched. We shall review English writing in these respects in a later section. At this point we may glance at the implications of these tendencies for the relation of spelling to phonology. With a limited set of alphabetic symbols, and with these symbols to occur as discrete units in a linear sequence only, the representation of morphological segments tends to be specifically phonemic: the contrastive aspects of the phonological system are those of which a writer will be most aware. Especially in the stressed portion of the segment, which in English is normally the stem or at least a part of it, the phonemic differentiation of one morpheme from another will tend to be reflected in the alphabetic representation. Phonetic details that are not significant to the distinctive representation of the morphological structure will tend to be disregarded for linguistic and practical reasons: they are of no linguistic significance and the luxury of recording them is a burden to both writer and reader.

OLD ENGLISH SPELLING

23.3 The nature of spelling conventions leads directly to the character of the earliest spelling of English and implies a great deal about the subsequent history of spelling of the language. At the outset of the one main tradition of writing English, an alphabet in use for writing principally Latin was available to writers; this alphabet was a set of graphemic symbols that by convention stood for the various phonological units of Latin. The writing of English was in effect the use of these same symbols with their phonological significations in the representation of the language segments of Anglo-Saxon speakers. The working out of the constituent sounds of Old English morphological structures would necessarily have been more deliberate than it subsequently became for practiced writers, since there were no previous spellings of English words; that is, the conventions of spelling the English segments of discourse had to be developed. The theoretically predictable nature of the spelling of Old English corresponds to the historically determined nature of the spelling: the texts of Old English reflect a spelling that is essentially phonemic, and the conventions are much simpler than they have been at subsequent times in the traditionally evolved conventions of writing English.

A perfect one-to-one match did not exist between each phoneme of Old English and each grapheme in Anglo–Saxon writing. The inventory of phonemes of Latin and that of Old English were not identical. Old English /þ/, for example, manifest in the allophones [θ] and [ð], had no Latin counterpart. A digraph *th* was the earliest expedient, apparently, for representing the phoneme. Subsequently two monograph symbols took the place of the digraph: *þ* was borrowed from the runic alphabet, and the special marking of *d* by a stroke through the ascending line produced *ð* to distinguish it from *d*, the symbol for the homorganic stop consonant. That these two symbols for the spirant, *þ* and *ð*, were never assigned to allophonic differences [θ] and [ð] attests to the essentially phonemic rather than phonetic principle of representing the phonological structure of words. Consonantal /w/ was represented by *u* or *uu* until another runic symbol ƿ "wen, wynn" was appropriated for it. The other symbols, including *æ* and (very early) *œ*, were essentially of Irish adaptation of the Latin alphabet.

The least satisfactory fit of the alphabet to English was a carry-over from Latin—the limitation to five vocalic graphemes for a language that had many more than five vowels. Development of *y* as a vocalic symbol was one expedient for distinguishing vowels in spelling, and two-letter symbols such as *eo* was another. Contrasts between long and short vowels were not represented, however. The subsequent history of English spelling reflects at all points the inadequate set of vocalic symbols.

MAJOR CHANGES IN SPELLING CONVENTIONS

23.4 It would be far beyond the scope of the present study to detail the changes in spelling conventions and the changes in the relations of spelling and speech through the thousand years and more of extant writing of English. The major developments will have to be characterized by selected examples. The developments fall into two broad types: change in conventions of alphabetic representation of phonological units, and change in the phonological shapes of morphological structures with or without corresponding change in spelling. The relationships between changes in phonological shapes of morphemes and changes in spelling are among the most unsystematic of the aspects of English.

Changes in representation of phonological units have been of many kinds from many causes. So simple a matter as distinguishing two graphemes that stood alternately for each of two phonemes occurred roughly five hundred years after the phonemes were distinct. Curved *u* and angular *v* were in effect variant shapes of a single letter ("allographs") until assigned (principally) vocalic and consonantal designations respectively, an assignment made only in relatively late Modern English; normal *i* and elongated *j* have much the same history. The disuse of *þ* and ð is attributable to spelling conventions of Anglo-Norman scribes during the period of Middle English using the digraph *th* for the sounds [θ] and [ð]. When the single dental spirant split into /θ/ and /ð/, no new spelling was devised to distinguish them; five to six hundred years later we still have only the one digraphic spelling *th* for both. The letter *q* was also introduced by French scribes, and continues to occur in spelling in English only with a following *u*. One of the significations of *qu* has continually been /*kw*/, occurring only at the beginning of a syllable; it supplanted the spelling *cw* in native English words. Another chance for sorting out sounds and letters came with the introduction of *g* in Anglo-French scribal tradition. It was a different shape of an historically identical symbol that appeared in English writing as *ȝ*. But after a complex variety of changes, only one letter shape *g* was retained and a symbol of potential utility in representing new consonant phonemes was lost. Also attributable in the main to Anglo-French traditions were *ch* for postvocalic /x/, ultimately *gh* for the same phoneme, and *wh* to replace *hw* spelling of /hw/. From these and the instance of *th*, it will be apparent that the *h* part of the digraphs signaled spirant manner of articulation; the first part of the digraphs marked the approximate position of articulation —*th* = dental spirant, etc. *Ch* in prevocalic position supplanted *c* for /ċ/, to distinguish it from /k/. A trigraph *tch* also was devised (as for *ditch*) for postvocalic /č/ when the vowel was "short"; otherwise *ch* was used. *Sh* supplanted *sc* for prevocalic /š/, and *sh, ssh, sch,* and even *ss* were at one time or another used for postvocalic /š/. For writers of Old English and for Anglo-Norman writers *z* represented /ts/ (Anglo-Saxon scribes seldom used it except for writing Biblical names). The signification /z/ was acquired only much later for a variety of reasons generated in the histories of both French and English, but is still used only sparingly to spell /z/. Among the changes of a less elemental kind are the *gh* for /g/—an invention by Dutch printers of English—and spellings retained from literate borrowings: *ch* in *chaos, ph* in *graph,* and many more.

Vowel spellings show no more rationality in their historical development. The inventory of graphemes was inadequate from the beginning, as has been mentioned. Among the principal changes, the use of *o* (as well as *u*) for the vowel /u/—eventuating in Modern English *son,* beside *sun*—was an Anglo-French innovation; the symbol represented approximately in French the vowel sound spelled *u* in English, and the distinctive letter shape of *o* made it useful for clarifying the vowel amidst letters characterized by short downstrokes—*m, n, i, u.* Perhaps there is no better example of the uncoordinated changes in sound and spelling than those associated with the digraph *ou.* It was introduced as the Anglo-Norman alternative to *u* for /ū/. After it had become the established spelling, the shift of [u:] to [aʊ] did not occasion spelling change.

The most significant innovation—and potentially the most useful —was the doubling of vocalic letters to signify phonemically long (or tense, or free) vowels. The convention was established during Middle English and in some areas of England was used for any long vowel: *good, feet, wiis* 'wise,' *taake* 'take,' etc. In the more influential areas of England, however, particularly around Oxford and London, only *oo* and *ee* were used regularly and the others were generally avoided. The subsequent history may be inferred readily from Modern English spellings. A Northern spelling convention marked a vowel as long by a following *i,* thus *guid* 'good,' *raid* 'rode,' etc., of which *build* is a relic in Modern English. From the earliest writing to the present, English has had no distinctive symbol for /ə/, the vowel now most frequent in occurrence in the language.

PERSISTENCE OF ESTABLISHED SPELLINGS

23.5 Established spellings tend to persist. The tendency increases with the increase of writing and literacy, a phenomenon of striking rate of acceleration in the past four hundred years. Persistence of spellings of morphemes increases also when the conventions of spelling are accorded the status of being authoritative. In the eighteenth century in particular current spellings were lent the weight of authority that is associated with eighteenth-century culture of English-speaking peoples. Much earlier, at the end of the ninth century, the spelling of Wessex English gained a short-lived authority by its being nearly a sole-surviving tradition, together with the prestige of King Alfred and Wessex that was associated with it. Apart from these landmarks in establishing spellings, any conventions of spelling, given currency and any sort of prominence, are likely to leave some mark in the history of English orthography. Change in spelling has followed change in speech at rates closely contingent upon the presence and prominence of established conventions of spelling morphological structures: the more prominent the conventions, the slower the change.

The tradition of characterizing Middle English as "chaotic" apparently stems as much from the spellings of Middle English texts considered collectively as it does from the linguistic diversity among the dialects of Middle English. The melange of spelling conventions, from native traditions, French innovations for English, and the permutations of the native and foreign traditions, is indeed forbidding, even in the light of the still greater diversity of conventions reflected in standardized spelling of Modern English. But the attribution "chaotic," in so far as it is associated with Middle English spelling, arises from the varieties of the dialects and the absence of a standard dialect with standardized spelling. However diverse and unsystematic the spelling of Middle English may appear in a variety of texts, spelling was nevertheless basically phonemic, within a more complex set of conventions of sound-and-symbol association than Old English had had. When English was not the prestige language, when differentiation of dialects had become extensive, and when no single dialect was dominant (or "standard"), spelling reflected closely the phonemic makeup of morphological structures in any single dialect. With the linguistic and orthographic state of affairs during most of the period of Middle English, it will be apparent why spellings established during the period of Old English have not persisted into Modern English: there was a complete and prolonged absence of a prominent set of conventions for spelling morphological structures. Only with the establishment of a new set of prominent conventions did spellings again come to be fixed and to persist for writing English, whatever differences in pronunciation there may be.

The conventions that came into prominence had as their basis a particular regional dialect (more accurately, a set of dialects)—the speech of London and the surrounding areas principally to the north. The emergence of a fairly uniform set of spelling practices was a development tied to practical affairs of government: from about 1400, the principal writing by government clerks was increasingly regularized and became increasingly influential, and the clerks wrote London English. Conventions of letter-sound association were then somewhat mixed, but two other factors have had more to do with the "nonphonetic" spelling that English has subsequently had. The principal one, of course, has been change in pronunciation: *night, neighbor, through, though* exemplify but one aspect of change, reflecting pronunciation of these words when they still had /x/ as part of their phonemic makeup. The other one has been dialect mixture reflected in change of pronunciation of morphs and in spellings of words in a nonstandard dialect adopted by writers of the emerging standard dialect: *bury* is a specially telling example, the *u* reflecting a spelling established for a front rounded vowel when it was current in a western English dialect as the stressed vowel of the word.

The history of Modern English spelling comprises essentially a slow process of reducing various spellings of any morphological structure to a single spelling that is accorded the status of "standard" or (popularly) "correct." The selection of single spellings has followed almost every conceivable principle. A phonological principle has operated for many word spellings, but it has never been dominant. The practice of "best" writers is another, though this principle has been inoperative for at least the last two hundred years. Etymology has also been the deciding factor for some spellings; in some celebrated instances—*debt, doubt, indict, parliament, fault,* and others—the etymology has been inaccurate, to be sure, but none the less decisive. Most striking circumstance is that the spelling of English within the past five hundred years has not been systematically remodeled, despite the extensive changes in the phonemic structure of morphs, the proposals of reformers, the increasing, enormous burden English spelling imposes on people who write, and the ease and wisdom with which revision of spelling could be carried out. In the face of these factors, established spellings persist to an extent unprecedented in the earlier history of English, unprecedented, in fact, in the history of any other living language.

Chapter 24

STRUCTURE MARKING: MODERN ENGLISH

TWO LEVELS OF STRUCTURE MARKING

24.1 Some kinds of structure marking have been described in earlier chapters. One is the occurrence, or potential of occurrence, of an inflectional morpheme marking the boundary of a stem, whether the stem is a single root form or a derivational or compound sequence of morphemes: the inflectional morpheme occupies only the final position in a fixed combination of morphemes. In earlier periods of English this kind of marking operated with adjectives—including "compared" forms—as well as nouns and verbs. When verbs still had person- and number-signaling inflections in past tense forms, the sequence requirement was strictly that tense-indicating inflection precede person- and number-inflection; the latter inflection was thus specifically a boundary marker of the "verb word." Another kind of marking is implicit in the clustering patterns of consonants. A sequence of consonants that does not conform to one of the clustering patterns marks a syllable boundary in any case, and marks a fairly high probability of morpheme boundary. Even the occurrence of a short, "checked" vowel in a stressed syllable provides negative marking, that is, that a syllable or morpheme boundary is not present but may occur only after one or more following consonants. Still another kind of marking that has been mentioned inheres in stress variation. Inflectional syllables have always had relatively weak stress (as well as word-final position); in compounds and derivatives, one morpheme (or one syllable of it) has greater stress than any other in the fixed sequence.

Structure marking of these kinds defines boundaries of relatively short series of morphemes. The series thus defined are by and large of the kind that, for English, the term "word" is an appropriate label. Moreover, in indicating only boundaries, these markings identify no more than the attachment or nonattachment of morphemes to each other when those morphemes occur in adjacent positions in the linear sequence of utterances. They mark whether the forms are welded together or not (to use a metaphor from mechanics); they cannot mark, though, any structural relations with noncontiguous morphemes —whether morphemes separated from others are wired somehow in simple or complex circuits (to use a metaphor from electronics). It is to the structure marking of normal, major units of discourse that we shall turn in this and the next two chapters, the units of utterance that are "wired"—sometimes in complex ways—rather than "welded" into words.

What have just been referred to as "normal, major units of discourse" will be of several kinds and sizes as we proceed. The primary one will be that of the "sentence" and others will be principal constituent parts of sentences. Thus, within the sentence unit, for example, noun phrases, verb phrases, and prepositional phrases are susceptible of separate analysis. Before we limit ourselves to the maximum units of average sentences, it will be instructive to examine some exceptionally long but linguistically normal utterance units. That the first sample is *one* sentence may be determined apart from the punctuation that graphically marks the utterance as a single sentence; it is from an anonymous translation, published in 1608, of Belleforest's version of the Hamlet story.

> Fengon, brother to this Prince Horuendile, who onely fretting and despighting in his heart at the great honor and reputation wonne by his brother in warlike affaires, but solicited and prouoked (by a foolish ielousie) to see him honored with royall aliance, and fearing thereby to bee deposed from his part of the gouernment: or rather desiring to be onely Gouernour: thereby to obscure the memorie of the victories and conquests of his brother Horuendile; determined (whatsoeuer happened) to kill him, which hee effected in such sort, that no man once so much as suspected him, euery man esteeming that from such and so firme a knot of alliance and consanguinitie, there could proceed no other issue then [= than] the full effects of vertue and courtesie. (The Hystorie of Hamblet, Prince of Denmarke (London, 1608); reprinted from the unique copy preserved in the Library of Trinity College, Cambridge, with the kind permission of the Master and the Fellows of Trinity College, Cambridge.)

Although this sentence is very long (and somewhat exhausting) by standards of modern English standard prose, it is not obscure and poses no special problems for construing its structure accurately and fully. At the simplest level of analysis, for instance, the core of subject-predicate structure emerges readily—"Fengon . . . determined . . . to kill him [Horuendile]"—despite the seventy-four words intervening between *Fengon* and *determined*. A diagram of the sentence, showing the structural relations of its word parts, would be far too large and complex to fit any ordinary page; but for all the graphic complexity of a diagram, the structural complexity does not exceed practical limits of immediate comprehension. A second sample is also one sentence and is punctuated to so appear in writing; it is in verse, a portion of Chaucer's Prologue to "The Wife of Bath's Tale" in *The Canterbury Tales* (c. 1400).

> But me was toold, certeyn, nat longe agoon is,
> That sith that Crist ne wente nevere but onis
> To weddyng, in the Cane of Galilee,
> That by the same ensample taughte he me
> That I ne sholde wedded be but ones.

[Gloss: *toold* told; *agoon* ago; *sith* since; *onis* once; *ensample* example; *ne sholde* should not; *ones* once.]

Apart from its being a somewhat shorter sentence than the first one, this one utilizes simpler principles of structuring, notably in the multiple uses of *that*. The layering of the sentence, by which "[To] me was toold . . . that . . . Christ . . . taught . . . me that I ne sholde wedded be but ones" appears straightway as the core, is plainly marked: as the sentence progresses, all the intervening parts have structural signals that (among other things) inform us 'completion of sentence-core is delayed.'

One more sample of a lengthy utterance may be given. This one, unlike the two preceding, is not literary composition; it is part of an annal in The Parker Chronicle (a version of "The Anglo-Saxon Chronicle(s)"), written about 900 A.D. In this excerpt there is no capitalization; minimal punctuation, occurring as a point, is reproduced here as it occurs in the manuscript. The translation that follows it gives segment-by-segment equivalence, with the punctuation of the original text.

þa hie ðа fela wucena sæton on twa healfe þære e ond se cyng wæs west on defnum wiþ þone sciphere þa wæron hie mid metelieste gewægde ond hæfdon micelne dæl þara horsa freten • ond þa oþre wæron hungre acwolen • þa eodon hie ut to ðæm monnum þe on east healfe þære e wicodon ond him wiþ gefuhton ond þa cristnan hæfdon sige ond þær wearo ordheh cyninges þegn ofslægen ond eac monige oþre cyninges þegnas ofslægen ond se dæl þe þær aweg com wurdon on fleame generede • þa hie on east seaxe comon to hiora geweorce ond to hiora scipum • þa gegaderade sio laf eft of east englum ond of norð hymbrum micelne here onforon winter • ond befæston hira wif ond hira scipu ond hira feoh on east englum ond foron [etc.]

'Then when they stayed several weeks on the two sides of the river and the king was (in the) west in Devon against the ship-army then they were distressed with famine and had eaten up a great share of the horses • and the others were dead from hunger • then they went out to the men who were encamped on the east side of the river and fought against them and the Christians had the victory and there Ordheh the king's thane was slain and also many other of the king's thanes slain and the part who there came away were saved in flight • then they came to Essex to their fortifications and to their ships • then the remnant gathered again from East Anglia and from Northumbria a large army before winter • and secured their wives and their ships and their property in East Anglia and went [etc.]'

Without the structure marking of modern conventional punctuation, and even in the face of points occurring sometimes where we should put them but sometimes where we would not, the passage nevertheless is intelligible; the principle difficulty in understanding the passage is in sorting out whom the pronouns refer to, but that is only because we now lack general knowledge that the historical context originally supplied. The structure markings that hold this run of sentences in shape, the markings that enable the reader to understand a long sequence of words (and morphemes), are much different in their particulars in the Old English and the Modern English renderings. What is important to notice is that there are markings, even without modern punctuation (and without voice inflection and the like), sufficient to enable us to make good linguistic sense of the moderately long utterance.

"PROMINENCE" AND INTONATION FIGURE MARKERS

24.2 To "make sense" of a linear string of morphemes is to put all (or at least most) morphemes of the string into comprehensive structures that we recognize. It is in the nature of a natural language that the markings or signals should be sufficient so that a hearer may expect to put the morphemes into a structure that is approximately the same as the structure that a speaker somehow has for the string. In the rest of this chapter we shall take inventory, so to speak, of the principal types of structure marking devices for English other than those delimiting fixed morpheme combinations on the order of words.

By what signals, then, may we be instructed—or give instruction —in "making sense" of the forms that are perforce strung out single file in speech? Above all, some marking must signal just how much is to be built into a principal unit, that is, a signaling of the boundary of the type of structural unit to be construed before proceeding to another unit of the same type. The practical unit is that of the "sentence." The first two samples in the preceding section were marked for termination by the occurrence—in writing—of a full stop, or period. In speech, some other signal or signals mark the termination; normally one signal is a conspicuous drop or rise in voice pitch, commonly followed by a longer than average interval between the final syllable of the unit thus marked and the beginning syllable of the next comparable unit. The correlation is something less than perfect, but the distinctive rise in pitch generally corresponds to a question mark, the distinctive drop in pitch (as for the samples, above) generally corresponds to a full stop. These signals convey roughly the meaning 'END' with respect to sentence units. Until such a signal occurs, the utterance unit is understood still to be in progress. To represent these structure markings of speech we may select the symbols ⟨↗⟩ for rising pitch, ⟨↘⟩ for falling pitch.

In addition to the specific 'END' marking by pitch glide (and usually timing) signals, English utilizes—in speech but not in conventional writing—another marking to signal imminent end of a linguistic sequence. This marking may be analyzed variously, for it may have several acoustic attributes: greater intensity of sound (more stress), higher voice pitch, or prolongation of a syllable (increased duration). All three may occur, but the linguistic marking still occurs if any one of these factors is suppressed; quite probably, any two could be suppressed and the marking would still be perceived. The occurrence of any or all these factors in English in the marking function we are concerned with has been labeled "prominence" by Philip Lieberman, in *Intonation, Perception, and Language*. It is called "sentence accent" by Kurath, in *A Phonology and Prosody of Modern English*. (It has had many other labels and definitions since phonetic aspects of sentences came under close study chiefly since the 1930's.) The feature is represented most economically in linear typography by the acute accent symbol ⟨ ′ ⟩, which we shall use here. The relation of the marking "prominence" to that of the intonation figures of conspicuous rise and drop in voice pitch is generally as follows. While the intonation figure occurs in the voicing in the final syllable of the series being marked as "sentence," the feature of prominence may occur in conjunction with any syllable up to and including the final one. Again, while prominence may involve higher voice pitch, it is the relative pitch rather than rise or fall of pitch that is distinctive. And finally, prominence always precedes the intonation figure. Together these two types of marking signal the termination of a sentence unit.

In terms of the structure markings of prominence and the two alternate intonation figures, the following are then identified as sentences.

↘ Nó
How ↘ múch
How ↗ múch
I ↘ thínk so
The book is on the ↘ táble over there
Darwin's *Origin of Species* was published in eighteen fifty- ↘ níne
Darwin's *Origin of Species* was ↘ públished in eighteen fifty-nine [but planned years earlier]
Darwin's *Origin of Species* was published in eighteen fifty- ↗ níne [*Response:* Yes, that's right]

The Chaucerian sentence in 24.1, presumably, concluded thus:

. . . that I ne sholde wedded be but ↘ ónes.

In these short sentences the structure marking of the sentence unit by prominence and intonation figure is quite simple. In the first two long sentence samples in 24.1 it will be obvious that prominence marking occurs a great number of times, yet there is only one sentence termination. At the outset, for instance, *Fengon* and *Horuendile* both (when read in present-day speech) are thus marked. Termination of a structural unit does follow each one, but the unit is less than that of a sentence, as that unit has been defined thus far. The termination (again, in present-day English) is marked differently, however. The voice pitch figure at the end of the unit is neither conspicuously a rise or drop like that symbolized by ⟨↗⟩ and ⟨↘⟩. The figure may be represented as ⟨→⟩. Thus, → *Féngon, brother to this Prince* → *Hóruendile, who* (etc.). This third intonation figure customarily signals 'end of a major nonfinal constituent of a sentence'; contrasting with ⟨↗⟩ and ⟨↘⟩ signaling 'END,' ⟨→⟩ signals '(From here) GO ON.' It too is commonly followed by a longer than average interval before the syllable string of the next major constituent unit begins. The interval is normally shorter than that following ⟨↗⟩ or ⟨↘⟩, but its relative length is not decisive in identifying the structural boundary.

OTHER TYPES OF MARKERS

24.3 The three intonation figures just described (each preceded by a marking of "Prominence") are sufficient to mark the boundaries of ordinary sentences and their principal constituent parts. They are certainly not the only structure-marking devices of English, however, and the more complex and long a sentence is, the more other devices are needed. As we proceed in this informal inventory of structure-marking features of nonfixed morpheme combinations it is to be understood that extensive redundancy in structure marking may occur in any given sentence. In any sentence of even moderate length, at least partial redundancies ("overlaps") of marking are the rule rather than the exception. Where overlapping markings occur, it is often beside the point to attempt a ranking of types of markings. While intonation figures with prominence markings are probably primary (at least statistically), the redundancies of various structure markings are a normal feature of language; suppression or deletion of one (or more) of them need not leave an utterance unmarked for structure.

It is because of redundancies, in fact, that writing is feasible without marking "prominence," for example, or without complete correlation of pitch rise or fall with (written) question mark and full stop, respectively. The Old English sample in 24.1, without punctuation (including capitalization) corresponding to modern conventions, can be construed in sentences nevertheless; in the next chapter we shall "construe" some samples of Old English from evidence in Anglo-Saxon writing. Modern conventions of punctuation supply the graphic marking of the Chaucerian sample sentence given earlier; an editor of the fourteenth century text can find ample clues for the graphic marking of structure by punctuation. In what do these clues inhere?

"Function words" constitute a type of structure markers: *But, that, ne, to, in, of, by* are of this kind in the Chaucerian sentence. The prepositions in this list are solely function words; *ne* is also an unambiguous marker of negation; the first *but* is conjunctive, the second *but* prepositional; *that* occurs several times with what is commonly called "relative" function. Even the word *the* can be included among function words since, whatever else it may signify, it also marks the structural fact of a noun or nominal closely following without (among other things) the intermediate occurrence of a finite verb or a preposition.

Potential membership in one of only a limited set of "parts of speech" is another device for marking structure. Aside from prepositions, conjunctions, "definite articles," negating particles, and the like, *certeyn, weddyng, ensaumple, onis – ones, nevere, taughte, sholde,* and others are limited in possibilities of structural functions. *Sith* 'since' is likewise limited; in combination with a following *that—sith that*—the probabilities are very high that the "core" of predication will be delayed until after the occurrence of an ensuing ⟨→⟩, or that it has preceded *sith (that)*.

We are already overlapping not only marking by "function words" and "parts of speech" categories, but marking by sequence patterns as well. *But* as conjunction as well as *but* as preposition precede elements with which they are most closely structured; *ne* precedes a finite verb without any other forms intervening between it and the verb form that structures most closely with it; *nat longe* are intimately structured in that order so long as no other grouping marker (such as ⟨→⟩) accompanies *nat,* while the reverse order of the words would not signal closest structural relation of the two words.

Finally, inflection provides significant structural marking. In the first line of the sample, *me* cannot be subject of a verb; *he* and *I* in the later lines, by their case forms (subjective), mark the occurrence of clause subjects. Most inflections that had appeared in Old English are not present in this late Middle English example, but *toold* is distinct from the finite preterite form *tolde,* hence identified here by its inflection as participial. And so on.

Our inventory now includes intonation figures, "prominence," "function words," "parts-of-speech" categories, word order, and inflection (quite apart from devices belonging to writing); these are probably all the devices. The array of structure-marking devices and their normal degree of overlap are sufficient to signal the structure —in speech—of even the very long and elaborate sample sentence given first in 24.1. For that sentence only a few matters need be remarked. One is the distinctly participial forms that "downgrade" so many of the constitutent parts of the sentence, that is, they signal nonindependent constructions. Another is the marking of "infinitives" by a preceding, adjacent *to,* by which the form is excluded from the potential function as predicator. Another is that, once the principal or "core" subject-predicate construction has been completed—*Fengon . . . determined . . . to kill him*—the use of ⟨→⟩ will make clear the delays in sentence termination that are not otherwise overtly marked.

Implied in the variety of devices to mark sentence structure and in the redundancy that the devices may have in any given sentence is one further aspect of structure markers: they operate as complex systems, not as strings. To take a simple example, the morph *to* has several potential marking functions. Its relative stress in an utterance may partially limit its specific function; its position relative to other morphemes, in turn in relation to the following intonation figure, may also define its function; in addition, the "part of speech" and inflectional features of morphemes within the bounds of a preceding intonation figure (or silence) and a following intonation figure also may signal its specific function. At the same time, the occurrence of *to* operates to define the specific structural features of other parts of the morpheme sequence. The interaction of structure markers thus provides the means for signaling utterance structure with great precision for nearly any kind of sentence a (native) speaker may construct as a natural utterance.

Only an extremely limited set of sentence types of English cannot be "disambiguated" by structural marking of the kinds listed. Best known, probably, is a pattern involving an *–ing* morpheme: *He is always engaging in discussions.* Why the ambiguity 'constantly engaging, participating in' beside 'constantly engaging, attracting interest, winning' should be unavoidable is a long lesson in the history of English. But aside from these rare examples, sentences in normal speech carry structure marking even sufficient to compensate for errors or for differences from the norm of a dialect. A child's impromptu sentence goes like this: *That's* (or *Thát's*) *the girl* (→) *whose hand I held going across the* ↘ *stréet's house.* A change of order and inflection produces normal *That's the house of the girl whose* (etc.); but the prominence-marking of *streét–* provides marking enough to clarify the structure of the child's sentence. A nonstandard construction of the type *Me and Bill bought a horse* is not ambiguous despite the pronoun inflection in any of the prominence and intonation contour patterns that will occur.

SYNTAX AND PROSODY

24.4 The interaction, or interrelation, of structure markers has been only lightly touched upon, since broad generalization in this matter serves our purpose but little. Less broad generalization produces descriptions of the language that traditionally go under the heading "syntax" of English. For example, a syntax describes the case inflections of nouns or pronouns following prepositions, the requirements of concord ("agreement") of inflections of words of different form classes that are related, the "government" of case inflection of nouns occurring as "object of verb," the extent to which word-order patterns are fixed and obligatory, and the like. These patternings concern all the markers except for the ones here called intonation figures and "prominence." The description of these two as they operate in English is probably best labeled "prosody" of English. It will not be possible to provide in the ensuing chapters either a syntax or a prosody of English; neither space nor the purpose of our study permit them. These two aspects of the English language, it may be added, have had far less thorough formulation than have the phonological, morphological, and lexical aspects, at any and all stages in the historical development of the language. With an inventory of the structure-marking devices of English, our next task will be to consider to what extent the inventories in Old English and Middle English are like that of Modern English. Then, by comparing developmentally related features of syntax (and inferred prosody), we can examine some of the ways in which the systems of structure marking of non-fixed morpheme sequences have evolved in our language.

Chapter 25

STRUCTURE MARKING: OLD AND MIDDLE ENGLISH

PROSODIC FEATURES AND WRITING

25.1 The inventory of structure markers in the preceding chapter is drawn up from analyses of Modern English. All the marking devices except "prominence" and intonation figures are by nature recorded in alphabetic writing, apart from punctuation, in the linear representation of morphemes phonologically distinguished: both the morphemes and their sequence pattern record the data that are analyzable as function words, parts-of-speech categories (form-class membership), inflection, and word order. It follows, then, that from the alphabetic writing of Middle English and Old English the structure markers of these kinds should be fully recoverable. But what of the prosodic features, those that are not by nature recorded in alphabetic writing? Punctuation of Modern English only roughly approximates the recording of terminal contours ⟨↗⟩ and ⟨↘⟩ and is not a reliable guide to ⟨→⟩, while "prominence" is not represented at all by graphic means. Punctuation by writers of Middle English recorded no features that modern punctuation does not also record, and the conventions during the period of Middle English were somewhat less systematized and thorough. The one sample of Old English in 24.1 was fairly typical of Anglo-Saxon writing in respect to punctuation—limited use of a point (a raised full stop) not necessarily confined to sentence boundary, lack of capitalization at sentence beginnings, and no marking, again, of "prominence." Nevertheless, several instances of tenth and eleventh century writing provide some evidence for the prosodic features of Old English. The evidence, as will appear shortly, is of a kind not found in subsequent writing of English. However, having graphic evidence provided by contemporary speakers of Old English and certain general—perhaps universal—characteristics of language, we can reconstruct the prosody of Old English with some assurance. To the extent Old English and Modern English prosodic features correspond both in nature and in deployment, we may infer the same features for Middle English.

OLD ENGLISH PROSODY: SAMPLE TEXT

25.2 The sample of Anglo-Saxon writing we shall examine for evidence of Old English prosodic features comes from an early eleventh century copy of the earliest grammar of Latin to be written in any of the modern vernacular languages in Europe: the *Grammar* by Ælfric, Abbot of Eynsham. (The manuscript selected is British Museum MS. Royal 15B.xxii.) Figure 25A is a freehand imitation of four lines of the manuscript, in which the spacing between letters and points has been carefully reproduced. The passage from the *Grammar* is the opening of the description of prepositions.

Prepositio est pars orationis
indeclinabilis · prepositio mæg beon gecweden on englisc
fore set nyss forðande he stent · æfre on fore weardan ·
swa hwær swa he bið · beo he gefeged to oðrum worde ·

Figure 25A. Freehand reproduction of a sample of British Museum MS. Royal 15B. xxii, illustrating variations in spacing.

The irregularity of spacing between groups of letters will be immediately apparent, but the relation of occurrence or nonoccurrence of spacing at word boundaries (and between parts of words) will appear only in the transcription that follows. Instead of imitating the spacing characteristics of the manuscript, the transcription provides notation to record the spacing characteristics. Superscript numerals indicate the width of spacing measured on a scale in which the space required for one downstroke—the space for an *i*—counts as 1, the space required for an *n* (or other two-minim letter) counts as 2, and so on; at word boundaries a 0 spacing (no space) occurs several times. Hyphenation indicates that spacing occurs between parts of a word. The symbol 7 is equivalent to an ampersand, and italic represents expanded abbreviations. A translation is also given, with sacrifice of smoothness and idiom to the requirements of explication.

Prepositio est pars orationis indeclinabilis •
Prepositio^{2} mæg^{1} beon^{1+} gecweden^{2+} on^{0} englisc / fore–$^{1/2}$
set–^{1} nyss^{2} for^{0} ðan^{0} ðe$^{1/2}$ he^{0} stent •^{3} æfre^{1} on^{0}
fore–$^{1-}$ weardan • / swa^{1-} hwær^{2-} swa^{1-} he^{0} bið •^{3} beo^{1+}

he^{0} gefeged^{2} to $^{1/2-}$ oðrum$^{1/2}$ worde • / ne^{0} beo$^{1/2}$ he •^{3}
Hwilon^{1} he^{0} ge–^{1} eacnað •$^{2+}$ 7^{0} gefylð^{1} þæra^{2} worda^{2}
andgyt/þe$^{1/2}$ he^{0} to^{2-} • cymð $^{2+}$ 7$^{1/2-}$ hwilon^{1-} he$^{1/2}$ awent^{1+}
heora^{1} getacnunge •$^{2-}$ 7^{0} hwilon / wanað •^{3}
is healic
Celsus •^{2} do$^{1/2}$ þær$^{1/2-}$ to^{2-} *pre*positio^{2} .ex.^{3} þon*ne*$^{1/2-}$ bið$^{1-}$
swiðe healic
hit^{2} •excelsus • / her^{1-} he^{0} ge–$^{2-}$ fylð$^{2+}$ þ*æ*t$^{1/2}$ andgyt •^{3}
is rihtwis
Iustus •$^{2+}$ do$^{1/2-}$ ðær$^{1/2}$ to^{2-} prepositio^{2-} .in. / þon*ne*$^{1/2}$
unrihtwis
bið$^{1+}$ hit^{1} iniustus •^{3} her^{1-} he^{1-} awent^{2} þ*æt*$^{1/2}$ andgyt •^{3}
ic hliche
rideo •^{3} do / þær^{0} to^{2+} prepositio^{2} .sub.^{3} þon*ne*$^{1-}$ bið$^{1-}$
ic smercige
hit^{2-} subrideo •$^{2+}$ her^{1-} he^{0} ge– / wanað^{2} þ*æt*$^{1/2-}$ andgyt •^{4}

'Prepositio est pars orationis indeclinabilis • A preposition may be called in English "(something-) set-in-front," because it stands always in the front (position), wherever it may be, be it joined to another word, be it not. Sometimes it increases and fills out the sense (*or* meaning) of words to which it comes and sometimes it changes [into the opposite] their signification, and sometimes diminishes [the meaning]. *Celsus,* [which] is "high," put the preposition *ex* thereto, then it is *excelsus* "most high"; here it fills up the sense. *Iustus,* [which] is "justice" [right-wise], put the preposition *in* thereto, then it is *iniustus* "injustice" [un-right-wise]; here it reverses the meaning. [***R***]*ideo,* "I laugh," put the preposition *sub* thereto then it is *subrideo* "I smile"; here it diminishes the meaning.'

With the assistance of the translation one may trace a number of patterns into which points and the varied spacings fall, of which the following are only some. A point and a following capital letter occur at sentence boundaries, those boundaries being independently inferable from the syntactic signals; words that are cited are set off by points, a practice equivalent to italicization in the modern conventions of printing, or to underlining in modern handwriting. The latter half of the passage in which three illustrations are offered (beginning *Celsus . . .*) consists of three complex sentences, each paired with a short simple sentence following, in exactly parallel construction. The variations in spacings within the three sentence pairs are almost congruent as well, if proportions rather than precise measures are observed. The congruence suggests that something in the linguistic signaling is represented by the variations in spacing. Furthermore, the various ranges of spacing correspond in several ways to various syntactic features. On the one extreme, the widest spaces occur at boundaries of major syntactic constructions—"clauses," whether sentence-final or not. On the other extreme the determinative *þæt* and the following noun *andġyt* have narrow space separating them in each of the three occurrences. The space between each *þæt* and the preceding verb is regularly 2 (+), the syntax being that of predicate followed by direct object *(þæt andġyt)*. In the first half of the passage, prepositions and their immediately following objects are not separated; by contrast the form *to* is separated from the following verb *(þe hē tō cymð)* where the prepositional object, relative particle *þe,* precedes *tō* by a rule of word order.

FEATURES OF OLD ENGLISH PROSODY

25.3 Several inferences about Old English prosodic features may be made from the patterns in the passage above. Since the degrees of spacing correspond in a number of consistent ways to varieties of structures signaled syntactically, spacing features in writing are probably based on prosodic features in speech that include (or can be manifest in part by) timing features. What has been marked for Modern English as ⟨↘⟩ corresponds to maximum spacing in the manuscript evidence. (In the sample above, it also corresponds to the position marked by a point and a following capital letter.) What has been marked for Modern English as ⟨→⟩ regularly corresponds to spacing wider than other spacings except those at sentence boundaries. As in Modern English, where prolongation of syllable or pause between syllables is inadmissible, spacing is minimal. Thus, besides preposition and following object, pronoun subject and immediately following finite verb are separated either not at all or by only slight spacing: *hē stent, hē bið, hē ġe-ēacnað, hē āwent,* etc.

Among the variety of known acoustic features that may have guided the Anglo-Saxon scribes in the systematic variation of spacing, timing has been inferred as the one most likely to have been operative. Timing is probably a universal feature of language because of the physiological requirements of grouping segments of utterances into breath groups; it is also a feature shared by the Germanic languages. It is the one feature, as well, whose translation into spacing variation is a priori most probable. That the widest range of spacing occurs at sentence boundaries and the next widest range occurs at boundaries of nonfinal clauses implies that Old English employed timing features comparable to normal sentence- and clause-final intonation features. Whether we are also warranted in inferring intonation features for Old English comparable to those marked ⟨↗⟩, ⟨↘⟩, and ⟨→⟩ for Modern English, can be decided on several grounds. One is the fact that all descendant varieties of present-day English utilize intonation-feature marking, and this marking, in turn, is more regularly employed than is the factor of pause that is deleted in rapid, steady speech. That Old Englsh marking was congruent with that of Modern English is implied in texts of rhythmic speech—verse —when sentence boundaries do not have wider spacing only if the number of syllables intervening between rhythmically timed stresses is great enough to preclude the usual timing interval between the sentences. Another is, again, the physiological conditioning of breath groups; the details of this conditioning and its acoustic correlates are much too complex to be rehearsed here (but they may be found fully described in Lieberman's *Intonation, Perception, and Language*). Still another is the general linguistic characteristic of prosodic marking seldom being carried by a single acoustic factor. All things considered, the evidence converges upon the conclusion that intonation figures—whatever their particular acoustic shapes—were operative in Old English, and that they were coordinated with timing factors to mark clause (including sentence) termination.

Whether prosodic marking of "prominence" can also be inferred for Old English is a more complicated matter. Again, the fact that it is marked in all varieties of present-day English is relevant, and the marking in all varieties of the living language by means of the same set of factors—conspicuous timing, pitch variation, and stress—provides presumptive evidence that "prominence" was a prosodic device (manifest in much the same ways) in Old English. The general characteristics of language mentioned in the preceding paragraph are also relevant. The trends of historical development in phonological shapes of words, as mentioned in an earlier chapter, clearly imply stress accent as an operative suprasegmental factor from the earliest eras of English to the present. Of particular relevance is the evidence provided by scribes who were native speakers of Old English.

The sample of manuscript text given in 25.2 illustrates the kinds of graphic evidence from which prosodic marking of "prominence" may be inferred. The feature is not represented by a separate kind of diacritic such as an acute accent; a mark of that kind is used in most Anglo-Saxon manuscripts, but its function as a prosodic marking can be ruled out conclusively. It is to spacing characteristics that we may turn once more for evidence. At this point the pedagogical motivation for carefully varying spacing may be mentioned; that inferred motivation, though not necessary to the following argument, may yet be germane and helpful. The *Grammar* was carefully composed, and since instruction from it would proceed best if it were read with a deliberate, "didactic" speaking manner, the fullest prosodic marking in a copy of the *Grammar* would provide the maximum guidance for a lector. The manuscript seems to be spaced in a way providing fullest marking. The three pairs of sentences concluding the sample passage are parallel in structure, parallel in substance or topic, and congruent in spacing patterns. The contrast in substance is in the differences being illustrated—how what Ælfric calls "prepositions" (and we may call prefixes) expand, or reverse, or diminish the meaning of a word (that is, a base form) when joined to it. Let us then infer that contrastive purposes place the "prominence" marking of parallel clauses on the contrasting verbs—*ġe–fylð, āwent, ġe–wanað*. Next let us assume that, like the spacing features at clause terminations, a spacing factor based on timing may be operative here. But unlike a timing factor between clauses—between final syllable and initial syllable of successive clauses—the timing factor in "prominence" occurs as prolongation of the stressed syllable of a word. The vowel of the stressed syllable could be, of course, set off in writing by spacing (or doubled or tripled in spelling), but that would seriously conflict with other principles of alphabetic writing. If spacing is to show prosodically pertinent prolongation, it must occur following the written word carrying the marking of "prominence." It is just there that the distinctive spacing does occur in the manuscript text. Taken in conjunction with syntactic marking, other spacing characteristics, pointing and capitalization in this manuscript, and rhetorical and semantic probabilities, some spacing characteristics indeed seem to imply a marking of "prominence" whose empirical attributes included prolongation of the syllable. The use of additional factors of stress and pitch variation, something like those of Modern English, is then a reasonable further inference.

PROSODIC FEATURES AND VARIATION IN SPACING

25.4 A brief excursis here may be in order on the "writing" of prosodic features by variation in spacing. The system of varying spacing, along with some pointing and capitalization, was somewhat more accurate for representing structural aspects of natural, extended utterances than was the system of punctuation marks that subsequently developed. The system of spacing was inherently impractical, however, in at least three important ways. In handwriting, a mistake in spacing was difficult to correct, requiring erasure; unless the mistake were corrected before a subsequent spacing had been left, correction short of rewriting was almost impossible. The variations would not be readily distinguished in mechanical, routine copying, since the variations are governed by analytical "listening"—by the consideration of how the text is to be said and heard: the spacings are determined by an active analysis by the writer of the linguistic sample. (The skill of the scribe of the manuscript of the *Grammar* mentioned above was of the highest order: there are very few errors of writing or inconsistencies in spacing.) In printing, the justification of margins imposes arbitrary spacing factors that interfere with prosody signaling; and again, the mechanical nature of the "writing"—that is, the typesetting or typewriting—is such that appropriate variation of spacing could be expected only if copy were overtly marked for spacing—something like the marking given the sample in 25.2.

SYNTACTIC MARKINGS OF OLD ENGLISH

25.5 The syntactic markings of Old and Middle English are made from the same inventory of devices as are those of Modern English. They will be only briefly illustrated here, using still the short sample from Ælfric's *Grammar*. Inflection is prominent in the short passage in Old English, notably in the variant morphs belonging to the paradigm of the verb "(to) be"—*bēon, bið, bēo;* person- and number-inflection occurs with every finite verb; contrasts between dative and accusative case inflections are matched to differences in prepositions to which the noun or pronoun is directly structured; the third person pronoun forms *hē, heora, hit* are distinguished. The adjective form *ōðrum* has distinctive dative inflection that links it in concord with dative-inflected *worde* in the prepositional phrase *tō ōðrum worde*. Subject and predicate concord is consistently marked, as is concord of pronoun and antecedent. The function words can be inferred from the translation. Form-class membership is marked extensively by inflection when it is not implicit in such noninflectable words as *þonne* 'then,' *hēr* 'here,' and *hwīlon* 'sometimes.'

The other major device is that of word order. No demonstration of the degree to which it marked structural aspects of utterances is possible, of course, from the very small sample before us. The recurrent patterns in these few sentences nevertheless are indicative of what has been determined from analysis of extensive evidence: that word order, far from being free, operated as a principal structure marker in Old English, as it has throughout the history of English as well. The last three pairs of sentences (beginning *Celsus . . .*) exhibit exactly parallel word order. The simple sentence (one-clause sentence construction) in each pair has, following the initial adverbial *hēr,* the following consistent order of constituents: pronoun-subject, finite verb (predicate), and complement consisting of determinative + noun. The predicates of these declarative single-clause sentences are distinctly of the mode traditionally called "indicative." The complex sentence in each pair consists of two clauses with contrasting word order patterns. The first clause with a predicate modally marked as "imperative" has the verb form in the initial position, and a subject does not occur; adverbial *þǣr-tō* immediately follows, succeeded in turn by the complement of the verb. The second clause has the "indicative" verb form as predicate preceded by adverbial *þonne,* a pattern that regularly requires the subject (pronoun) *hit* to follow immediately, followed in turn by the complement of the copula verb *bið.* The other clause in the passage may be seen to follow related patterns of word order. The more conspicuous instances are those involving modally marked "subjunctive" *bēo,* the sentence-initial *hwīlon* (like *hēr*). The patterns involving prepositions, the negative particle *ne,* and the determinative forms have been commented on earlier.

STRUCTURE MARKING IN MIDDLE ENGLISH

25.6 Since the inventory of structure-marking devices of both syntactic and prosodic kinds appears to be the same for Old English as for Modern English, and nothing in the evidence for Middle English points to additional devices during that intervening era, we shall make the obvious inference that the same inventory of devices has been present throughout the history of the language. That the particular uses, including the "load," of any one kind of structure marking have changed during the past thousand years and more will be obvious from the preceding chapters in which the history of inflections has been outlined. Changes may be readily inferred as well from the order of sentence elements just illustrated from Old English differing from the order of the same elements in Modern English sentence structure. It is to some main lines of historical development in syntax and prosody that we shall turn next.

Chapter 26

CHANGE OF SYNTACTIC STRUCTURES

A BRIEF REVIEW

26.1 Several aspects of syntax of English have appeared in earlier chapters, especially in those describing the morphology of the language through its recorded history. The fixed word order of constituents of noun phrases was described (13.3–4) in accounting for the reduction of determiners-pronominals from complex to simple sets of forms: the structure signaling inherent in rigid word order was seen to be sufficient to mark relational features of a string of forms when the elaborate system of concord manifest in the inflections of determiners, adjectives, and nouns disappeared with the loss of inflections. A supplementary description of noun-phrase word order was provided (14.3) in connection with the history of English adjective inflection. The word order characteristics involving negative particles and adverbs had to be brought into description of the evolution of clause negation (18.2); negation was introduced, in turn, in connection with the point that there is intergrading of morphological, syntactic, semantic, and phonological features and that that intergrading is relevant even to lexical study. Further structure marking in the match-up of inflections has been described in the frequent mention of requirements of concord between sentence subject and predicate, and between pronoun or pronominal and referent. To describe the functional shift of verbs from intransitive to transitive (20.3), some syntactic aspects of clause structure were perforce introduced. In this chapter we shall select only those additional aspects of historical syntax and prosody whose intrinsic interest and illustrative value specially recommend them.

SUBJECT AND COMPLEMENT PRONOUNS WITH COPULA VERB

26.2 Let us first consider a relatively simple sequence of changes eventuating in two construction types that alternate in present-day English as solely stylistic variants: *It is I* (or *he, she, they, we*) and *It's me* (or *him* etc.). The divergence of these two types of construction belongs to the period of Modern English, and the shibboleth character of the alternation belongs only to the past two centuries. Both the course of development and the basis of the shibboleth lie in the unusual nature of the construction pattern.

The copula verb *(to) be* with pronouns as subject and complement imposes a systemic anomaly whenever the pronoun forms belong to different person categories. To the extent that the pronouns are semantically identified or equated by the copula verb, the person category distinction is contradicted; and since in almost all inflections of the verb, both past and nonpast, there is person distinction in the singular forms, the occurrence of at least one singular pronoun form as subject or complement introduces at least quasi-anomaly in concord of person (and sometimes number) inflections of pronouns and verb. Even so, the anomalous nature of the construction has never threatened its persistence: from the beginning of English to the present, the systemically neuter singular form *(hit* >) *it* has been employed in this very common kind of utterance. That *it* should be selected to fill either the subject or complement slot apparently results from its having the broadest scope of semantic reference among the pronoun forms. That a form such as *it* always occurs is an obligatory condition of the syntactic pattern involving the copula verb.

At the outset of the recorded history of English the normal construction was *iċ hit eom,* literally 'I it am.' The word order was fixed, and the concord of inflections shows that *iċ* is subject, *hit* is complement. There is some evidence that the sentence stress occurred normally on *iċ* and that it never occurred on *hit,* and there is no contrary evidence relevant to position of prosodic prominence. The first change in this construction type occurred in the fourteenth century, consisting simply of modification of word order: *(h)it am I.* Concord of inflections again defines *I* as grammatical subject, *(h)it* as complement; so far as can be ascertained, sentence stress remained on *I*. Why the change in word order occurred just when it did is a question obviously requiring a very complex answer, one that still awaits full formulation. Whatever its cause, the revision of word order created a syntactic and prosodic structure of a statistically minor kind—complement + copula + subject. The utterance type, however, for its frequency, utility, and simplicity, could be expected either to become fixed in a formula that would persist as a nearly anomalous structure type, or to undergo further change to conform to the statistically dominant syntactic pattern of brief sentences—subject + copula + complement. The construction *(h)it am I* did not "freeze" into a formula, and in fact was obsolete approximately a century after it developed. It was superseded by the simple alternative in which subject + copula + complement word order was created by a single change, this time in the verb inflection: *(h)it is I.* Selection of this particular change seems to be attributable to two factors. One is the dominance of the syntactic feature of word order, such that the pronoun (now) preceding the verb was reinterpreted as sentence subject and the requirement of subject-predicate concord called for *is,* not *am.* The other is that that change was minimal, requiring no alteration of word order, pronoun case form, or (most importantly) location of the prosodic prominence marker.

In the fifteenth century the pattern *It is I* became established as the single, normal structure of the utterance type. Toward the end of the sixteenth century an alternate construction again developed: *It is me – It's me.* But for the conservative effect of later grammarians' strictures against it conveyed through schools to ever-increasing proportions of the speakers of English, it is quite likely that the newer construction should have by now superseded entirely the older *It is I* pattern. The change by which *It's me* developed as an alternate pattern was again a very simple one in substance—substitution of the "objective" case form of the complement pronoun for the "subjective" case form. The conditioning factors were anything but simple in anything like their full and combined functions. Possibly the word order pattern again contributed to the change, such that the analogy of noncopula constructions—*It hurt me, It pleased me,* for example—created a valence for the objective case form following the verb. The unlikelihood of this as a significant influence appears, however, in the difference in position of prominence marking in the sentence types: in the copula construction the pronoun other than *it* ordinarily has the marking and the verb does not, while in the type *It hurt me* the marking ordinarily comes on the verb. The difference in prosodic patterns all but cancels the similarity of word order patterns. It is even less likely that the analogy of French constructions typified by *c'est moi* had any appreciable effect (as has often been suggested), since French had not been a common second language in England for two hundred years prior to the change.

More likely as contributory factors are a related syntactic change and the development of stress attributes of pronouns in subjective and objective case forms. The one syntactic change that is both relevant and contemporary with the development of the pattern in *It is me* is one in which the case form of the identifying pronoun came to be influenced by an adjacent following clause: *It is me you saw* typifies the new syntactic pattern in which no relative pronominal form occurs to mark the complement of the second verb. Without the pronominal marker, especially if the sentence is uttered in only one prosodic phrase (*It is mé you* ↘ *saw*), the one pronoun stands as the only overt form with which to construe *saw,* thus establishing a valence for *me* and not for *I*.

The other major factor contributing to evolution of the pattern of *It's me* has been described in some detail by F. Th. Visser, *An Historical Syntax of the English Language,* Part I, §268; it involves what appears to be a difference between typically stressed and unstressed personal pronouns. The distinction does not, of course, affect the referential meanings in respect to person categories; it is rather a distinction of a different category attached to differences in stress, these differences in turn attaching to morphological contrasts of case inflection. The presumed history of the stress and morphological distinctions is briefly as follows. As subjects of clauses, pronouns most commonly were subjective case forms and came under relatively light stress in the sentence, typically without an immediately following intonation figure; nothing, that is, gave them emphatic or separate utterance in most sentence types except contrastive circumstances—*I* [*and not you*] *did it.* Conversely, objective case forms often carried prosodic prominence marking and often occurred as the final word in clauses, thereby being associated readily with emphasis that was not necessarily a result of contrastive utterances. Such constructions as *The real ME, Poor me,* or *Ah, me* and interrogative *(Who,) ME?* or *Would you like to try to be me?* will illustrate the development. Typical association of these kinds with the respective case forms produced a quasi-paradigmatic pattern. Instead of subjective or objective case forms of personal pronouns being selected solely by syntactic rules, they could also be selected by requirements of relative stress. In the sentence pattern *It is* ↘ ——, selection of the stressed form (technically an allomorph) was for *me* rather than for *I*. That name, noun, determinative, and nominal classes no longer had subjective vs. objective case distinction sharply reduced the force of the syntactic rules by which subjective case forms of complements of copula verb forms were required.

DISAPPEARANCE OF A SENTENCE PATTERN

26.3 A second instance illustrating syntactic and prosodic features under the perspective of history concerns the disappearance of a sentence pattern from the language. One of the sentence patterns in Old English that was common, though certainly not statistically dominant, was distinctive in having no overt subject. Nevertheless always it had a predicate and could have complements of a fully normal variety: the type must be regarded, therefore, as a major sentence pattern, not as a minor one such as those represented in *Yes, No, How much? Thirteen and a half, Stop! Why? Of course,* and the like. Some examples will show the main varieties of the type.

(1) Mē sceamað '[It] shames me' or 'I am ashamed.'

(2) Hīe forscamige ðæt hīe swā oft dōn 'They were (made) ashamed that they did thus so often.'

(3) Iċ wolde þæt þē sceamode swelċes ġedwolan 'I would that you be ashamed because of errors.'

(4) þā ġelustfullode ðām cyninge heora clǣne līf 'Their pure life pleased the king' or '[It] pleased the king, their pure life.'

(5) Hine ne lyst his willan wyrcan 'He was not pleased to carry out (*or* work) his will."

(5a) Himm lisste þa wel etenn off an appell 'He desired very much then to eat of an apple.'

The first one is a minimal, normal sentence which, as the inflection of the pronoun shows, has no overt subject, since *me* never occurs as sentence subject in Old English. The second adds a *that*-clause to the basic construction; the third adds a complement *swelċes gedwolan* with genitive case inflection; the fourth has complement *clǣne līf* in a different case (either nominative or accusative) ; and the fifth has an infinitive complement *(willan) wyrcan.* (5a is an early Middle English example of the same type.) Each of these examples has no overt subject. The variety of sentence types in the translations attests to the difficulty of rendering at once accurately and for explication of the original syntax any sentence in a structure that Modern English does not have.

The sentence type was restricted to a specific list of predicate words, those traditionally called "impersonal verbs" because of the distinctive syntactic structure of the clauses of which they could be the center. Another regular attribute of the constructions is the singular inflection of the verb, distinguished as third-person inflection in indicative mode. Also, the verb was most often preceded by a complement, either immediately or with only an interposed adverb; a noun (but not pronoun) complement sometimes followed the verb. The complement, in turn occurred in either accusative or dative case form, the particular case governed by the particular verb. The semantic field of the "impersonal verbs" (typified by 'be ashamed,' 'be pleased,' 'desire' in the example above) was such as to require a complement designating a person: a personal pronoun or *king, war-*

rior, people, father, and the like. (The inappropriateness of the term "impersonal" to describe these verbs will be apparent here.) The complement could be either singular or plural in form. Finally, the prosodic pattern seems to have placed prominence marking normally on the predicate and not on the preceding "personal" complement.

The number and variety of syntactic and prosodic characteristics of impersonal constructions may be emphasized by brief listing: no overt subject, a restricted list of predicate words, a single verb inflection independent of requirements of concord, a noun or pronoun in a nearly invariable position before the verb, inflectional government of that noun or pronoun by the verb, a restricted semantic field for verb and obligatory complement, and a regular prosodic pattern.

With all these normal structural attributes for constructions that essentially involved only two simple constituents—manifest often as only two words—it may be wondered what should have occurred such that the construction type disappeared altogether. Several different factors contributed to the obsolescence of the type. From the earliest records it is clear that alternate constructions were in use in which an "empty" subject *hit* 'it' occurred: *hit līcode him, hit him līcode* 'It pleased him,' with *hit* functioning much as it did in *iċ hit eom.* The *hit* form supplied an overt subject and matched, in concord, the verb inflection. Also, the verbs that functioned as predicates of the impersonal constructions were not limited to occurrence in this particular sentence type; they occurred with overt subjects of a "personal" kind, as *Hē mē wel līcað* 'He pleases me well,' and of other kinds, as *þām wīfe þā word wel līcodon* 'Those words well pleased the woman.' With the transition from Old English to Middle English a good proportion of the "impersonal verbs" fell into disuse. In terms of the statistics of sentence patterns, these "subjectless" sentences remained a minor type. All these factors, especially in combination, did apparently contribute to obsolescence of "impersonal" sentences.

Chronology and other data make it clear that the impersonal sentence type was not forced out of use, so to speak, by the factors already mentioned. Especially notable is the fact that a number of verbs were added in Middle English to the list associated with impersonal constructions, some of them functionally shifted—*nede(n)* 'need,' *boote(n)* '(to) avail, do good,' *wondr(i)e(n)* '(to) cause to wonder,' etc.—and some of them among the lexical borrowings from French—*mervaille(n)* '(to) cause to marvel,' *availe(n)* '(to) avail,' and others. Meanwhile another factor contributing to the loss of the sentence pattern began to operate. The loss of inflectional distinction of dative (and accusative) case for nouns, loss of all case inflections of adjectives, and loss of all case distinctions for the determinative and specifying forms (>*the, this – these, that – those*)—all these morphological changes together left no distinctive inflectional marking of a pre-verb complement of an impersonal construction, unless it were a pronoun. Earlier *þone man swā liste þæt ġecnāwan* would appear later as *the man so liste knowe that* 'The man desired so to know that.' Only pronouns still had inflectional markings to identify the form structuring most closely with the verb as a complement rather than as the subject: the force of the original syntactic rule was thus reduced in so far as all elements of noun phrases no longer had inflectional marking to distinguish complements from subjects. Under these circumstances, dominant word order patterns tended to redefine the noun phrase constituents of these constructions as subject.

That the impersonal constructions persisted long past the loss of inflectional marking as complements of nouns and their phrase-constituent adjectives and determiners and pronominals is testimony to the independence and salient position of the pronoun system among the sets of language habits. Impersonal constructions persisted well into the period of Modern English, a dozen or more generations of speakers after morphological changes we have been considering. When the change involving pronouns finally came about, generally in the sixteenth and seventeenth centuries, word order and the analogy of sentences with noun subjects (< complements) were primary causes: *me hungreth* > *I hunger, me semes* > *I seem* (or *It seems to me*), *him nedeth* > *he needeth – needs,* and so on. The process of obsolescence of impersonal sentence types was a gradual one in which all the factors we have enumerated contributed. In effect, the impersonal constructions were superseded by supplying grammatical subjects to "subjectless" sentences, or by replacement of impersonal constructions by similar alternate constructions having overt, if often empty, subjects.

HISTORICAL CHANGES IN MARKING OBJECTS OF VERBS

26.4 The history of the marking of the object or objects of verbs provides a third illustration of synoptic aspects of morphology and syntax. To examine the syntactic uses of the case forms other than nominative (> subjective), we will begin with an outline of the principal syntactic relations between verbs and nonsubject nouns, pronouns, and pronominals appearing as objects in clauses in Old English.

A noun object form in a clause in Old English might be inflected for any but the nominative case form; what is said of nouns will apply also to pronouns and pronominals and to determinative or specifying forms and adjectives that may accompany a noun. Selection of a specific case form of the object signaled the relation between the predicate expression and the object expression. To some extent a given verb may be said to "govern" its object by requiring dative, or instrumental, or genitive, or accusative inflection: some verbs with a single object occur with the object always in a single case-inflection category. Typically, *þancian* '(to) thank' has a dative-inflected object denoting to whom (or what) thanks are directed: *Hē Gode þancode* 'He gave thanks to God.' Some verbs, however, may have an object in one or another of its case inflections. When two objects occur with a single predicate, the inflections of the object words most often belong to different case categories: *Hē Gode þonciað blǣdes* 'He gives thanks to God for (the) glory,' with dative-inflected *God–* and genitive-inflected *blǣd–; Iċ hine his rīċes benam* 'I deprived (*or* took from) him his kingdom,' with accusative-inflected *hine* (masculine pronoun), genitive-inflected *rīċe–*. About any combination of variously inflected objects of verbs could and did occur. Consequently, verbs in Old English may be described as "taking" "dative of person and accusative of thing," thereby providing a rule of thumb with a fair degree of utility. The fact of the matter is that the selection of inflectional case forms seems to have been determined rather by the relationships conceived of by the speaker as existing between the referent of the verb and the referent of any object of the verb. Particularly when two object forms referred to persons, the reciprocal relations of these objects with the verb had to be specified. The specific categories of case, when the noun (or other form) occurred as object of a verb, can then be given labels reflecting the syntactic-semantic features that can be abstracted. The labels adopted (with reservation) by F. Th. Visser (*An Historical Syntax of the English Language,* §315 ff.) seem to be fully adequate. Dative inflection may be said to signal "indirect object," marking the referent of the base form as the recipient (actual or intended) of the action of the verb: *Ðā andswarode hē him* 'Then he answered (*or* gave answer to) him.' Genitive inflection correspondingly signals "causative object"; the term is less suitable as a basis for paraphrase of structural relations, but may be illustrated as follows. *Hē þāre gifena Gode þancode* 'He gave thanks to God for (*or* because of) the gifts'; *Se gomela Gode þancode þæs se man ġespræc* 'The old-man gave thanks to God for (*or* because of) that (which) the man said.' Accusative inflection signals "direct object," a simple descriptive formula for which has not been devised successfully; in Modern English the direct object corresponds to the form that in most sentences can be made the subject of the verb by transforming an active construction to a passive one. In Old English, *Hē hīe bereafade heora wǣpna* 'He bereft them of their weapons'; *Hē hine bescirede þæs rīces* 'He deprived him of his kingdom.' Instrumental case inflection (not distinctive for nouns, pronouns, or nominals) signals "ablative object," signifying generally 'place' or 'direction from': *ālȳs mē fēondum* 'release (*or* deliver) me from enemies.'

The historical changes can almost be inferred from the Old English samples and the accompanying translations that have been given. The principal changes, obviously, inhere in the reduction of case-inflection distinctions of nouns, pronouns, and pronominals, on the one hand, and the extension of the use of prepositions to signal the specific structural relations, on the other. While prepositions were used in Old English in many ways similar to their uses in Modern English, signaling by preposition to mark relation of verb and non-subject noun was far less frequent and was essentially redundant to inflectional signaling. Another signaling device for the verb-object relationships in Old English was sequence pattern ("word order"). It will not be practical here to demonstrate the extent of its operation, because other factors—principally contrasts in order for dependent and independent clauses—operated as well, making the number of rules and their hierarchical arrangement too complex to be included here. In broadest schematic statement, the history of verb-object marking is as follows: in Old English the marking was primarily by means of inflection (morphological selection), secondarily by word order, supplemented by function words (prepositions); in Middle English function words became dominant, complemented by inflection (for pronouns) and word order (genitive-inflected objects disappeared altogether at this time, leaving only "objective" case form for pronouns, none for nouns); in Modern English, word order and function words are primary markers, inflection operating only imperfectly among the pronouns.

That inflection should have undergone change from the primary signaling device to become a subsidiary one can be understood only in the light of redundancy among the various persisting devices of marking utterance structures. As should be clear from the example of functional shift of intransitive to transitive verbs, described in 20.3, other changes occurred in connection with the one we have been tracing.

MARKING OF MODE

26.5 A final illustration concerns chiefly the marking of mode of utterances. In Chapter 16 inflectional categories of mood and the progressive merging of inflections were described. As a result of this merging,

Modern English no longer has morphological categories of mood except for a few exceptions mostly limited to the speech of persons whose schooling has fixed morphological distinctions that are otherwise seldom encountered. The history of the marking of mode may therefore be expected to resemble partially the history of the marking of object(s) of verb: with the disuse of inflectional marking, some other kinds of marking assume a primary role.

Clarification of mode may be in order, especially in view of the various traditions of associating it exclusively with inflectional patterns or with semantic categories. Rules of thumb are again of fair utility in describing categories of fact-mood ("indicative"), thought-mood ("subjunctive"), and will-mood ("imperative")—to use Jespersen's terms; or "concession," "volition," "result," "purpose," "condition," and the like. These meaning-based categories nevertheless do not have consistent or simple match-ups with any one set of modal markers, and they are of negligible utility in accounting for changes in syntactic features of the language. The inflectional patterns of "mood" are also unsuitable as a basis for tracing the history of modal marking in English because morphological distinctions of mode have all but disappeared while modal distinctions are as much operative in Modern English as in any earlier periods of the language.

Mode in English can be analyzed as signaling of alternative relations between an utterance and the facts of existence. Syntactic devices are selected by a speaker and decoded by a hearer to indicate, as the primary distinction, whether a clause or sentence specifies the fact of existence or does not specify the fact of existence of the "contents" or symbolic reference of the utterance. In Modern English, for example, *The house burned down* specifies an existential state of affairs; the state of affairs of the house in fact being burned down is not specified in the following sentences:

If the house burns down (he will lose everything).
The house may burn down.
The house will burn down (someday).
Whether the house burns down or not (he will not leave the neighborhood).
He told me to burn down the house.
Burn down the house?
Burn down the house!

The binary distinction between existential specification and existential nonspecification should not be confused with negation, which is a separate and distinct aspect of utterances. *The house didn't burn down* specifies an existential state of affairs, while the negations of the other sentences listed above do not specify existence of the state of affairs. (It may be observed, too, that existential specification is independent of the truth of a statement.) For those sentences in which existence of a state or event is not specified, a secondary distinction will also be marked. The statement will be either "imperative"—a directive—or nonimperative. The nonimperatives are of the various kinds traditionally comprehended by the term "subjunctive."

In the course of the history of English, marking the mode of an utterance has been manifest in verb inflection, function words (of a generally "adverbial" character such as *if*), sequence patterns of sentence constituents ("word order"), or a small set of verbs whose meaning specifically marks modality. Just as with other types of relational signals, redundancy of modal marking is not unusual. Some illustration may be helpful. In the Old English sentence *þǣm lārēowe ġedafenað þæt hē symle wacol sȳ* 'It befits a teacher that he should be ever vigilant,' the inflection is *ġedafenað* distinctively marks existential specification and *sȳ* similarly marks existential nonspecification of a nonimperative type. Function word marking of "subjunctive" nonspecified existence, together with verb inflection marking, is represented in Old English *þēah man swā ne wēne* 'authough one (*or* people) do not think so,' Middle English *althogh it be me looth* 'although it is hateful to me'; in Old English *ġif se cyng swulte* 'if the king were to die,' Middle English *if such cause thou have* 'if you have such cause'; Old English *oþ þæt hē cwōme* 'until he should come,' Middle English *til he fynde it* 'until he finds it.' Word-order marking is clearly illustrated in early Modern English nonimperative *Had I gone . . .* and in imperative *Go (thou) to his house.* The verb words specifically marking existential nonspecification modality include (in Modern English) *can – could, may – might, will – would, shall – should, must, ought,* and in limited use, *need* and *dare*. The device of existential specification need no illustration, being marked by "indicative" inflection and absence of any of the markings for other modes.

Broad lines of the evolution of modal markings in English have again been implied in the citations and translations, but some of the important details must yet be supplied. So long as inflectional distinctions between mood categories persisted, inflectional marking could and did often provide the only marking of the mode of a clause. Particularly for the "subjunctive" mode, however, adverbial word or phrase marking, such as *if, although, whether, on condition that,* has always been common and sufficient by itself. Word order has always been a primary marking device of imperative mode, supplemented by inflectional marking so long as it was operative. The set of modal marking devices are related below in tabular form. (*I* represents "imperative," *S* represents nonimperative "subjunctive.")

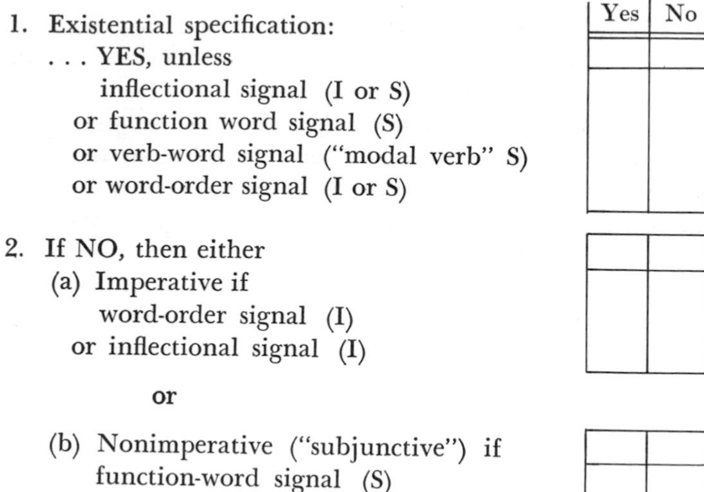

	Yes	No

1. Existential specification:
   . . . YES, unless
   inflectional signal (I or S)
   or function word signal (S)
   or verb-word signal ("modal verb" S)
   or word-order signal (I or S)

2. If NO, then either
   (a) Imperative if
   word-order signal (I)
   or inflectional signal (I)

   or

   (b) Nonimperative ("subjunctive") if
   function-word signal (S)
   or { inflectional signal (S), or
   verb-word signal ("modal verb" S)
   or word-order signal.

The logical-operator words in the schematic layout of modal marking devices are most important—*unless, or, if . . . then,* etc. For a "Yes" on existence specification ("indicative"), for example, there must not be a "YES" for any of the items that follow "unless." For a "YES" on Non-imperative ("subjunctive"), any item marked "Yes" is sufficient and more than one item marked "Yes" will produce that same mode.

Within the systemic relations of devices to mark mode there is obviously room for variations in the specific set of "Yes" or "No" conditions. It is within the range of variations that historical changes took place. To return to the marking device of inflection as the most familiar example, a "Yes" would be sufficient in all but later Modern English to mark "subjunctive" nonimperative, but the changes in verb morphology have been such that for present-day English a "Yes" cannot ordinarily be marked. For all three modes, redundancy of inflection with some other marking device has been reduced to almost zero in later Modern English.

The main trends in the history of modal marking in English are as follows. Inflectional marking was a primary device in Old English, still a regular device in Middle English and early Modern English, now nearly lost. Function-word signaling of "subjunctive" nonimperative was well established in Old English and has persisted to the present, progressively assuming most of the functional load earlier carried by inflection or by inflection and function word. Word-order signaling has been a primary marking device for imperative mode throughout the history of the language and now marks that mode without inflectional signaling that operated through Old and Middle English. Word order has never been a primary marker—though it did operate as a sole marker especially during early Modern English—for "subjunctive"; it has rather been a primary device for marking phrase and clause structure, as we saw earlier. Finally, "modal" verbs have also been primary modal markers throughout the history of English. At the outset, however, they were less frequently used—they carried less of the functional load of signaling nonimperative type of existential nonspecification. Modal verbs have become steadily more widely and exclusively used from earliest times to the present. If information about the occurrence of all the modal marking devices were available in statistical form and plotted on a graph, the "picture" would probably reveal two prominent trends: a decrease in redundancy of marking and a reversal of relative frequency of inflection as opposed to verb-word and adverbial function-word markings.

MODAL VERB WORDS

26.6 The sketch of the principal historical trends in modal marking has considered the various marking devices as they are related within a system. The history of one of the devices—modal verb-words—warrants some expansion, however, for some details and offshoots of it deserve special notice. The "modal auxiliaries," as they are called, still had in Old English some of the characteristics of "ordinary" verbs. In Modern English they are used exclusively in conjunction with another verb word (historically an infinitive form), but in Old English they could occur also as independent verbs. *Sceal – sceolde* (> *shall – should*), for example, with a direct object meant '(to) owe, have to pay'; *āgan – āhte* (> *owe – owed* > *ought*) meant '(to) own, possess; *magan* (> *may*) meant generally '(to) be able to do, be strong', *willan – wolde* (> *will – would*) signified an act of will or a desire with respect to something. The semantic content of these forms is clearly related to the modal "meaning" which they now have. With the disuse of these verbs as independent predicate words, their meanings have been not so much lost as transferred to the entire clause in which any one occurs.

Some change of meaning has occurred in consequence of exclusive use of these forms as auxiliaries. *Ought,* for example, now signifies obligation, particularly in terms of a moral scheme. The single most interesting change, however, occurred roughly within the period of

Middle English, with *shall* and later with *will.* The existential nonspecification marked by both forms was accompanied by signification of obligation or constraint in the case of *shall,* and a signification of volition or desire in the case of *will.* We cannot here go into the complex of circumstances attendant upon the change of meaning. Suffice it to say, with the loss of the specific meanings of constraint or obligation and later of desire or will, the existential nonspecification alone remained. Within the semantic field of modal verbs these forms then developed a specific meaning that can be paraphrased as 'existential nonspecification solely by reason of location in the time continuum.' How the use of *shall* and *will* as auxiliaries in a verb phrase should come to be construed as "future tense" will be immediately apparent. It will be recalled, however, that tense signification is limited morphologically to past and nonpast; "future" is marked only periphrastically with auxiliary forms that still can carry modal signification.

During Middle English the verb-words marking "subjunctive" came into full use; in later Middle English inflectional distinctions for "subjunctive" vs. "indicative" began to disappear, first for past-tense forms. These two factors appear to have been most important in bringing about still another change in modal marking. That change was the development of *(do)n* as a modal auxiliary. Prior to its development, the signaling of existential specification had inhered in distinctive inflection ("indicative") and *absence* of any of the markers signifying existential nonspecification. The coincidence of partial loss of inflectional marking (in past tense verbs) and the emergence of auxiliary ("periphrastic") *do* suggests casual relation between these changes. Unambiguous signaling of existential specification could be achieved in some utterances only by a supplemental device. Of the kinds of devices fully operative at the time, a specific verb-word was about the only one available. The meaning of *do(n),* like that of the "subjunctive" modal verb-words in Old English, was clearly related to the modal marking required. (While not the only word available nor the only one assigned modal function, from an historical perspective *do* is by far the most important instance.) In effect, to the inventory of mode-marking devices was added a verb-word that for the first time overtly marked existential specification. A diagrammatic representation of the increase in use of *do*-periphrasis is included in Alvar Ellegård's *The Auxiliary Do: The Establishment and Regulation of Its Use,* p. 162; at about 1400 its use in five sentence types was rare, but between 1500 and 1700 its use increased to nearly one hundred percent in four of the five sentence types. Once *do* was added to the modal-marking set of verb-words, its development has paralleled that of the "subjunctive" auxiliary verb-words; it has also come to serve, in its negated form, as a regular part of (negative) imperative sentences—*Don't start without me.*

SYSTEMIC NATURE OF THE CHANGES

26.7 These selected instances of change in the syntactic and prosodic features of English illustrate the familiar generalization that the features operate within systems and the systems intergrade with other aspects of the language, particularly those of morphology. This being so, historical change is to be viewed as a gradual process in the modification of individual features, any particular change conditioned to a great extent by the system or systems within which it operates.

Chapter 27

CHANGE, VARIATION, AND STANDARD ENGLISH

DISTINCTIONS BETWEEN VARIATION AND CHANGE

27.1 To identify a set of variations or to chart the course of change in language requires stipulation of what data are the same and what data are different. There is only apparent paradox in saying that linguistic change occurs only when differences exist between two or more samples of language that are yet the same. The "same" and "different" obviously apply to two or more aspects of a language system. Semantic change, it will be recalled, concerns differences in reference of a linguistic form that persists, that has historical identity. Comparison of adjectives has persisted in English while the norm of morphemic patterns for comparison has shifted from exclusively suffix forms to predominantly pre-posed function words (*more, most*). The obstruent system has persisted with losses and additions of individual consonants. Again, there is only apparent paradox when we say that American English /stæf/ and British English /staf/ are the same word *staff:* there is morphemic identity but phonemic difference. Variation and change of language materials have occupied a great deal of our attention in the preceding chapters and will provide the basis from which to consider the topics remaining.

The relations of variation and change may be briefly explicated by considering the following pair of sentences:

Linguistic change results from variations in speech.

Variations in speech result from linguistic change.

The apparent paradox in the pair of statements can be avoided again by making distinctions. Variation—"difference" among "sames"—in linguistic data can be regarded as an occurrence or as a state of affairs; it can be regarded as process or as effect of process; it can be regarded as a cause of change or as a result of change. Sentences defining variation and change may clarify the distinction still further: Variation consists of differences viewed without respect to their developmental aspects; change consists of differences viewed in the light of their developmental aspects. Thus distinguished, variation is a taxonomical concept, change is an evolutionary concept. The distinction is the same one made in Chapter 1. We are now in a position, however, to use the distinction for tying together some aspects of English and its history that have been mentioned frequently but not integrated in the intervening chapters: the rate at which the language has changed, the geographic distribution of variations, the notion of an "overall system" for the language, and the nature of "Standard English."

RATE OF CHANGE

27.2 If English—or any language—were a single, simply constituted entity, devising a way of measuring its rate of change would be easy enough. The problem of measurement would be analogous to measuring rates of growth, of hardening or dissolving, of movement in space, of specific learning processes, or any other of the familiar phenomena whose changes have long since been analyzed and timed. A language is not a single, "monolithic" entity; in it are systems and subsystems of many kinds. Intergrading occurs among some of the systems and their parts, for example, in the relations of morphology and syntax. Other systems may interact as in the relations of vowels and consonants and of phonology and morphology. There are also various degrees and types of autonomy as of the phonological system, for example. Further, some aspects of English are highly systematized: the systems of consonants and vowels and of inflections, in their differing ways, are closed systems; the lexicon is essentially an open system within which one change will not significantly alter the structure of the lexical "map" of the world that the language provides. The kinds of systems, their hierarchies, intergrading, interactions, and degrees of autonomy all show a language to be a complex "system of systems"; the history of English shows that any over-all system has neither the "tightness" nor the complete consistency by which a simple measurement of rate of change can be appropriately applied to a language.

A brief review of some of the changes we have traced earlier will illustrate the point. The wholesale borrowing of lexical items from French took place *during* the period of Middle English. In referring to "the period of Middle English" we imply that the changes by which we distinguish the principal periods of English were not, like borrowing, proceeding at that time at an unusually rapid rate. The "Great Vowel Shift" began at about the end of the period of Middle English, continued well into Modern English at a conspicuously rapid rate, but does not distinguish periods of English. The changes in inflectional systems, on which the convenient divisions of the history of the language into periods is largely based, show correlation with few but not most other aspects of the language. The different times and different causes of the development of paired voiced vs. unvoiced spirants (see 6.6) is particularly revealing about the nature of a language system and language change.

Apart from the structural relations of the many systemic aspects of English, other structural relations are inherent in population structure—the relationships of groups of speakers using similar language systems. Often in preceding chapters the statement has been made that such-and-such a change occurred at one time in one area, at a later time in another area, or that differences occur between Standard and nonstandard English. These geographic and social (or educational) distributions of variations will be considered more fully in succeeding sections, for they are less relevant to the matter of rate of change than are other aspects of population structure. Social stratifications of a geographically localized speech community may be reflected in language variations, as was mentioned in 7.4. Besides the linguistic conditioning that lay behind the Great Vowel Shift, a change in population structure may have also contributed to the modification of the vowel system: the developments in home industries, in farming, and in growth of cities brought persons of various ages into circumstances that defined age groups in new social and linguistic terms. The clearest example of the relation of population structure to rate of change lies in the size and degree of isolation of a speech group.

Variations arise in language as random occurrences. Those that persist do so by virtue of being repeated, and they become established in a language only as they appear in the speech of a major proportion of the speakers of the language. In a large speech community, any variation that does persist and spread throughout the language group will take longer to become established than the same process of change will take in a small speech community. Rate of change is thus correlated with size of a population. The matter of change is seldom that simple, however, except in the case of lexical items—best illustrated by slang terms—that may come and go independently. The incidence of variations is likely to be greater and the variations are likely to be more diverse in a large speech community than in a small one. If all other things were equal, we should therefore also expect differences in the changes that take place in large and small populations over the same period of time. To put a realistic example, let us suppose that from within a moderately large speech community a small group of speakers became detached by migration, by social customs, or whatever; they are to some degree *linguistically* isolated, that is, having less frequent and varied language contact with the members of the larger group. The rate of any change that does occur will be greater in the small group, the incidence of new variations will be less, and the particular variations that arise will tend to be different. If we add to this the relations among structural aspects of the language system, it will be clear that if one change conditions another one, and that one in turn conditions still another, the "chain" of changes will tend to work itself out more rapidly in a smaller than in a larger community. On the other hand, several changes not thus linked will tend to occur at a more rapid rate in the larger speech community. That the morphology of English reached nearly its "Modern" stage of development by the end of the twelfth century in northern English dialects, a dozen or more generations before the same stage of development was reached in southern dialects, seems to reflect in part a difference in population structure based on size and degree of isolation of speech communities.

The kinds and rates of changes within English during the first half of its recorded history are much the same as those within the Germanic dialects from which English thereby was differentiated as a separate language. While many of those kinds of change have continued (and presumably will continue in the future), another set of conditions has arisen in the latter half of the language's history by which the tendency to linguistic differentiation has been counteracted. Some of these conditions will be outlined in 27.5 in connection with the rise of a Standard English. Because English has never split into separate languages, however, the practical relevance of rate of change to the history of English lies in its implications for the systemic structure of the language and for the geographic distribution of its variations. It is to the latter topic that we shall turn next.

GEOGRAPHIC DISTRIBUTION OF VARIATIONS

27.3 Differential repetition of variations, both in rate and kind, is by nature characteristic of differing groups of speakers; one of the normal and most pervasive differences in groups of speakers lies in geographic distribution. Hence the mapping of language differences provides a useful and often fascinating study of language variations. The conventions of linguistic geography are generally as follows. Differences among "sames" are plotted on maps, simply recording the data of distribution. The data may concern any of the aspects of language—phonetics, phonemics, morphology, lexicon, syntax. Then the limits of distribution of differences are generalized by drawing lines to mark the boundary of the occurrence of a variation: such a line is an isomorph if it delimits a morphological feature, an isogloss if it delimits a lexical variation, an isophone if it delimits a phonological variation.

The mapping of linguistic variations is thus in principle a taxonomic procedure. As we have seen, the establishment of variations requires a process of language change; hence the distribution of variations implies differential histories of the items that appear on a linguistic map as different varieties of the same linguistic factor. The taxonomy represented graphically on a map implies evolution of the language differences.

Single differences in linguistic "sames" are only occasionally significant in either synchronic or diachronic study of the language. From the generalized aspects of language variations and change stated in the preceding sections, however, we may expect that an individual difference seldom lacks correlation with other individual differences. On a linguistic map of an area in which groups of speakers have lived for some time and in some significant degree of linguistic isolation, the isomorphs, isophones, and isoglosses ordinarily have the appearance of occurring in bundles or fascicles: several differences, in one or more of the major aspects of language, will be found to have generally congruent boundaries. On the basis of congruent sets of boundaries the taxonomic divisions of closely related features are made, the divisions referred to as dialects. Divisions of a sufficiently large order distinguish languages.

The boundaries mapped in linguistic geography are ordinarily correlated, in turn, with nonlinguistic factors. These factors may be topological—roads, forests, rivers, land ridges, deserts, large bodies of water, mountain passes—or they may be political boundaries, religious constraints, or other socially segregating forces: anything that effectively promotes or hinders linguistic intercourse may appear as a correlative of geographic distribution of language variation. Any of these nonlinguistic factors may not affect linguistic intercourse in a consistent way over an extended period of time. Territorial conquest changes political boundaries, a forest may be cut down, mobility of population may be increased or decreased, travel routes may change, and so on. For these reasons a dialect map will often show one or more bundles of boundary lines, and those bundles may be parallel, intersecting, concentric, fan-shaped, or in any other relation. From a single map (a synchronic analysis of distribution) the most plausible inference from incongruous sets of boundaries is that changes have spread from different directions or at different times, or both. Two or more maps showing distribution of a set of differences at different times will usually clarify the chronological and directional relations of noncongruent linguistic boundaries.

The broad principles of linguistic geography may be illustrated by the development of the dialects of Old English. The illustration and the general statement of principles are intended to be mutually amplifying. It should be mentioned at the outset that the traditional account of the origin of dialects in Old English, based on a section of Bede's *Ecclesiastical History of the English Nation,* does not fit very well the evidence now available from archeology and other sources: study of coin deposits, mode of burial, methods of land cultivation, sets of laws, styles of handwriting and decoration, and many more aspects of Anglo-Saxon culture. Settlement of three major Germanic tribal groups in separate areas of England, as Bede understood it, has been taken as the basis of dialect differences. The dialects seem to have developed, instead, in some other manner that may be outlined as follows. (This account owes much to David De Camp's "The Genesis of the Old English Dialects: A New Hypothesis.")

The Angle, Saxon, and other Germanic invaders of England in the fifth and sixth centuries came first as marauding bands, adventurers, mercenaries; gradually they settled in England, bringing over families. They were joined from time to time by still other emigrants from the Continent. Both the pattern of settlement and the structure of the Germanic tribal system indicate that the communities in the early stages of conquest of England were not homogeneous in tribal or dialectal origin. At this stage the language in England (in so far as it was Germanic as opposed to Celtic and Latin) was geographically a series of linguistic islands—or, probably, archipelagoes. The speech could be classified taxonomically as dialects of West Germanic, with many of the speakers still inhabiting the continental lowlands. In England, the speech areas were probably amalgams of Germanic dialectal variations.

The emergence of kingdoms was a contributing factor to the development of more uniform speech in the various areas. An increase in the density of communication, together with an increase in the number of members of the speech communities followed. While we have no direct contemporary evidence from the fifth through the seventh centuries, the earliest evidence that does survive indicates lesser differences among the linguistic areas in the early settled periods than in subsequent periods. The pattern or trend of the evidence of historical Old English (from the ninth century, in appreciable measure) is one of increasing divergence of geographical dialects.

By the time England was thoroughly settled by English speakers the norm of English speech was increasing in difference from speech of continental Germanic peoples; it was becoming sufficiently different to be classified as a distinct language. With relatively permanent settlement, subsequent linguistic influence across dialect boundaries originated in or was channeled through Kent, for the most part. Kent was for a time a dominant kingdom for its wealth and higher cultural developments; it was the area from which most English trade and contact with the Continent was conducted. The lines of travel and communication for England were heaviest in their connection with and convergence in Kent.

The Kentish peoples, through trade, political affiliations, and general cultural affinities, maintained close associations with Friesland, particularly, the Frankish kingdom, and other tribal groups. Linguistically, these connections of Kent with continental peoples and with the other English peoples constituted a density of communication in Kent greater than any other in England. By careful application of the principles of linguistic geography it has been shown that most of the phonological changes that appear in dialectal differentiation in England were changes imported into England through Kent and diffused along the principal lines of communication through England.

The densest lines of communication were northward through Mercia to Northumberland; the least dense were westward to Wessex. By the ninth century, Wessex differed more in dialect from the other three major areas than these three differed among themselves. The lines of influence had followed closely the principal routes of travel, and the influence was in proportion to the frequency of linguistic contact.

With the "Danish" invasions in the ninth century, however, the situation changed. Kent was already waning in its wealth, prestige, and cultural centrality. Subsequently the people of Wessex repulsed the Danish invasions and attained political prominence; soon after, with King Alfred's encouragement of learning, they achieved cultural prominence. The Wessex-led reconquest of areas held by the Danes established new patterns of density of communication. As a result, from approximately 890 to 940 the principal lines of influence were eastward and northward from Wessex to other areas. Northern England and Scotland, however, were not brought into this linguistic (and political) sphere of influence. When Wessex prominence extended the influence of the West Saxon dialect into the speech of other dialect areas, the effect was in part to reintroduce certain speech sounds which, from an historical point of view, were archaic elsewhere in England. Just as the extent of lines of influence of Kentish speech varied, so did that of the Wessex influence. The "breadth" of these lines varied, too, and many of them appear to have made jumps—that is, they appear in populous areas, leaving dialectal enclaves not subject to the influence.

In these ways the dialects of Old English seem to have developed, and the crossing and counter-crossing of England by successive and diverse lines of linguistic influence seems to provide the most satisfactory reconstruction of the evolution of dialectal variations in Old English. During much of the period of Middle English, when cultural domination in England belonged to speakers of another language (French), and when population groups remained relatively immobile, the dialectal differences increased. The divergences were sufficient, in fact, to render difficult any communication in English by speakers from opposite ends of England.

AN OVERALL LANGUAGE SYSTEM

27.4 One noun in English has a plural inflection /–ən/ *(oxen)*, about half a dozen nouns have "umlaut-plural" forms *(teeth, mice,* etc.), a few have Ø inflection for plural *(sheep)*, a few have singular and plural forms of the morphological system of the language from which the stem was borrowed (see 15.5); these variants from the simple systematic pattern of Modern English noun inflection illustrate the principal point to be made about an overall system of English. At all times there have been relics or innovations or alien items in the language that are not integrated into the dominant and productive systematic aspects of the language. The point is made with perhaps greater force by recalling the geographical distribution of differences—the dialects—and the fact that those differences resulted from differential repetition of variations; the differentiation of dialects results from difference in both the nature and number of variations that occur and the rate of change by which variations become established or lost.

As a natural language existing as the speech of a large number of people, English has never had an overall system manifest empirically. The historical, geographical, or social variations in English are not to be "reduced" to any existing system actually in use nor are they in fact derived from such a system. This is not to say that a set of deductive rules cannot be made for deriving the phonology of a dialect from a system of vowels and consonants abstracted from several varieties of English; James H. Sledd's "Breaking, Umlaut, and the Southern Drawl," for example, sets up a partially ordered set of rules for relating "old-fashioned Atlanta speech" to a generalized phonology of English. In the sense implied above, however, derivation is more suitable as an historical concept than as a taxonomic one.

STANDARD ENGLISH

27.5 Certainly "Standard English" is not the overall system—the "real" or "true" English—from which the dialects have been derived. From the point of view of classification, a standard English is one of the types (like dialects) which together constitute the English language. From the point of view of history, a standard English, like the regional and social dialects, evolved. With English, as with a number of languages, a "standard language" also has differences from the dialects in both its taxonomic and evolutionary aspects.

A "standard language" is said to exist when one particular system of language variations is employed uniformly by speakers (and writers) who constitute a dominant linguistic group among other, related linguistic groups; usually the sets of language habits of all the groups are closely related. "Standard English," then, is a particular version of English employed by a linguistically dominant group among users of all the language systems classified as English. A particular utterance may be classified as standard by its correlation with the type of usage designated as "standard." The "type" of standard English is a taxonomic concept, never merely a description of an observed utterance; the standard type is constructed by abstraction of a particular set of linguistic and cultural features. Whereas the description of a language consists principally of enumerating the typical patterns of its morphology, lexicon, syntax, and phonology, the description or definition of a standard language requires in addition an enumeration of nonlinguistic characteristics such as economic, political, social, and intellectual traits and behaviors of its users. The taxonomic description is based specifically on the *correlation* of linguistic and cultural features. For present-day American English, the characterization by Martin Joos (*The Five Clocks,* esp. Chapter IV) of "formal" style—one of five language styles—approximates what is called here (for historical study) "standard."

A "standard language" may differ in any linguistic aspects from any of the other divisions of a language made according to distribution of variations. There may be a standard pronunciation, not only distinct in the speech sounds but in the "standard" or fixed pronunciation for each of the lexical items. A principal cultural role played by dictionaries of the past two hundred years has been that of designating "correct" pronunciation in the standard language. In other aspects of the language the differences between standard and nonstandard features tend to appear piecemeal. In essence, the standard tolerates fewer free variations. While rules of grammatical concord of subject and predicate or of pronoun and antecedent, for example, hardly differ within the various divisions of English, any failure to observe a rule of concord is regarded as nonstandard. "Fixity" of usage in this context perhaps better describes "Standard English" than does the term "uniformity."

To enumerate distinguishing characters other than strictly linguistic ones is less easy, less precise, less certain; it requires that we deal in economic, political, social, and intellectual classifications which are notoriously unsettled and subject to more rapid change than are language features. Hence a general description, while necessarily somewhat vague, need not be incorrect. The standard type of a national language is the particular language system in which, by and large, governmental affairs are conducted, the activities of major commerce are carried on, the lives of certain (usually "superior") social classes are lived, the creations, studies, and exchanges of the intellectual world are transacted. It is a public language—public in a much larger and different sense than a regional or professional or social dialect may be said to be public. It is also often a less personal language. In a metaphorical sense, it is the language of the marketplace for a nation, as that is to be understood for the modern period of history. British "Received Pronunciation" is the clearest example of a standard, for its being distiguished in part as the only nonlocal dialect in England. But each national group of English-speaking peoples has its own standard as well.

ORIGINS OF STANDARD ENGLISH

27.6 The origin of a standard English was generally concomitant with the origin of the modern national political state of England, and the causes and sources for each are equally complex. Furthermore, both language and state mutually affected each other in various ways throughout their developments. It is as a national, public dialect that standard English emerged.

The familiar historical enigma in fixing the time and circumstances for the beginning of a broad public institution or set of customs obtains equally for a "standard language" in English. Extrapolations from early stages of what can be classified unquestionably as standard English, as well as from subsequent stages (since about 1600), show that a standard English had its origin in Midlands-London provincial dialects; it shares more features with the dialects of one particular region in its earliest stages than with other regional dialects of the same time. The dialect features of the Midlands-London region at about 1400 resemble those of the earliest identifiable "standard" so closely as to put the beginning of standard English at about 1400.

If we regard the early fifteenth century as the beginning of a standard English and the Midlands-London dialect type as its linguistic source, the developmental factors may be sketched as follows. The rise of the modern national state of England created an increasing need for full, natural, efficient communication on matters in the public domain, for people whose native language systems (dialects) differed sufficiently to inhibit full and natural communication. For many public purposes, persons would have to learn a dialect other than their native one and use it in carrying out those purposes. To the extent that those purposes were of a culturally eminent nature—having to do with national affairs, religion, schooling, trade, literature, learning, and the like—the incentives were sufficient to motivate persons to learn the dialect in which these affairs were conducted. It was thus as a relatively uniform auxiliary dialect that a standard English developed in its early stages.

A concomitant of this development was the growth of population centers. The centers in which national affairs were most commonly conducted—London and the surrounding counties, principally to the north during the periods from late Middle English into Modern English—were also the population centers with most rapid growth. The increase of population density had, in turn, an effect on the language spoken in the areas. Because distances were less, social relationships were more complex, and linguistic contact was far more frequent and diverse, the language system became more uniform throughout the area. Because it became increasingly fixed while it contained an unusually wide range of variations, it came to have as established features many compromises, fossilizations, and innovations that, in their totality, did not exist in any of the component or contributing dialects. Again, because the population centers continued to draw in members speaking various regional dialects, the amalgamation of diverse dialectal characteristics continued until the stability, uniformity, and authority of the standard language became firmly established. In standard British English the amalgamating process continued well into the seventeenth century.

Although writing had some effect on the standard language from the first and had increasing effect after the introduction of printing, it did not have its fullest effect until the graphemics were both standardized and widely distributed through printing, and literacy had reached a moderately high rate. Once that stage for the written representation of the language was reached—in the eighteenth century, roughly—writing could and did exercise an important and steady influence on spoken English; on the basis of written records, most of the dictionaries, grammars, and handbooks since the eighteenth century have been constructed.

STANDARD AMERICAN ENGLISH

25.7 Before the nineteenth century there could be only one major national standard type of English. When additional English-speaking nations became established and culturally independent, conditions for emergence of additional national standards came into being and new standard "languages" gradually developed. The principal and earliest instance was American English. While the different conditions of its development may be traced in nearly every difference between early fifteenth century England and early nineteenth century America, two factors are especially prominent. The first is the place of writing in the definition, shaping, and perpetuation of a standard type of the language. The standards fixed in the "standard" writing of English were modified only in minor ways in the public national language of the United States. The exceptions most remarked upon are in spelling, thanks largely to the nationalistic fervor of Noah Webster (whose spelling-book and dictionary were extraordinary influential) and in lexical differences; the latter are mostly confined to new terms required by technological advances. Otherwise the standards of written English differ in linguistic aspects hardly at all between British and American usage. Differences between the two national standards are greatest, of course, in pronunciation—both in the phonological systems and in the pronunciation of individual lexical items. These differences reflect in large part the second main factor operative in the rise of an American standard. Because no one regional dialect (including, of course, London English) retained linguistic eminence either through cultural dominance of its speakers or through central geographic position, as had been the case earlier in England, a single standard pronunciation of American English can be stipulated only in terms of numerical dominance and systemic centrality; since the advent of radio and television, the pronunciation typified by that used by network announcers may be taken as the best illustration of that standard. By any other criteria than number and systemic average (and perhaps wide distribution), multiple, local standard pronunciations must be recognized.

The nature of standard American English and its relation to dialects is far from unchanging at the present time. Three cultural developments have begun to have specially significant effects on the varieties of American English (and, in turn, on the collective varieties of English). The invention of electronic voice-amplifying devices has nearly done away with "public address" or "platform" pronunciation as the standard; instead of essentially a spelling-pronunciation in which each syllable is articulated with a vowel based on the standard written form of words, speech for public purposes has come to approximate the norm of personal address. A different but equally effective factor inducing change in the standard is a change in attitude toward the language by its "guardians" of several kinds. Since about the 1930's there has been a gradual spread of recognition of variations in the language as normal and attributable to historical change rather than to perversity or to "corruption" of the "pure" language. The effect has been to reduce the influence of the putative "correct" language model embodied in eighteenth and nineteenth century prescriptive treatments of English. That this cultural change has not advanced smoothly is well attested by responses to *Webster's Third New International Dictionary,* a collection of which has been edited by James Sledd and Wilma R. Ebbitt under the title *Dictionaries and THAT Dictionary.* The cultural change nevertheless is most likely to continue and its rate may be expected to increase. The third cultural development of special significance lies in changes in population structure. Its two main dimensions are increase in geographic and social mobility and increasing concentration of population in ever-growing major cities.

Some effects of these cultural changes on the language can be predicted with reasonable assurance, but the mutual effects of cultural and linguistic change cannot be forecast very far into the future. The evolution of English is in a most interesting stage just now, a process that can be observed and understood best by those with a knowledge of English and its history.

BIBLIOGRAPHY

The listing that follows serves two main purposes: to identify fully all publications cited by title and author in the chapters of this book, and to list a selection of materials of immediate utility for students using this book. The listing of materials for further reading has been kept short because of the availability of a recent, extensive bibliography, *Linguistics and English Linguistics,* compiled by Harold B. Allen (New York, 1966); approximately 2000 titles (including other bibliographies) are listed in that volume, grouped under special topics, and indexed and cross-referenced.

1. Some Basic Reference Sources—Data

(a) Alphabetical

A Dictionary of American English on Historical Principles, ed. Sir William Craigie, J. R. Hulbert, et al. Chicago, 1936.

A Dictionary of Americanisms on Historical Principles, ed. Mitford M. Mathews, 2 vols. Chicago, 1951. (One volume edition, 1956).

Kurath, Hans, and Sherman M. Kuhn, eds. *Middle English Dictionary.* Ann Arbor, 1954—— (Issued in fascicles).

Jones, Daniel. *Everyman's English Pronouncing Dictionary; Containing 58,000 Words in International Phonetic Transcription,* 11th edition. London and New York, 1956.

Kenyon, John S., and Thomas A. Knott, eds. *A Pronouncing Dictionary of American English.* Springfield, Massachusetts, 1953.

Oxford English Dictionary. A Reissue, corrected and expanded, of *A New English Dictionary on Historical Principles.* Oxford, 1933.

Skeat, Walter W. *Etymological Dictionary of the English Language,* 4th edition. Oxford, 1910.

Toller, T. Northcote. *An Anglo-Saxon Dictionary Based on the Manuscript Collections of the Late Joseph Bosworth.* Oxford, 1898, with Supplement, Oxford, 1921.

Wentworth, Harold, and Stuart Berg Flexner, eds. *Dictionary of American Slang.* New York, 1960.

Wright, Joseph, ed. *The English Dialect Dictionary,* 6 vols. London, 1898–1905. (Rëissued, New York, 1963).

(b) Topical

Campbell, Alistair. *Old English Grammar*. Oxford, 1959.

Greenough, James Bradstreet, and George Lyman Kittredge. *Words and Their Ways in English Speech*. New York, 1902. (Reprinted, New York, 1961, and Boston, 1962).

Jespersen, Otto. *Growth and Structure of the English Language*. 9th edition. Oxford, 1948.

———. *A Modern English Grammar on Historical Principles,* 7 vols. Copenhagen, 1909–1949. (Reprinted, London, 1954).

Kurath, Hans. *A Phonology and Prosody of Modern English*. Ann Arbor, 1964.

———. and Raven I. McDavid, Jr. *The Pronunciation of English In the Atlantic States*. Ann Arbor, 1961.

Marckwardt, Albert H. *American English*. New York, 1958.

Moore, Samuel. *Historical Outlines of English Sounds and Inflections,* revised by Albert H. Marckwardt. Ann Arbor, 1951.

Mossé, Fernand. *A Handbook of Middle English,* translated by James A. Walker. Baltimore, 1952.

Mustanoja, Tauno F. *A Middle English Syntax,* Part I: Parts of Speech. Helsinki, 1960.

Skeat, Walter W. *English Dialects from the Eighth Century to the Present Day*. Cambridge, 1912.

Visser, F. Th. *An Historical Syntax of the English Language,* Parts I–II. Leiden, 1963–1966. (Part III is forthcoming).

Wright, Joseph, and Elizabeth M. *An Elementary Middle English Grammar,* 2nd edition. Oxford, 1928.

Zandvoort, R. W. *A Handbook of English Grammar,* 8th edition. London, 1961.

2. Some Basic Reference Sources—Analysis

Bach, Emmon. *An Introduction to Transformational Grammars*. New York, 1964.

Bloch, Bernard, and George L. Trager. *Outline of Linguistic Analysis*. Baltimore, 1942.

Bloomfield, Leonard. *Language*. New York, 1933.

Chomsky, Noam. *Aspects of a Theory of Syntax*. Cambridge, Massachusetts, 1965.

Gleason, H. A., Jr. *An Introduction to Descriptive Linguistics,* 2nd edition. New York, 1961.

Hill, Archibald A. *Introduction to Linguistic Structures: From Sound to Sentence in English*. New York, 1958.

Hockett, Charles F. *A Course in Modern Linguistics*. New York, 1958.

Hoenigswald, Henry M. *Language Change and Linguistic Reconstruction*. Chicago, 1960.

Joos, Martin. *Acoustic Phonetics*. Language Monograph No. 23. Baltimore, 1948.

Lehmann, Winfred P. *Historical Linguistics: An Introduction*. New York, 1962.

Lieberman, Philip. *Intonation, Perception, and Language*. Cambridge, Massachusetts, 1967.

Marchand, Hans. *The Categories and Types of Present-Day English Word-Formation: A Synchronic and Diachronic Approach*. Wiesbaden, 1960.

Nida, Eugene A. *Morphology: The Descriptive Analysis of Words,* 2nd edition. Ann Arbor, 1949.

———. *A Synopsis of English Syntax,* 2nd edition. The Hague, 1966.

Pedersen, Holger. *Linguistic Science in the Nineteenth Century,* translated by John Webster Spargo. Cambridge, Massachusetts, 1931. (Reissued as *The Discovery of Language,* Bloomington, Indiana, 1962).

Pike, Kenneth L. *Phonemics: A Technique for Reducing Languages to Writing*. Ann Arbor, 1947.

Sapir, Edward. *Language: An Introduction to the Study of Speech*. New York, 1921.

Smalley, William A. *Manual of Articulatory Phonetics,* revised edition. Tarrytown, New York, 1963.

Stern, Gustav. *Meaning and Change of Meaning, with Special Reference to the English Language*. Göteborg, 1931. (Reprinted, Bloomington, Indiana, 1963).

Ullmann, Stephen. *Semantics: An Introduction to the Science of Meaning*. New York, 1962.

Weinreich, Uriel. *Languages in Contact: Findings and Problems*. New York, 1953.

3. Some Additional References

Abbott, Edwin A. *A Shakespearian Grammar,* 3rd edition. London, 1870. (Reissued New York, 1966).

Allen, Harold B., ed. *Readings in Applied English Linguistics,* 2nd edition. New York, 1964.

Baker, Sydney J. *The Australian Language,* 2nd edition. Sydney, 1966.

Baugh, Albert C. *A History of the English Language,* 2nd edition. New York, 1957.

Bloch, Bernard. "English Verb Inflection," *Language,* 23 (1947), 399–418.

Bolinger, Dwight L. "Disjuncture as a Cue to Constructs," *Word,* 13 (1957), 246–55.

———. *Forms of English: Accent, Morpheme, Order*. Cambridge, Massachusetts, 1965.

Carroll, John B. *The Study of Language*. Cambridge, Massachusetts, 1953.

Cassidy, Frederic G. *Jamaica Talk: Three Hundred Years of the English Language in Jamaica*. New York, 1961.

Chafe, Wallace L. "Phonetics, Semantics, and Language," *Language,* 38 (1962), 335–44.

Chrétien, C. Douglas." Genetic Linguistics and the Probability Model," *Language,* 42 (1966), 518–30.

DeCamp, David. "The Genesis of the Old English Dialects: A New Hypothesis," *Language,* 34 (1958), 232–44.

Diver, William. "The Modal System of the English Verb," *Word,* 20 (1964), 322–52.

Ellegård, Alvar. *The Auxiliary* DO: *The Establishment and Regulation of Its Use*. Stockholm, 1953.

Fisiak, Jacek. *Morphemic Structure of Chaucer's English.* University, Alabama, 1965.

Francis, W. Nelson. *The Structure of American English.* New York, 1958.

Fries, Charles C. "On the Development of the Structural Use of Word-Order in Modern English," *Language,* 16 (1940), 199–208.

———. *The Structure of English: An Introduction to the Construction of English Sentences.* New York, 1952.

Gleason, H. A., Jr. *Linguistics and English Grammar.* New York, 1965.

Hall, Robert A., Jr. *Introductory Linguistics.* Philadelphia, 1964.

———. "American Linguistics, 1925–50," *Archivum Linguisticum,* 3 (1951), 101–125.

Haugen, Einar. "The Analysis of Linguistic Borrowing," *Language,* 26 (1950), 210–31.

The Hystorie of Hamblet, Prince of Denmarke, an anonymous translation of F. de Belleforest, *Le Cinquiesme Tome des Histoires Tragiques;* the translation was published in London in 1608.

Hoijer, Harry, ed. *Language in Culture.* Proceedings of a Conference on the Interrelations of Language and other Aspects of Culture. Chicago, 1954.

Jacobson, Roman, and Morris Halle. *Fundamentals of Language.* 's–Gravenhage, 1956.

Jespersen, Otto. *Negation in English and Other Languages.* Copenhagen, 1917.

———. *The Philosophy of Grammar.* London, 1924. (Reprinted, New York, 1965).

Juilland, Alphonse G., and James Macris. *The English Verb System.* 's–Gravenhage, 1962.

Jones, Daniel. *The Pronunciation of English,* 4th edition. Cambridge, 1956.

Joos, Martin. "Description of Language Design," *Journal of the Acoustical Society of America,* 22 (1950), 701–708.

———. *The Five Clocks, International Journal of American Linguistics,* 28, No. 2 (1962). (Reissued New York, 1967).

———. *The English Verb: Form and Meanings.* Madison, Wisconsin, 1964.

———. *Readings in Linguistics: The Development of Descriptive Linguistics since 1925,* 4th edition. Chicago, 1966.

Kenyon, John S. *American Pronunciation,* 10th edition. Ann Arbor, 1950.

Kökeritz, Helge. *Shakespeare's Pronunciation.* New Haven, 1953.

Kuhn, Sherman M. "On the Syllabic Phonemes of Old English," *Language,* 37 (1961), 522–38.

Kurath, Hans. "The Loss of Long Consonants and the Rise of Voiced Fricatives in Middle English," *Language,* 32 (1956), 435–45.

Labov, William. "Phonological Correlates of Social Stratification," *Ethnography,* 66 (1964), 164–76.

Ladefoged, Peter. *Elements of Acoustic Phonetics.* Chicago, 1962.

McKintosh, Angus. "A New Approach to Middle English Dialectology," *English Studies,* 44 (1963), 1–11.

Martinet, André. *A Functional View of Language.* Oxford, 1962.

Mencken, Henry L. *The American Language: An Inquiry into the Development of English in the United States,* 4th Edition and Two Supplements. An abridged edition by Raven I. McDavid, Jr., New York, 1963.

Moulton, William G. "The Stops and Spirants of Early Germanic," *Language,* 30 (1954), 1–42.

Reed, Carroll E. *Dialects of American English.* Cleveland, 1967.

Roberts, Paul. *English Syntax,* alternate edition. New York, 1964.

Robertson, Stuart. *The Development of Modern English,* 2nd edition, revised by Frederic G. Cassidy. New York, 1954.

Samuels, M. L. "Some Applications of Middle English Dialectology," *English Studies,* 44 (1963), 81–94.

Sapir, Edward. "Language and Environment," *The American Anthropologist,* 14 (1912), 226–42.

Scott, Charles T., and Jon L. Erickson, *Reading for the History of the English Language.* Boston, 1968.

Sledd, James H. "Breaking, Umlaut, and the Southern Drawl," *Language* 42 (1966), 18–41.

———. *A Short Introduction to English Grammar*. Chicago, 1959.

——— and Wilma R. Ebbitt. *Dictionaries and THAT Dictionary*. Chicago, 1962.

Starnes, DeWitt and Gertrude E. Noyes. *The English Dictionary from Cawdry to Johnson*. Chapel Hill, North Carolina, 1946.

Stevick, Robert D. "The Morphemic Evolution of Middle English *She*," *English Studies*, XLV (1964), 381–88.

Stockwell, Robert P. "The Middle English 'Long Close' and 'Long Open' Mid Vowels," *Texas Studies in Literature and Language*, II (1961), 529–38.

Twadell, W. Freeman. *The English Verb Auxiliaries*. Providence, Rhode Island, 1960.

Vendryes, Joseph. *Language: A Linguistic Introduction to History*, translation by Paul Radin (1925). New York, 1951.

Whorf, Benjamin Lee. *Language, Thought, and Reality*, ed. John B. Carroll. Cambridge, Massachusetts, and New York, 1956.

Wyld, Henry Cecil. *A Short History of English*, 3rd edition. London, 1927.

INDEX

This index has been compiled as a complement to the *Contents*. Because the book is organized topically, a full listing of chapter and section headings in the *Contents* provides a guide to principal topics as they occur seriatim. For the *Index*, topics are sifted yet another way and listed alphabetically.